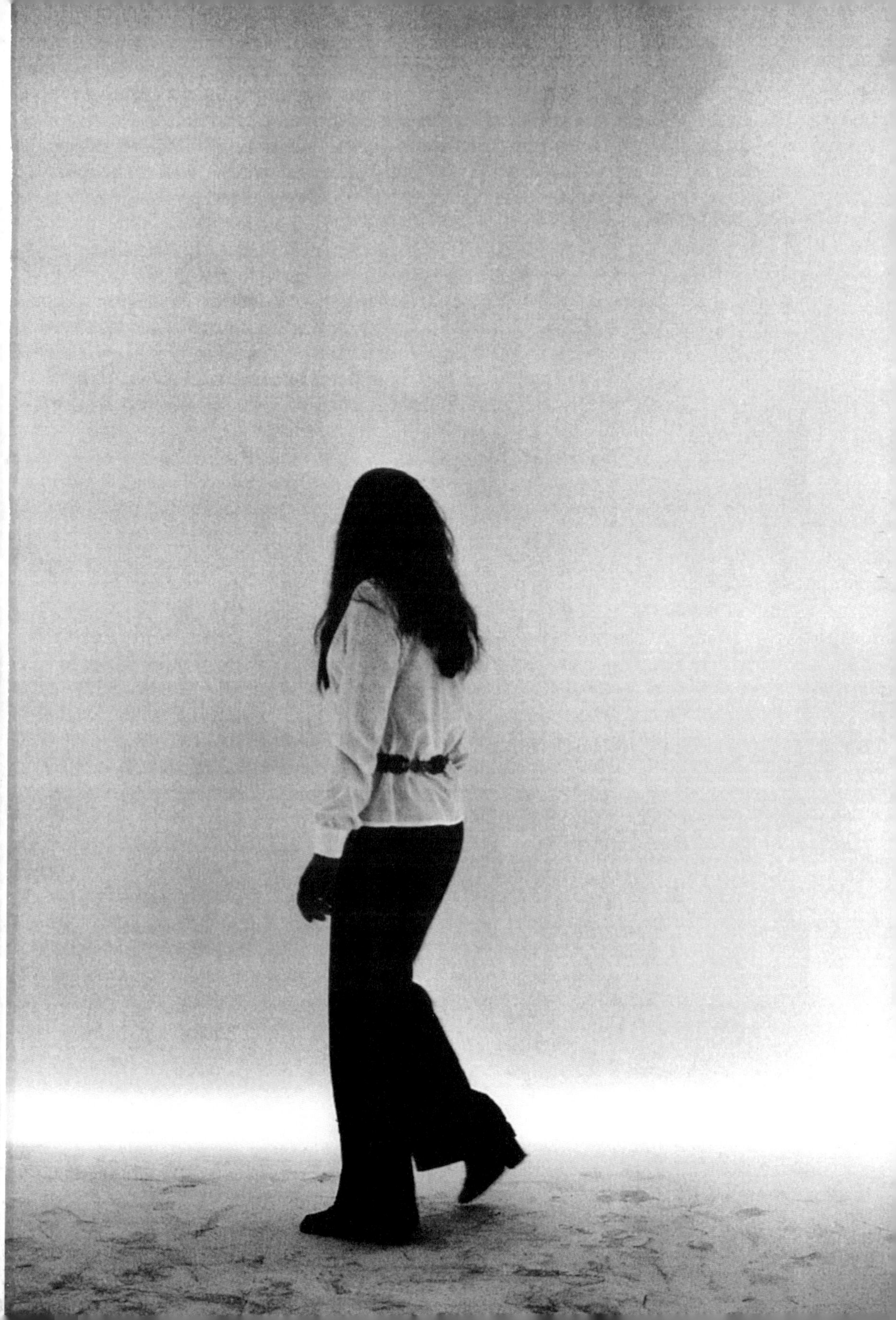

← **Laura Grisi in her installation *Volume of Air*, 1968**
Exhibition view, *Nuovi Materiali, Nuove Tecniche*, Caorle, 1969

Laura Grisi

Marco Scotini,
with Clément Dirié (eds.)

jrp|editions

Table of Contents

A Reserve of Air: Laura Grisi and the Order of the Imponderable

Marco Scotini

Make 100 different people say the same four words.[1]

1969: Laura Grisi creates a cubic room that is completely white.[2] In theory, this is nothing more than the pure containment of a space. On the walls, a white fluorescence reflects the luminous radiations on an increased wavelength, while a thin neon tube—with an even more intense light—runs around the entire perimeter of the room, highlighting the joints of walls, ceiling, and floor. There is no desire to give any form to the space and even less to define any image inside it.

The glimmer of light in the environment is anything but the sign of something. As the artist says, "it modifies its volume only by one cubic centimeter less."[3] In reality, the effect it produces is the dematerialization of the walls, transforming the space into an undefined and limitless site: in other words, deprived of a frame. No images, nor any other thing, appears to those who cross the room, so much so that one might think that there is nothing—here—other than an absence. Nonetheless, thanks to the neon light, a sort of whitish (diaphanous and transparent) haze permeates the environment, defining a body that is both dense and elusive. Anything but a sign of emptiness, this aerial matter, that eludes appearance, is rather a condition (the medium) through which everything can be made visible, tangible, audible—except itself. And possibly, by being too evident, this invisible support of everything that appears is always disregarded, omitted, removed from our thoughts. What is so enigmatic, in this place, that makes its foundations disappear from view?

The element that can be perceived without manifesting itself is nothing other than air, this invisible resource that we can take as the latest given in Grisi's artistic research, in her cosmology. It is a subject that the artist approaches, between the 1960s and 1970s, through successive approximations, asymptotic progressions, imperfect translations of the original, without ever providing a tangible mold or duplicate. The artist is well aware that air (its uninterrupted becoming) is not objectifiable, locatable, cannot be reduced to a presence: or only at the cost to decreeing the oblivion of air as such. In this sense, the entirety of her work appears to be a gargantuan effort to account for the breadth, the unlimited nature, the imperceptibility, as well as the endless proliferation of all "the possible." Nonetheless, her practice departs from precise constraints, paradoxical gaps, different linguistic and semiotic limitations—from all that knowledge that has led the Western male theoretical presidium to the domination of nature and the oblivion of air.

Far from the mystical nature of Yves Klein's *Raum der Leere* (made in Krefeld in 1961), and equally from the psychologism of the Californian Light and Space movement's contemporary environments (Doug Wheeler, Robert Irwin, and James Turrell, among others), Grisi's *Volume of Air* (1968) is an environment at the degree zero of life. Air is present as a limitlessly available medium, everywhere. But, above all, as the basic element of organic existence and sensorial experience that we pass through, and which, analogously, passes through us. In this way, a dynamic system of flows and forces becomes the site of all the events that, uninterruptedly, feed and define the world in which we live, in contrast to the solid and inert terrain on which classic Western thought locates the materiality of things.

It is no surprise, therefore, that this environment only represents a phase, however paradigmatic, in the cycle of metamorphosis through which Grisi gives space to the atmosphere, to its changes of pressure, temperature, evaporation, condensation, and so on. Or, rather, it represents only one out of all the instances where the artist uses the atmosphere as the generator of spaces, giving rise to a series of environments in which natural phenomena are artificially reproduced and transposed from outside to inside exhibition spaces—all responses to the different impacts of the climatic conditions she encountered at diverse latitudes. The wind is central to her intervention for the *Teatro delle mostre* at Galleria La Tartaruga in 1968, and to a 16mm black and white film made in the same year. Fog appears, together with luminous columns, in 1969 in the courtyard of the Marlborough Gallery in Rome; rain is presented in Grisi's solo exhibition at the Galerie E. M. Thelen in Cologne in 1970. On the other hand, the whirlpool is the subject of a 16mm color film projected onto the floor inside a circular space.[4] But, once again, it is the medial nature of air that Grisi visualizes in the optical, auditory, and sensorial effects to which it gives rise. The rainbow recreates, inside a room, "all the colors of the spectrum that the air, which is colorless, lets pass through."[5] In her 1970 solo exhibition at the Galerie E. M. Thelen, refraction is obtained using light and the insertion of metal tubes into circular, transparent basins of water. Lastly, stars are the effect of diffraction when high intensity sources of light encounter and perforate a lead plate. The theater of this event was the environment *Luce + Calore = Tempo di Fusione* that Grisi created in 1970 at the Galleria del Naviglio in Milan.

These are all chapters from a broader yet incomplete project, given that the artist promised, but unfortunately never produced, further stages—"there will also be hail, and the condensation and cooling of air."[6] "I didn't want a painting or a sculpture containing air, earth, or water"—the artist commented, in differentiating her work from Arte Povera—"I didn't want air, earth, or water to become objects. I wanted to recreate the experience of natural phenomena."[7] Neither reifying it as an artistic object, nor as the exclusive subject of scientific knowledge, for Grisi air is more broadly a vital, shared medium. It is the invisible dense space between two subjects that relates the whole with itself. It is the fluid casing (the *virtual*) that keeps things alive and makes them recognizable, that allows them to be perceived each time as different and singular, evading the unequivocal meanings or codifications attributed to them. The feminist theorist Luce Irigaray speaks explicitly on this subject: "Is not the air the whole of our habitation as mortals? Is there a dwelling more vast, more spacious, or even more generally peaceful than that of air? Can man live elsewhere than in air?"[8] However, here the question doubles up. For what reason should the vital function of breathing remain outside Grisi's encounter with air, given that it is the unequivocal condition of existence? And, is there any other sign that, more than the voice, is the direct emanation of breath? Of its urgency?

When Grisi began to record the micro-sounds of nature in 1971, she wrote the following instructions for the execution of her piece in one of her typewritten texts: "Make 100 different people say the same four words and record them. Listen at reduced speed." With every enunciation, the voice always surpasses the word. The immaterial caliber of the voice keeps the semiotic equivocality of what is said alive, it singularizes and renews it, it makes it exist. It nullifies its univocal nature and opens up an unforeseen field of possibilities.

Thus, beginning with *Volume of Air*, a rereading of Grisi's artistic and cultural profile provides us with a two-fold opportunity. On the one hand, it allows us to perceive the more conceptual turn of her work not as a bifurcation (the infamous *eclecticism*), but as continuity with respect to her previous activity, liberating us from all those normative canons that have made placing her (when she has not been excluded) so difficult within the hegemonic and universalizing narrative of a modernist and male-oriented historiography. On the other hand, it forces us to recognize air (and its forms) as a typical trait (a paradigmatic relocation?) of the inscription of her artistic and feminine activity that escapes the normative assumptions of visual identification.

There is no wish to fill a gap with the return of a female artist to the official history that decreed her exclusion. The purpose is the deconstruction of the parameters in order to pluralize the narratives, the representations, the differences. This then permits a whole genealogy of works to emerge in which Grisi's research appears pioneering: the *Atmospheres* (1968–1971) series by Judy Chicago, *City of Clouds* (1968) by Maria Nordman, *Structures of Air* (1970) by Teresa Burga, *Rhythm 4* (1974) by Marina Abramović, through *Be Careful With What You Wish For* (1998) by Monica Bonvicini, *A Wind Woman* (2003) and *To Breathe–A Mirror Woman* (2006) by Kimsooja, or *Structure for Communicating with Wind* (2012) by Céline Condorelli. The list could probably go on. However, is Laura Grisi herself (like all the female artists of her generation) not ultimately proof of an *absence* within the history of art, despite being part of it? There are many aspects in her work that undoubtedly define an alternative to the patriarchal order, and a rejection of a solid and measurable cognitive basis, the decentralization of the creator-subject, an opposition to chrononormativity, and the privileging of listening over enunciation.[9] Within a multiplicity of activities that take the "journey" (from remote locations crossed to the variety of media used) as their fundamental condition, Laura Grisi embodies a sort of stateless and nomadic female subject who defies the politics of identity, the univocal nature of representation, and the unidirectionality of time. It is the urgency of themes such as gender, ecology, and interculturalism that currently determines the contemporary nature of her rediscovery that goes far beyond the conceptual nature of her work. In Grisi's work, the tension between macro and micro-scale, between given and possible, law and chance, universal and particular, past and future, is presented each time by means of a radical policy of paying attention to the minimal, the marginal, the zero degrees: four pebbles, the sound of water drops, the color of mango leaves, the direction of the wind, the perceptive passage between sensations, the sounds produced by the movement of ants on the earth. Such extreme attention is always the subject of an anthropological ritual whose cultural coordinates escape us: counting grains of sand, measuring the strength of the wind, distilling sensorial perceptions, rephotographing pictures already taken with a different lens, switching things and objects, listening to the inaudible. It is as if the incommensurable is always the latest given (the unforeseen outcome) of a tireless measuring process where signs and languages are nothing more than the initial limits of the possible. As Lucy Lippard wrote in 1979, "her work is poised between possible alternatives and the lack of alternatives. She usually chooses the permutational system and then accepts the consequences."[10]

If it is true that Grisi's work exposes us to an ecology of the virtual,[11] this is not because it contains an aspiration to abstraction, but rather due to an adherence to the physicality of the experience that calls representation into question. Is *Volume of Air* not something that requires the sensorial participation of the observer? Is it not proposing a presence that, as such, balks at being photographed?[12]

Standing still in the same place. Observing the passing of time through the movements of one's shadow.

In a black and white photograph from 1961, we are entranced by the gaze of a young Fula woman who moves her head slightly to the right—and her eyes with it—to look into the lens. She has very dark skin, a kerchief on her head, earrings, and a necklace. She has scarifications at the edges of her mouth and her temples: the same as her sleeping daughter bound to her shoulders by a broad colored cloth tied at breast height. In another photograph of the same period, a young woman is shown again, no longer with nomadic and tribal signs, but with the urban and Westernized ones of a megalopolis such as Lagos. The same twisting of the head, the same framing of the subject at shoulder height. However, in this case, the gaze is flirtatious and self-satisfied, her hairstyle is fashionable with a yellow side bow and hairband. The background to the portrait is a large advertisement bearing the words "African Records" and an oversized painted vinyl. This is a nightclub in the Nigerian capital where, between the twist and the tam-tam, the Yoruba girls from the nearby lagoon villages are forced to act as hostesses, their tribal origins identifiable from the bow on their heads. In yet another photograph, a strange initiation ceremony is captured by a series of snapshots taken in the Boni village in Burkina Faso (former Upper Volta). The initiates are naked children lying flat on the ground, while those officiating, acting as animal divinities, wear Bwa masks in carved and painted wood over wide vegetable fiber costumes.

Between 1958 and 1959, Laura Grisi spent an entire year traveling through the Andes in Bolivia and Argentina—where she encountered the gauchos of Las Pampas—the province of Misiones, the region of the Iguazù Falls where she met the Guarani indios, and finally reached Buenos Aires. In 1960–1961, a new journey took her for several months to Chad, Cameroon, and southern Tunisia. In 1961–1962, she spent a year in the Pacific Ocean in the Polynesian Leeward Antilles. Her journey to South East Asia was in 1962: Vietnam, the Malesia region, Malesia, Thailand, and in 1963–1964 she was again in Africa: Nigeria, Upper Volta Republic (now Burkina Faso), Niger, Dahomey (now Benin), and Togo. During these travels searching for the traces of disappearing populations, Grisi accompanied her husband, Folco Quilici, a popular film, TV-program, and documentary maker. This network of lengthy itineraries at various latitudes continued uninterrupted through 1973. However, the way the artist related to them changed completely from 1965 onward. The traces of these travels remain an indelible element throughout her further activities, influencing her "way of thinking and of visualizing life."[13] Similarly, her photographic experiences were destined to underscore every step of her subsequent artistic journey (the importance of light being just one example) until, in the 1970s, the medium was retrieved in a completely conceptual way. Photography, stripped of every attribute and reduced to being only self-referential of what it depicts, comes to be used by Grisi mechanically and impersonally (without any arbitrariness). As a repeated element within a numerical progression, the photograph becomes part of visual sequences that develop permutations and variations of the same object (or the same constellation of objects). Equally, it might become the place for a specular series that infinitely reflects itself, as in the "De More Geometrico" series (1977). In either case, it is no longer the single image (or the image as such) that is important, but the way it relates to every other case of the possible. Thus, the photograph becomes the outcome of a preestablished, arithmetical procedure, rather than the prey captured at the "decisive moment" as pursued by Cartier-Bresson.

Between 1958 and 1964, Laura Grisi temporarily abandoned painting. Armed with a Hasselblad and a Rolleiflex, she dedicated herself to Magnum-style documentary photography. Many of her authorial photographs were published in her photographic book *Pasos por Buenos Aires* (1959), in illustrated weeklies, and in some books of essays by Folco Quilici such as *I Mille Fuochi dal Sahara al Congo* (1965). Alongside her photographic production, there are her illustrated magazine reports and a book published in 1964, *I Denti del Tigre*, written in the form of a popular ballad and set in the Polynesian Tuamotu Archipelago.

The subjects of Grisi's initial photographs are the ancestral rites, costumes, social roles, the female condition, work, and the ecosystems that characterized the tribal populations still existing at the time, although already threatened by Western modernism. There was no doubt that the photographic medium was the most appropriate for recording these traces before they disappeared. However, it was precisely her confrontation with these multiple non-Western cultures that led Grisi to question the assumed objectivity and "true to life" nature of the medium used, together with its implicit representational limitations. It was possibly the photograph itself that revealed her own state of privilege (as a white woman with an automatic, out-of-place visual device representing domination) as a limitation. Despite having accumulated a body of photographs numbering more than five thousand (an authentic "inventory of the world"), in 1964–1965, Grisi abandoned photography and returned to painting with an emblematic exhibition in the Galleria dell'Ariete in Milan, which followed her first solo exhibition at Galleria Il Segno in Rome. The pictorial works and preparatory drawings from this period look like anatomical charts in which, rather than the "represented space," the photographic "space of representation" lies at the center of an emotionally detached analysis undertaken in pictorial terms. The very titles of the works refer to filters, lenses, shooting angles, and types of camera. The visualized object is an abstract and indiscernible image (a photographic macro?) surrounded by the concentric circles of the lens, while the entire focus is turned on the deconstruction of the recording medium. As Grisi states, "this was a world seen through a lens with an altered focal distance. The rest of the canvas, on the other hand, was filled with precise, meticulous diagrams and descriptions of all kinds of lenses, photographic calculations, times of exposure, aperture widths, and so on, all the media and methods that could eventually help to give focus to objects and forms."[14] By demonstrating that there is no naturalism behind the mechanical gaze, Grisi questions the presumed objective and universal nature that we attribute to it (its power of credibility), when, in fact, the photograph is nothing more than the final outcome of an entirely Western history of vision. In the same way, the artist also begins to distance herself from the freezing of time that the photographic image impresses on the temporal duration and the continuum of its extension. Not only does the optical trace impressed on the film snatch a single space-time of the real from its mutation by recording it, but it even dates it. In the photographic act, the frozen instant and the framed space are infinitely and doubly robbed. The instant is embalmed and, as such, in the words of André Bazin, preserved forever "as the bodies of insects preserved intact, out of the distant past, in amber."[15] So, from this moment onward, the search for something that is not given in advance and definitively installed in temporality (in contrast to Roland Barthes' "that has been" noeme[16]) will mark, day by day, Grisi's itinerant destination in the reclaiming of air.

Look at the ocean until the sun sets.
Don't be distracted by the surrounding landscape.

1966: Grisi presents a large format, "variable," mobile, and multi-material diptych at the 33rd Venice Biennale which—in theory—the observer can change by means of sliding panels. The two large pictorial compositions entitled *Landscape Omaggio a Gainsborough* and *Seascape Omaggio a Constable*, put on display the temporary and incomplete nature of an image that is always in a state of potentiality: on the point of mutating into something else, equal and different at one and the same time. A fractured totality that only the involvement of the observer can provide with a temporary structure (layout) because nothing in it is fixed or lastingly framed. In contrast to the prevailing critics of the time, who placed her within the Nuova Figurazione of the 1960s, these works (indebted to, but not part of Pop art) continue to question the perceptive moment as such. They push the distancing from mirroring the world and the univocal image that the artist had begun with the previous cycle, even further. It is no coincidence that the titles of the works make reference to two great masters of landscape painting who, according to art historian Peter Galassi,[17] are examples of a pre-photographic trend: both in the meteorology of Constable's cloud studies and in Gainsborough's atmospheric qualities. However, in Grisi's works, the machine-picture is the emergent reference, so that the visualization of a theme (the represented landscape) is transformed *into* the theme of visualization (the representational conditions).

De facto, in contrast to the photographic shot's freezing of time and the static nature of painting, in these works Grisi proposes a temporalization of the image as a montage of an indefinite number of preestablished and superimposable frames. Turning to the window-frame model, the artist imposes on the landscape (clouds, waves, and earth) a geometric subdivision into panels covered in Plexiglas that over-frame, reframe, and multiply the effect of the image within the image, as in a sort of *mise en abyme*. The plane is divided into a multiplicity of subplanes in accordance with an idea of fractioning the space already present in the layout of Grisi's first solo exhibition in Rome. The viewpoint is effectively not fixed in any definitive way. It changes a certain number of times, opening up to a plurality of readings. Nonetheless, the freedom of variations of the image is proportional to the condition of the invariability of its elements. The figures that define the landscape are reduced to silhouettes that stand out from the plane, using flat acrylic colors with little depth. They are character-signs capable of separating and combining themselves with every new movement of the panels, like patterns on a visual score. In the alteration of the "picture" Grisi wants to give form to, many elements of this painting make an indirect reference to photography: the recursive silhouette of the artist (spectator or actor?) as a shadow projected on the object of observation, the idea of the filter connected to the use of the transparent Plexiglas, the traces of the geometric optics of the lenses, and the de-subjectivation of the pictorial treatment. The structure that supports this construction remains visible to the observer while the image is always the result of the rhythmic combination of geometric figures emphasized by the periodic return of the same elements, in accordance with the literary methods of the *école du regard* [Nouveau Roman].

Grisi also continues to develop her work on the surface of the pieces in relation to time in her subsequent pictorial cycle that she calls "Neon Paintings." Here she adds superimposing layers of different materials to the previously introduced sliding panels: Plexiglas outlines in different textures (transparent, corrugated, shiny, opaque), panels in enameled aluminum, neon lights. All are cold and unconventional materials that Grisi pioneeringly imports into painting. The bidimensional nature of the work is thus transformed into a sort of three-dimensional plastic relief, jutting out from the wall into space, in accordance with contemporary research into the refutation of painting. In place of the window format typifying the previous series, box-like structures now appear, moving the view of the external landscape inside. Comparable to doors, cabinets, and booths, these demarcations of the image are all life-size. *Subway*, *Top Floor*, and *East Village* (all 1967) are all eloquent examples of this.

In the "Neon Paintings" series, Henri Bergson's concept of doubling time is defined by Grisi using a two-fold strategy. On the one hand, there is a temporality at work where the artist still uses mobile panels that can be superimposed on each other, and circular outlines that can be rotated (*Glosty*, 1966). On the other hand, working on the depth of the pieces with neon tubes and various filters or screens, Grisi creates supplementary spaces inside the surfaces. These are actual inserts giving form to a virtual temporality, full of potential. The nebulous effect of the image (atmosphere, vapor, air) is produced by the dynamic play between clarity and lack of focus, transparency and opacity, refraction and distortion, shadow and light. The silhouettes of the represented figures (in groups or in isolation) remain in place, but appear and disappear thanks to the perceptive conditions of the observer moving in front of them. This gap between the image and the surface, made possible by the effects of the light on plastic materials, forms the neuralgic center of this work.

Thanks to Alan Solomon, the "Neon Paintings" were presented in 1968 at the Institute of Contemporary Art in Boston and at the Jewish Museum in New York in the *Young Italians* exhibition, where Grisi was the only woman among a host of male artists, including Enrico Castellani, Jannis Kounellis, Michelangelo Pistoletto, and Pino Pascali. Udo Kultermann, who wrote the catalogue for the artist's solo exhibition the same year at the Galerie E. M. Thelen in Essen, saw in this series the coexistence of "technique and atmosphere."[18] However, it was Maurizio Fagiolo dell'Arco who perfectly captured the temporal aspect by means of which Grisi "achieves the blurring of memory without forgetting the cold projection of reportage."[19] For the Italian critic, there is a formal principle (shadow) and a device (the camera) at the basis of these works. In fact, with the "Neon Paintings," it is the imponderable that insinuates itself into the visual texture of the picture. It is no surprise therefore, that, in 1968, Grisi decided to radically abandon any type of representation and convert signs into forces, the plane into an environment, the exhibition into a situation, the long-lasting into an event. Grisi began to place the intangibility and immateriality of phenomena at the center of her research, in close continuity with her previous works. If we take the representational space as the narrative thread of her artistic experiments, it becomes clear that there are no fractures, no bifurcations in this passage, but simply a common underlying design. 1968–1969 saw the start of her environments with natural elements such as fog, wind, water, air, heat, and other atmospheric phenomena such as rainbows, whirlpools, diffracted light. These works partially came together in her 1971 participation in the seminal exhibition *Earth Air Fire Water: Elements of*

Art at the Museum of Fine Arts in Boston, in which Grisi participated together with Robert Smithson, Dan Graham, Hans Haacke, Newton Harrison, Alan Sonfist, Dennis Oppenheim, Nicolás García Uriburu, and many others.

Count the grains of sand in an hourglass and count the time needed to do it with another, similar hourglass.

Decentralization and listening are the conceptual devices the artist puts in place for the exploration of those perceptive and cognitive mechanisms not subjugated to hegemonic knowledge, and which we can read in the light of a feminization of observation times and location spaces. On the one hand, the methods of fractioning (the whole and the parts) and dispersion (aerial and fluid substances) pursued by Grisi in contrast to seeing the work as something closed in on itself, is accompanied by her recourse to the plurality of mass communication methods that Germano Celant recorded as the *Offmedia* trend at that time. The artist's books such as *Distillations: 3 Months of Looking* (1970) and *Distillations: Choices and Choosing 16 from 5000* (1970), the 16mm films *The Measuring of Time* (1969) and *From One to Four Pebbles* (1972), as well as the multiple of two magnetic tape audio cassettes *Sounds* (1971), are all part of Grisi's research phase that is increasingly speculative and decidedly conceptual. In other words, the trajectory follows the artist's desire to overcome the static nature of the artwork and to demonstrate the insufficiency of the visual as an exclusive perceptive moment. When, in one of her text works on display at the Rome art festival *Mappa 72*, she requires her interlocuter to "tie two adjacent rocks underwater with a rope," she makes clear the principle that underlies her practice. The piece is typical of the text works of this period, and although the script may seem banal and absurd, the instructions are meant to be followed to the letter. The removal from the gaze of the connection (made underwater) defines the creation of an invisible relationship between the parts (the two rocks) and the whole that the water has eroded. It passes from multiplicity to unity. This direction is reversed when, in her photographic book on ethnographic material *Distillations: Choices and Choosing 16 from 5000*, Grisi invites the observer/reader to study "the varieties in sameness" or, when, in *Distillations: 3 Months of Looking* she asks them to calculate the number of times a flame's color repeats itself while a fire burns, and is presenting them with the dilemma expressed in the film *The Measuring of Time* (1969). This 16mm film documents the artist alone on a seashore and working on an endeavor worthy of Sisyphus that is apparently endless, beyond calculable time. In this beautiful film "fragment," that alternates close-ups of the hands counting out every grain of sand, and panoramic sweeps of the beach, there is not merely a female figure working on an operation beyond the possible—counting all the grains of sand on a beach. There is not just a challenge to the passing of time which, as such, can never be recorded in the duration of such an arduous program. The sandy expanse that appears completely homogeneous (recalling all the deserts Grisi visited) is, in contrast, infinitely divisible, in each layer of its sedimentation. In fact, every grain of sand repeats itself while—at one and the same time—never being identical to any other. How can one grain be chosen and isolated over another? Grisi's obsession with the negligible detail, with the differential gaps to which she pays extreme and repeated attention (equal to the depth and sensitivity of observation by indigenous peoples) is equivalent to that of the incommensurable, the infinite variety of phenomena. But what is this "whole" for Grisi? It seems that the expression "whole" does not allow for any declension as it aims not to exclude any parts. Nonetheless, in this case, the whole never coincides with unity. No totality, no univocality, no single directionality—only proliferation, infinite repetition without a subject. The "cool," de-subjectivizing nature of Grisi's work is an explicit demonstration of this. The multiple cannot be recomposed, the void of the subject cannot be filled, the ethereal cannot become solid. Behind every presumed uniformity lies only the innumerable divisibility of things, of time and of space.

Use someone else's handwriting to write your own ideas.

Grisi patiently, meticulously, and unwaveringly accumulates: heteroclitic materials, ethnic groups, animal and vegetable species, landscapes, perceptions and concepts, signs and forces, games and rituals. She organizes and redistributes the parts without ever finding in the increase of the wholes the single element that unites them. She uninterruptedly transcribes texts from one field to another, from one language to another: visual ideograms, musical notation, mathematical symbols, alphabetical writings. She never ceases to translate even herself. Certain character-signs, such as a bird's flight inscribed in a triangle or the form of a hexagon, present as patterns in *Geometric Landscape* (1966), ten years later become the generators of space in artistic cycles such as *Hypothesis about Space* (1975) and *Blue Triangle* (1980). In the same way, *Distillations: Choices and Choosing 16 from 5000* translates Grisi's photographic archive in three different ways. A similar translation process takes place with the reduction of the *Rainbow* (1968) environment into the changeable signs of *Stripes* (1974); with the transformation of the *Tempo Reale* (1975) photograph into the silkscreen cycle *One Minute* (1975–1994). In *Pebbles*, presented by Leo Castelli in Grisi's first solo exhibition in 1973, five pebbles are taken as both natural elements and arithmetical symbols. They are the numerical unit of a mathematical permutation, making a spatial order possible within a succession. It is not the artist who provides a preestablished order, who chooses any one combination over another. She rather adheres to the possible extension of all those combinations provided by the permutation process. She attempts to establish a relationship between the order of the mind and the natural order of things, without superimposing the one over the other. She surrounds the alignment of a finite number of stones with ever new, increasingly extended, virtual circles (as in *Drops of Water*): a "nebulosity" of images, to use Gilles Deleuze's word.[20] In this, the limits and resistances can dissolve into uninterrupted openings where the exchange between real data and numerical units presupposes common properties in both fields. In this passage of things into signs, Grisi calls into play the accomplishable and the thinkable, the aesthetic power of sensitivity and the abstraction of the intelligible, in accordance with that assumption of the *bricoleur* as a paradigm much loved by Claude Lévi-Strauss.[21]

In this sense, *Stripes* transforms the optical phenomenon of the rainbow into an abstract sequence of six colors painted on canvas in which the artist visualizes all the possible permutations within a single space in the format of an oriental scroll. The artist adapts to the finite repertoire available and, adding nothing more, uses a mathematical operator to reorganize it. In this way, *Stripes* provides an overall picture of 720 sequences, stimulating the spectator to imagine other combinations. During this period, the constant cumulative nature of Grisi's work (inventory, list?) reaches its maximum degree of expression, allowing us to appreciate its origins. Permutation is effectively the opposite of selection. The latter's purpose is to take a few elements from a wide group of choices for certain ends—therefore, a subtraction. Permutation, on the other hand, is an operator that generates the many from the few, acting as a multiplier, an opening up of possibilities.

This is why the original photographs of Grisi's activities are a constant problem for the artist in their freezing of time, isolating of space, in their fixing of an identity which, as such, excludes all others. If it was Benjamin who claimed that "the concept of traces finds its philosophical determination in opposition to that of aura,"[22] Laura Grisi's entire research moves in the opposite direction.

The photographs of *Hypothesis about Time* (1975) and *Endless Dialogue* (1977) close the 1970s. On the one hand, the same frontal image of a blue chronometer is obsessively repeated 360 times, one next to the other, permitting the minimal, temporal unit of a second to fill the whole room. On the other, the image of a chessboard is layered, self-reflecting, multiplied on itself as in a game of Chinese boxes, one inside the other. In contrast to chrononormativity, *Hypothesis about Time* visualizes the permutation of a temporal interval, calling into question the linearity of time. Therefore, in the new series, the future comes before the present, the past follows the future, the present precedes the past, and so forth. Similarly, *Endless Dialogue* ensures that the distance between the first and the last squares on the chessboard are divisible into ever increasing parts, opposing any pretext of the commensurability of space. Due to a well-established paradox, a tortoise having to cross the chessboard would always find itself at the starting point.

Play and the ritual have the same type of relationship: their underlying rules make an unlimited number of games or ceremonies possible, beginning with the same number of elements. Here the tending to infinity is endless. If there is an ecology (and undoubtedly there is) to which we are exposed along this journey, it is precisely that of the virtual, the anti-determinist adhesion to the multiple, to all that exists in a potential state without being visible. In her insistence on reclaiming air from oblivion, Grisi's nomadic research does not cease to "finally give back some infinity to a world that threatened to smother it." [23]

1 The titles of the essay's five sections are quotes from a textual work by Laura Grisi on display in the Rome exhibition *Mappa 72*, curated by Incontri Internazionali d'Arte, Palazzo Taverna, Rome, November 20–December 18, 1972. The title of the third section is the only exception, and is taken from the artist's book *Distillations: 3 Months of Looking*, Artestudio, Macerata 1970.

2 *Volume of Air* was created for the exhibition *Nuovi Materiali, Nuove Tecniche*, Caorle, 1969. The only time it was reconstructed was for the exhibition *Artificial Nature*, curated by Jeffrey Deitch and produced by the Deste Foundation for Contemporary Art, The House of Cyprus, Athens, 1990.

3 Laura Grisi, "L'aria è la certezza visiva di uno spazio," in *Qui–Arte Contemporanea* 6, Rome, September 1969. The text was previously published in the catalogue of the *Nuovi Materiali, Nuove Tecniche* exhibition.

4 The film, *Whirlpool*, was shown with the title *Gorgo* at the Rome Quadriennale in 1973 and almost five decades later in the exhibition *The Measuring of Time,* Muzeum Susch, 2021. It is a video of a 16mm color film projected onto the floor; it covers the entire surface of the environment and reproduces a circular whirlpool into which the public is invited to enter. Once in the center of this virtual, atmospheric condition (with changing color and concentric speed), totally sucked into the vertiginous depth of the vortex, the spectators cease to perceive themselves as outside the phenomenon. They begin to feel themselves to be part of a process that it is difficult to stop, and lose track of meters and measurements. This permanent flow does not simply alter the conditions of perceptive stability of the environment, disabling our sense of orientation. Neither does it limit itself to contrasting the spatial limits of the exhibition room with the limitless transformation of natural phenomena. The fundamental aspect of this work lies in placing us face to face with a basic dilemma: that thought, per se, is movement, the inexhaustible resource of a nomadic being.

5 Grisi in "Essay–Interview by Germano Celant," in *Laura Grisi. A Selection of Works with Notes by the Artist*, trans. Marguerite Shore, Rizzoli, New York 1990, p. 31.

6 Laura Grisi, "L'aria è la certezza visiva di uno spazio."

7 Laura Grisi, "Essay–Interview by Germano Celant," p. 24.

8 Luce Irigaray, *The Forgetting of Air in Martin Heidegger* [1983], trans. Mary Beth Mader, University of Texas Press, Austin 1999, p. 8. Irigaray's text is liberally used here.

9 This is not to judge Grisi's adhesion or otherwise to the feminist movement, but to highlight the inherency of orientations and practices of subjugation to the frameworks of epistemological gender reference in the 1970s. The politics of listening as a moment privileged over enunciation is not only the subject of the feminism of difference, but also and principally of Carla Lonzi. On chrononormativity, see Elizabeth Freeman, *Time Binds. Queer Temporalities, Queer Histories*, Duke University Press, Durham 2010, p. 3.

10 Lucy R. Lippard, *Intricate Structure/Repeated Image*, Tyler School of Art, Temple University, Philadelphia 1979.

11 Felix Guattari talks of an "ecology of the virtual" in *Chaosmosis: An Ethico-Aesthetic Paradigm* [1992], trans. Paul Bains and Julian Pefanis, Indiana University Press, Bloomington and Indianapolis 1995.

12 Robert Barry had created photographs of his *Inert Gas Series* (1969) in the Mohave Desert, precisely to demonstrate that they would not provide any visual evidence. Nonetheless, in contrast to Grisi's work, the *Inert Gas Series* does not provide for any physical presence or interaction with the spectator.

13 Grisi states: "This is how I came into contact with so many peoples and cultures that were distant from my own cultural context, an experience that strongly influenced my way of thinking and of visualizing life," in "Essay-Interview by Germano Celant," p. 13.

14 Laura Grisi in "Essay–Interview by Germano Celant," p. 17.

15 André Bazin, "The Ontology of the Photographic Image," in *What is cinema?* [1958–1965], trans. and ed. Hugh Gray, University of California Press, Berkeley 1967.

16 Roland Barthes, *Camera Lucida* [1980], trans. Richard Howard, Hill & Wang, New York 1981.

17 Peter Galassi, *Before Photography: Painting and the Invention of Photography,* The Museum of Modern Art, New York 1981.

18 Udo Kultermann, essay in the exhibition catalogue, Galerie E. M. Thelen, Essen 1968.

19 Maurizio Fagiolo Dell'Arco, *Laura Grisi*, exh. cat., Premio Provincia di Trento–Mostra Nazionale di Pittura, Trento 1967, p. 56–57.

20 Gilles Deleuze, "The Actual and the Virtual," trans. Eliot Ross Albert in Gilles Deleuze and Claire Parnet, *Dialogues II* (1977), trans. Hugh Tomlinson and Barbara Habberjam, The Althlone Press, London 1987.

21 Claude Lévi-Strauss, *The Savage Mind* (1962), The University of Chicago Press, Chicago 1966. Laura Grisi was familiar with the author's idea of the "science of the concrete," which she witnessed on her many travels. "These photographs," she confessed to Celant, "were the result of the impact on me of many different cultures, with their various rituals and modes of behavior in various cultural contexts and traditions. They were also the sum of my personal reactions to a wide range of environmental situations. I was interested in finding affinities between ethnic groups that were both very different from each other and also often alike, with similar mythologies, rituals, customs, and habits," in "Essay–Interview by Germano Celant," p. 31.

22 Walter Benjamin, "Lettera ad Adorno del 9-12-1938," in *Lettere 1913-1940*, Einaudi, Torino 1978, p. 280. Published in English in *The Correspondence of Walter Benjamin, 1910–1940*, University of Chicago Press, Chicago 1994.

23 Felix Guattari, *Chaosmosis*.

Traveling with Laura Grisi 1958–1959

Laura Grisi, Las Pampas, Argentina, 1958

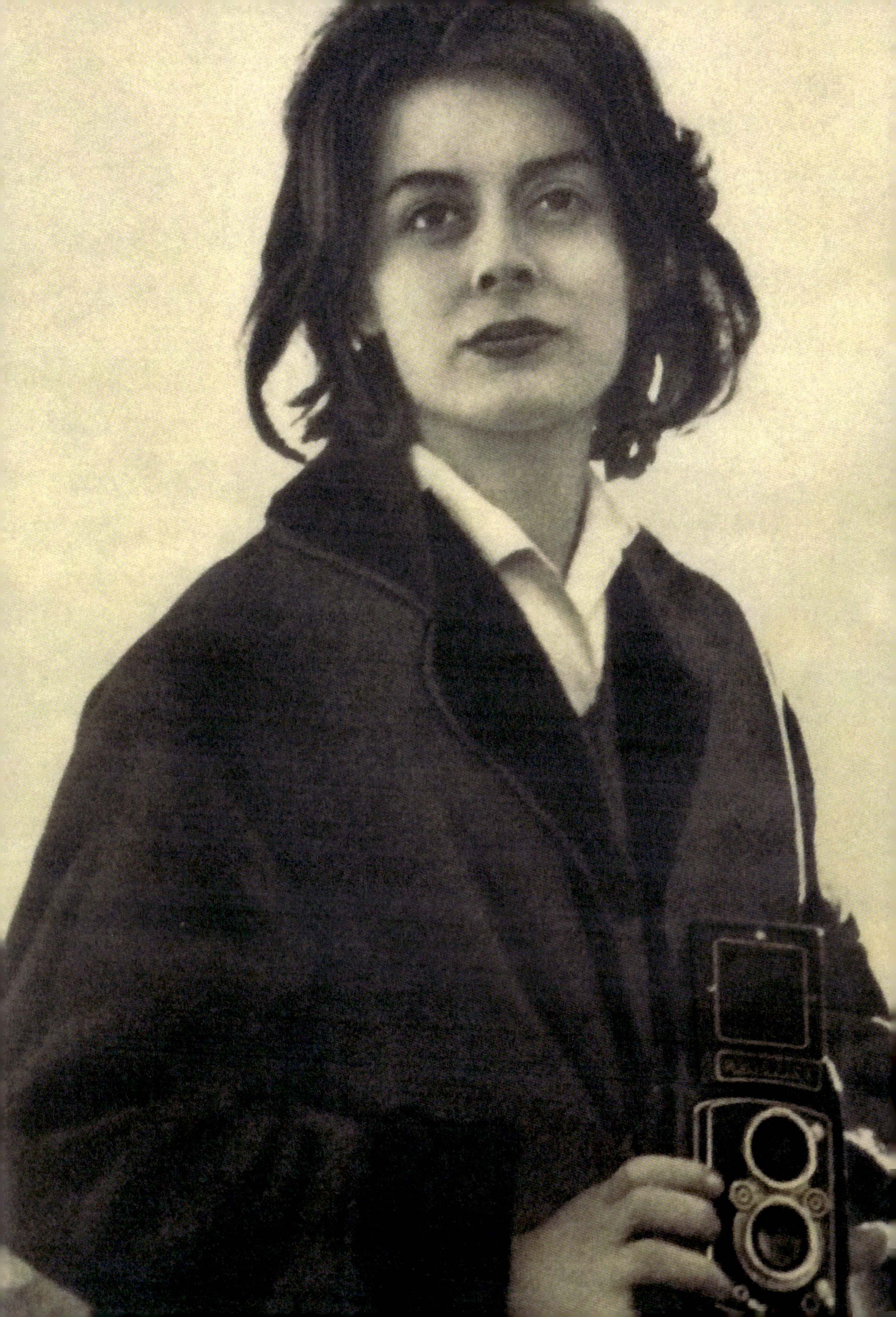

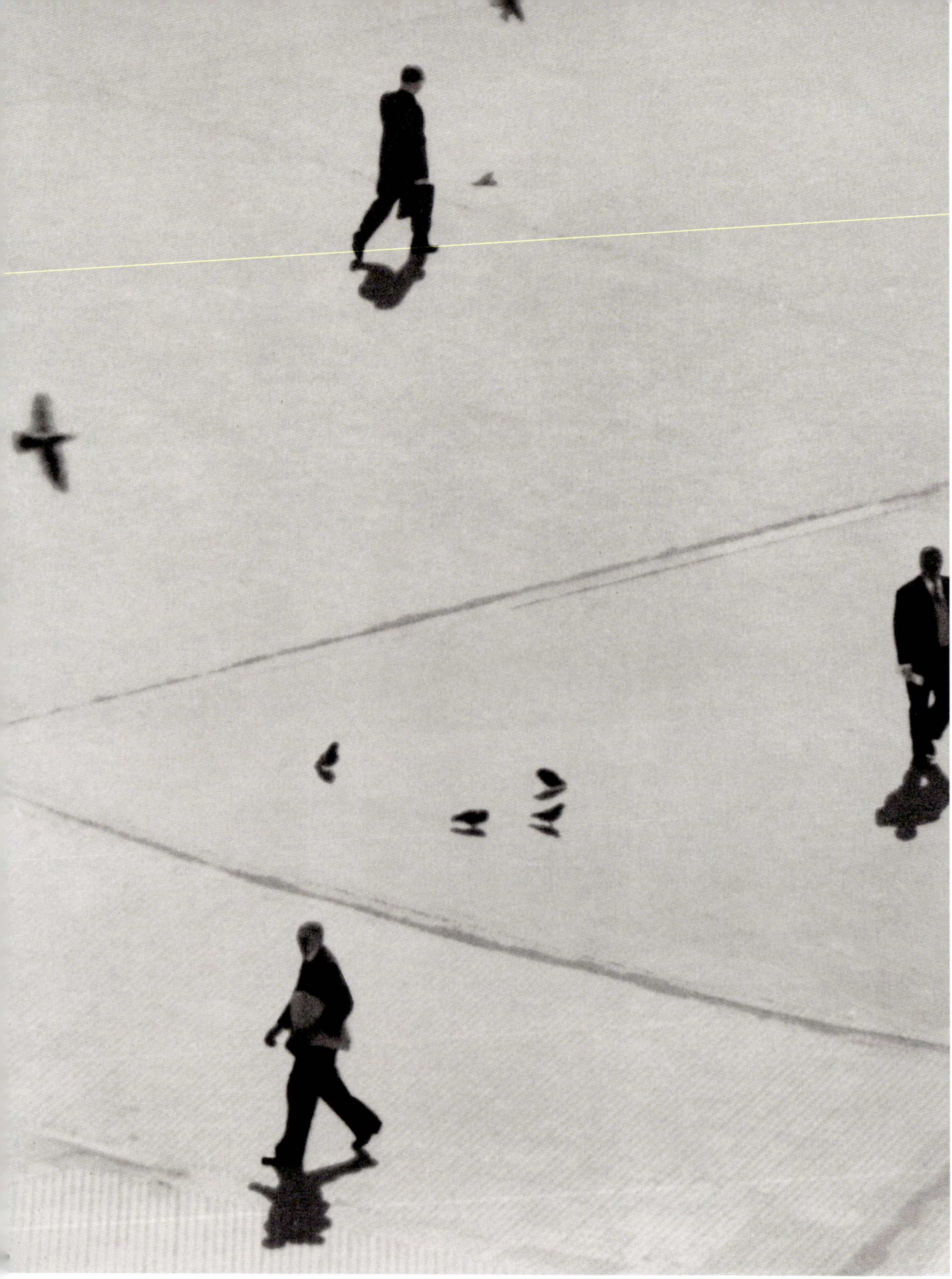

Men's Friends (Mayo's Square)
Pages 24–29: all photographs from the book *Pasos por Buenos Aires*, Capricornio, Buenos Aires 1959

Make Believe and Reality
Snack on the River Side
Children's Corner

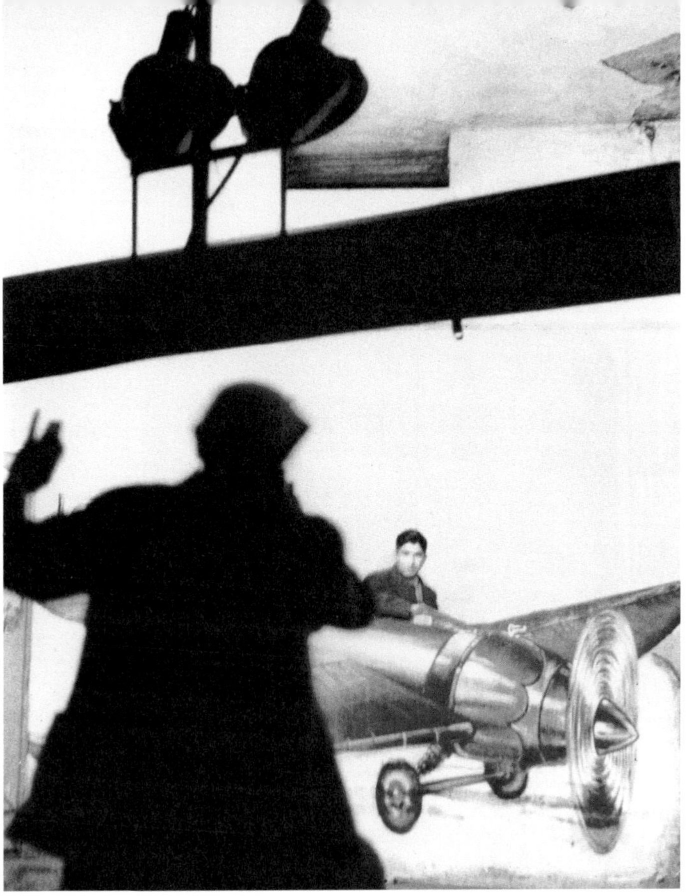

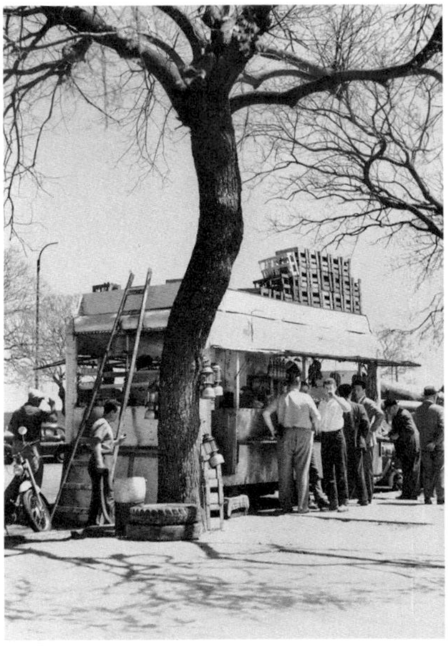

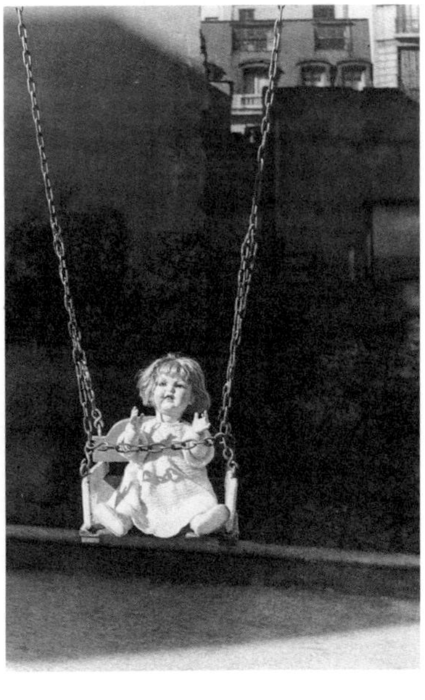

Waiting for Clients
The Inevitable Indigence (Dock Sud)
The Cradle of the Tango (Dock Sud)

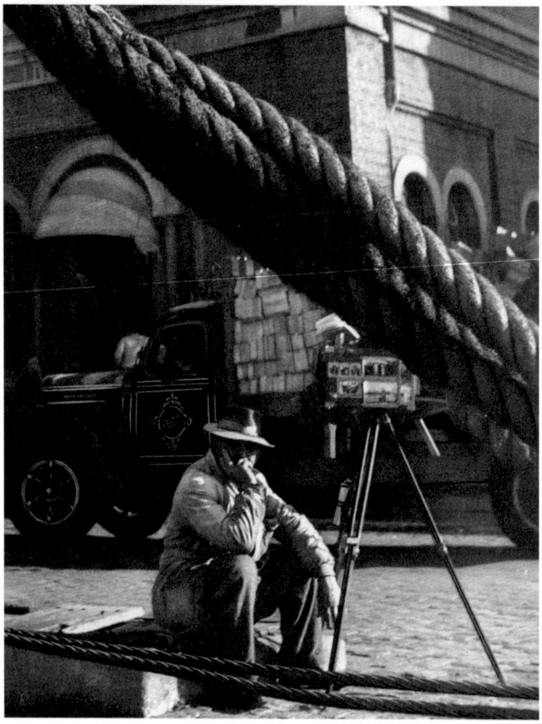

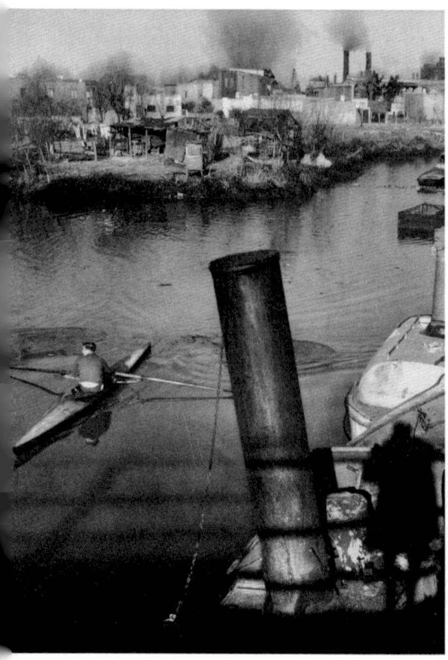

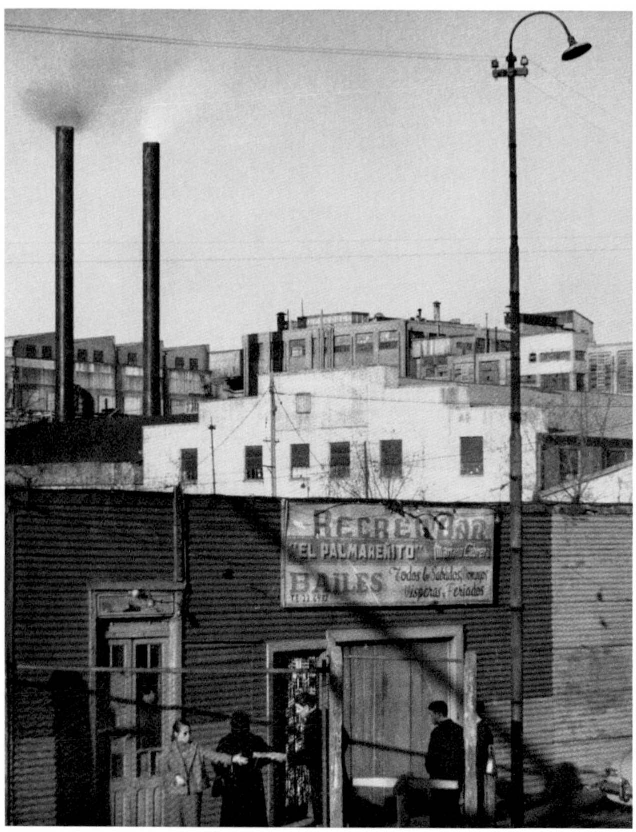

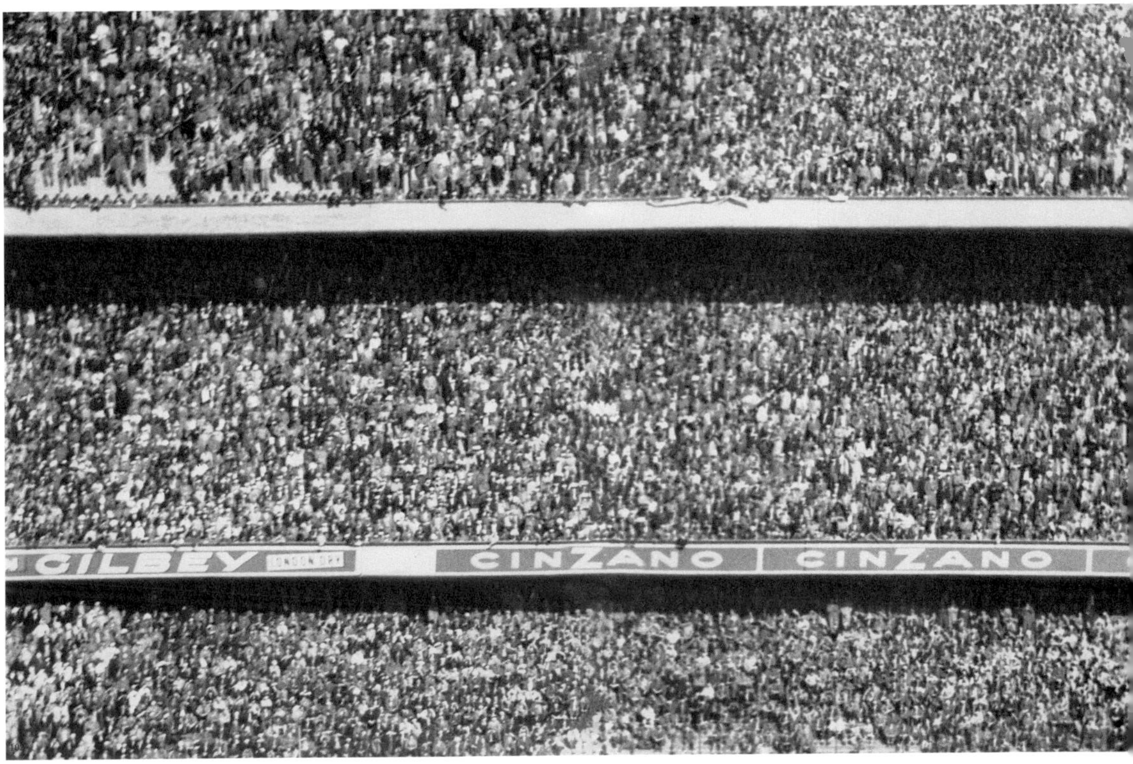
GILBEY
LONDON DRY
CINZANO
CINZANO

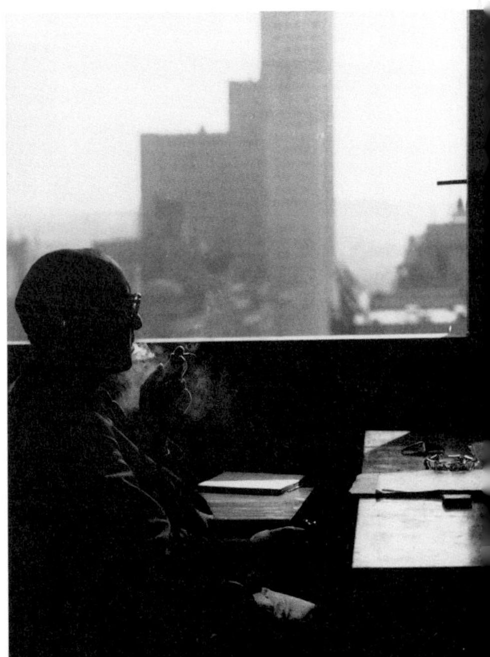

The End of a Night or the Beginning of a New Day?
Precautions
Ivory Tower

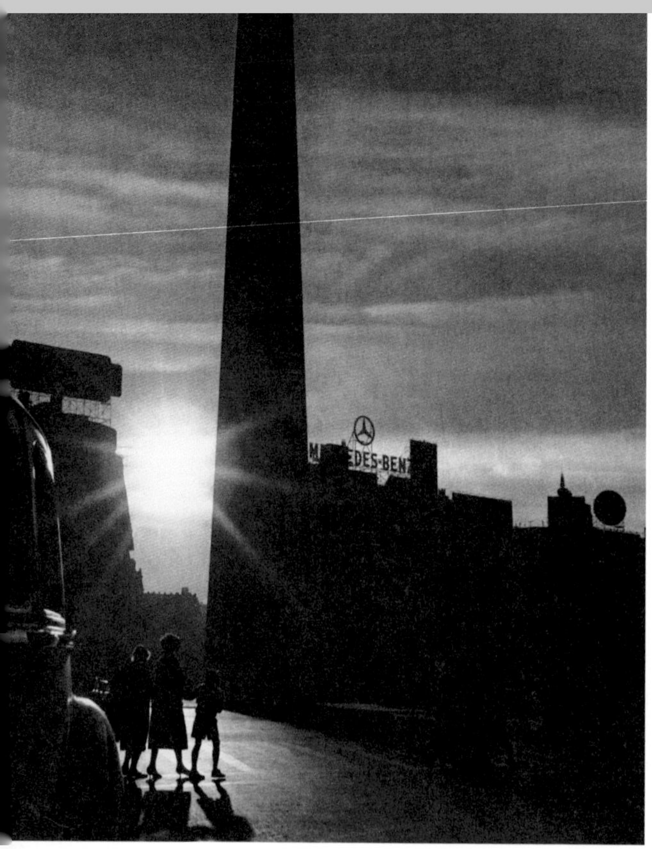

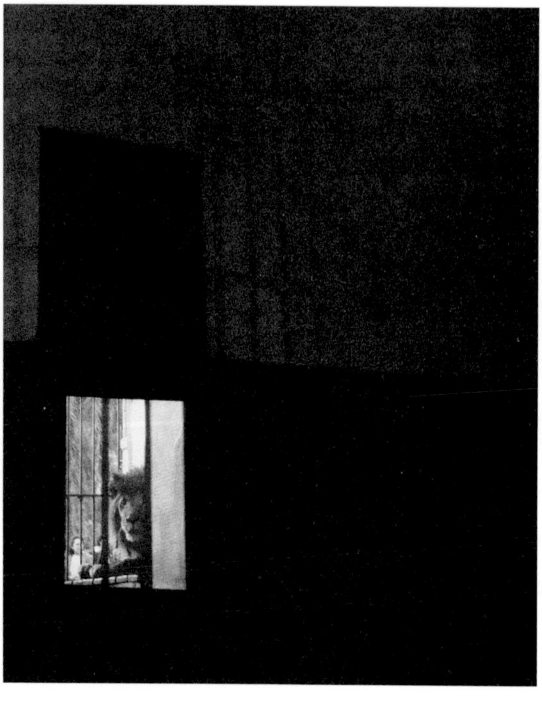

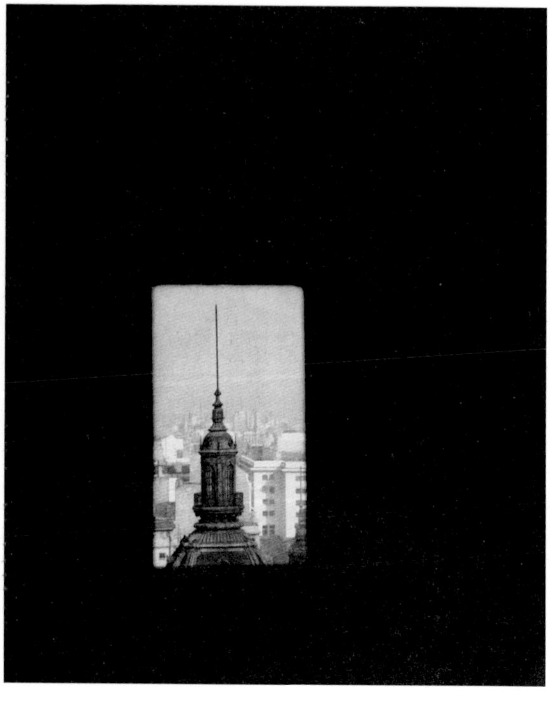

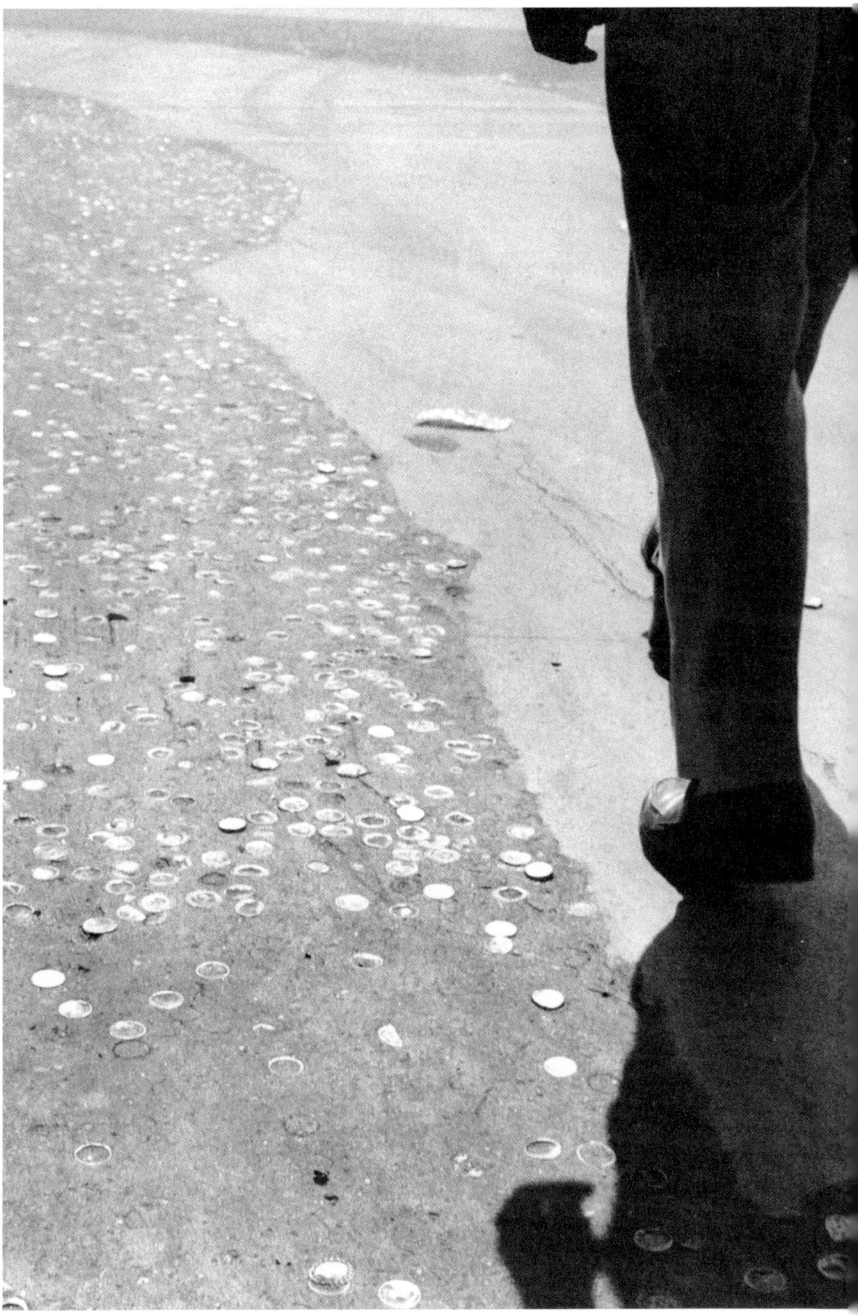

Traveling with Laura Grisi 1960s

Laura Grisi, Sahara Desert, 1963

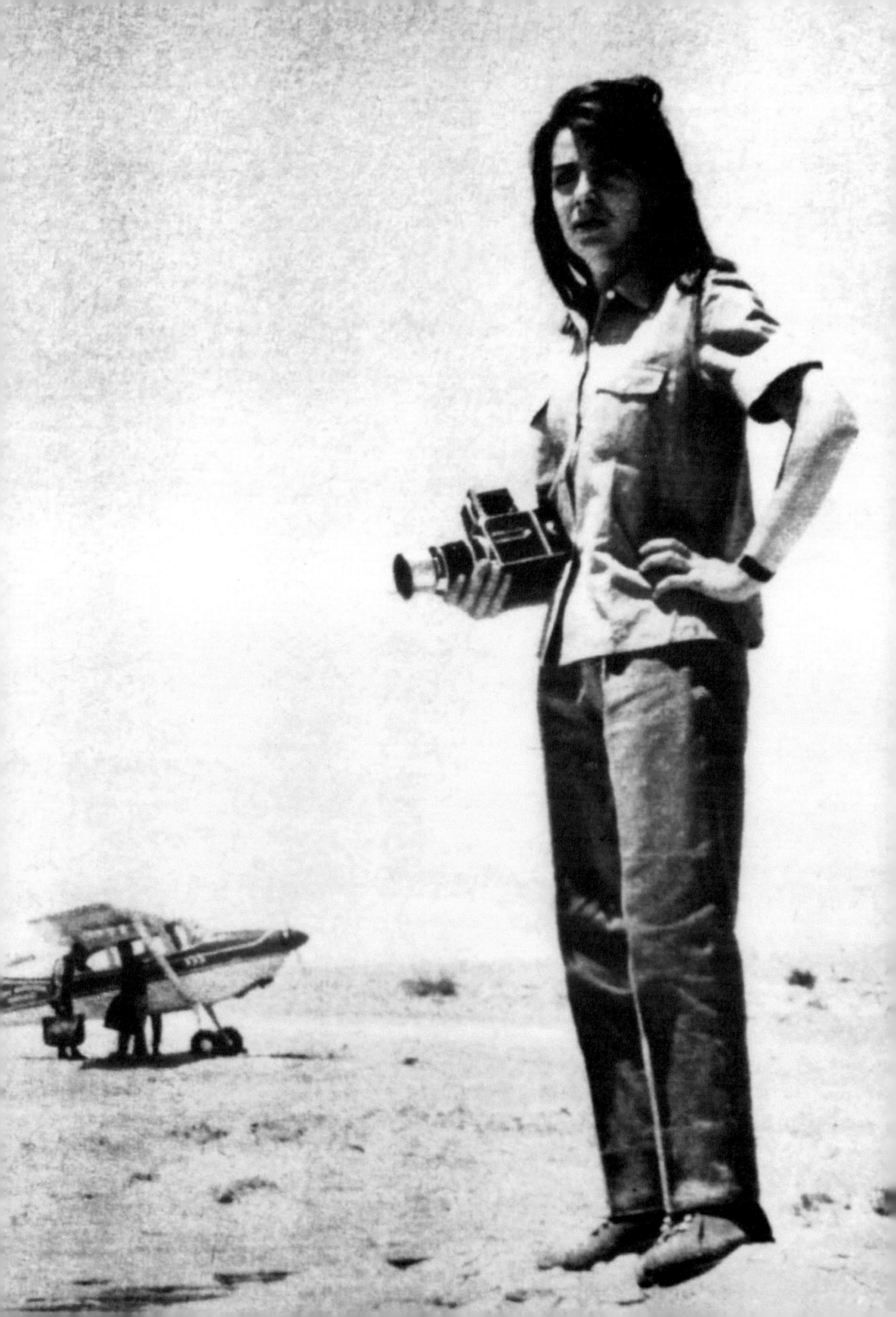

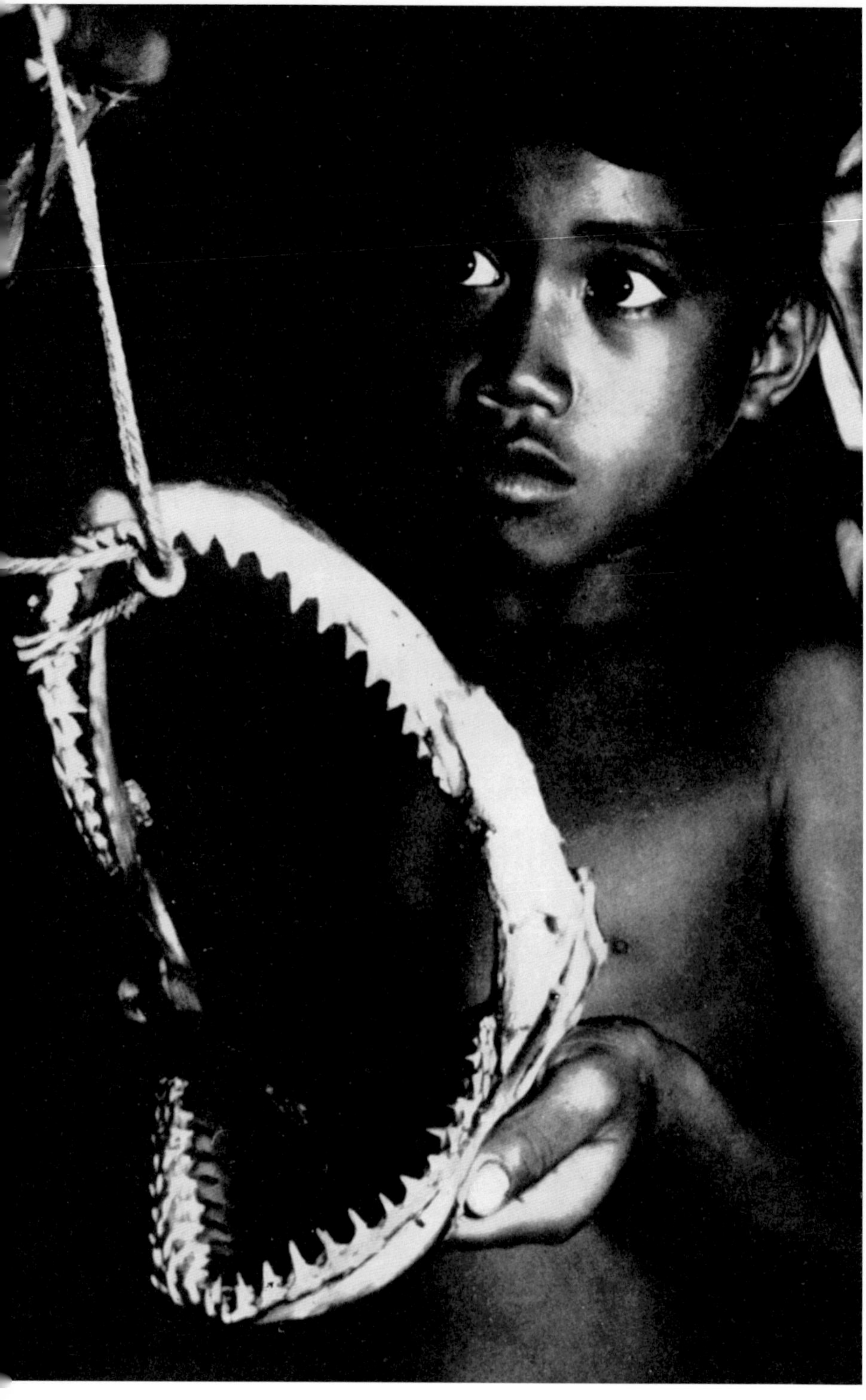

Pages 32–34: all photographs from the book *I Denti del Tigre*, Lerici Editore, Milan 1964

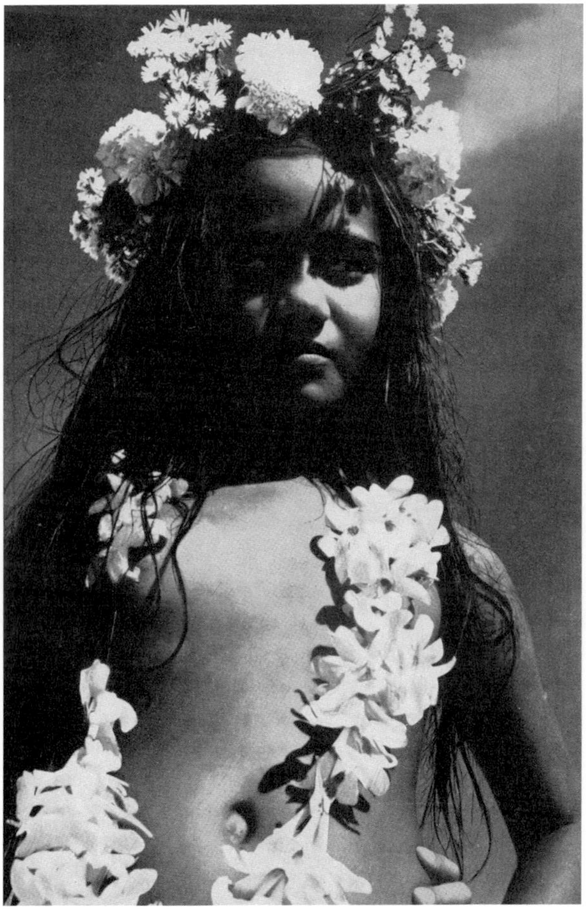

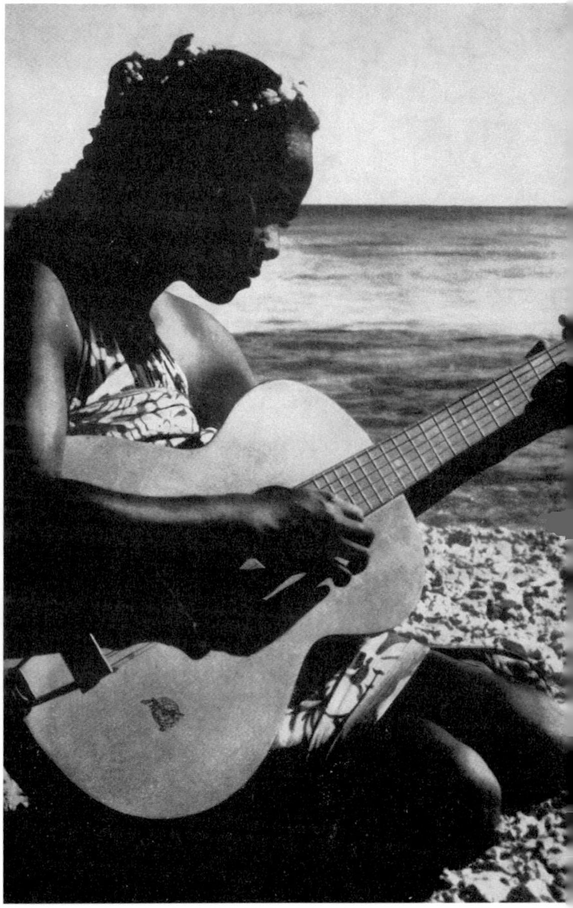

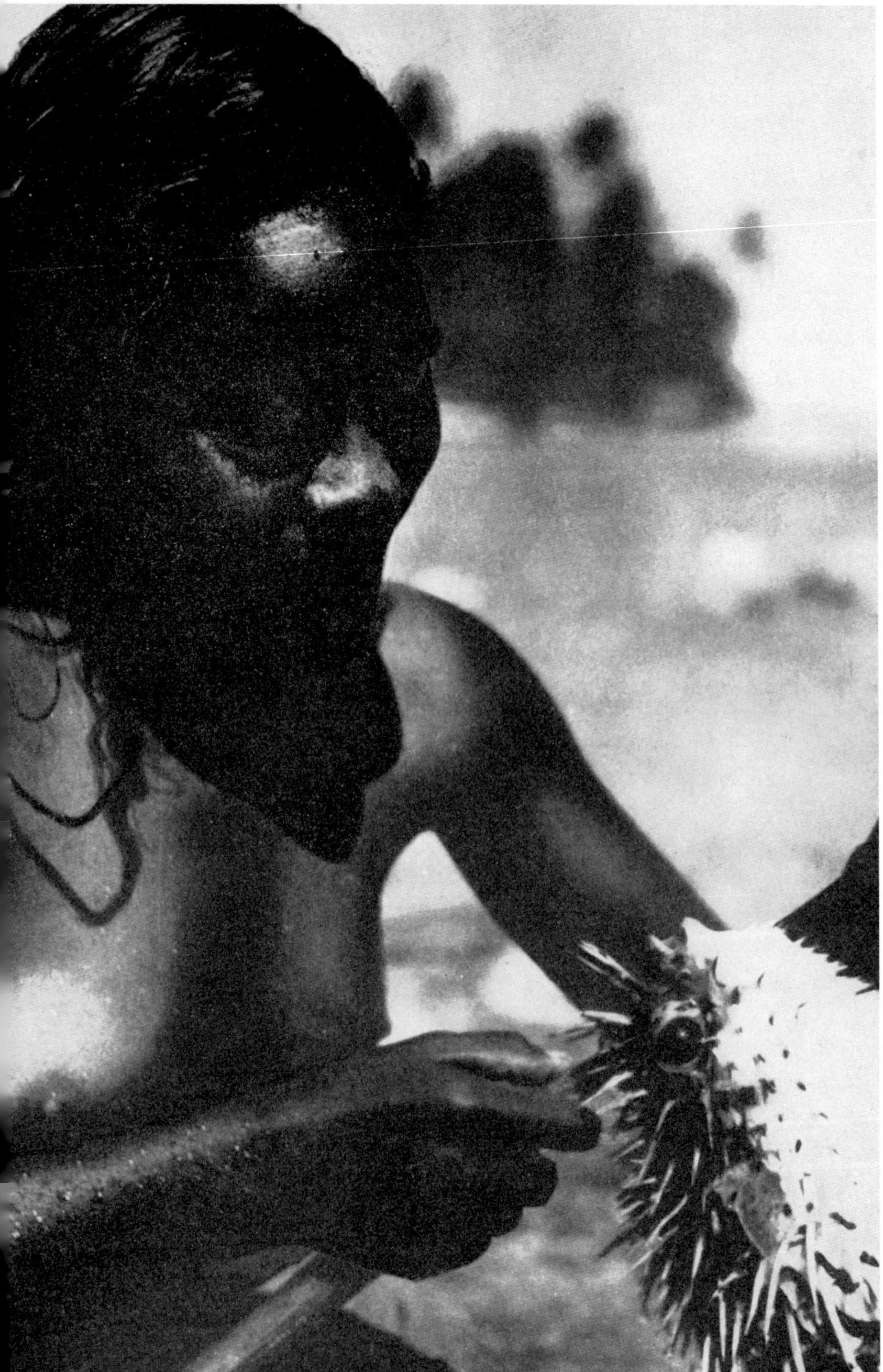

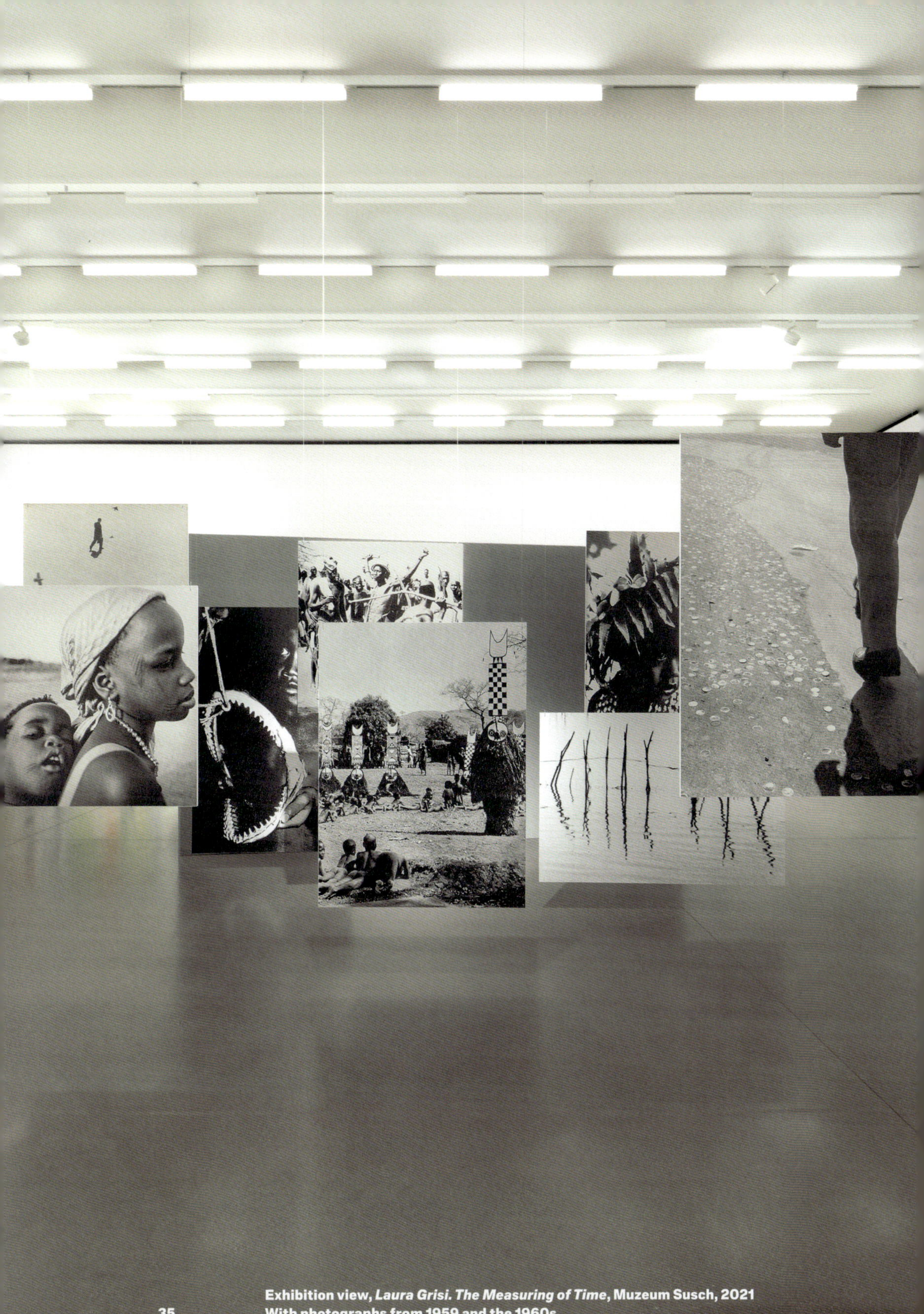

Exhibition view, *Laura Grisi. The Measuring of Time*, Muzeum Susch, 2021
With photographs from 1959 and the 1960s

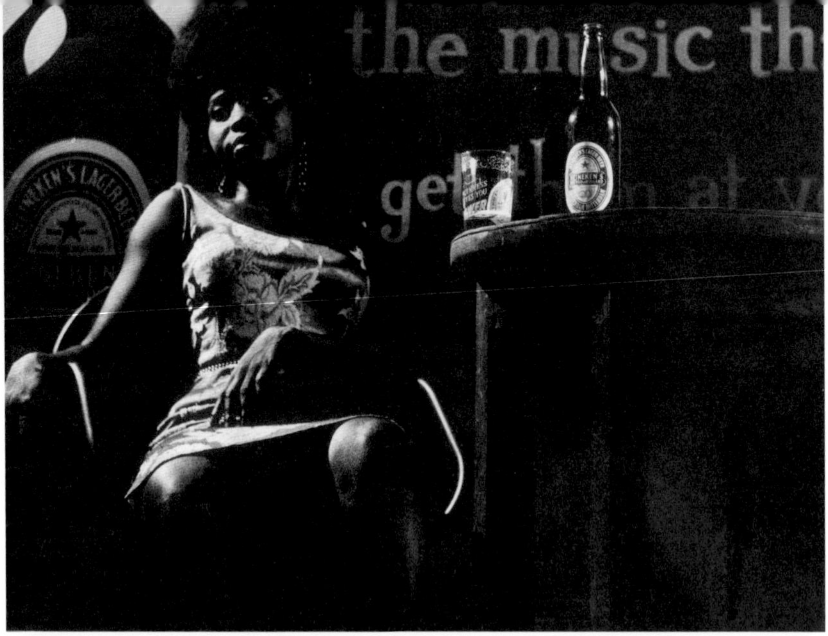

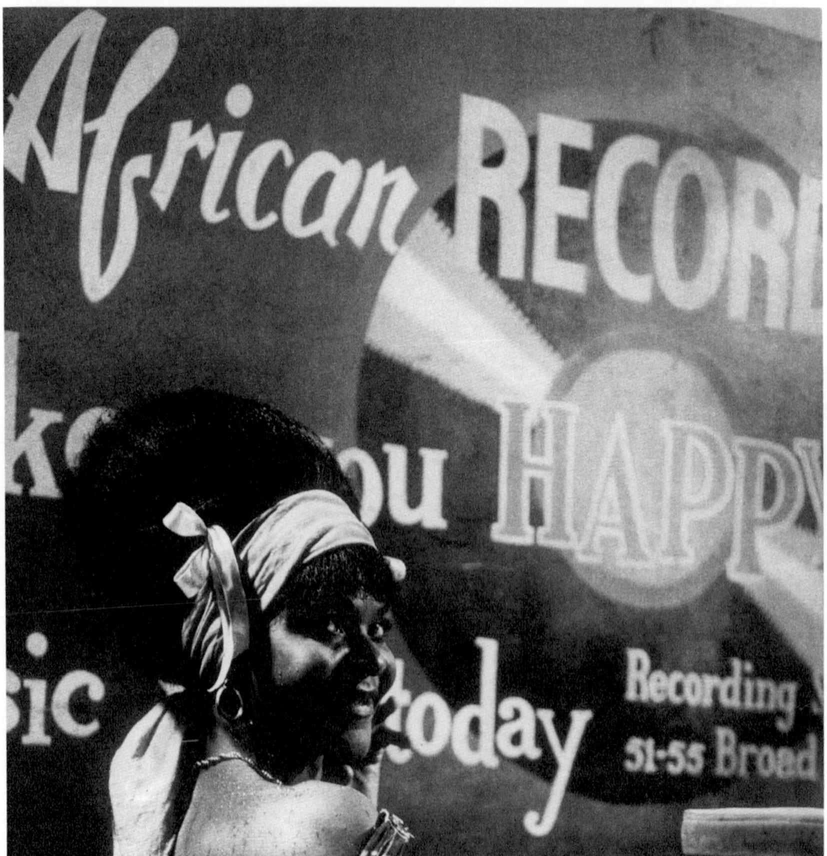

Yoruba Girls and Twist Fatigue at the Lagos Lido, Nigeria, 1963
Hully-gully Soloist at Fort Lamy's Olimpus, Nigeria, 1963
Pages 36–37: all photographs from *I Mille Fuochi dal Sahara al Congo* by Folco Quilici, Leonardo Da Vinci, Bari 1965

Baby Carried on Shoulders, Nigeria, 1961
A Bedouin Woman with All the Goods of Her Tent Follows A Caravan Heading to Gabes, Sahara Desert, 1961
A Mossí Girl Sifts Millet by Pouring it into an Outdoor Barn, Upper Volta, 1963

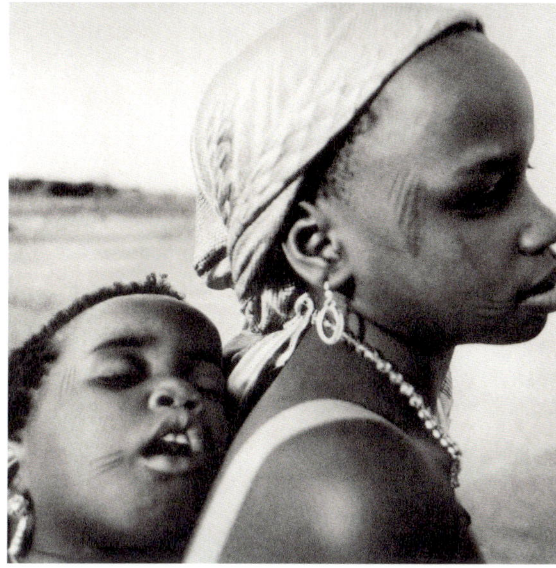

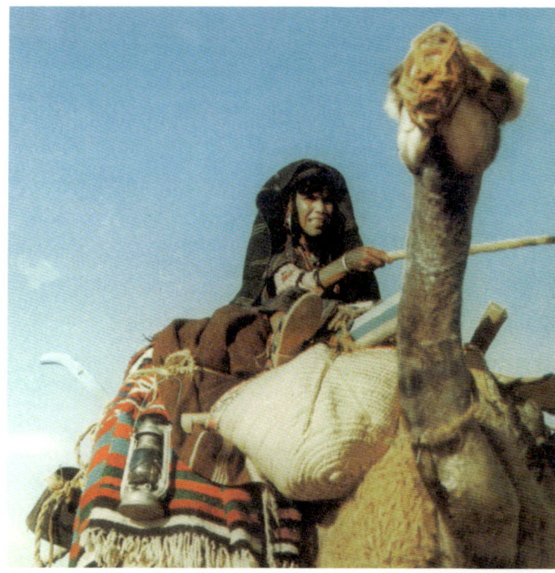

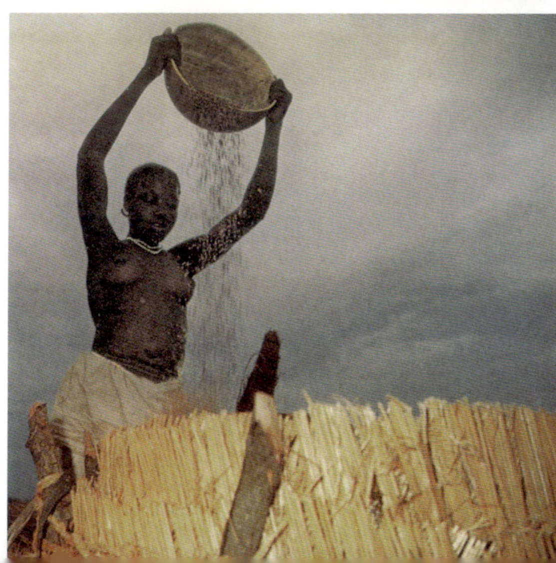

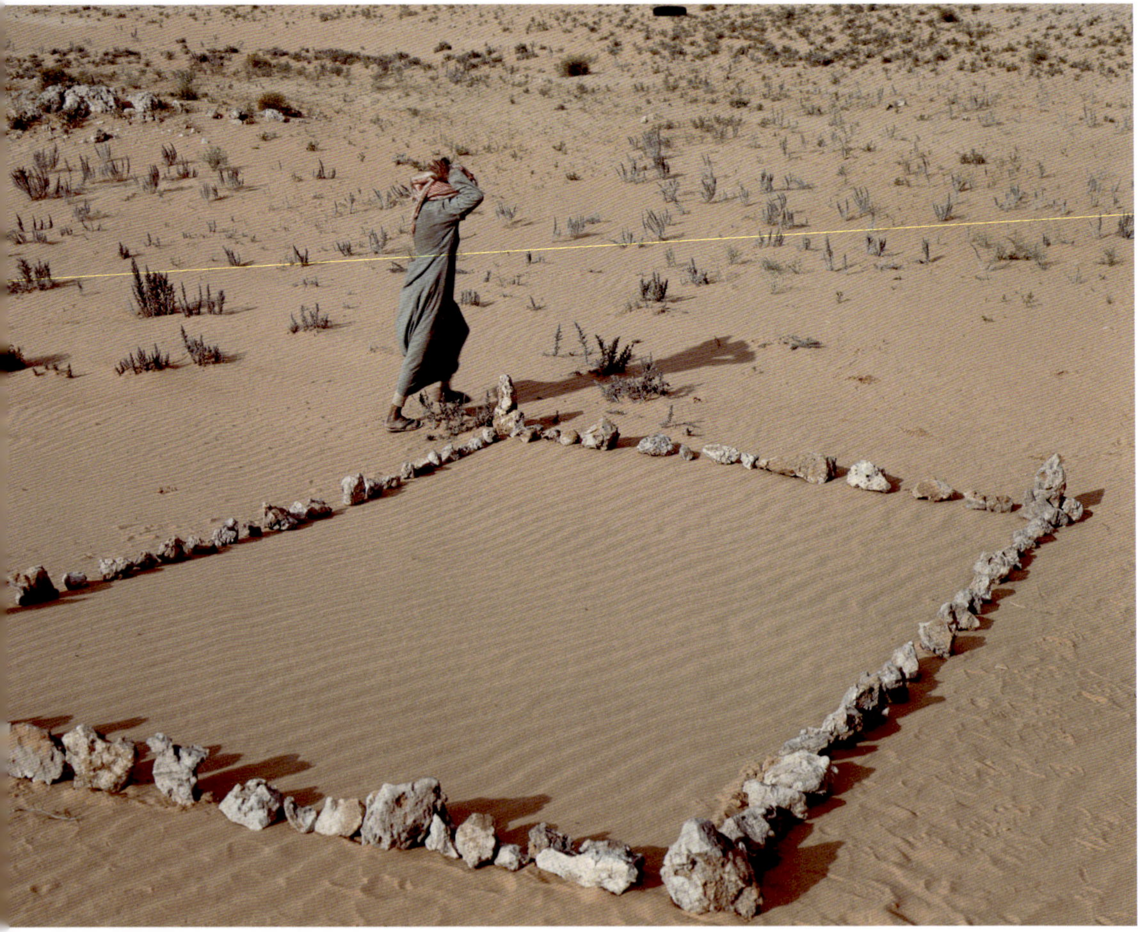

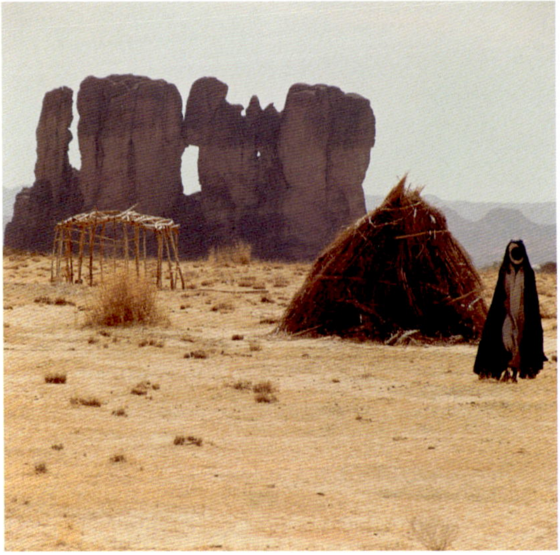

***A Nomad and "His Mosque" (A Stone Square in the Desert)*, Saudi Arabia, 1966**
***Ennedi Plateau*, Chad, 1960–1961**

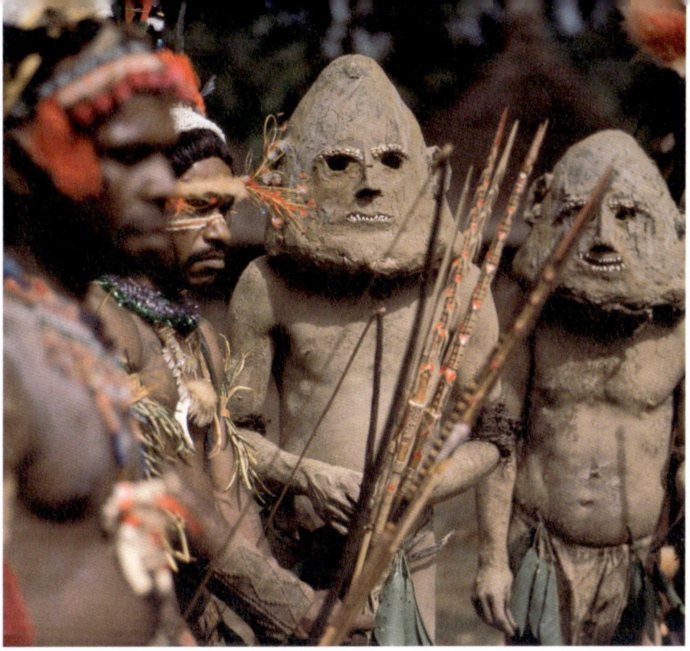

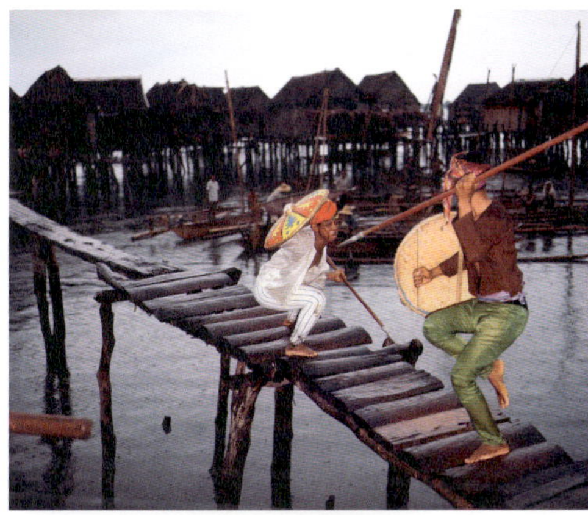

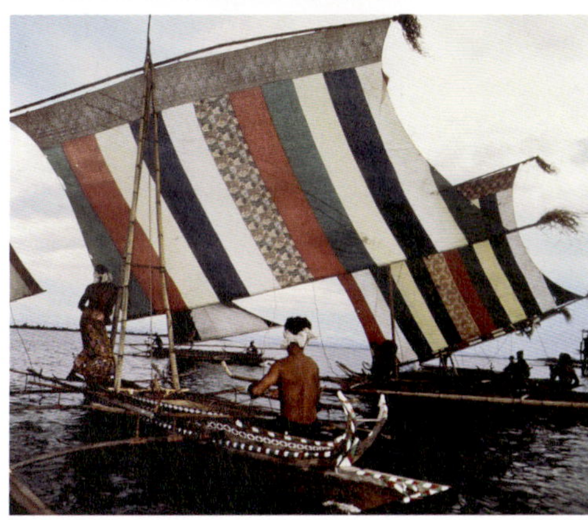

Mudmen in Ritual Mud Masks, **New Guinea, 1969**
Muslim Warrior Dance, **Sulu Islands, 1967–1968**
Vintas, the Distinctive Boats of the Badjaos, the Nomads of the Sea, **Mindanao, 1967**

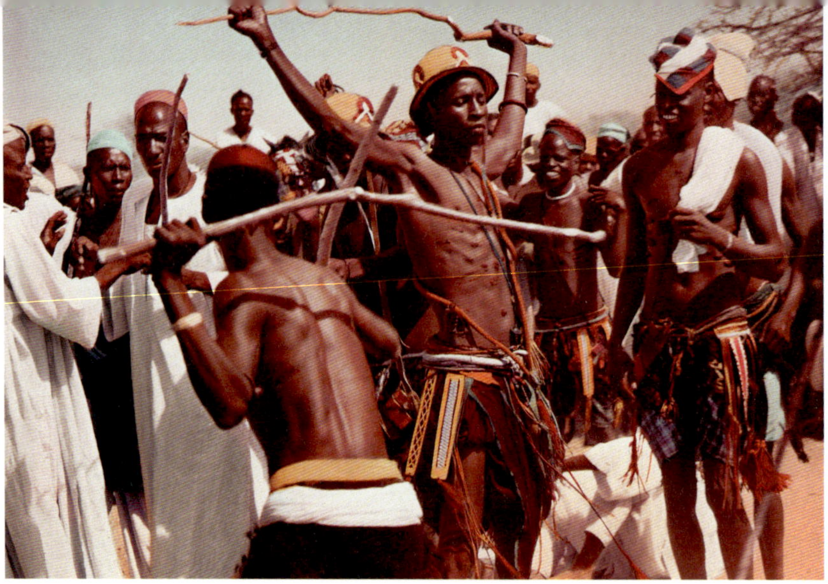

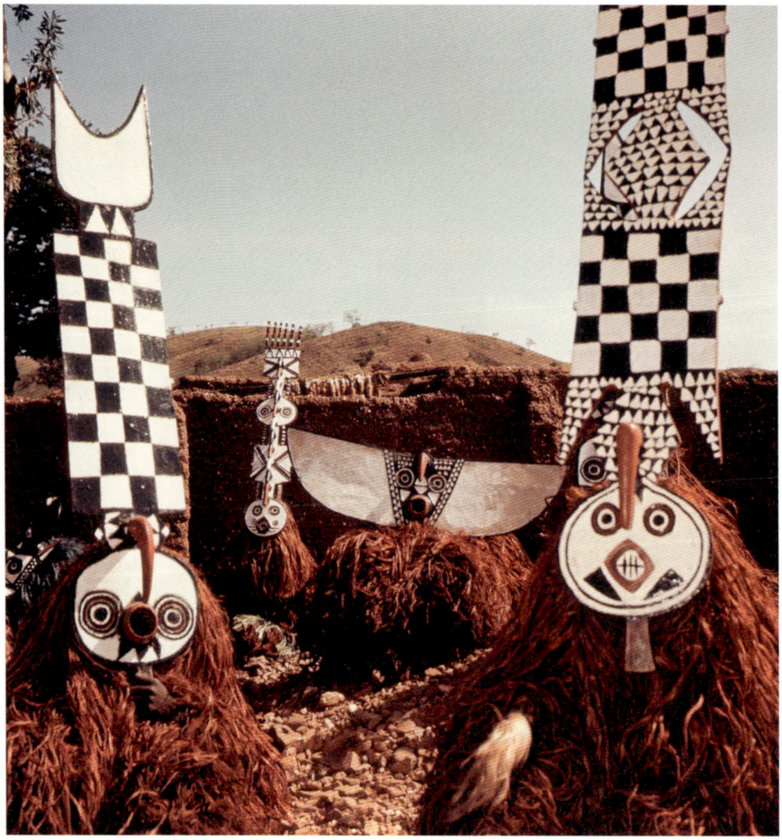

***Peul Shepherds Prove their Courage in the Sha-ròt Ceremony*, Niger, 1963**
Children's Initiation Ceremony, Boni the Bobò Masks
***Represent Forest Gods and Wild Animals*, Upper Volta, 1963**
***Lake Chad*, Chad, 1968** **→ p. 114–119**

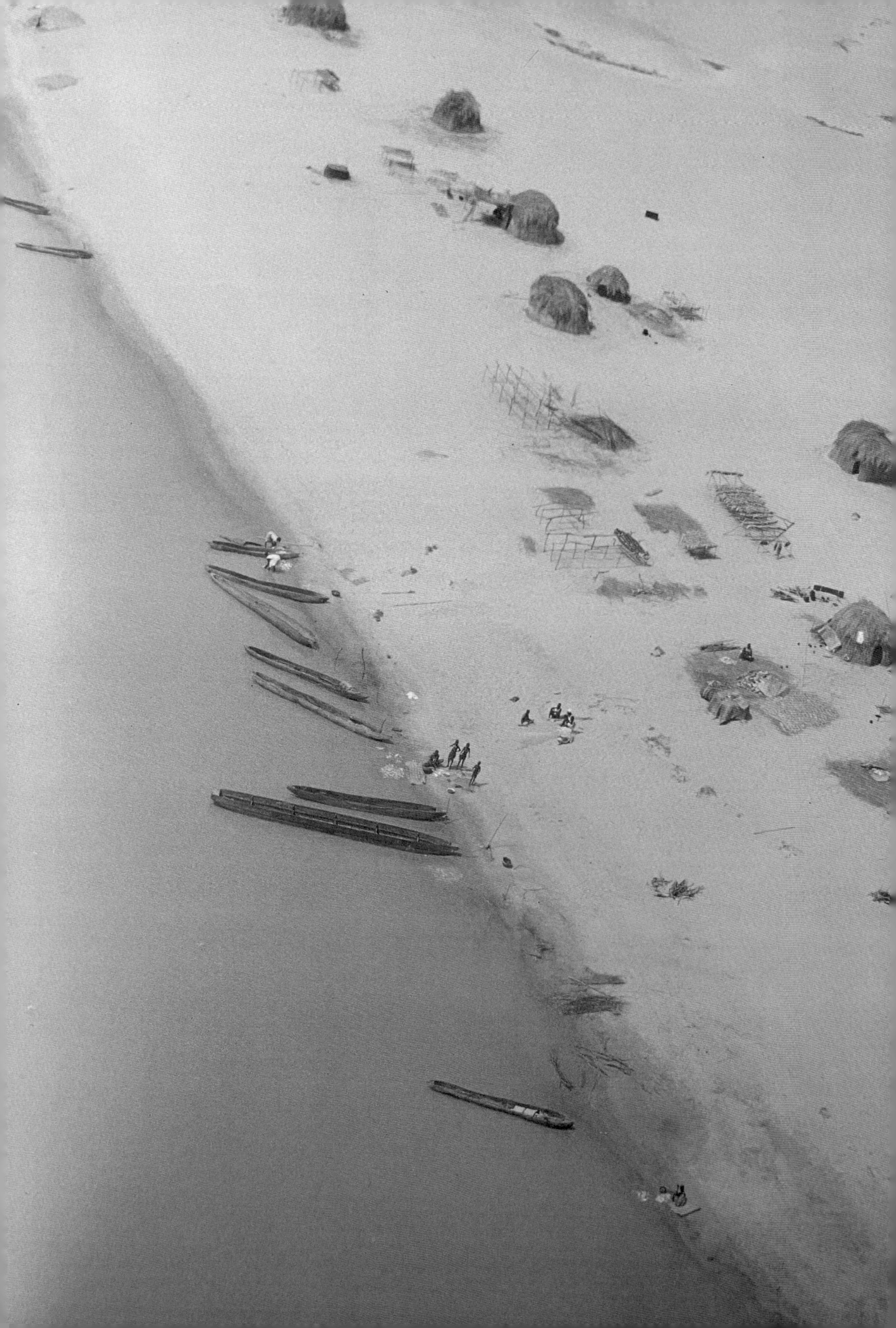

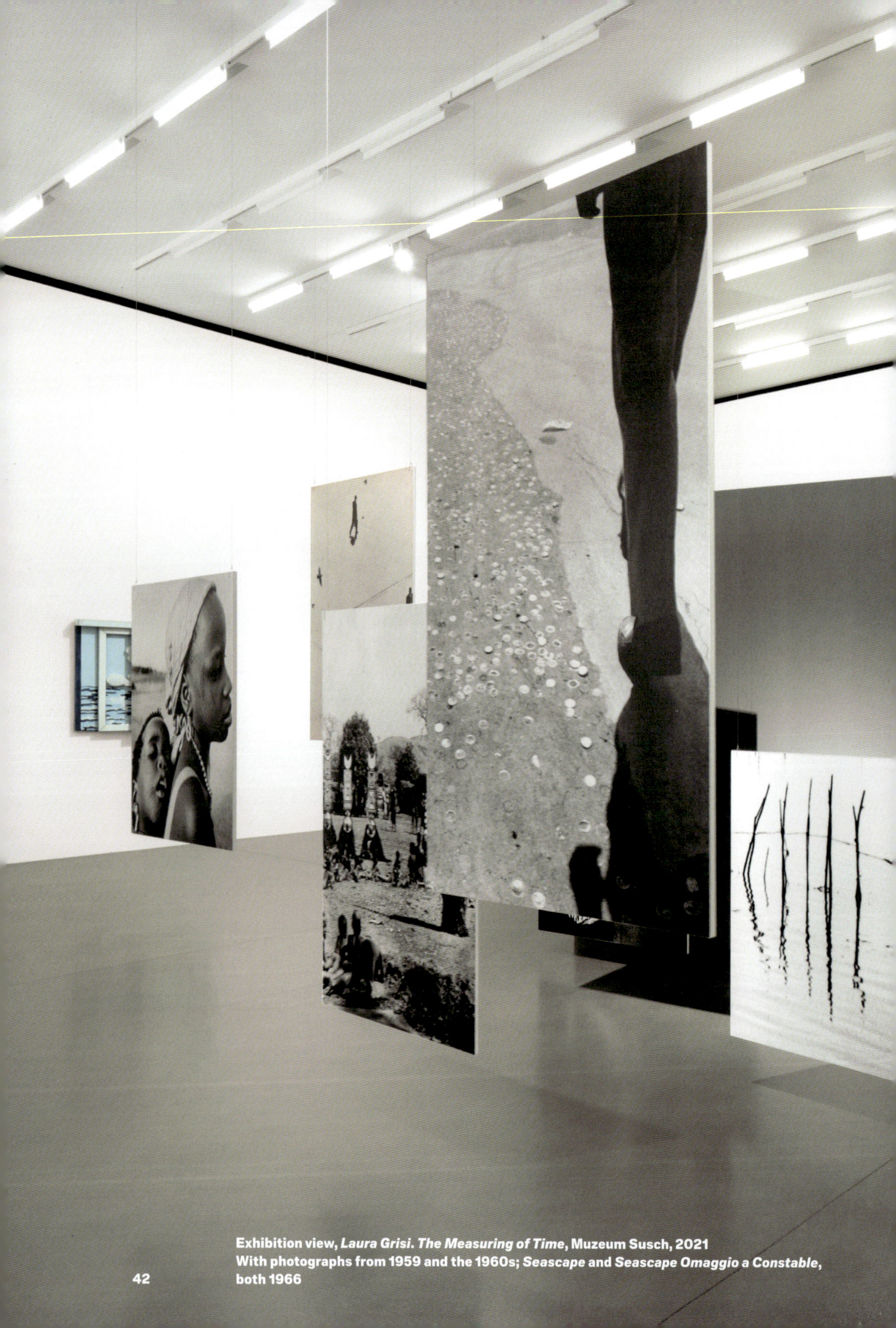

Exhibition view, *Laura Grisi. The Measuring of Time*, Muzeum Susch, 2021
With photographs from 1959 and the 1960s; *Seascape* and *Seascape Omaggio a Constable*, both 1966

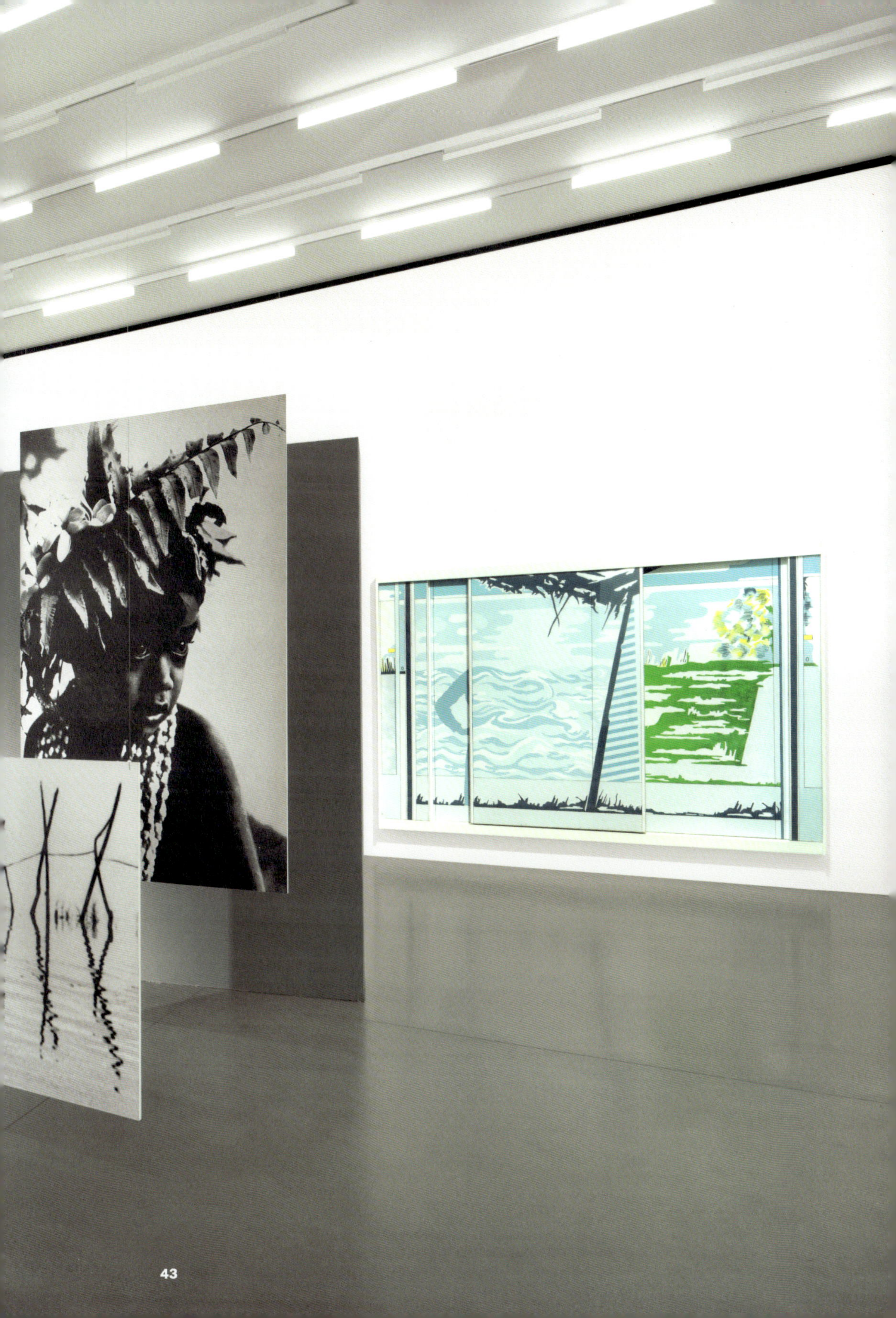

Laura Grisi: In and Ahead of Her Time
Valérie Da Costa

June 1968: the 34th Venice Biennale opened in chaos. Four young people—Michelle Coudray, Piero Gilardi, Laura Grisi, and Pino Pascali[1]—are sitting on the terrace at the Caffè Florian. The last three represent a new generation of artists. Pascali takes center stage in the snapshot: he is presenting a solo exhibition in the Italian pavilion and has just spoken to a crowd of students and journalists in the Biennale Giardini to make the case for opening his space.[2] It is a time of protest, the "inaugurazione della prima biennale del poliziotto," ("the biennale of the policeman") as the leaflets handed out by protesters claim. The pavilions are to stay closed for several weeks, eventually reopening in July.

Two years previously, Grisi had shown her work at the 33rd Venice Biennale alongside Umberto Bignardi, Mario Ceroli, and Michelangelo Pistoletto. The prize for painting that year went to Lucio Fontana, and the Grand Prix to Julio Le Parc, then at the beginning of his career. Having shown her work at Milan's Galleria dell'Ariete the previous year, Grisi took the opportunity in Venice to present her first geometric landscapes (*Landscape Omaggio a Gainsborough*; *Seascape Omaggio a Constable*, both 1966), characterized by bright colors on layered, painted Plexiglas panels with moving parts. The themes of these works—her own shadow and those of plants, trees, and birds—affiliate them with Italian Pop figurative painting, foregrounding an art of the silhouette also found in the work of Bignardi, Giosetta Fioroni, Renato Mambor, and Mario Schifano, as if the aim were to strip figurative art back to its simplest, flattest self, as a single pictorial projection. Grisi's visual compositions strive to reach beyond painting in the strict sense, imagining the effects of volumes of color in a similar vein to Cesare Tacchi's painted fabric pieces (*Paola e poltrona*, 1964) and Pascali's paint-on-polyurethane-foam series "pezzi anatomici di donne" (*Labbra rosse*; *Omaggio a Billie Holiday*, both 1964), shown in 1965 at the group exhibition *Revort 1* at the Galleria Civica d'Arte Moderna, Palermo. This was where Grisi first met Pascali. Palermo was also hosting a lecture by the Gruppo 63,[3] where she met the writers Alberto Arbasino, Furio Colombo, and Umberto Eco. This marked the beginning of her friendship with Pascali, strengthened some years later by their mutual interest in using the four elements, earth, wind, fire, and water—also key features in the development of Arte Povera, from which Laura Grisi was surprisingly absent.

In the mid-1970s, Grisi's work took a new direction, less installation-based and participative and more pictorial and sculptural, making her a somewhat marginal figure on the Italian art scene of the 1980s and 1990s. Even so, in a lengthy interview with Germano

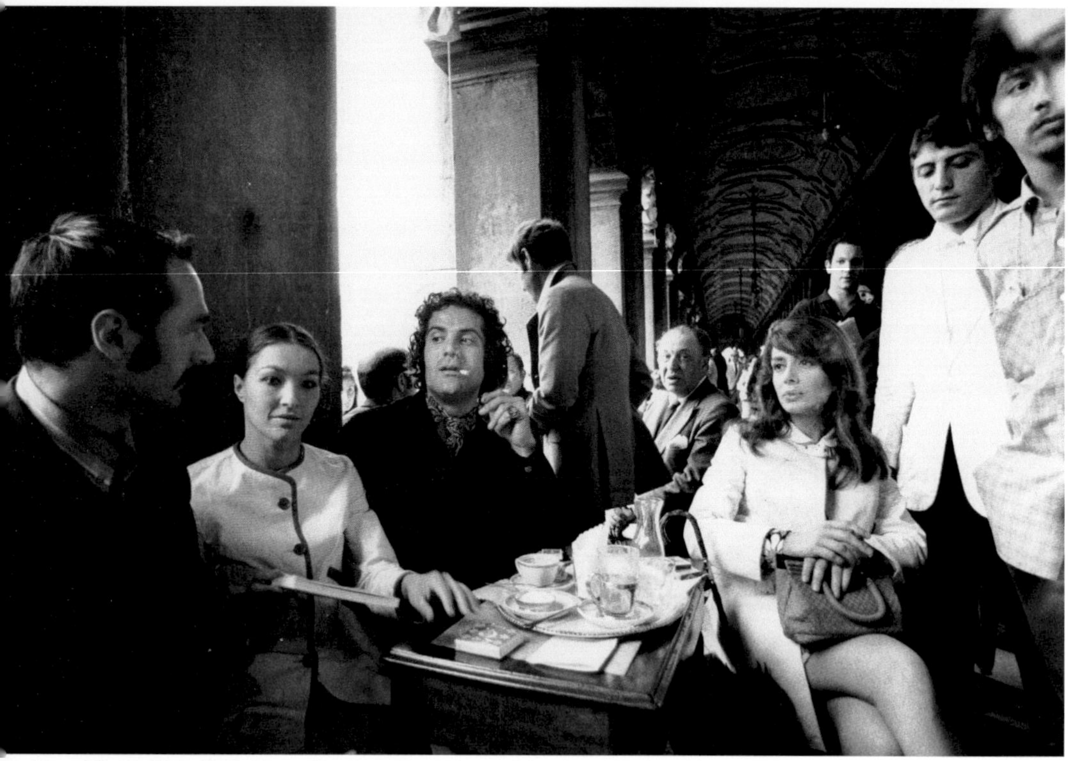

Piero Gilardi, Michelle Coudray, Pino Pascali, and Laura Grisi, Caffé Florian, Venice, 1968

Laura Grisi and Lucio Fontana, Galleria dell'Ariete, Milan, 1965

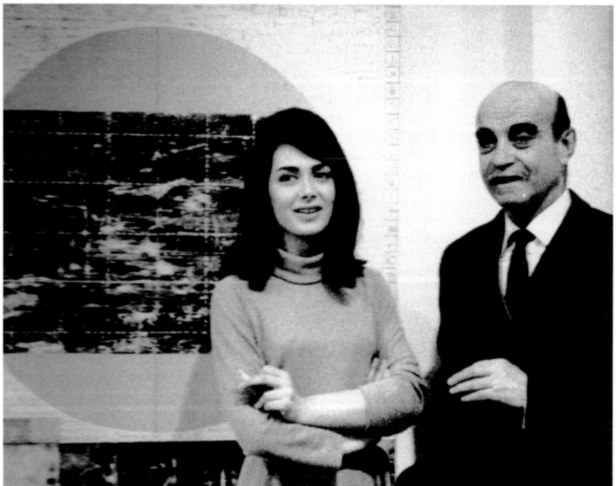

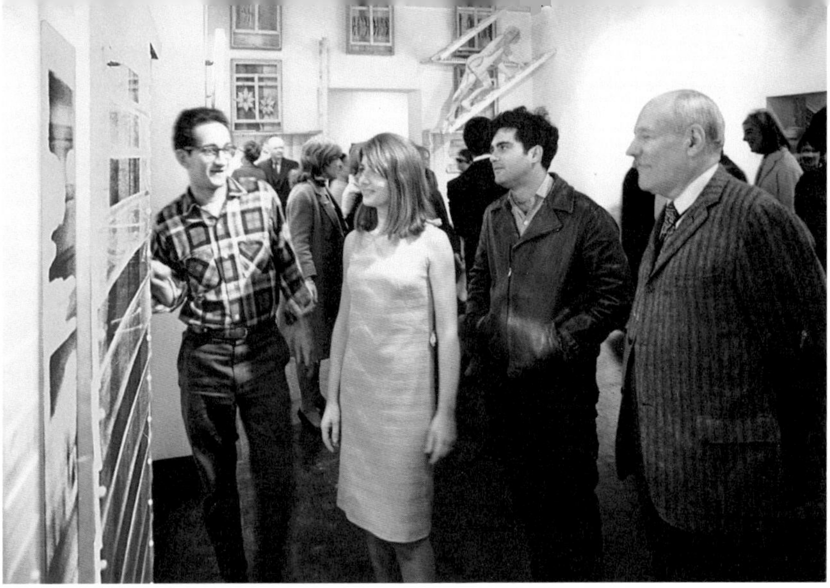

Frank Stella, Laura Grisi, Larry Poons, and Barnett Newman at the exhibition *Italy: New Tendencies*, Galleria Bonino, New York, 1966

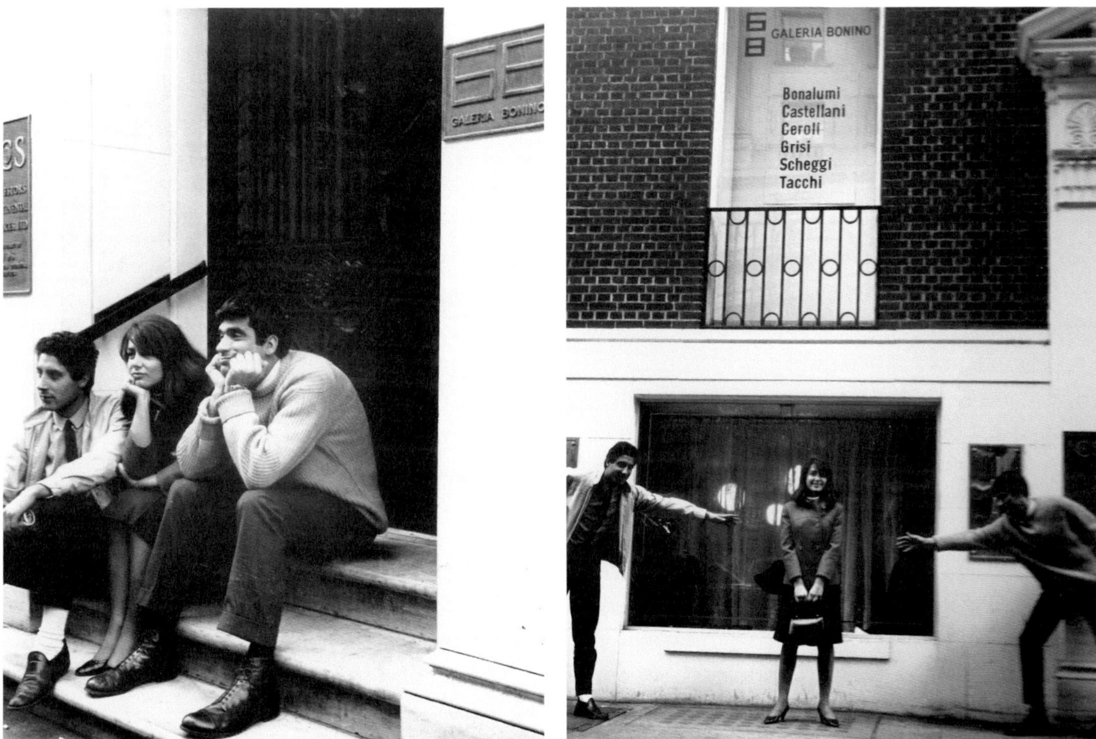

Laura Grisi with Renato Mambor to her left during the exhibition *Italy: New Tendencies*, Galleria Bonino, New York, 1966

Celant in 1989, in the sole monograph on her work available to date, Grisi looked back at Pascali's visits to her studio: "He sometimes came to visit me at home, where I had a large zebra skin on the floor, which I had brought back from Africa. One day he looked at it carefully, then made a gesture, tracing its outline in the air. Seeing that he was drawing it mentally, I gave him a pencil and a sheet of paper, but he once again repeated the outline in the air, answering that he didn't need paper and pencil, the form was now imprinted in his mind and he would remember it. Sometime later he made a piece,[4] representing an animal skin with thick fur, that hung on the wall. I always wondered whether it was my zebra."[5]

Grisi resumed traveling in Africa in 1968, after her first travels in the early 1960s. Pascali shared her fascination with the culture of a continent he never visited: his imagination stirred, he referenced Africa several times in his drawings of animals of the steppes for Radiofortuna advertisements (1964–1965) and in his steel wool and fake fur sculptures representing archetypal, dreamlike, primitive realms of hanging bridges, creepers, and tanned animal hides (*Ponte*; *Liane*; *Pelle conciata*, all 1968).

Spending time in Africa let Grisi think about and experiment with light and, more broadly, the elements of nature that came to dominate her work from the late 1960s on.

Neon was instrumental in her work on light. Fontana was the first to use neon in art in his *Ambienti spaziali* of the early 1950s, which had a profound influence on an entire generation of young artists in Italy and beyond. They included Grisi and Mario Merz, who in turn began working with neon in the late 1960s; Fontana in fact supported them by buying their first works.[6] Grisi's first neon pieces combined paint and movable Plexiglas panels. The light-filled works capturing New York's urban nightlife were both shown at the 1968 exhibition *Young Italians* curated by Alan Salomon, first at the Institute of Contemporary Art in Boston, and later at the Jewish Museum in New York. This was the first group exhibition in America to reflect the diversity of the new Italian art scene, looking beyond Arte Povera to include artists working in Kinetic art and the Rome school of painting. As at the 1966 Venice Biennale, Grisi was the only woman in the group, alongside artists such as Getulio Alviani, Jannis Kounellis, Francesco Lo Savio, Mambor, Pascali, and Pistoletto. That same year, the German art critic Udo Kultermann chose to showcase her work in a solo exhibition at the Galerie E. M. Thelen (Essen), having exhibited Pascali the previous year. At the group exhibition in New York, she met Leo Castelli again, who began representing her and hosted her first solo exhibition in New York in 1973.

Women were few and far between on the Italian art scene at that time—Carla Accardi, Marisa Busanel, Lisetta Carmi, Fioroni, Titina Maselli, Marisa Merz, Marinella Pirelli, Carol Rama, Cloti Ricciardi to name just a few—and by no means all achieved a high profile in a realm dominated by men. Grisi's career is an exception: she played a leading role not only in Italian art circles, but also internationally in the 1960s and 1970s. The rediscovery of her oeuvre in recent years—sadly too late for the artist, who died in 2017—raises the question of why she was overlooked in histories of Italian art in the latter half of the 20th century that seek to foreground the achievements of female artists.[7]

Laura Grisi pioneered the use of natural elements in Italian art, beginning with the creation of neon columns (*Un'Area di Nebbia* [*A Space of Fog*], 1968) placed outside in artificial fog, like light-filled landmarks. These were the starting point for her approach to the use of fog, wind, air, and rain, since, as she explained to Germano Celant, she did not want to produce paintings or sculptures containing air, earth, or water *per se*: "I didn't want air, earth, or water to become objects; I wanted to recreate the experience of natural phenomena."[8] The artist's endeavor is not bound up with the form of a given object, but rather involves recreating a natural environment indoors, and this is where Grisi's work differs from the Arte Povera theorized by Celant in the same period. She is not part of the Arte Povera narrative of origin or its historicity[9]; nor was she part of the group exhibition *Fuoco Immagine Acqua Terra* at the Galleria L'Attico in Rome in June 1967, which featured Kounellis' work on fire and Pascali's work on earth and water, foreshadowing her adventure that was begin a few months later. Her travels in Africa, including Nigeria, the Sahara, Niger, and Chad, prompted her to recreate her experience of light, water, wind, and more broadly, time.

In May 1968, Grisi was invited to join the *Teatro delle mostre*, a month-long event organized by Plinio De Martiis at La Tartaruga, his gallery in Rome, which featured a different artist every day between 4 and 8 pm. The series heralded a profoundly new understanding of the art exhibition as an ephemeral event lasting just a few hours.[10] Grisi's exhibition followed on from Mauri's installation, *Luna.*[11] On Monday, May 27, she showed an installation recreating a southwesterly wind with a speed of 40 knots (*Vento di s.e velocità 40 nodi* [*Wind Speed 40 Knots*], 1968). Photographs of the event show Pascali, hair blowing in the wind: he was not in the program himself, but he visited every day to see his friends' work. Grisi placed the experience of elemental forces at the heart of her practice, shooting the effects of the wind as part of her 16mm film

(*Wind Speed 40 Knots,* 1968) and presenting the results as part of her installation at the *Teatro delle mostre*.

Filming nature was something she shared with her contemporary Pirelli, who has likewise recently been rediscovered.[12] Like Grisi, Pirelli was interested in studying light in films such as *Sole in mano (o appropriazione, a propria azione, azione propria)* (1970–1973). Their art takes account of the nature with which they interact—light in Pirelli's case; wind, earth, and sand for Grisi—as they immerse themselves in such spaces without considering them merely as a terrain for action in front of the lens, as Luca Patella does in his films *Terra animata* (1967) and *SKMP2* (1968), dating from the same period. All these films are connected to nature, featuring filmed actions and thereby affirming that the issues raised by Land art are not solely an Anglo-American concern. Grisi was in fact the only Italian artist included in the group exhibition *Earth Air Fire Water: Elements of Art* at the Museum of Fine Arts, Boston, in 1971, alongside Dennis Oppenheim, Robert Smithson, and Dan Graham. She presented the 1968 work *Drops of Water*, a circular pool into which drops of water fall, echoing the sound of rain. Other films (*The Measuring of Time*, 1969; *From One to Four Pebbles*, 1972) and installations (*Refraction*, 1968) would suffice to justify her centrality in the handful of studies focusing on the relationship between artistic practice and time.

In this sense, she is a significant absence from Lucy Lippard's *Six Years: The Dematerialization of the Art Object from 1966 to 1972* (1973), the first and only study to date to catalogue the works, exhibitions, publications, and events to emerge from Conceptual art, Land art, and Arte Povera from 1966 to 1972. Alighiero Boetti, Gilardi, Merz, and Emilio Prini all feature in the study, which aimed to document the movements in America and Europe equally.

Grisi and Fioroni are the only two Italian women on the lengthy list of artists to have shown their work at the 1973 *Contemporanea* exhibition in Rome, curated by Achille Bonito Oliva. The event, international in scope, is now widely remembered for being held in the Villa Borghese car park. Grisi also showed the same work of sound art, *Sounds* (1971), at a smaller exhibition with a clear political dimension, *Pollution. Per una nuova estetica dell'inquinamento,*[13] held outside on the Piazza Santo Stefano, Bologna, in October 1972. Gilardi, Ceroli, Ugo La Pietra, Gino Marotta, and Claudio Parmiggiani were among the 24 artists featured at the event, an early example of art in dialogue with environmental issues. Grisi's sound art was discreet, barely audible, merging into the noises of the city from a tape recorder that played two cassettes featuring the sounds of stones, ants, and trees.

1 The artists quoted in the present essay are Carla Accardi (1924–2014), Getulio Alviani (1939–2018), Umberto Bignardi (1935), Alighiero Boetti (1940–1994), Marisa Busanel (1933–1990), Lisetta Carmi (1924), Mario Ceroli (1938), Michelle Coudray, Giosetta Fioroni (1932), Lucio Fontana (1899–1968), Piero Gilardi (1942), Dan Graham (1942), Jannis Kounellis (1936-2017), Ugo La Pietra (1938), Julio Le Parc (1928), Francesco Lo Savio (1935–1963), Renato Mambor (1936–2014), Gino Marotta (1935–2012), Titina Maselli (1924–2005), Mario Merz (1925–2003), Marisa Merz (1926–2019), Dennis Oppenheim (1938–2011), Claudio Parmiggiani (1943), Pino Pascali (1935–1968), Luca Maria Patella (1934), Marinella Pirelli (1925–2009), Michelangelo Pistoletto (1933), Emilio Prini (1943–2016), Carol Rama (1918–2015), Cloti Ricciardi (1939), Mario Schifano (1934–1998), Robert Smithson (1938–1973), and Cesare Tacchi (1940–2014).

2 See Valérie Da Costa, *Pino Pascali: retour à la Méditerranée,* Les presses du réel, Dijon 2015, p. 9 ff.

3 Gruppo 63, founded in Palermo in the autumn of 1963, was a group of young writers and intellectuals including Alberto Arbasino (1930–2020), Nanni Balestrini (1935–2019), Furio Colombo (1931), Umberto Eco (1932–2016), and Elio Pagliarani (1927–2012). They set out to write a new chapter in Italian literature, then dominated by the postwar neo-Realist movement that lasted throughout the 1950s, experimenting with new forms in novels and poetry. See Nanni Balestrini and Andrea Cortellessa (eds.), *Gruppo 63. Il romanzo sperimentale* [1966], L'orma, Rome 2013.

4 *Pelle conciata*, 1968.

5 "Essay–Interview by Germano Celant," in Germano Celant, *Laura Grisi. A Selection of Works with Notes by the Artist*, trans. Marguerite Shore, Rizzoli, New York 1990, p. 18.

6 Ibid., p. 13. See also Valérie Da Costa, *Écrits de Lucio Fontana,* Les presses du réel, Dijon 2013, p. 76 ff.

7 See for example Laura Iamurri on the feminist critic Carla Lonzi: Carla Lonzi, *Autoritratto*, et al/Edizioni, Milan 2010; Carla Lonzi, *Scritti sull'arte*, et al/Edizioni, Milan 2012, with Lara Conte and Vanessa Martini; *Un margine che sfugge. Carla Lonzi e l'arte in Italia 1955-70,* Quodlibet, Macerata 2016; and Raffaella Perna on feminism and photography in Italy: *L'altro sguardo. Fotografe italiane 1965-2018,* Palazzo delle Esposizioni, Silvana Editoriale, Rome 2018; *The Unexpected Subject. 1978 Art and Feminism in Italy,* FM Centre for Contemporary Art, FlashArt, Milan 2019, curated by Raffaella Perna and Marco Scotini, and the latest Rome Quadriennale, *Fuori*, Quadriennale d'arte, Treccani, Rome, 2020, curated by Sarah Cosulich and Stefano Collicelli Cagol.

8 "Essay–Interview by Germano Celant," p. 24.

9 Celant's monograph on Laura Grisi was published by Rizzoli in 1990. Arte Povera had long drawn to a close and could by then be read as a period in Italian art history.

10 See Ilaria Bernardi, *Teatro delle mostre, Roma, maggio 1968,* Scalpendi Editore, Milan 2014.

11 On Fabio Mauri's installation *Luna,* see the chapter "Au-delà de la toile : *Luna* et le *Teatro delle mostre"* in my book *Fabio Mauri : le passé en actes/The Past in Acts,* Les presses du réel, Dijon 2018, p. 43–57.

12 *Luce Movimento. Il cinema sperimentale di Marinella Pirelli,* Museo del Novecento-Electa, Milan, 2019, curated by Lucia Aspesi and Iolanda Ratti.

13 Based on an idea by Gianni Sassi, a music producer who founded the art and politics journal *Bit*.

1964–1969

Laura Grisl working on *Sunset Light*, 1967

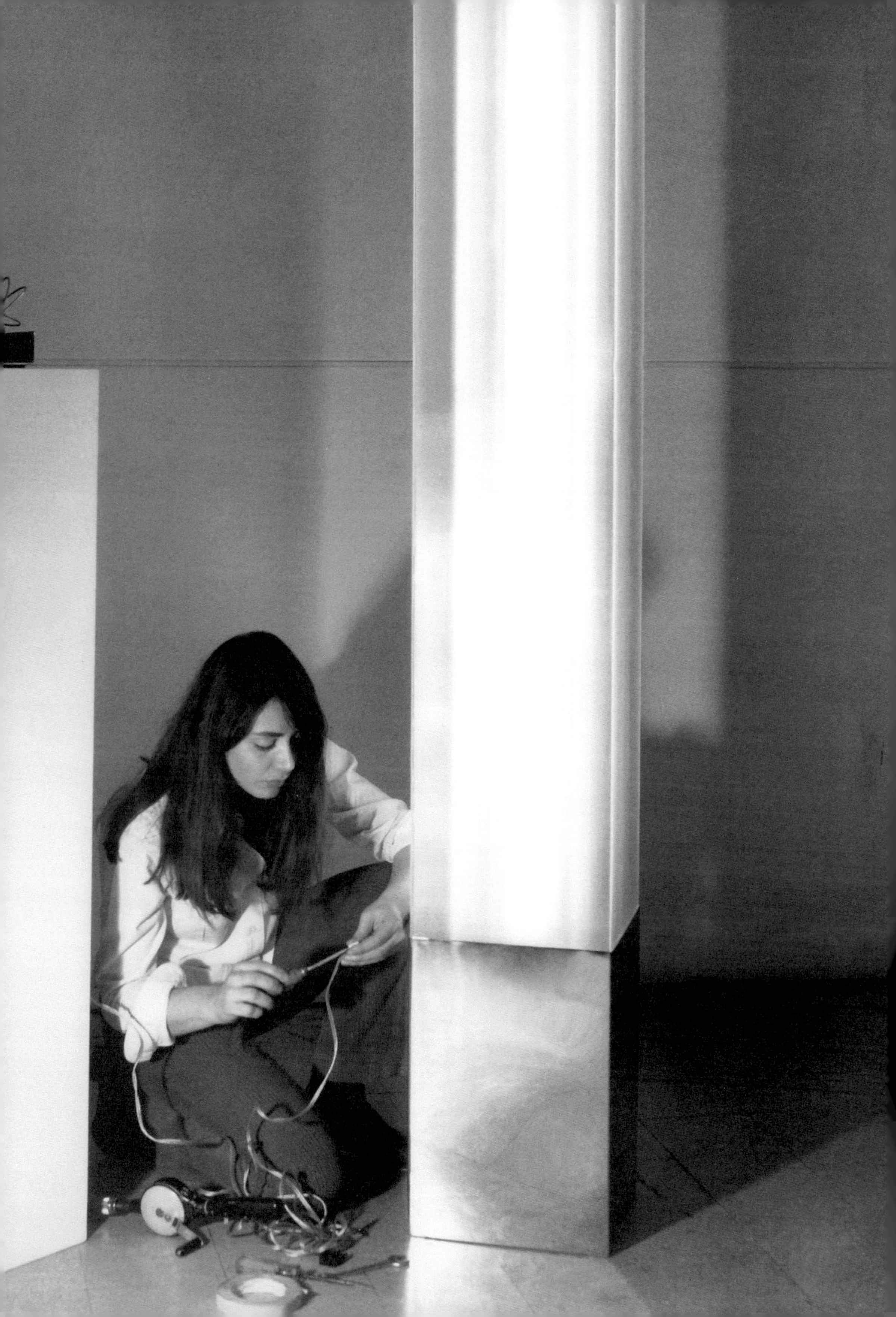

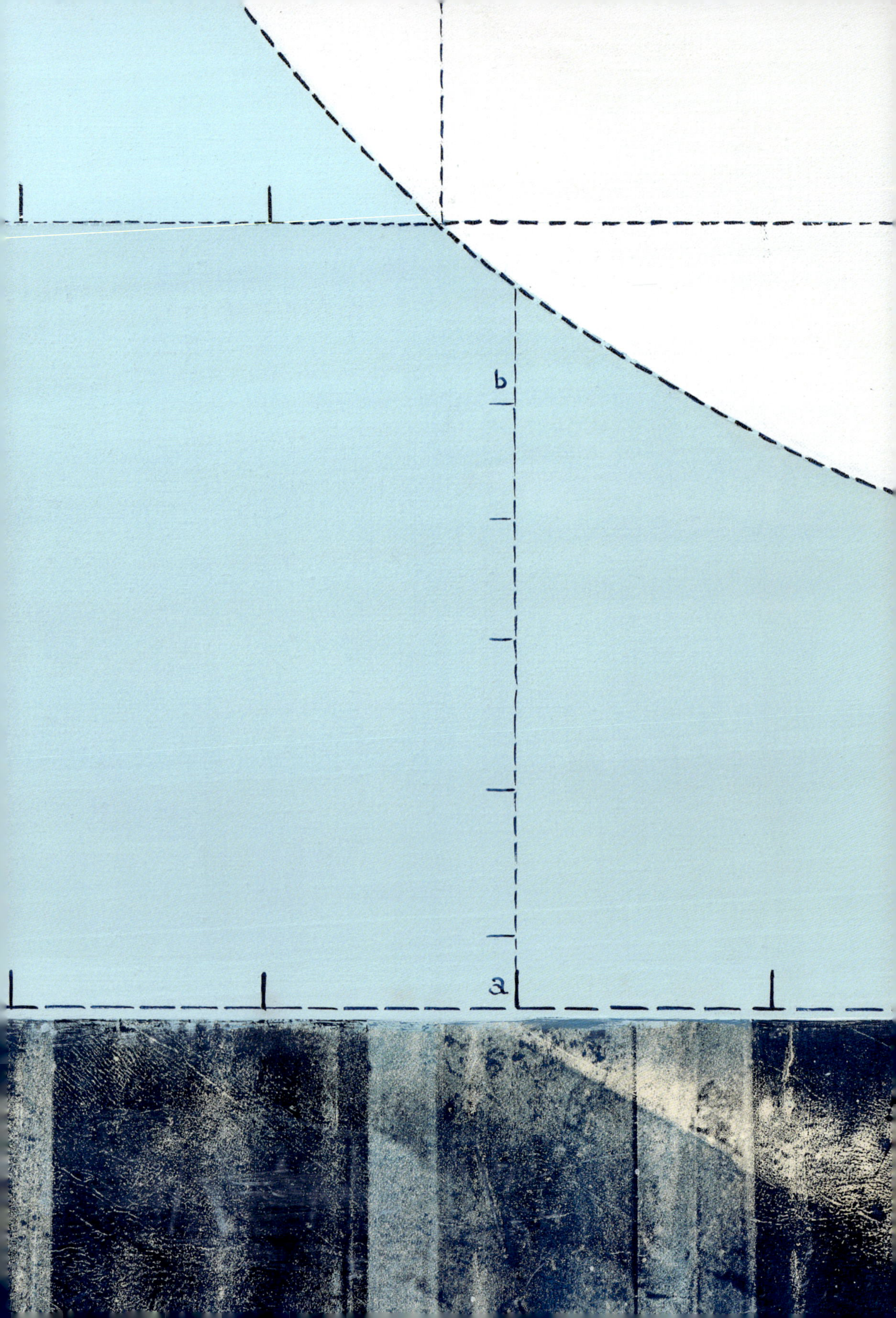
b
a

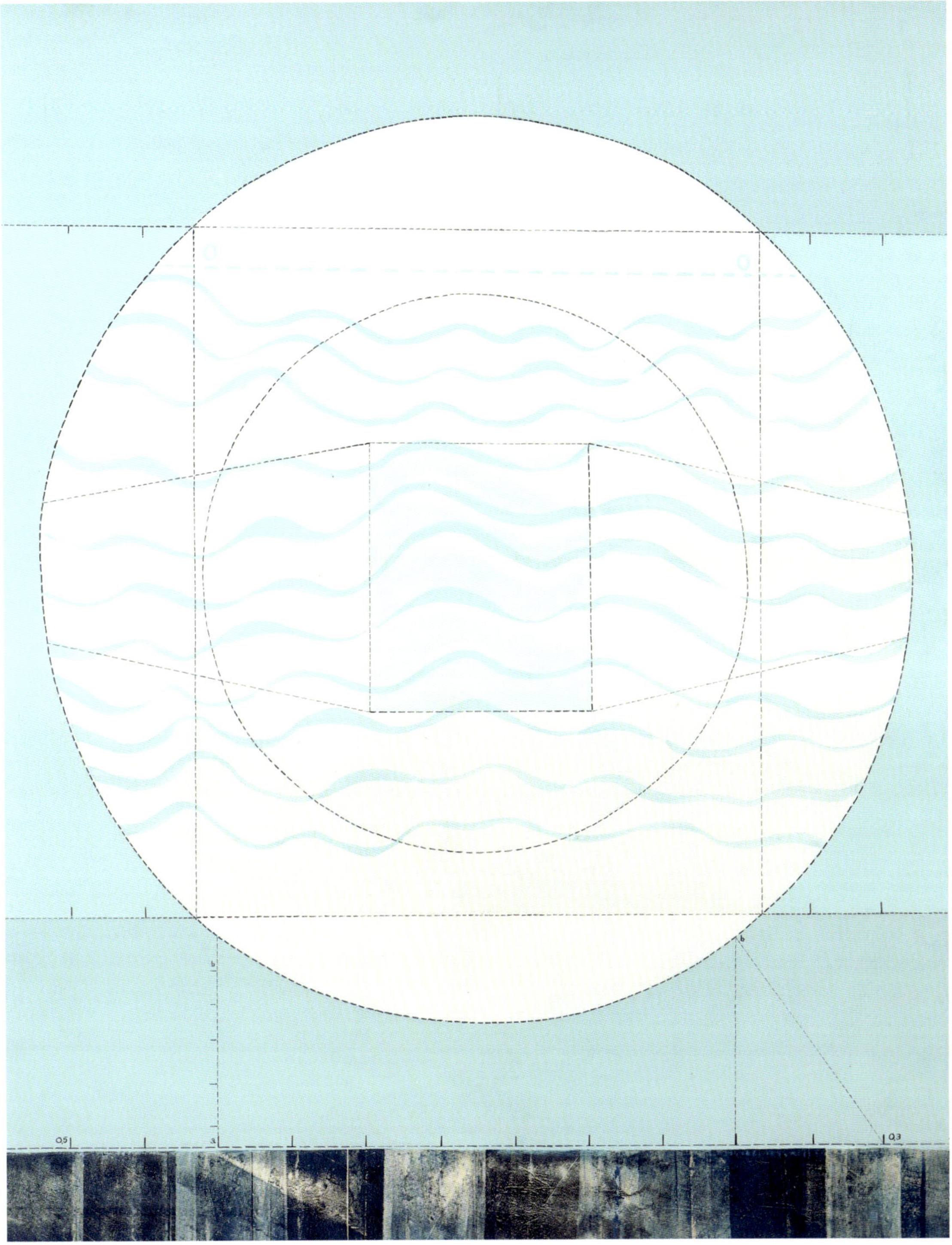

 Grande Reflex, 1964

Untitled, (1964–1965) →

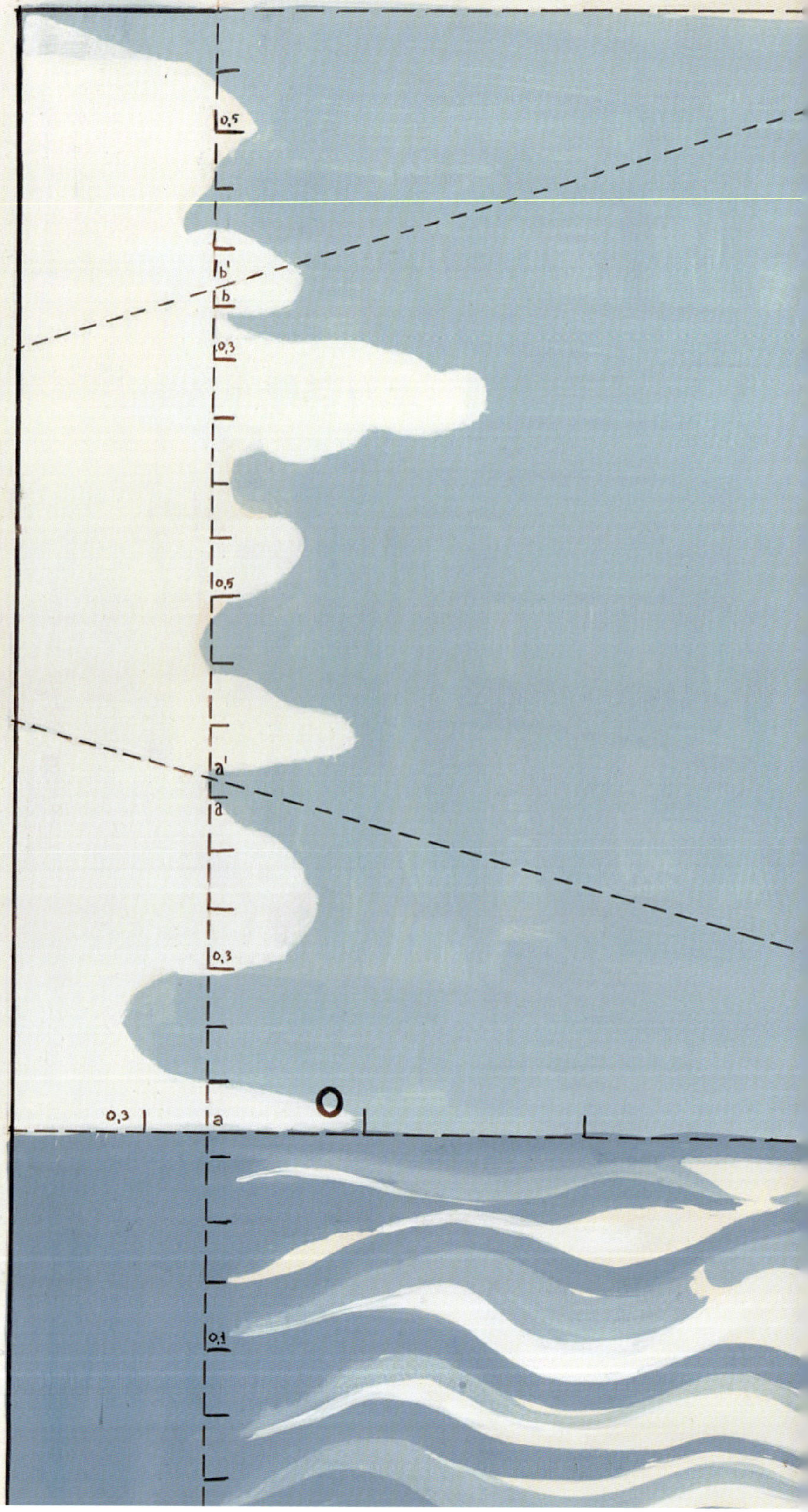
0,5
b'
b
0,3
0,5
a'
a
0,3
0,3
a
0
0,1

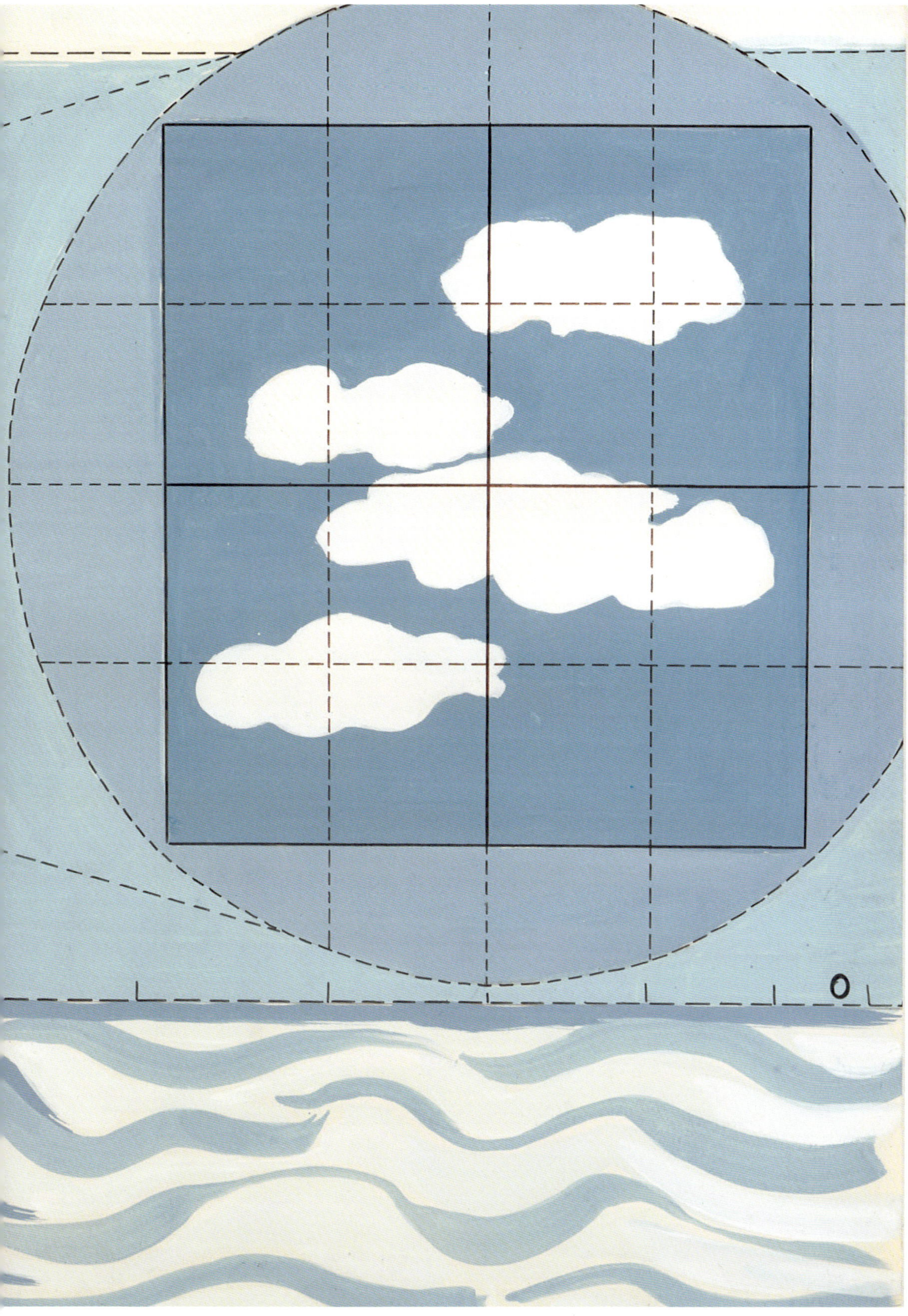

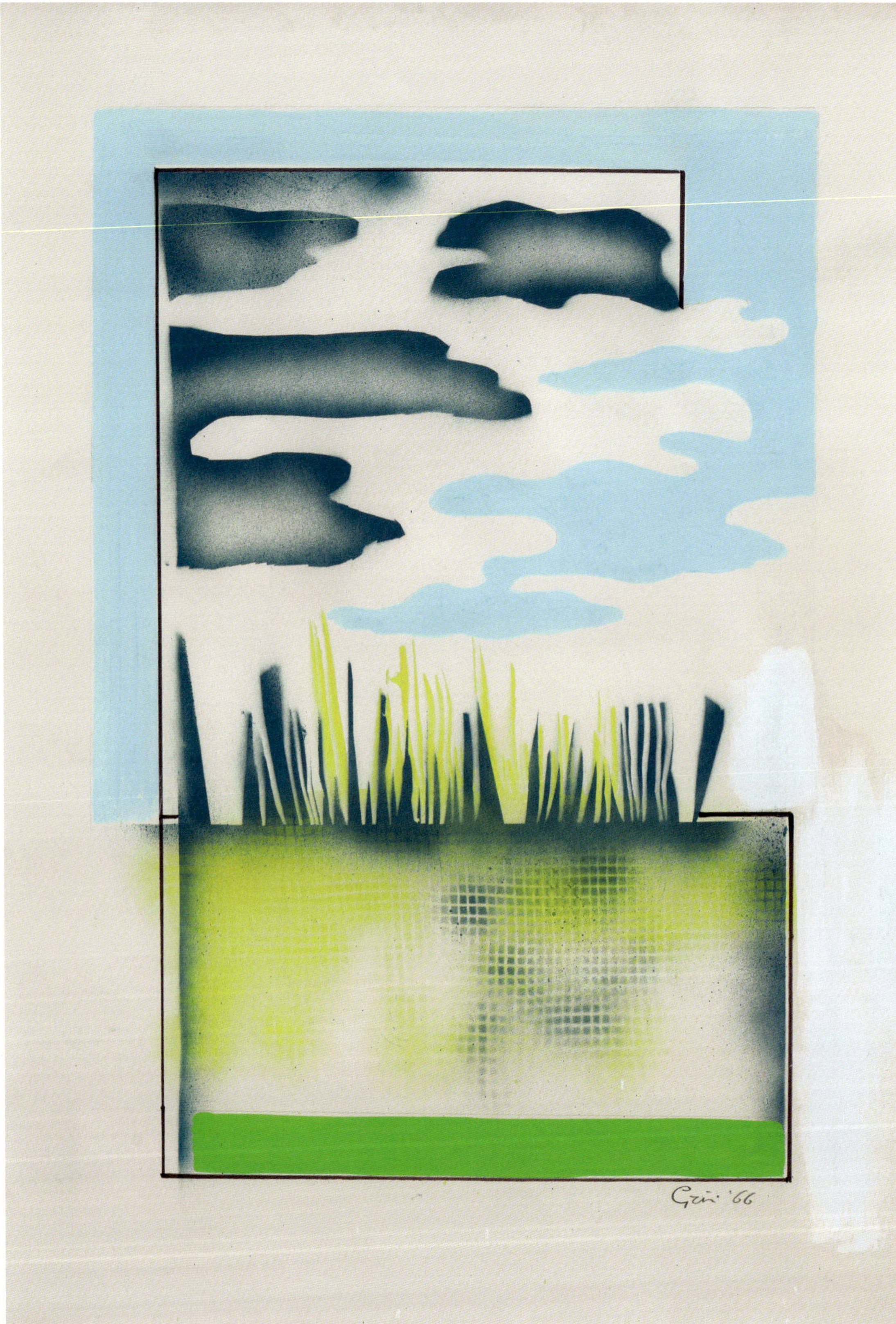

Untitled, 1966

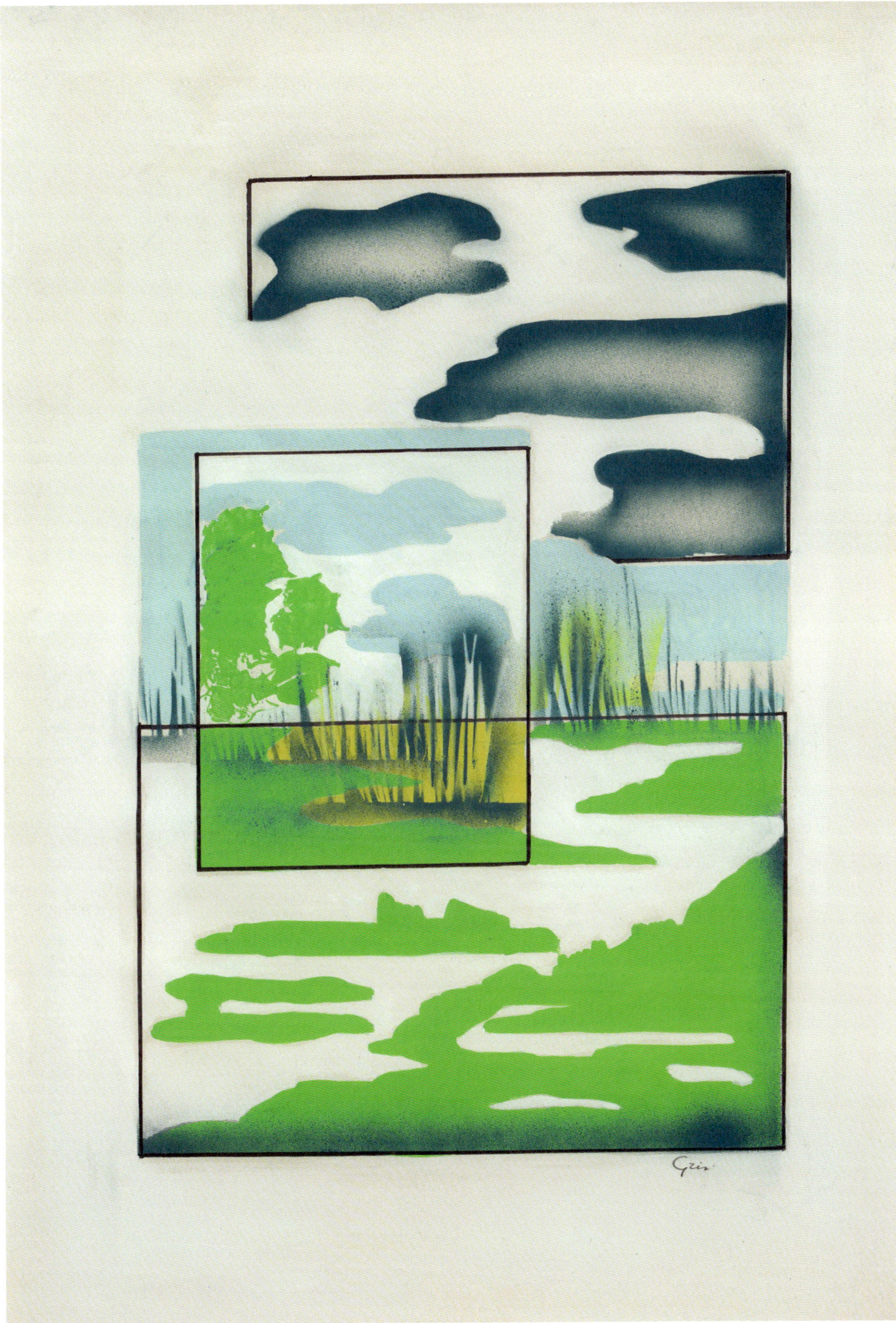

59 *Untitled*, (1966)

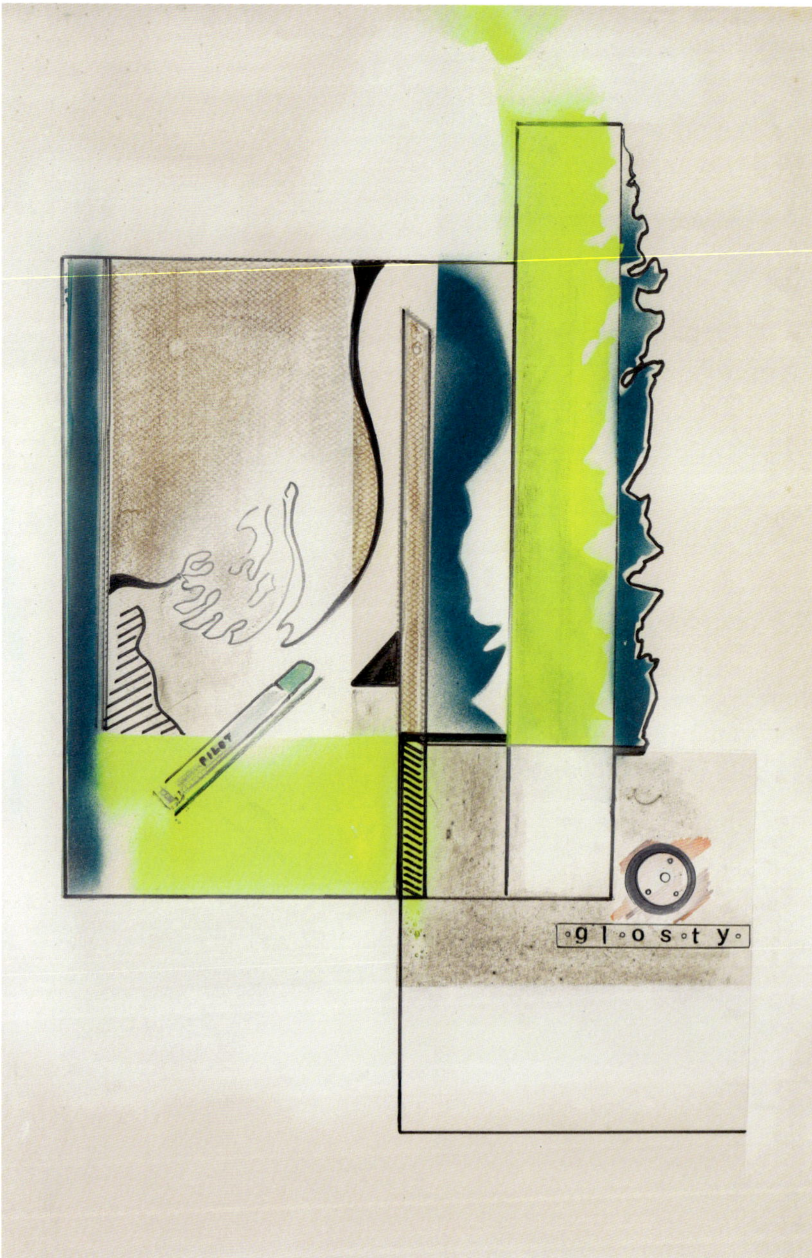

 Untitled, (1966)

Untitled, 1966

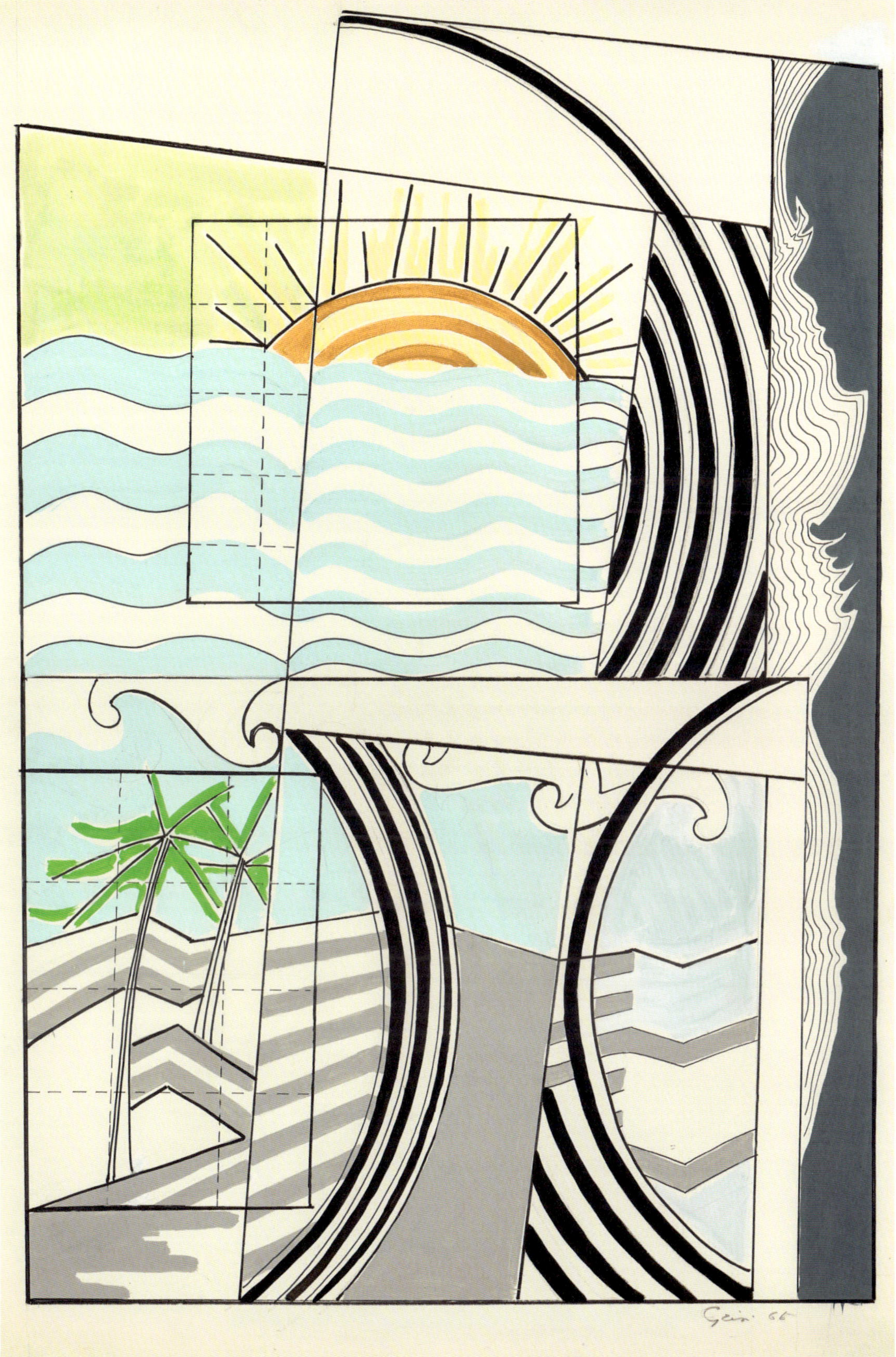

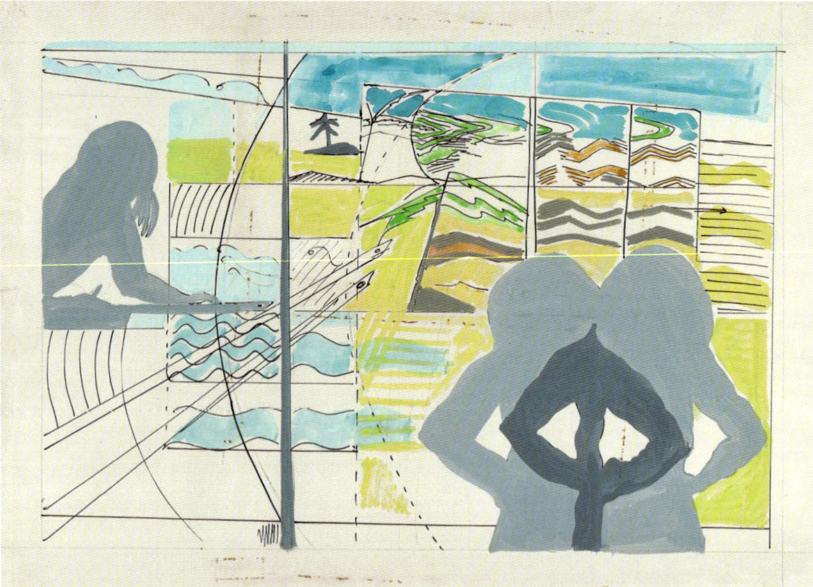

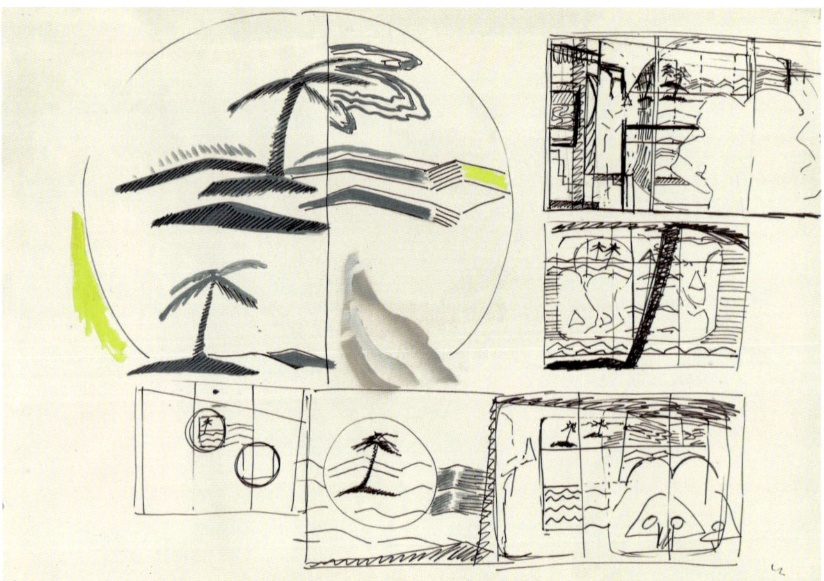

Untitled, (1965-1966)

Untitled, (1965-1966)

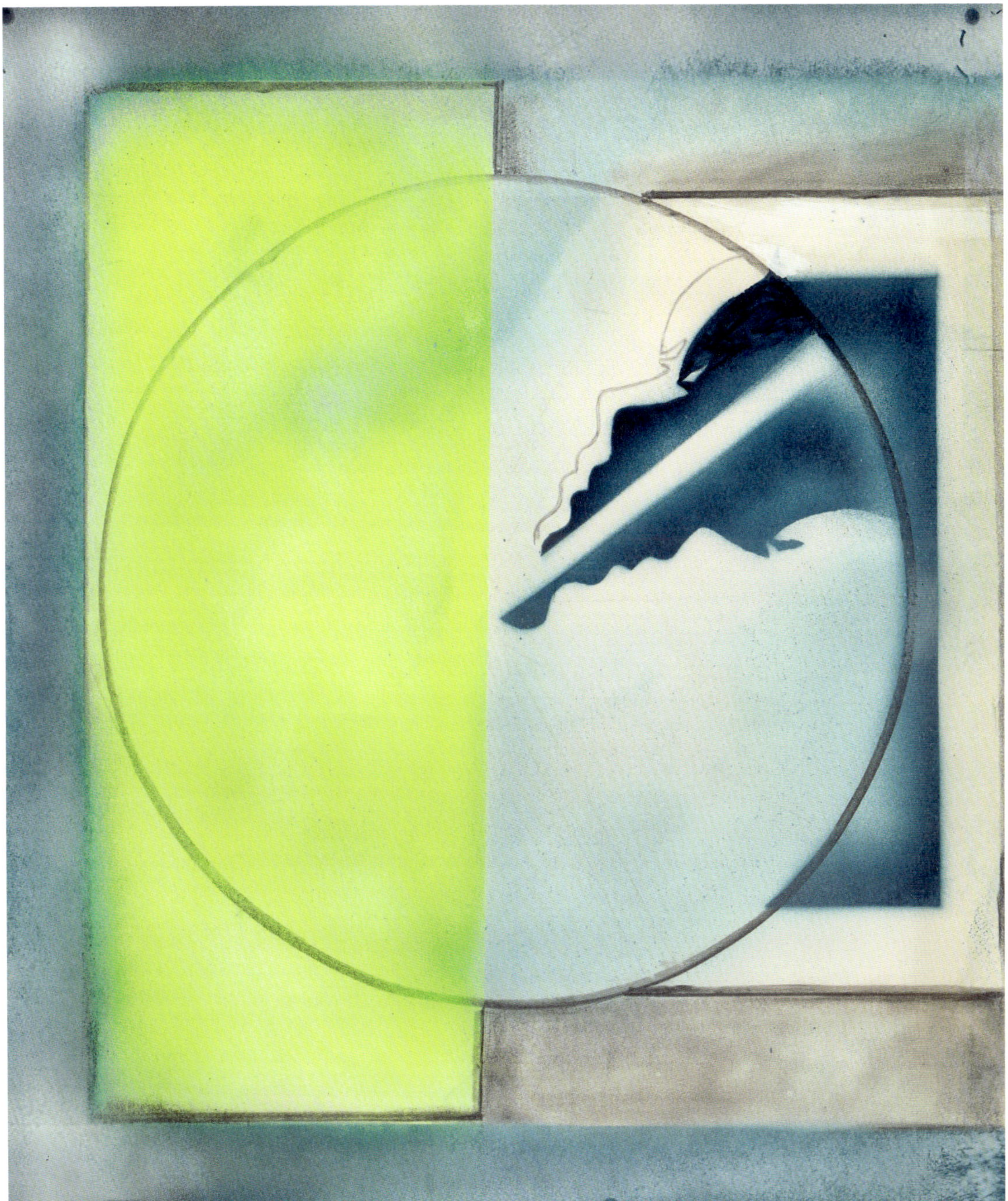

63 *Untitled*, (1965-1966)

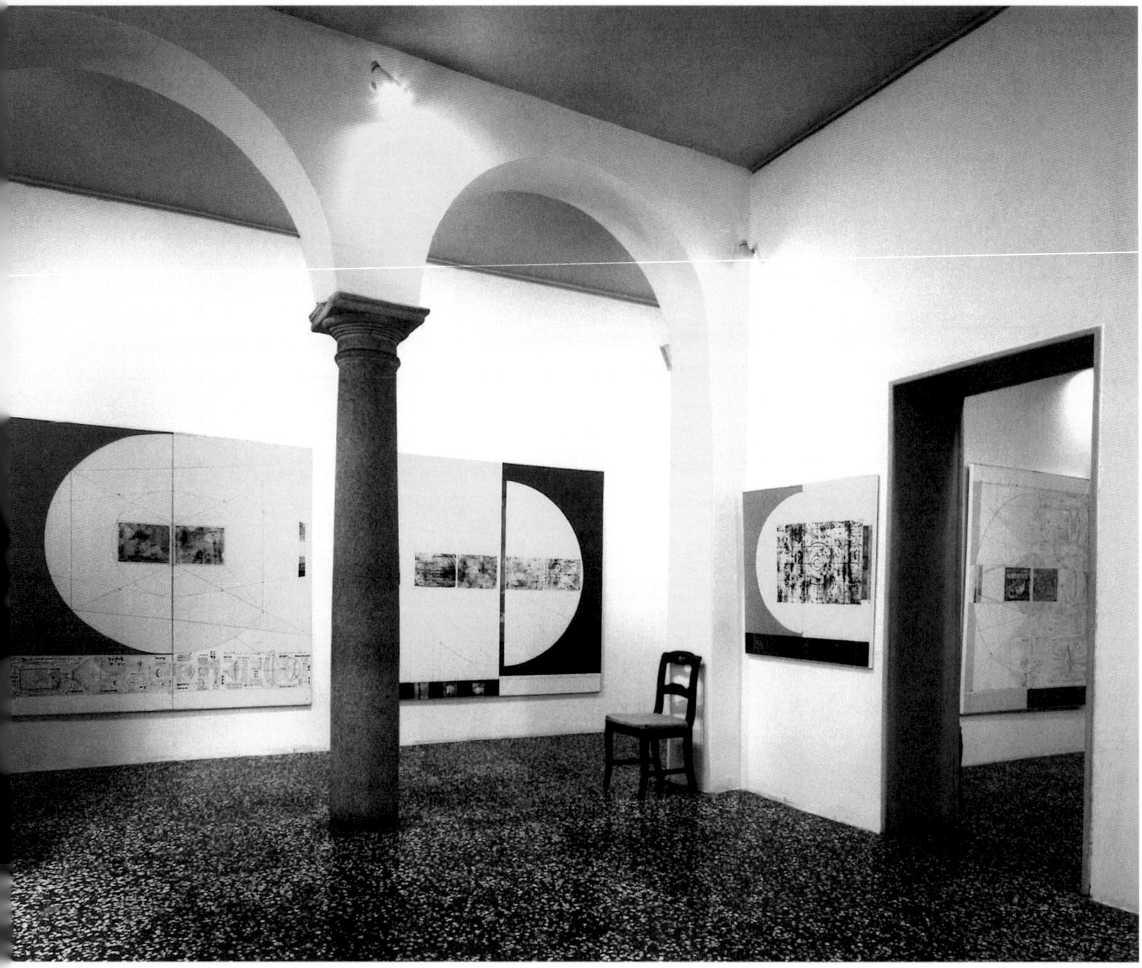

Exhibition view, Galleria dell'Ariete, Milan, 1965

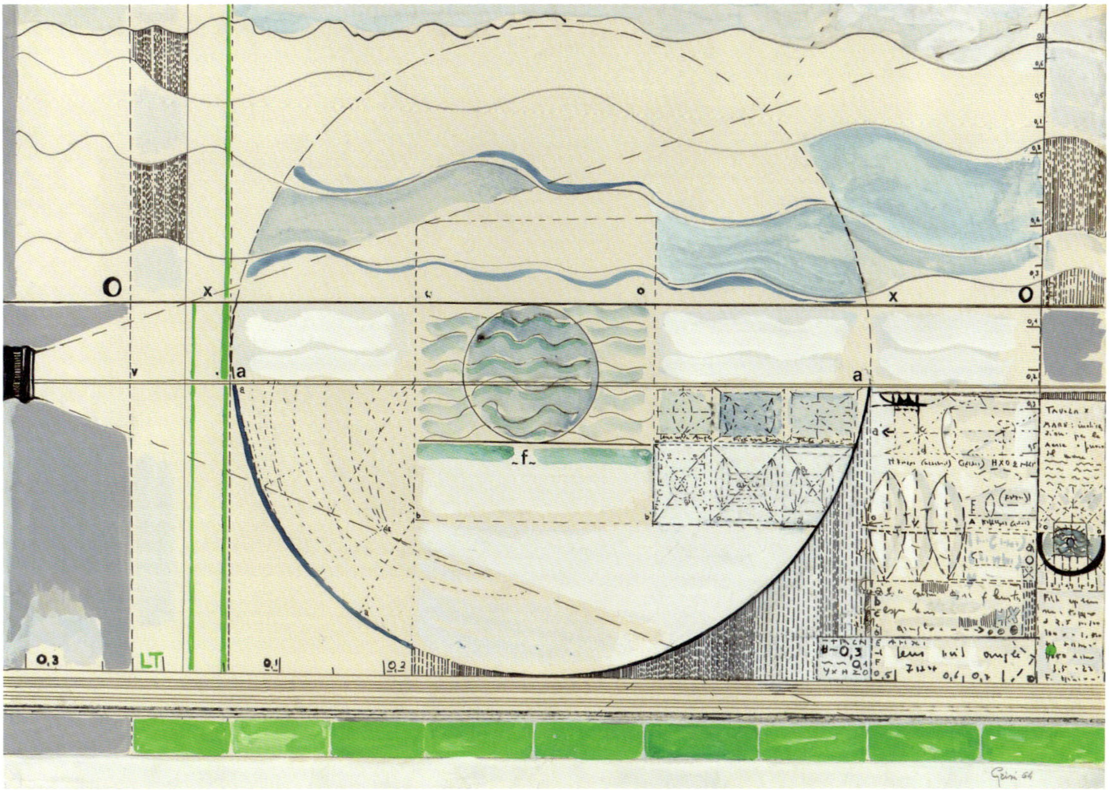

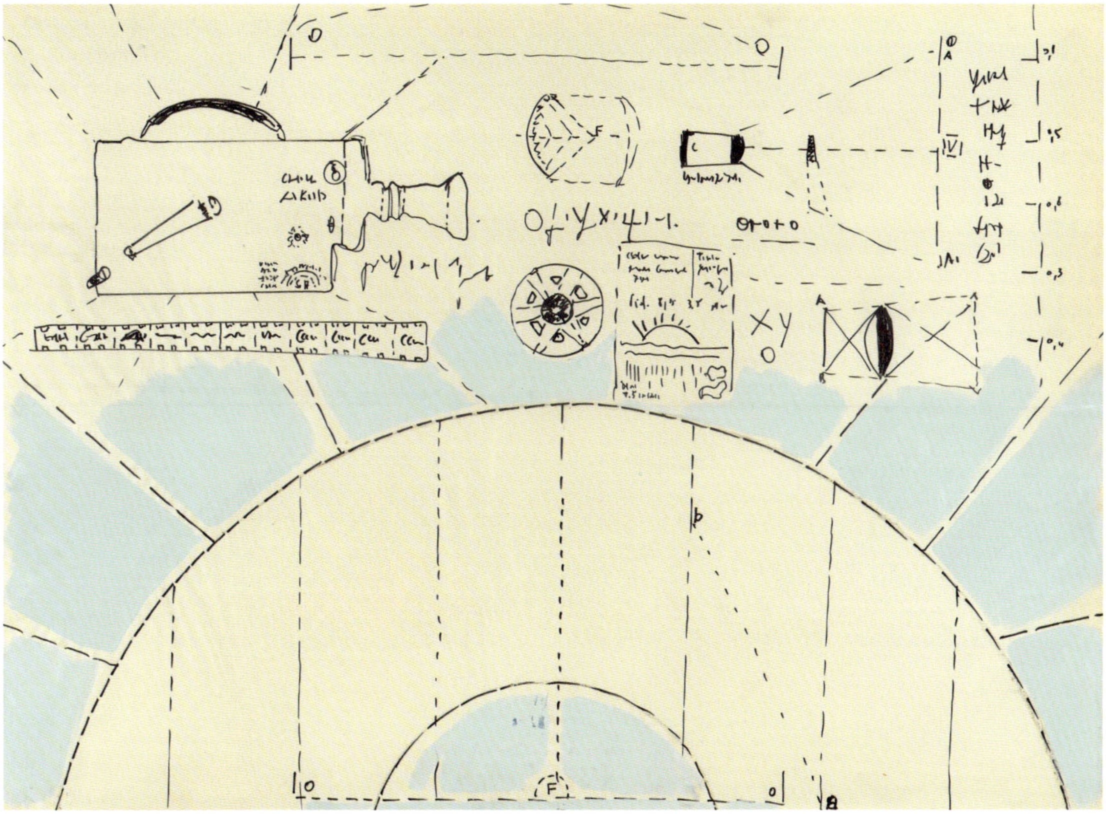

Untitled, 1964
Untitled, (1964–1965)

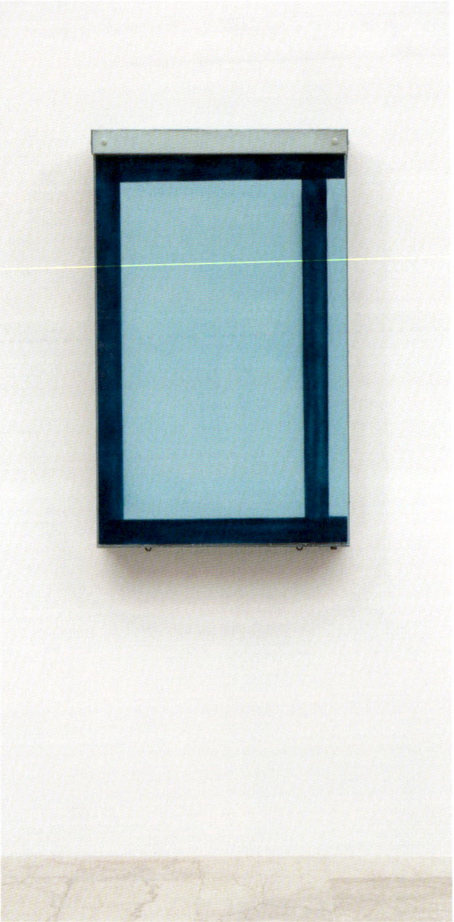

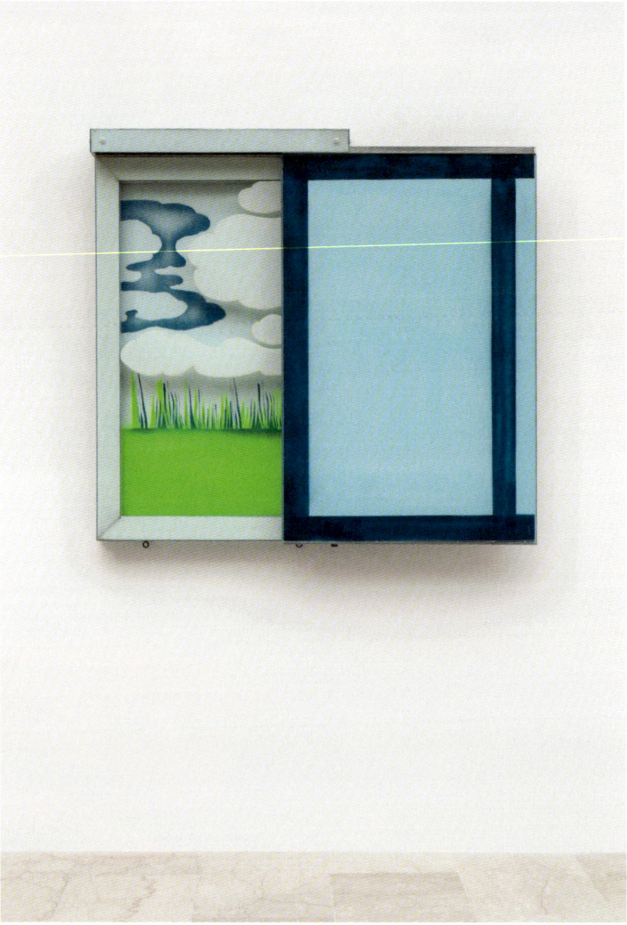

***Grass Field*, 1966**

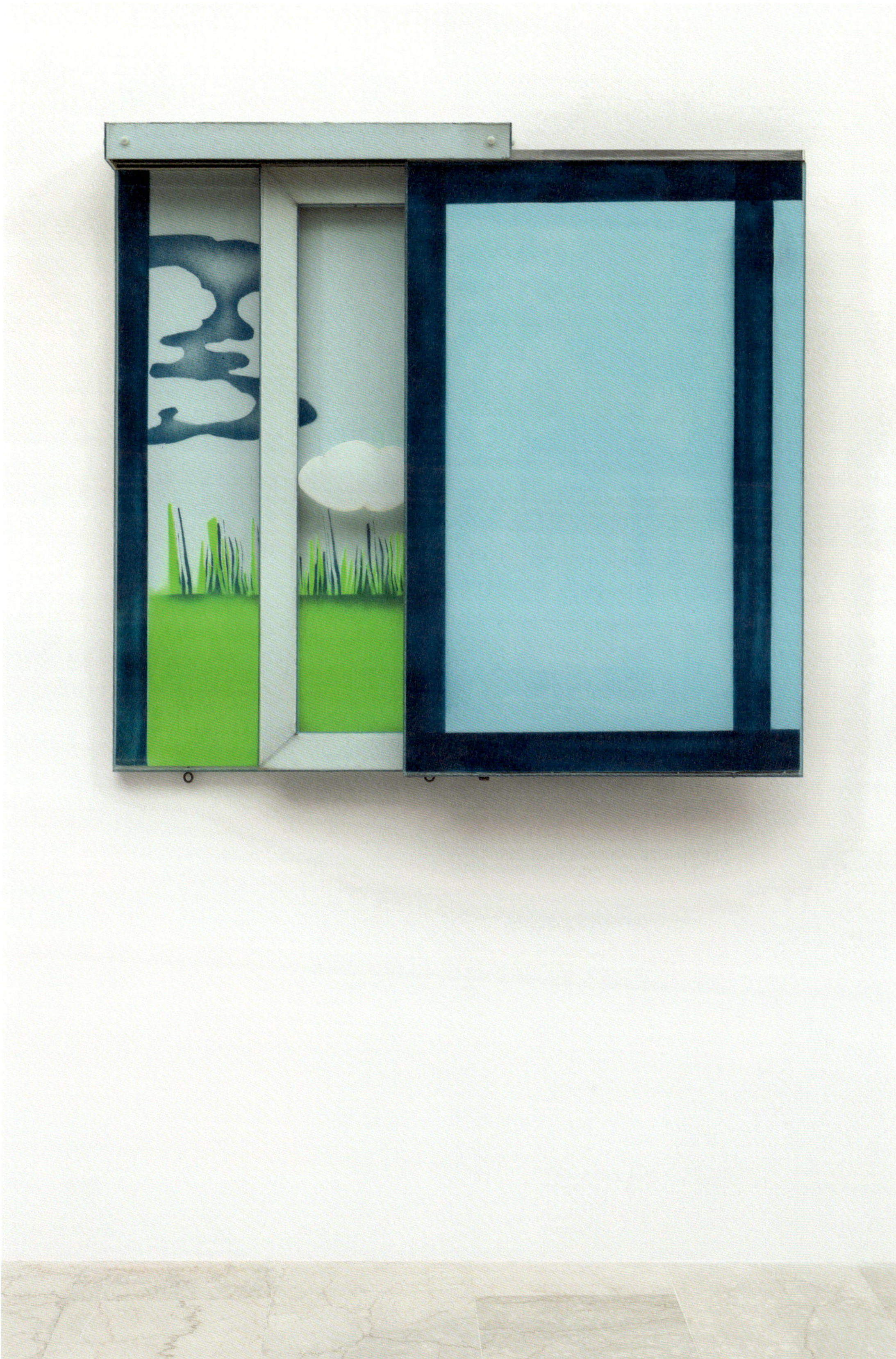

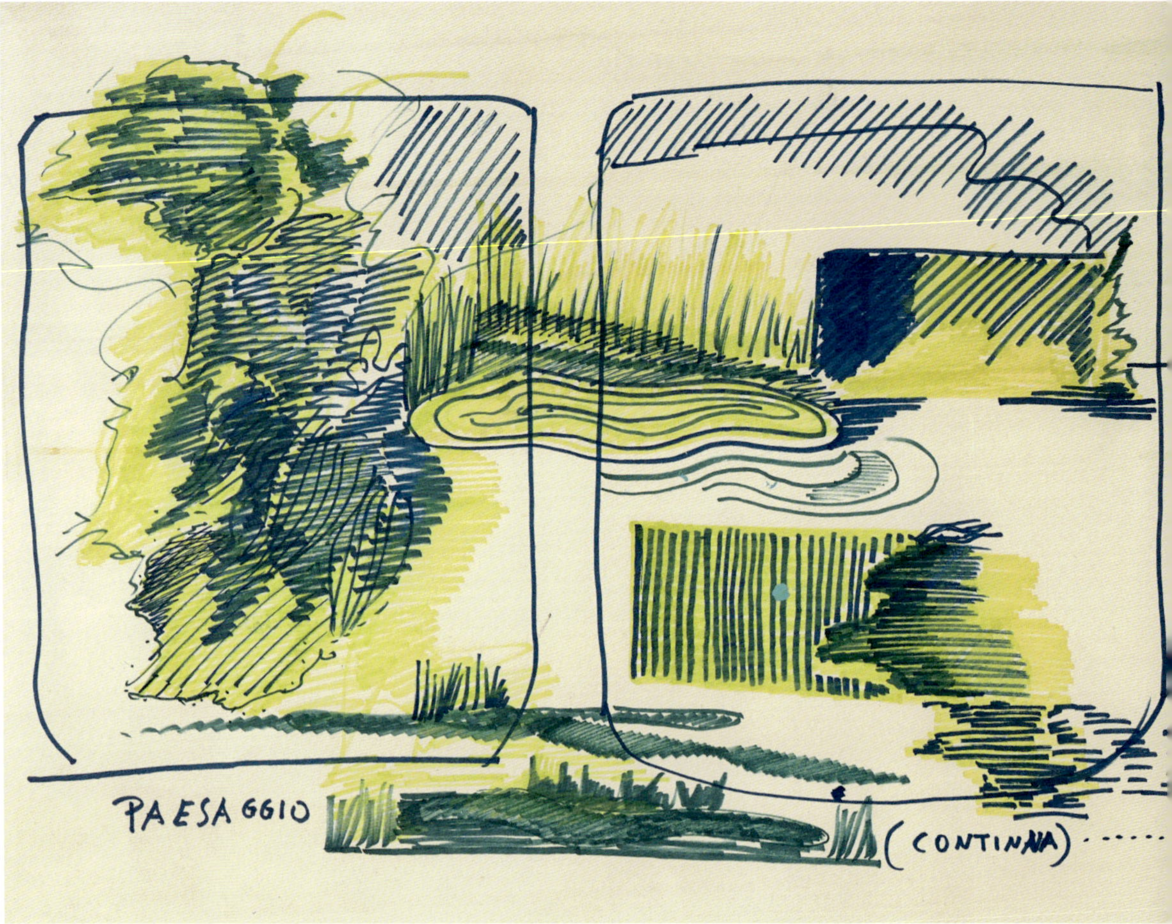

 Untitled, (1965–1966)

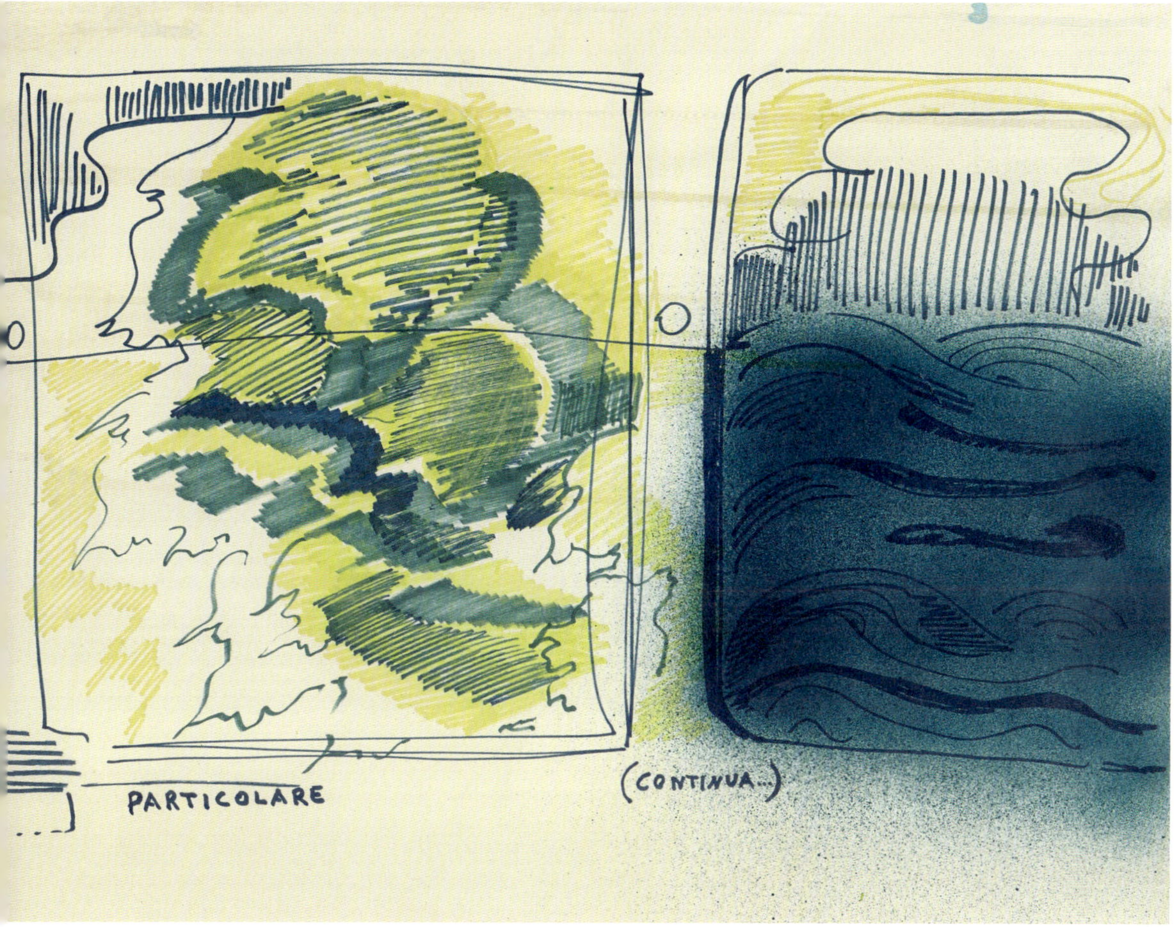
PARTICOLARE
(CONTINUA...)

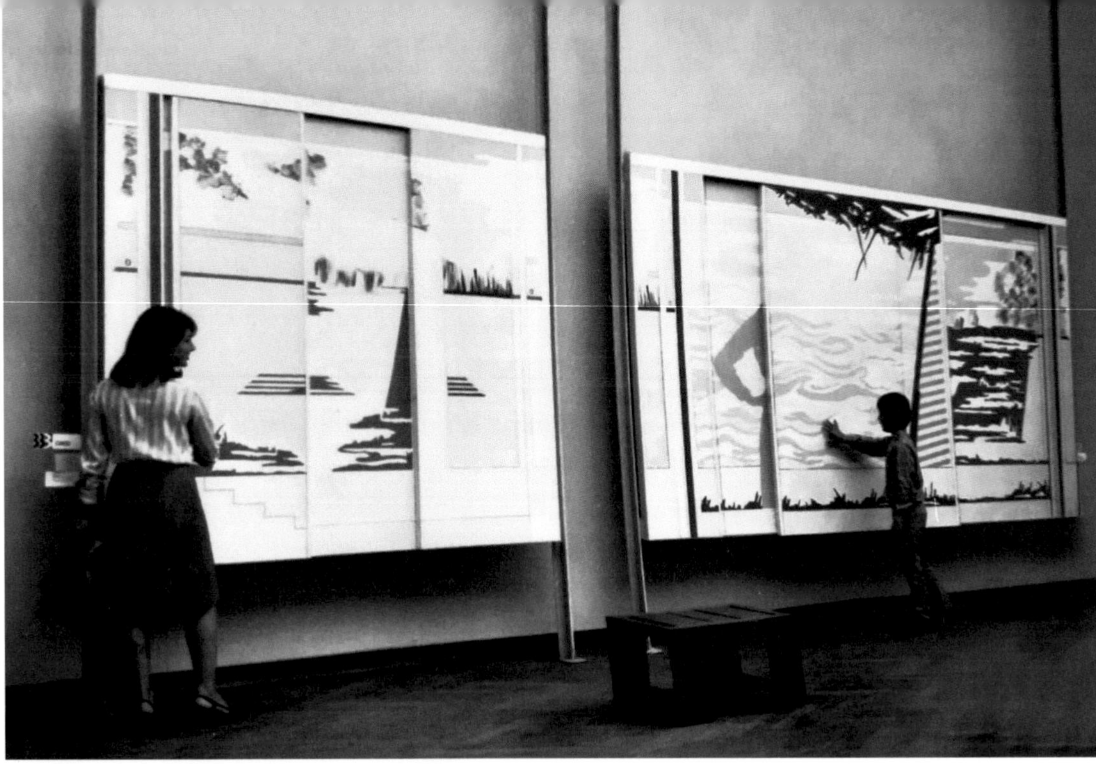

Laura Grisi at the 33rd Venice Biennale, Venice, 1966
With *Landscape Omaggio a Gainsborough* and *Seascape Omaggio a Constable*, both 1966

Laura Grisi moving *Transparent Door*, 1965

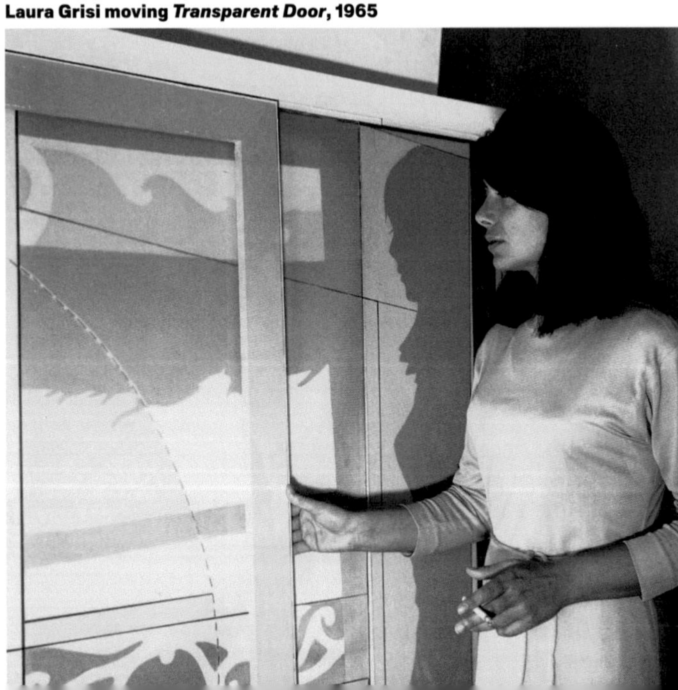

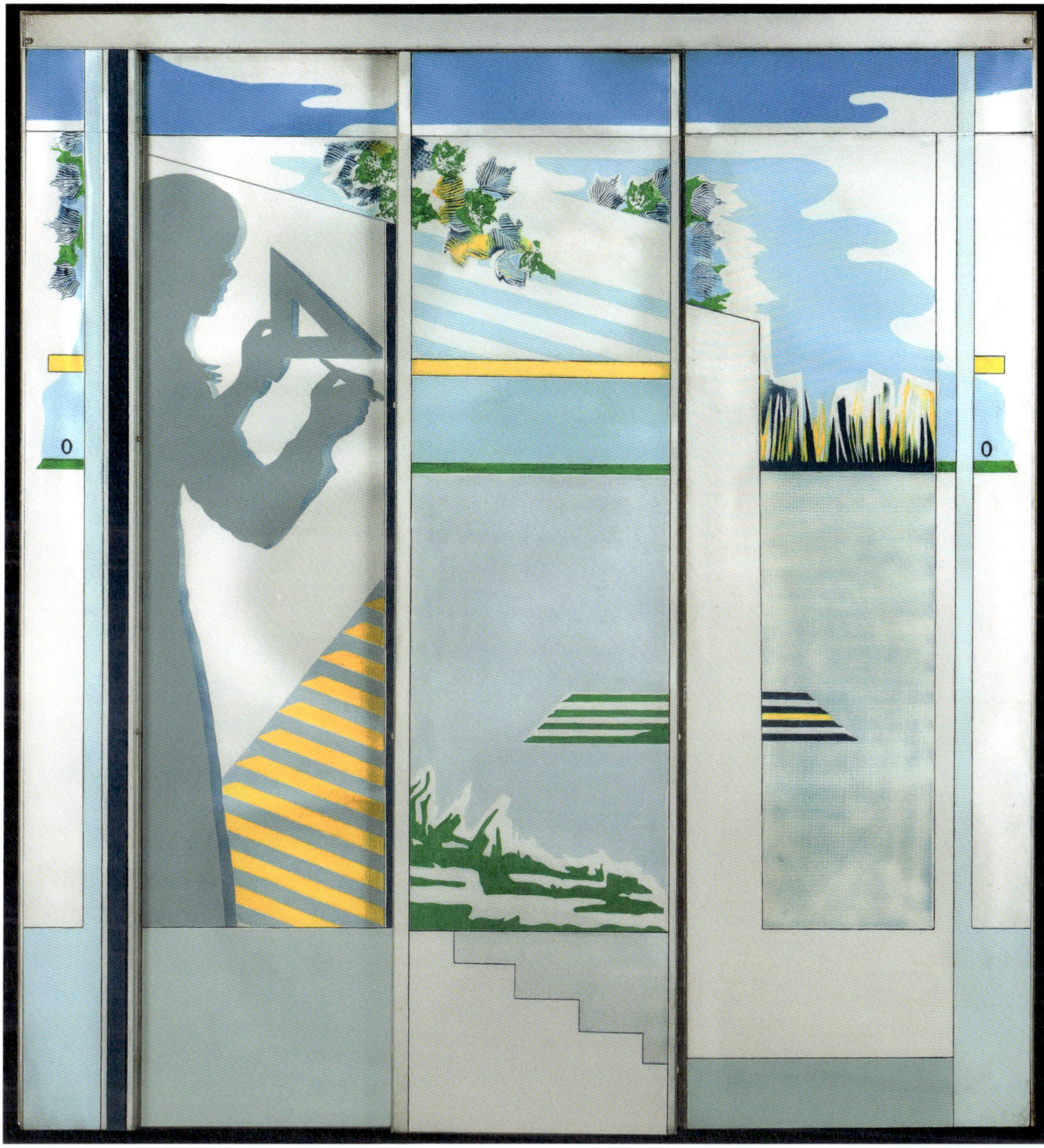

71 *Landscape Omaggio a Gainsborough*, 1966

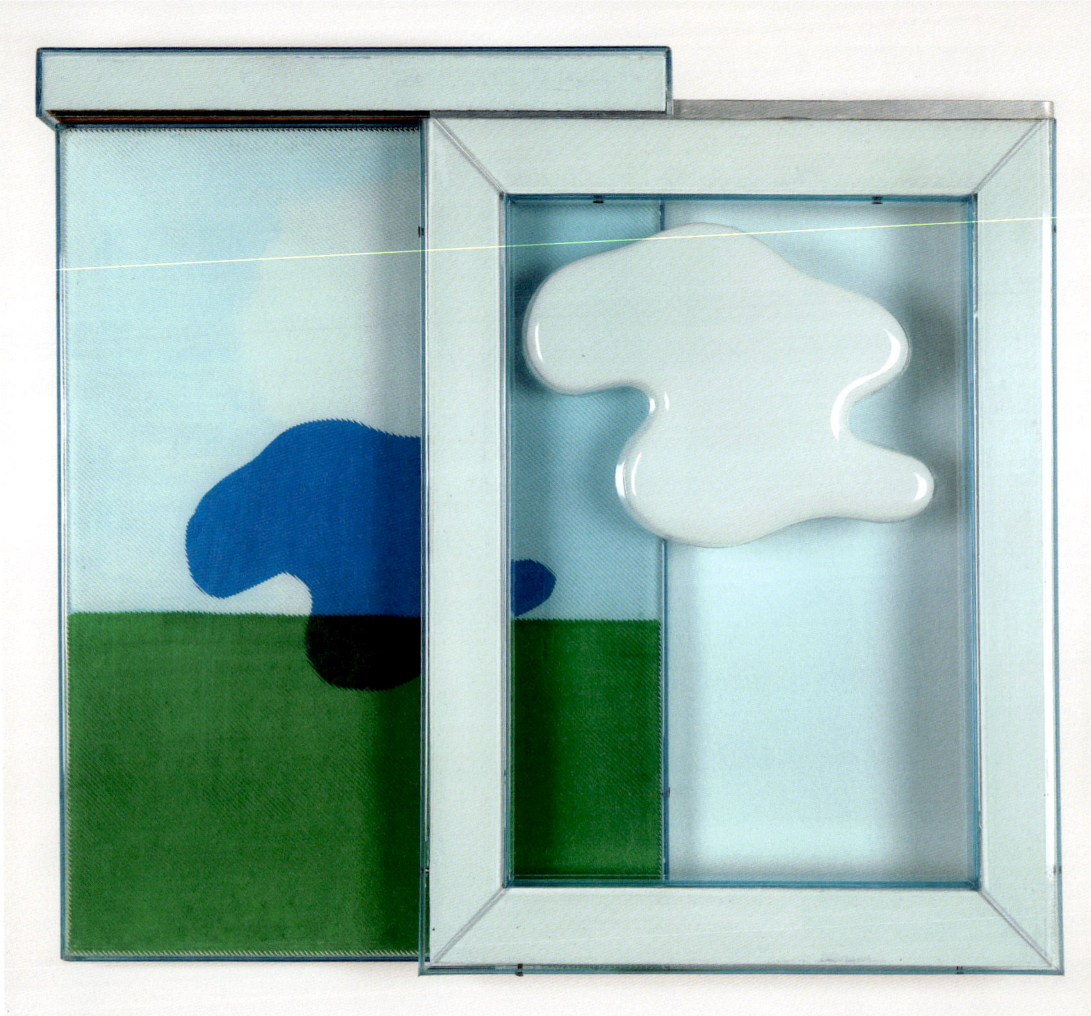

 Untitled, 1966

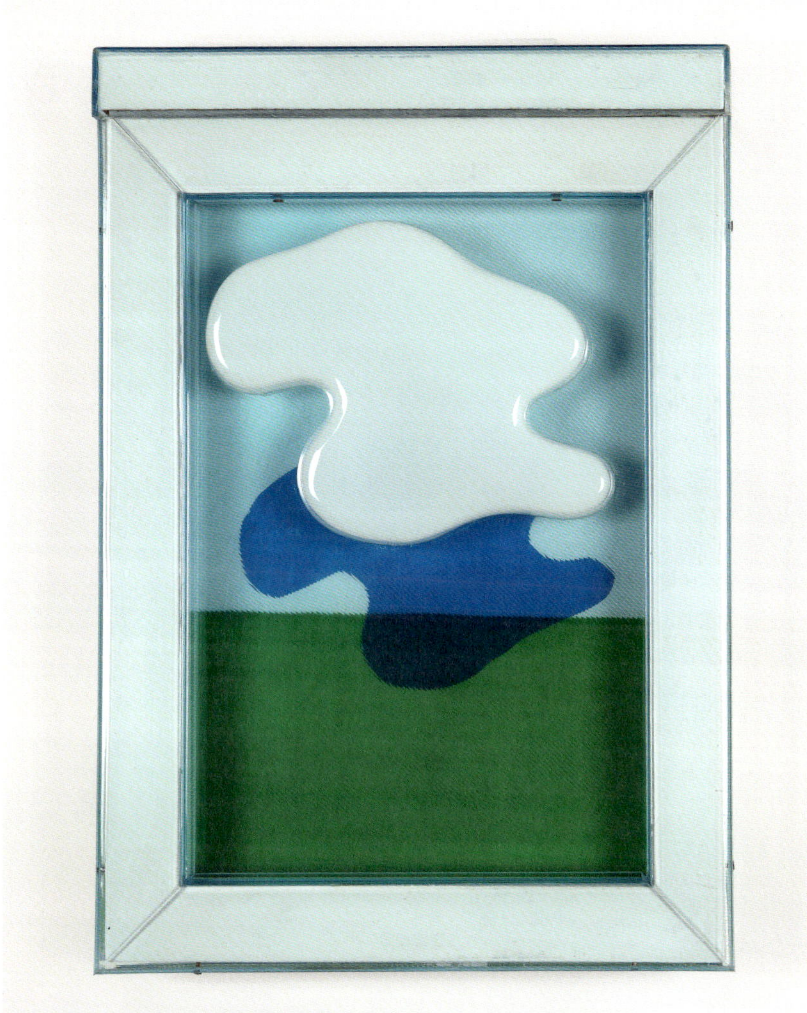

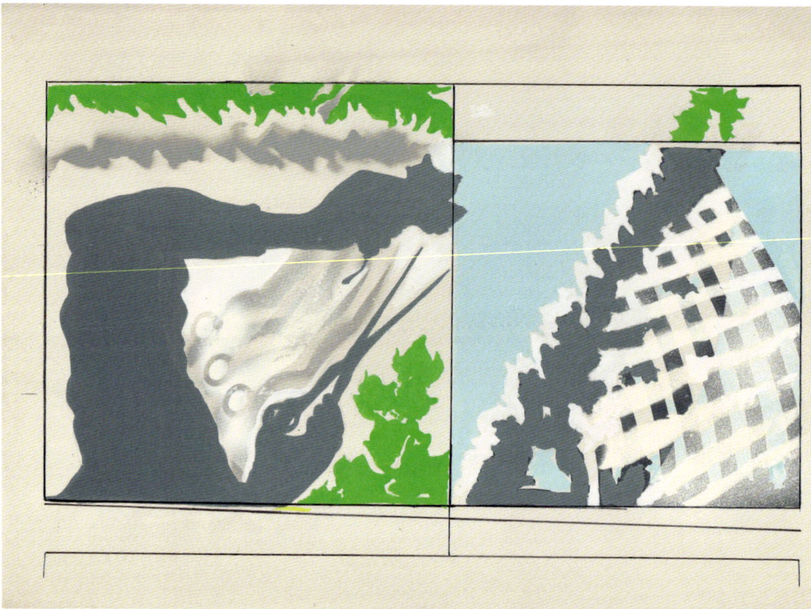

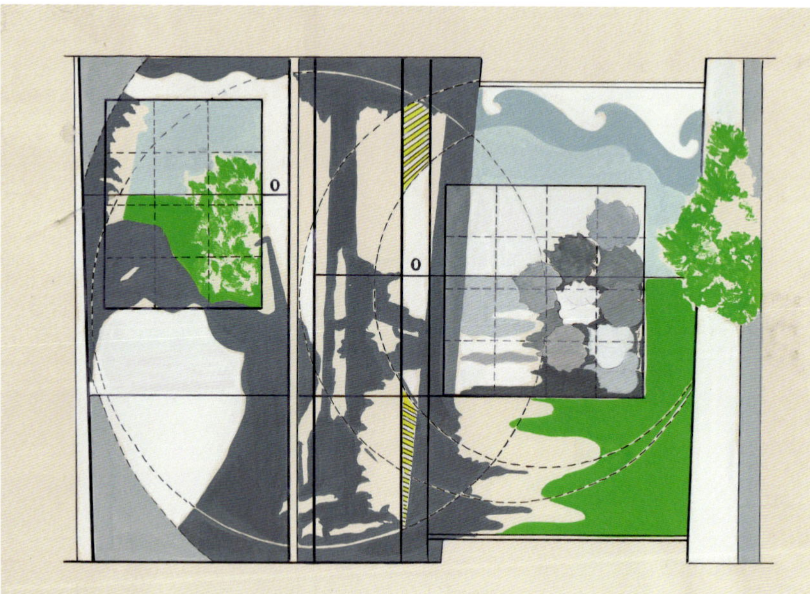

Untitled, (1965–1966)
Untitled, (1965–1966)

Untitled, 1966

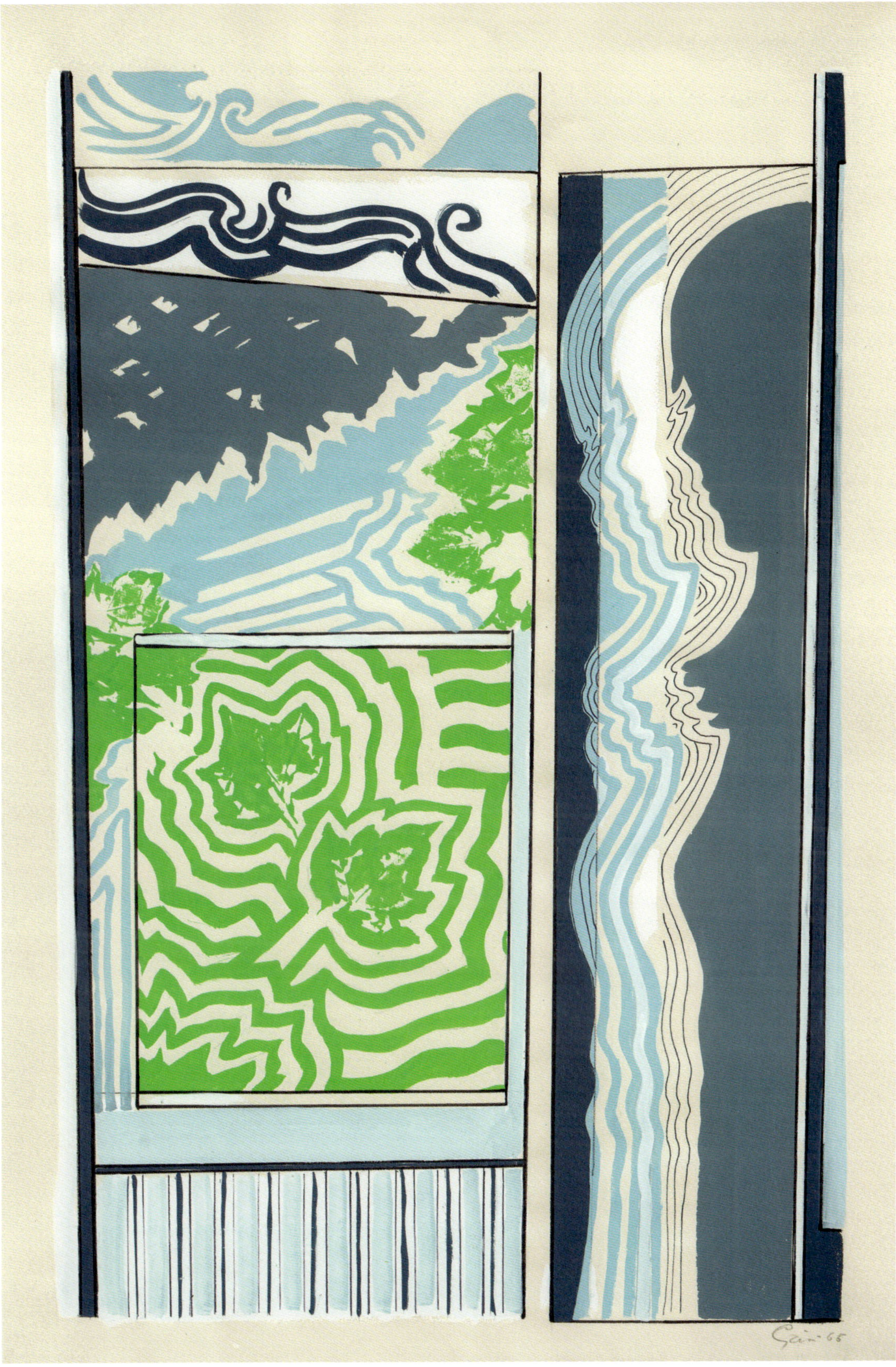

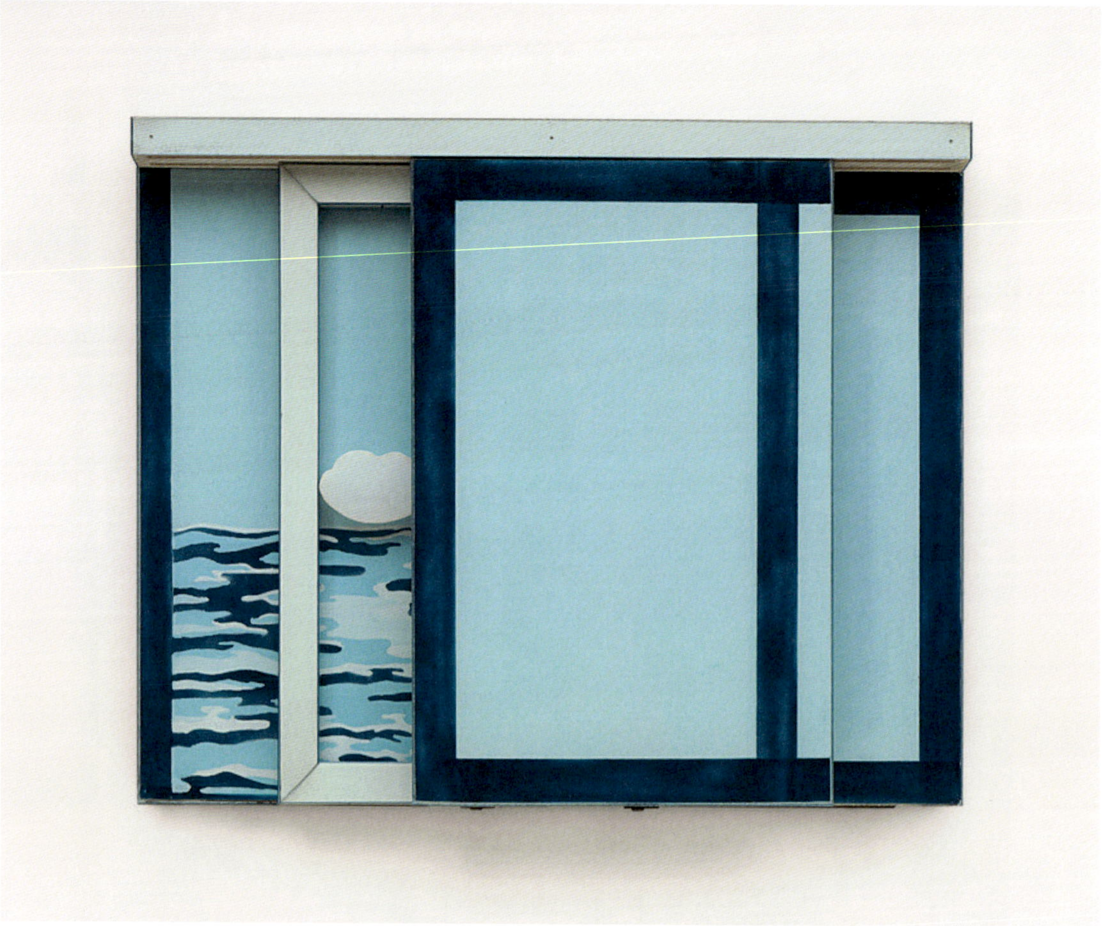

 ***Seascape*, 1966**

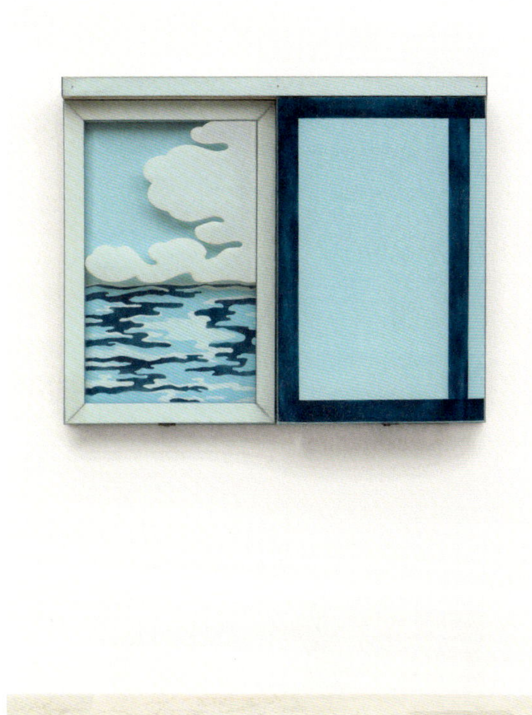

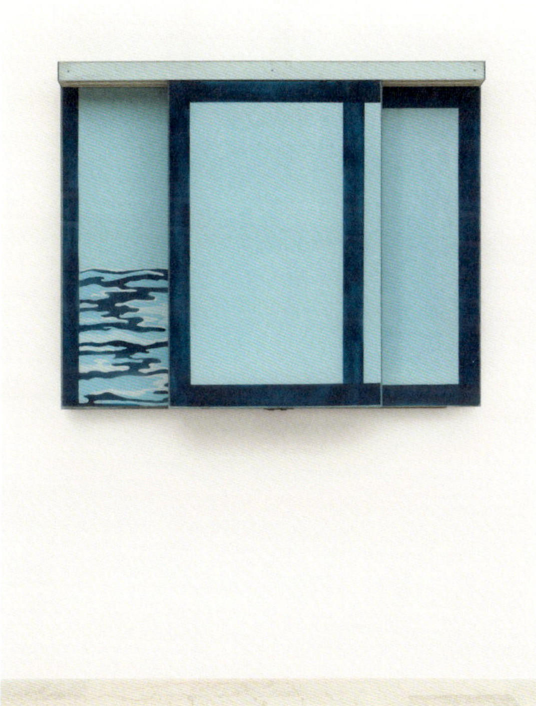

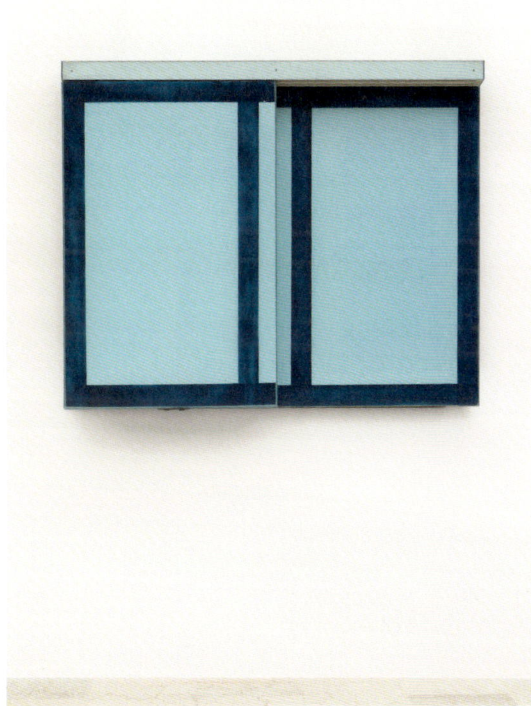

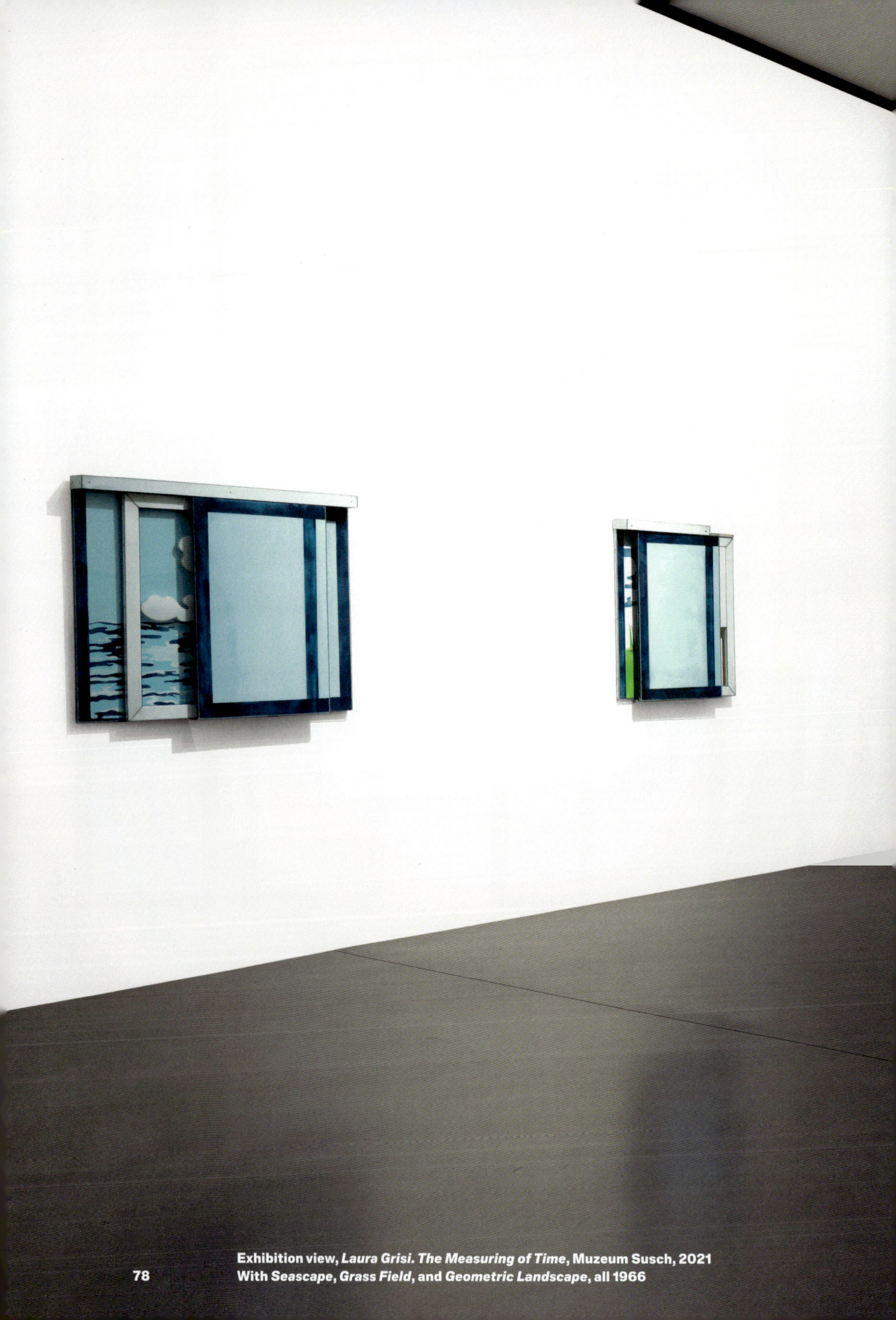

Exhibition view, *Laura Grisi. The Measuring of Time*, Muzeum Susch, 2021
With *Seascape*, *Grass Field*, and *Geometric Landscape*, all 1966

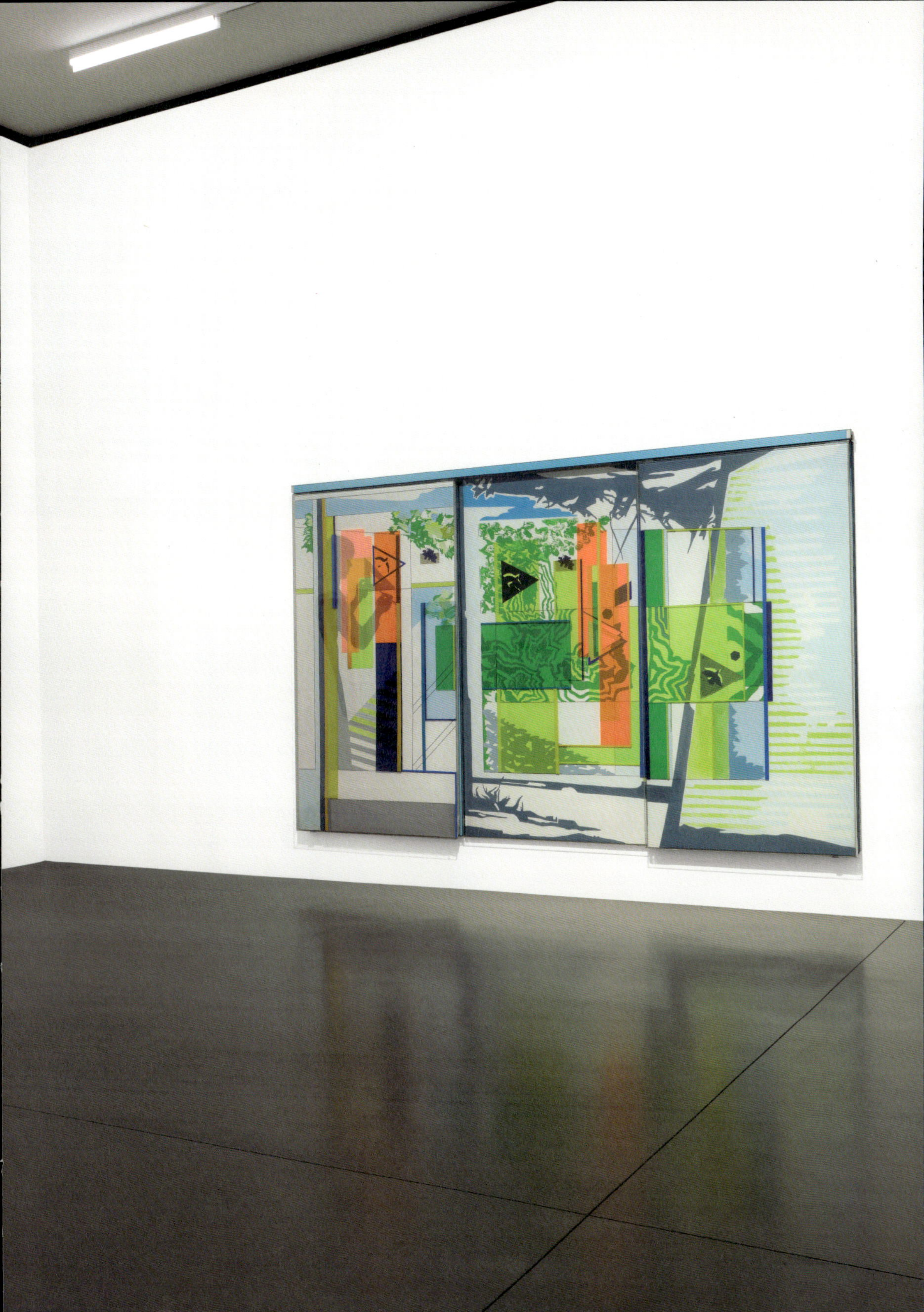

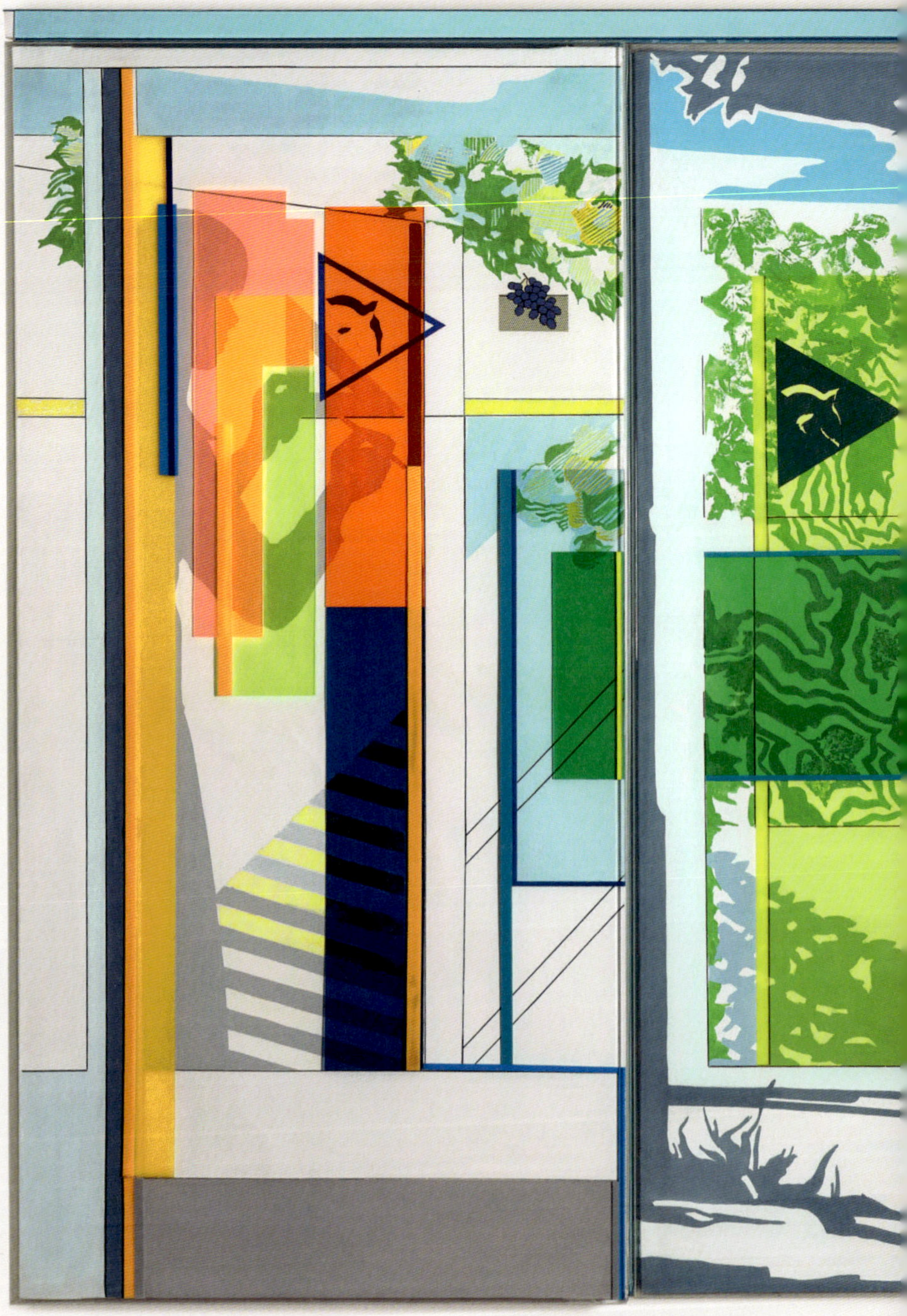

***Geometric Landscape*, 1966**

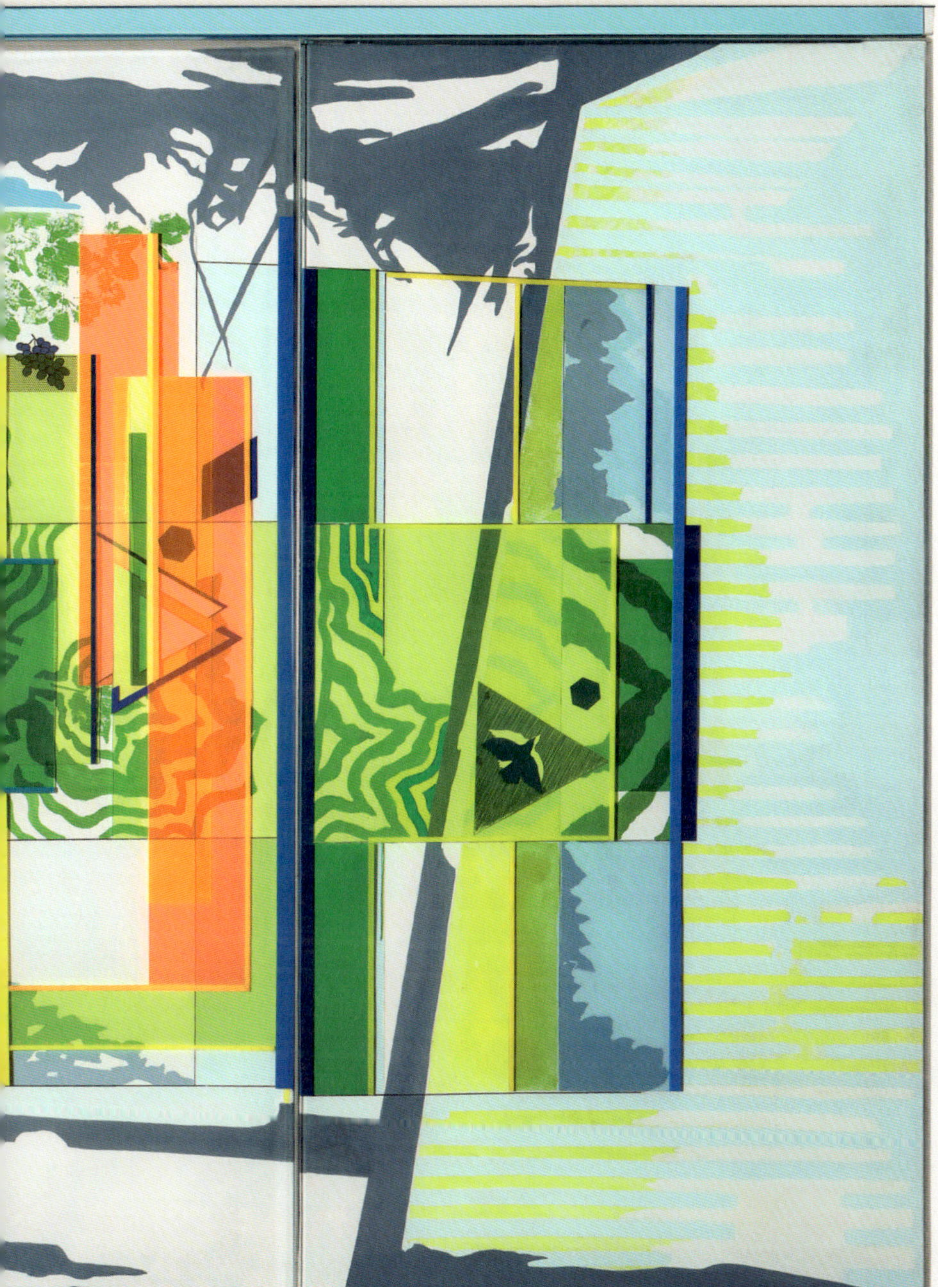

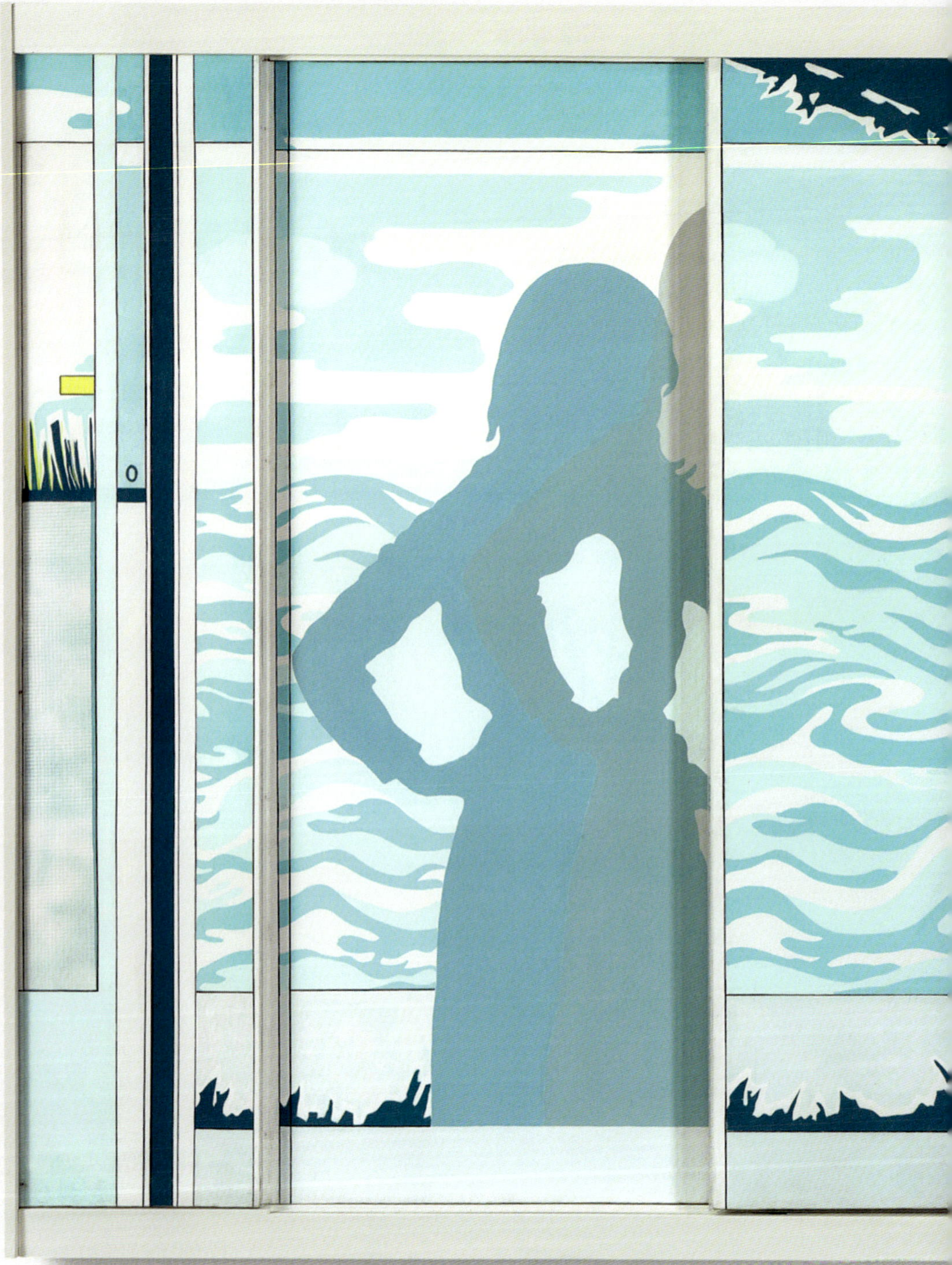

Seascape Omaggio a Constable, 1966

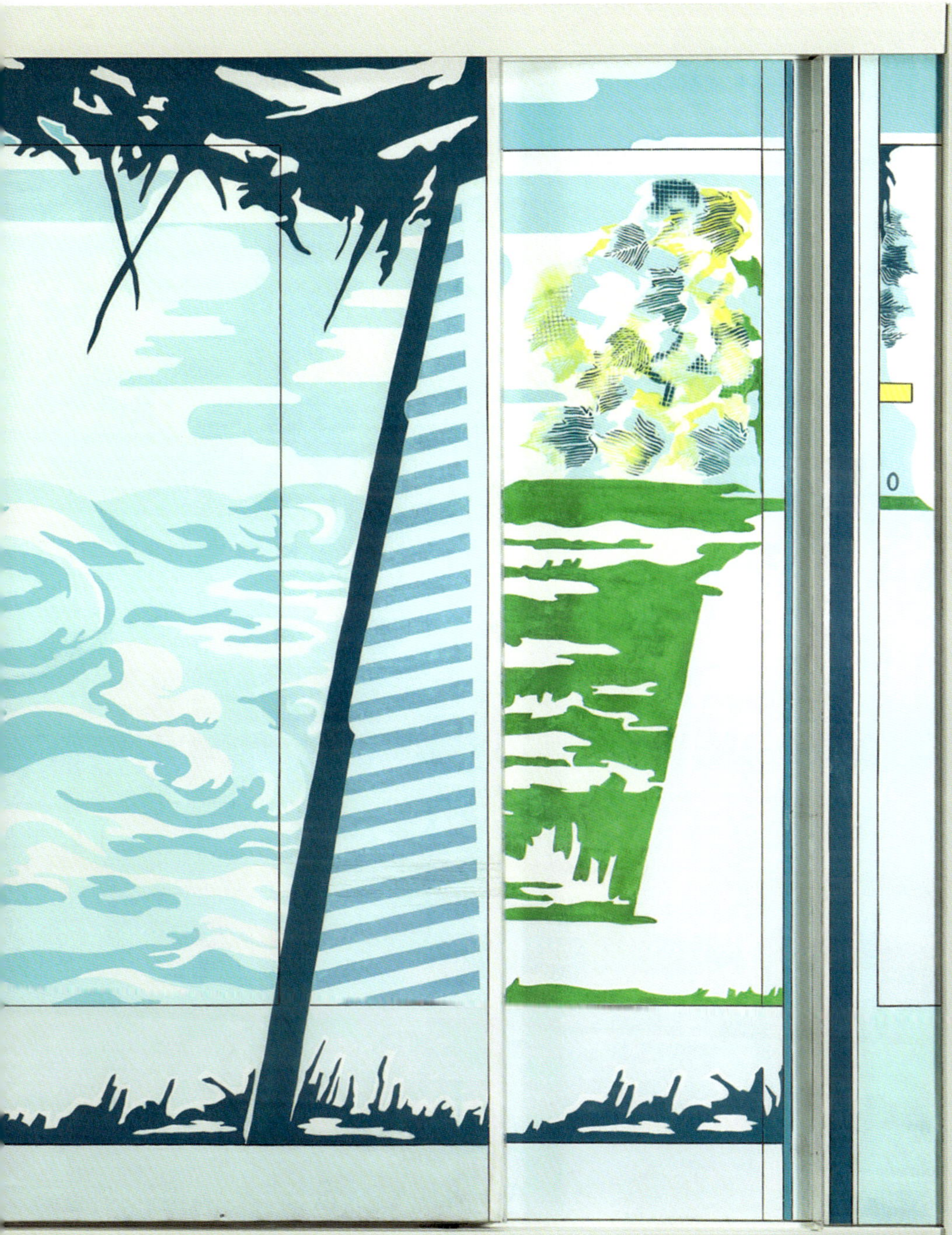

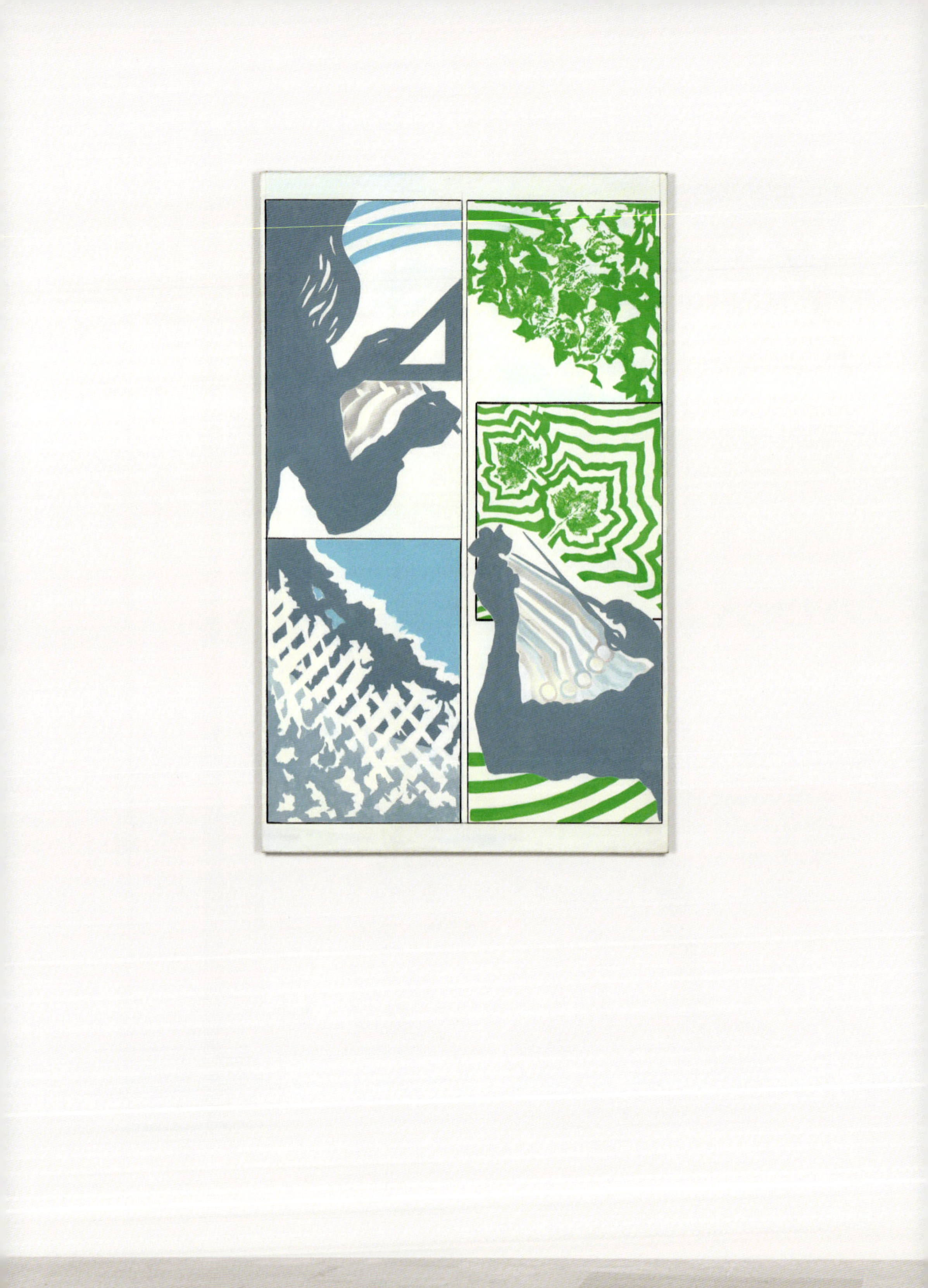

 Untitled, 1965–1966

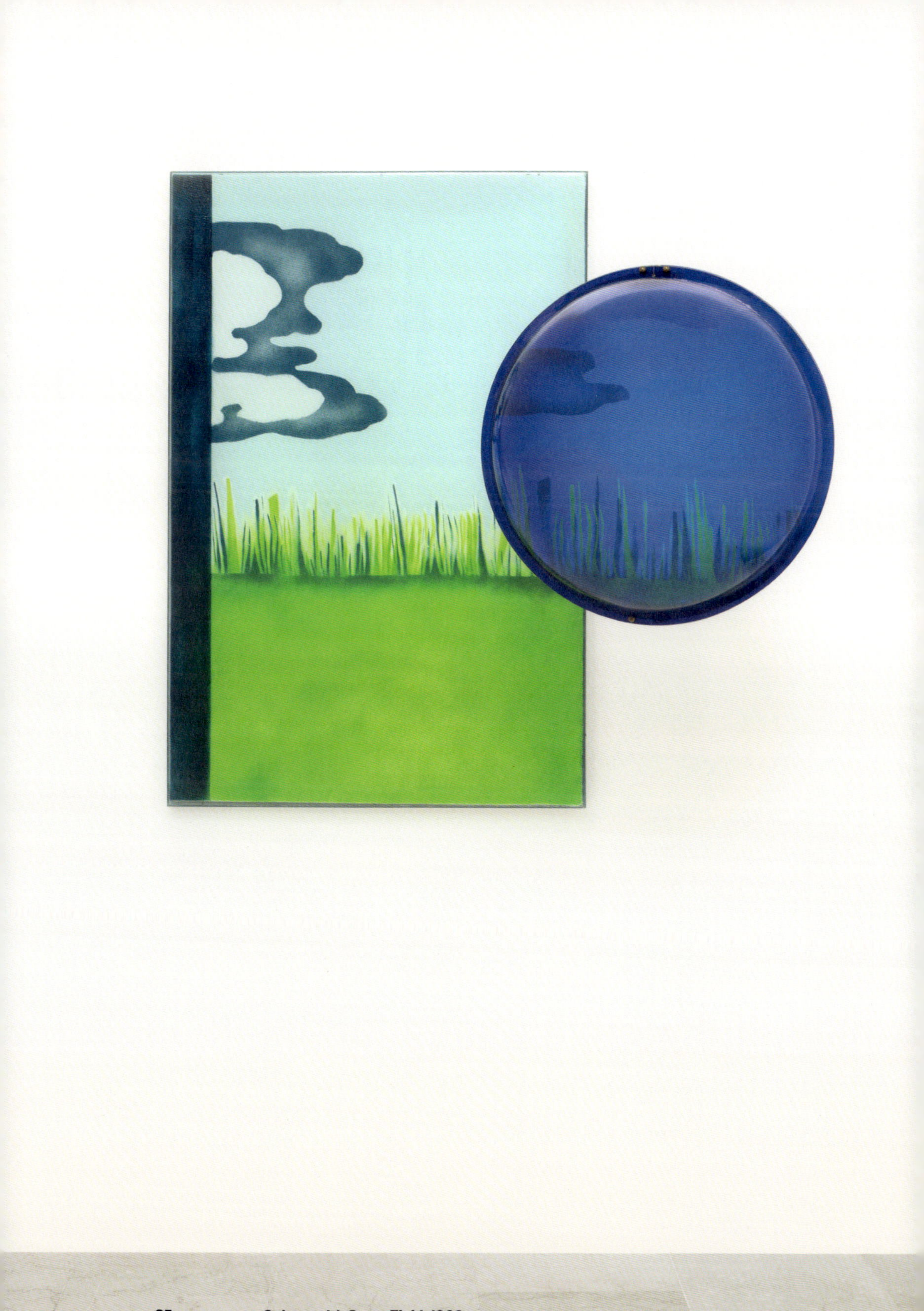

***Sphere with Grass Field*, 1966**

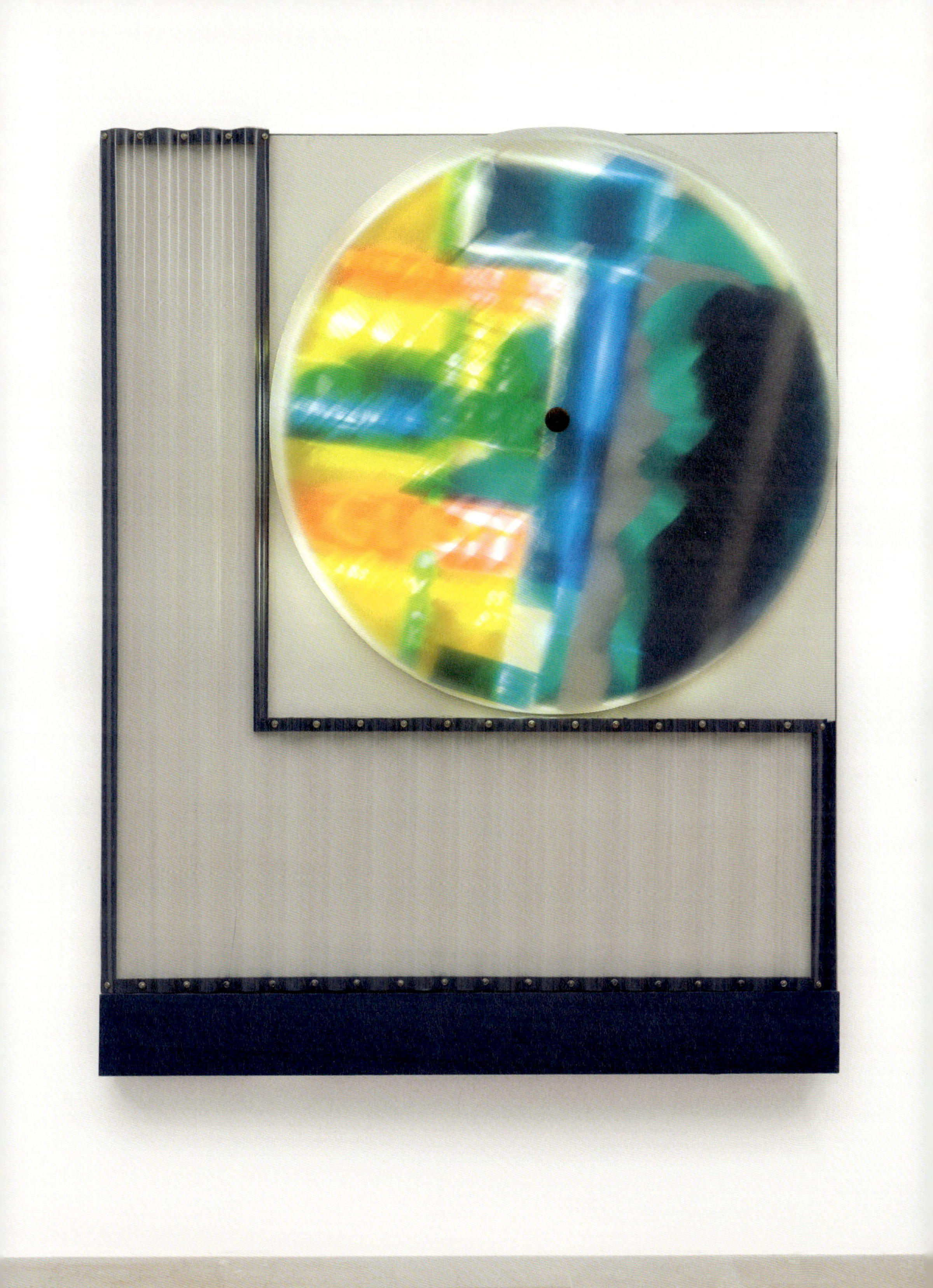

87 *Glosty (East Village Series)*, 1966

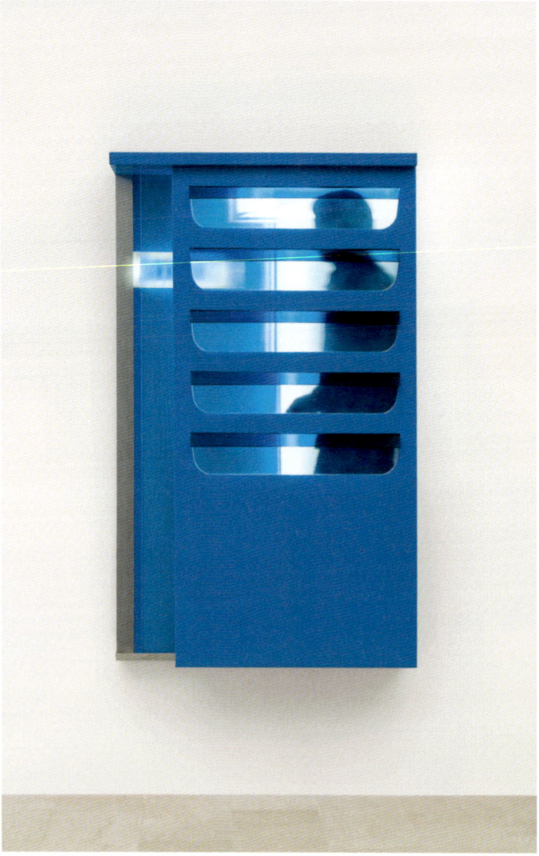

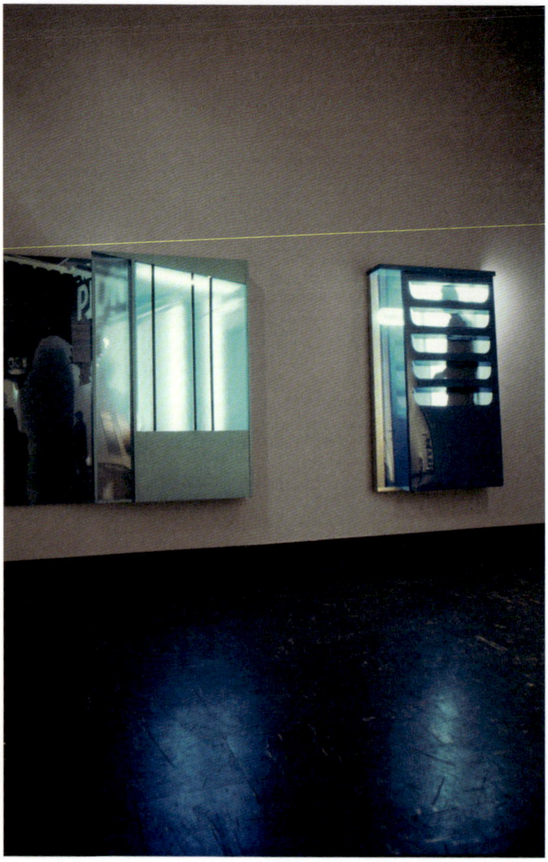

Subway, **1967**
Exhibition view, *Young Italians*, Institute of Contemporary Art, Boston, 1968
With *East Village and Subway*, both 1967

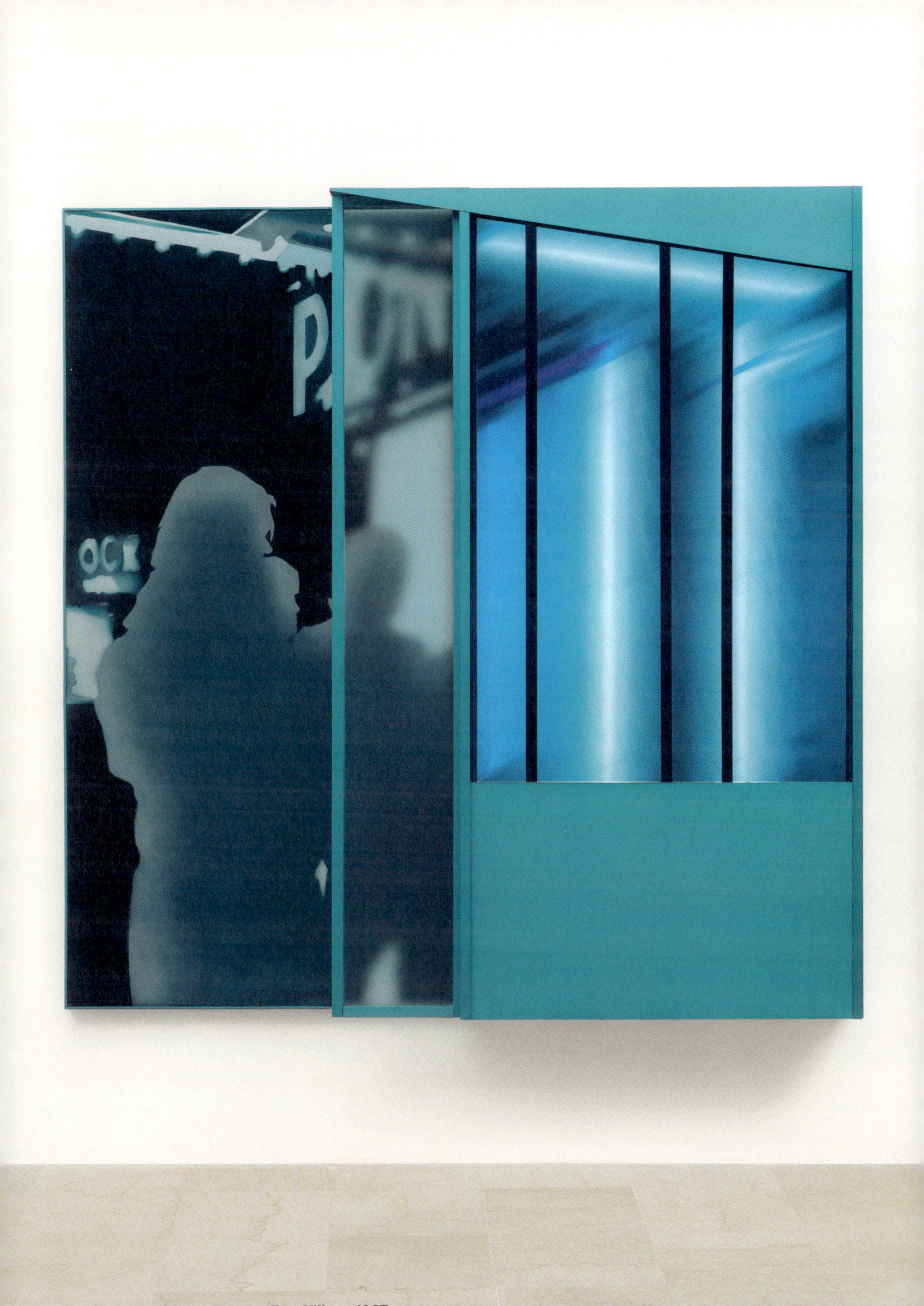

89 *East Village*, 1967

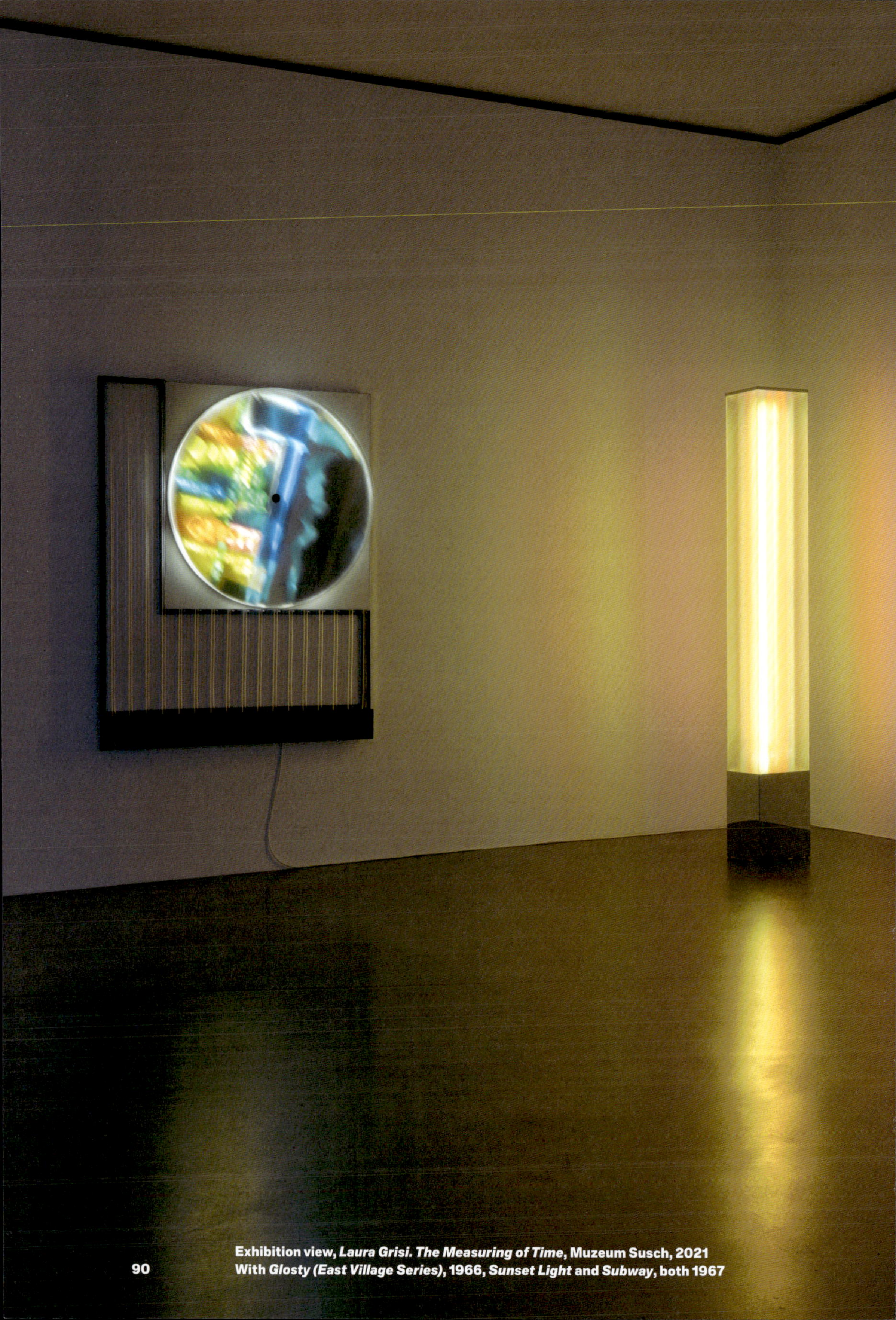

Exhibition view, *Laura Grisi. The Measuring of Time*, Muzeum Susch, 2021
With *Glosty (East Village Series)*, 1966, *Sunset Light* and *Subway*, both 1967

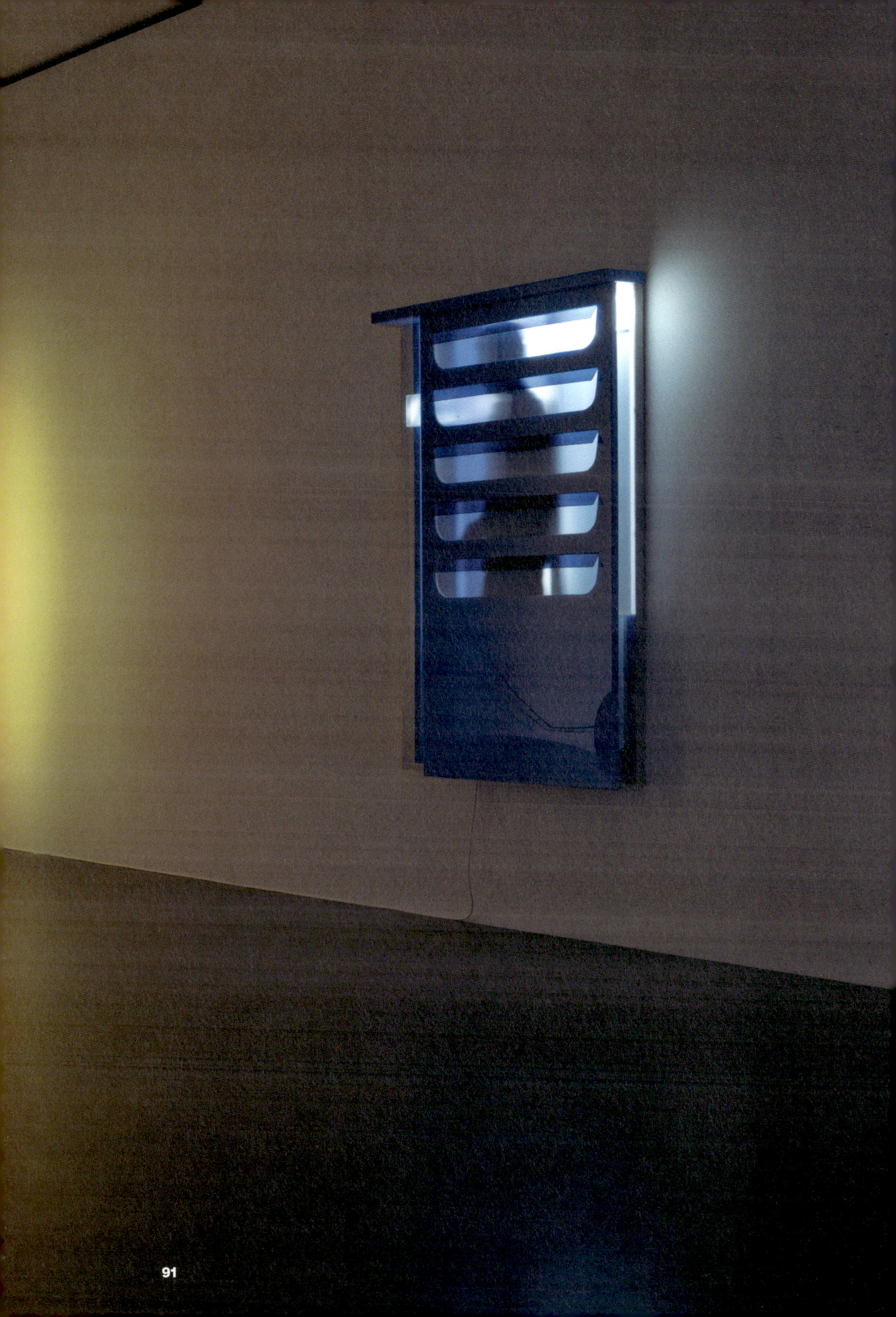

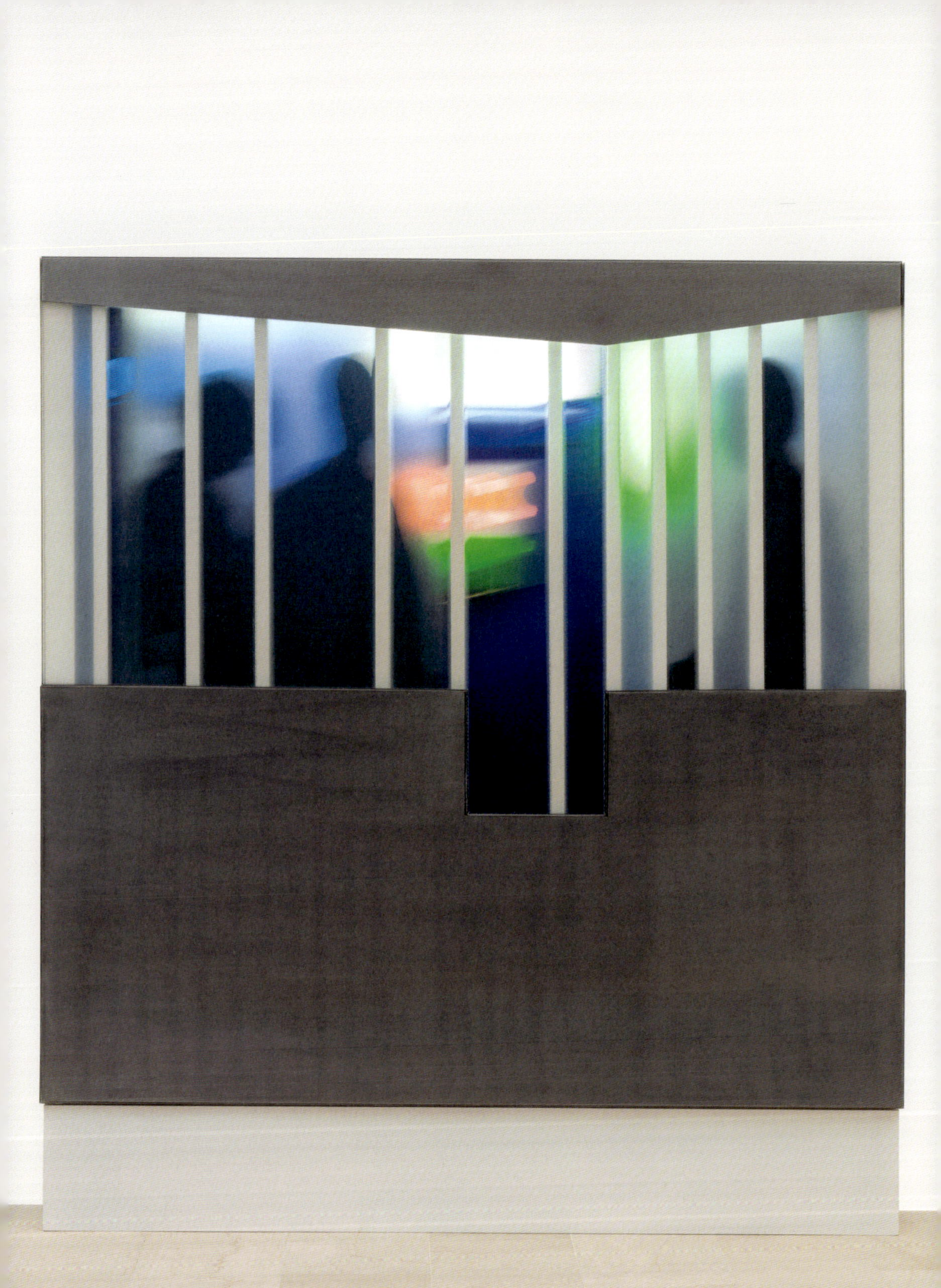

 ***St. Marks Place (East Village Series)*, 1967**

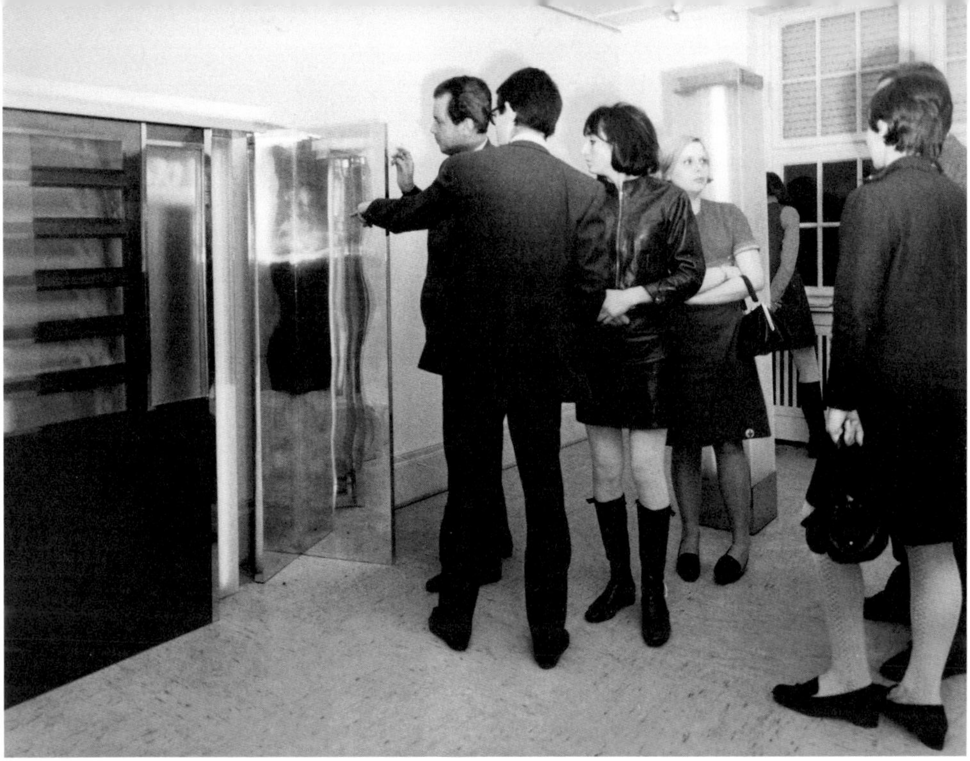

Exhibition view, Galerie E. M. Thelen, Essen, 1968
With *No. 470, Angolare*, 1967, and *Antinebbia*, 1967

Laura Grisi, Galerie E. M. Thelen, Essen, 1968
With *No. 470, Angolare*, 1967, and *Antinebbia*, 1967

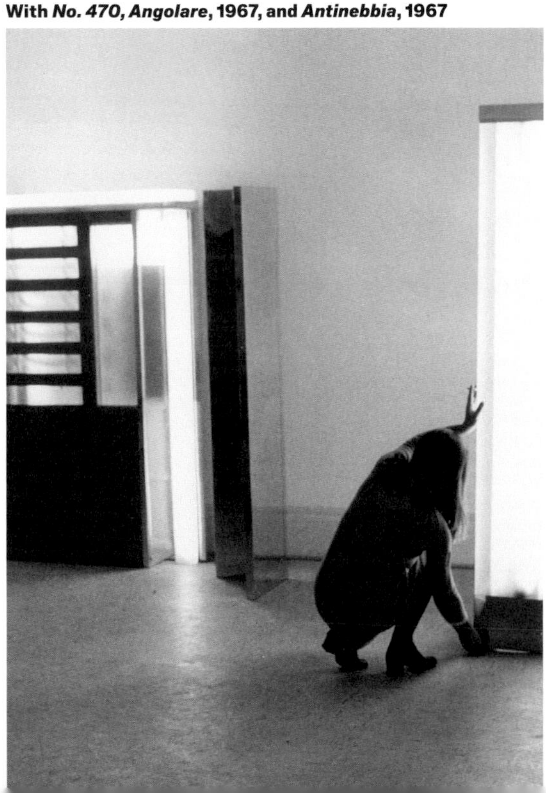

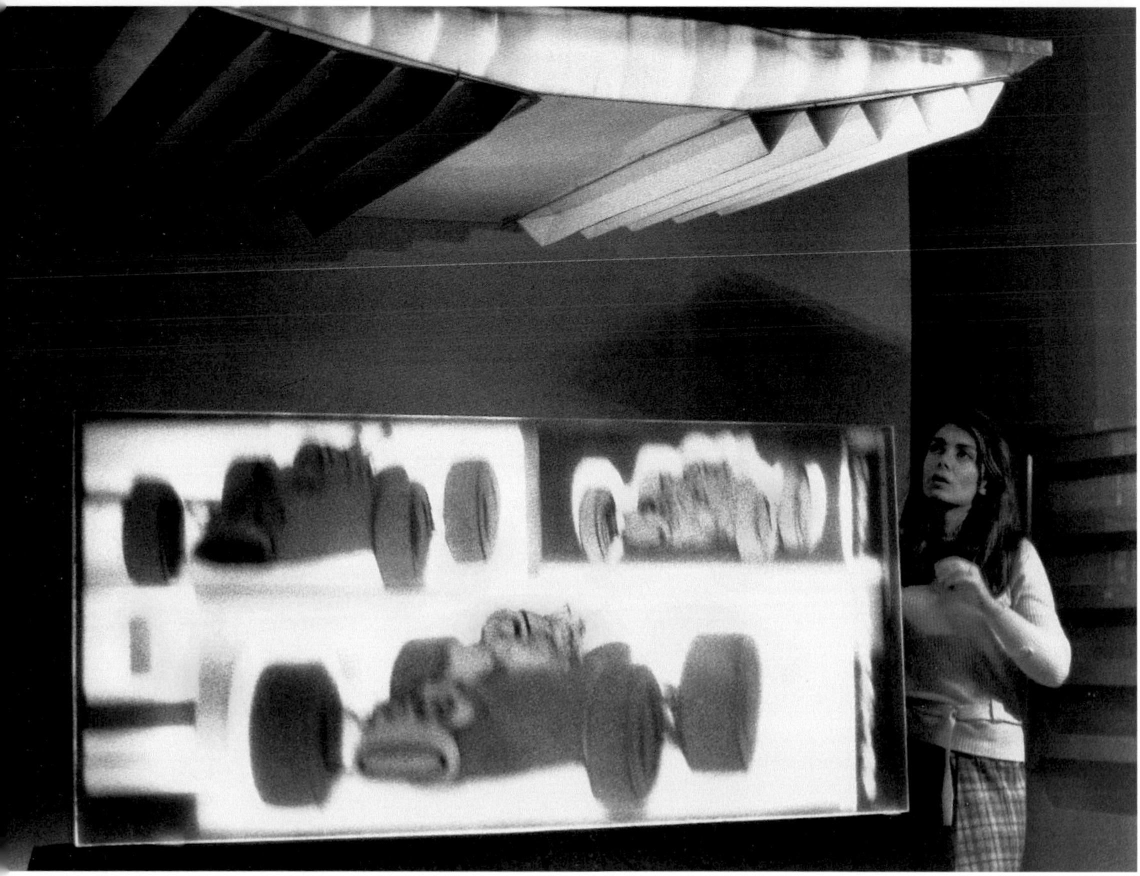

Laura Grisi in her installation *Racing Car Room*, Galerie E. M. Thelen, Essen, 1968
With *Model Car Racing* and *Blue*, both 1967

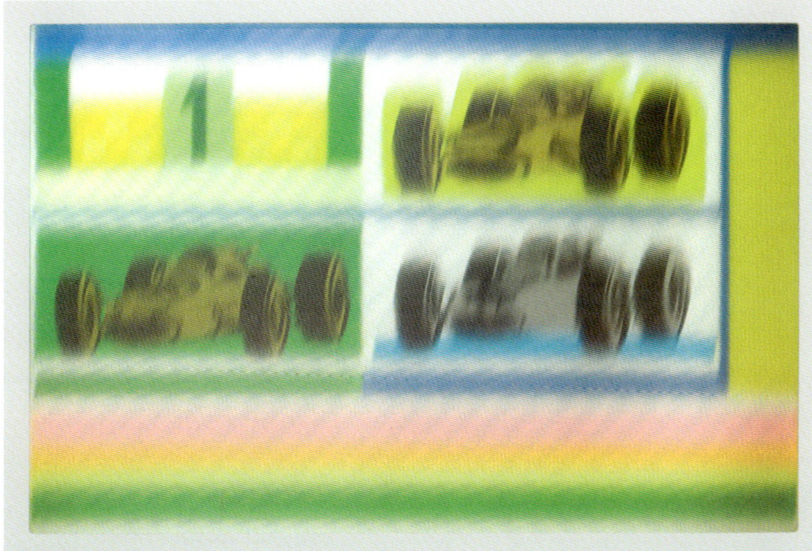

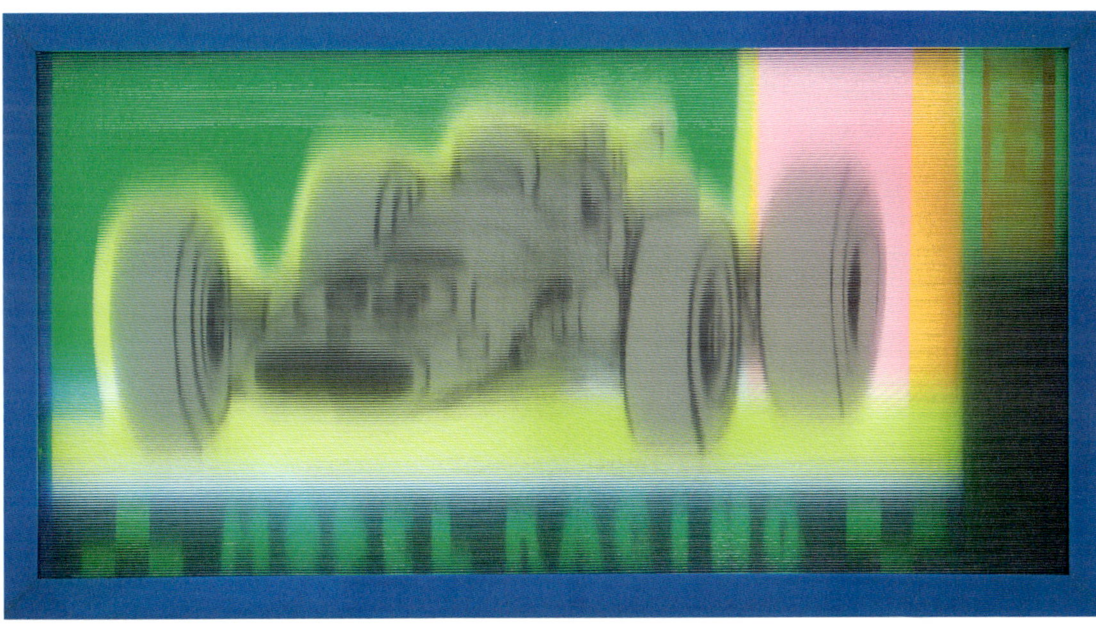

Model Car Racing, 1967
Model Car Racing, 1967

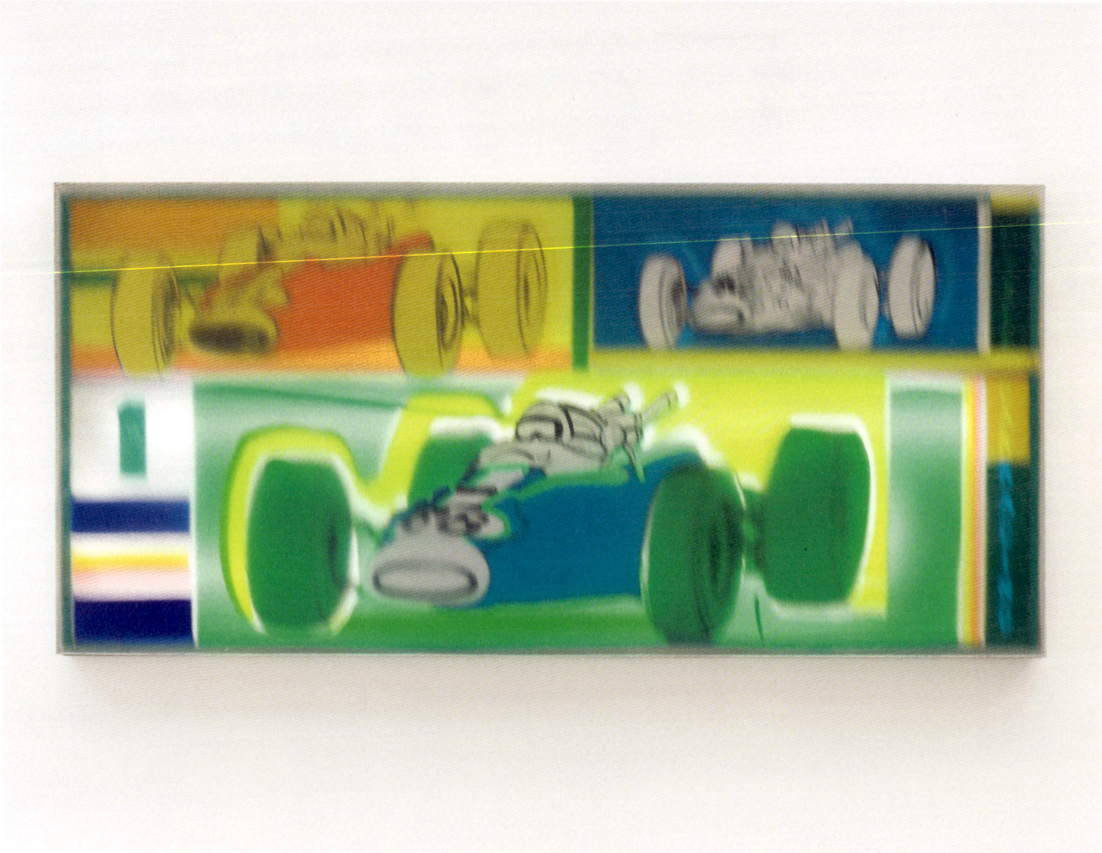

***Model Car Racing*, 1967**

***Top Floor*, 1967**

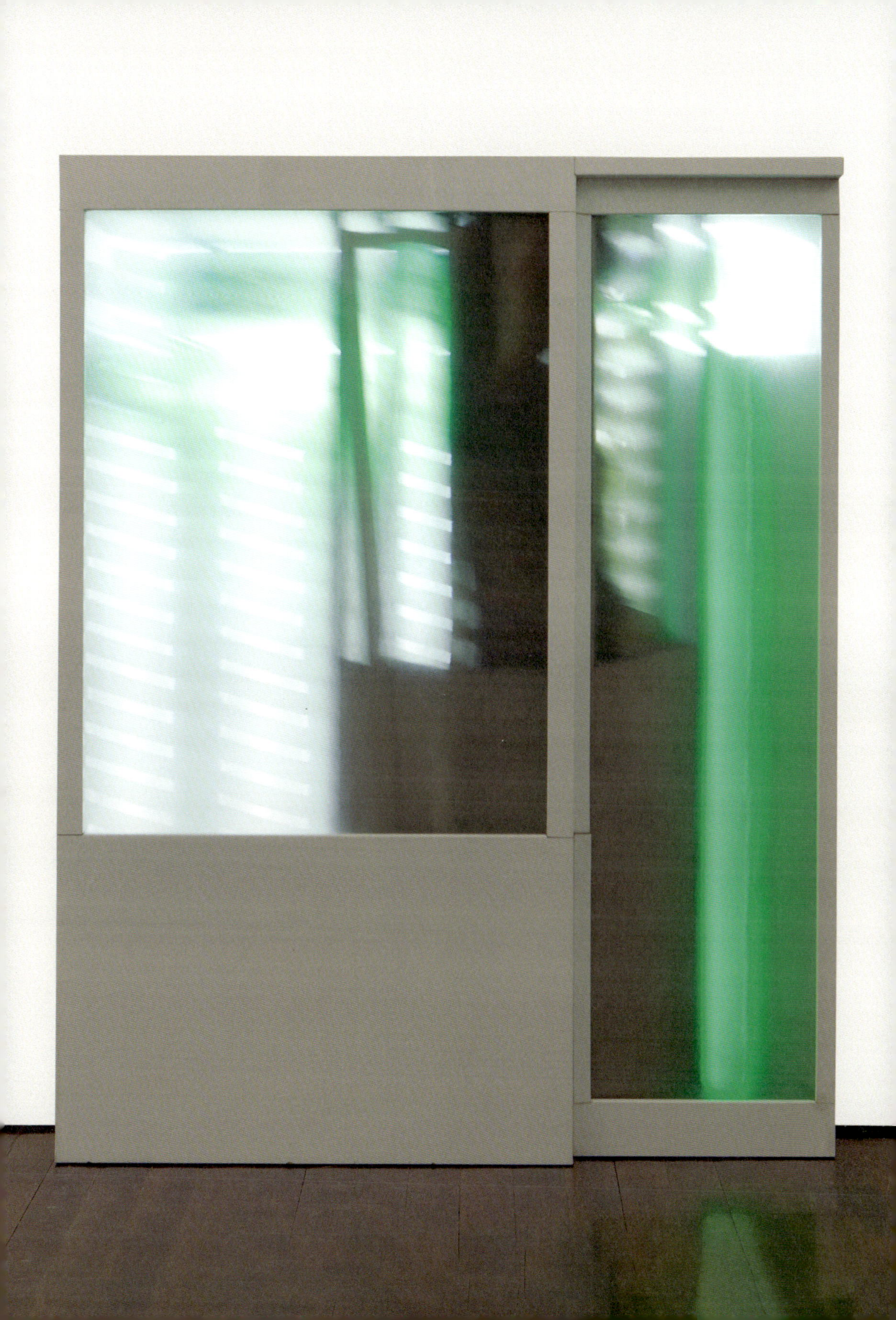

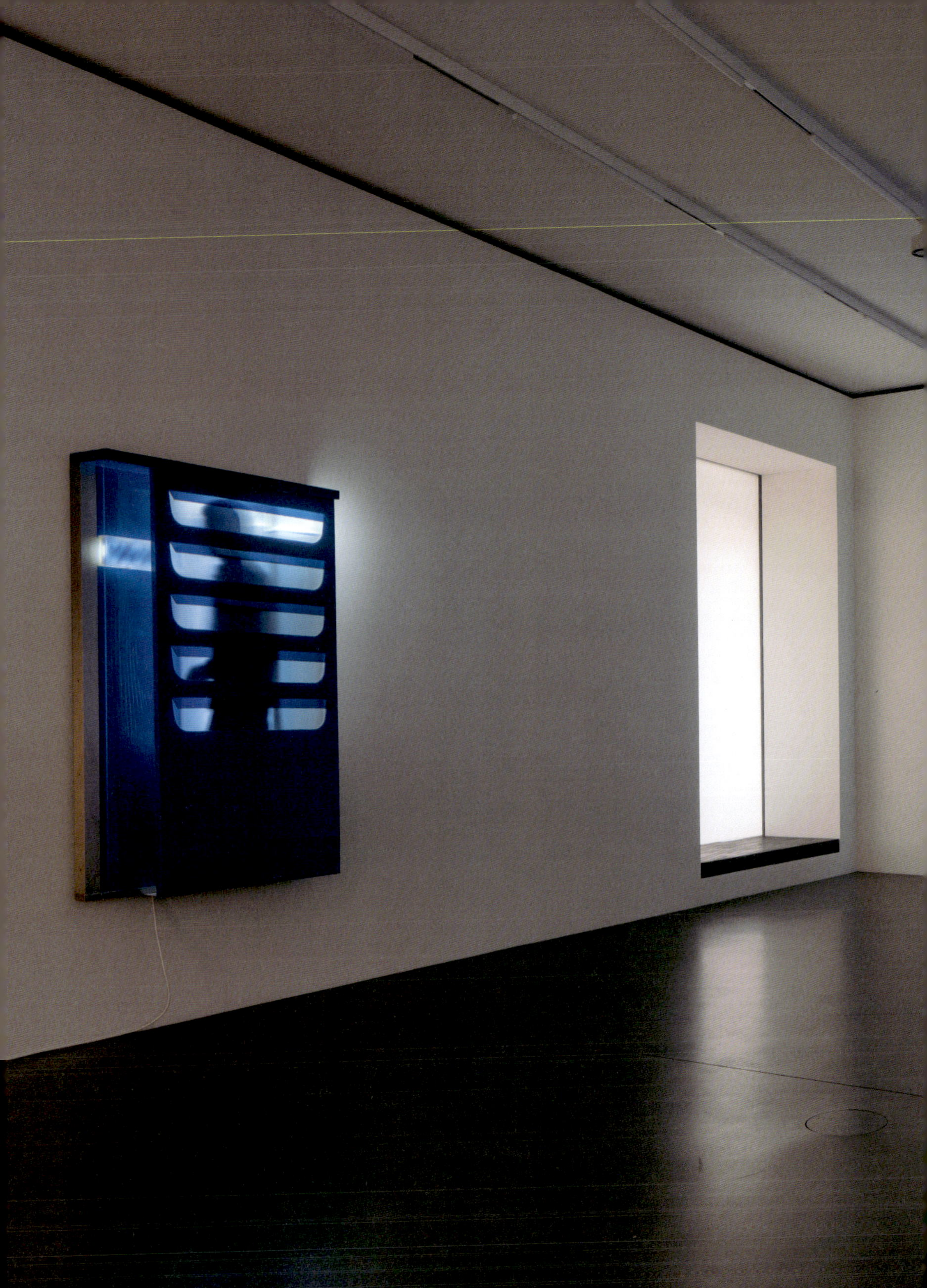

Exhibition view, *Laura Grisi. The Measuring of Time*, Muzeum Susch, 2021
With *Subway* and *East Village*, both 1967, and *Un' Area di Nebbia (A Space of Fog)*, 1968

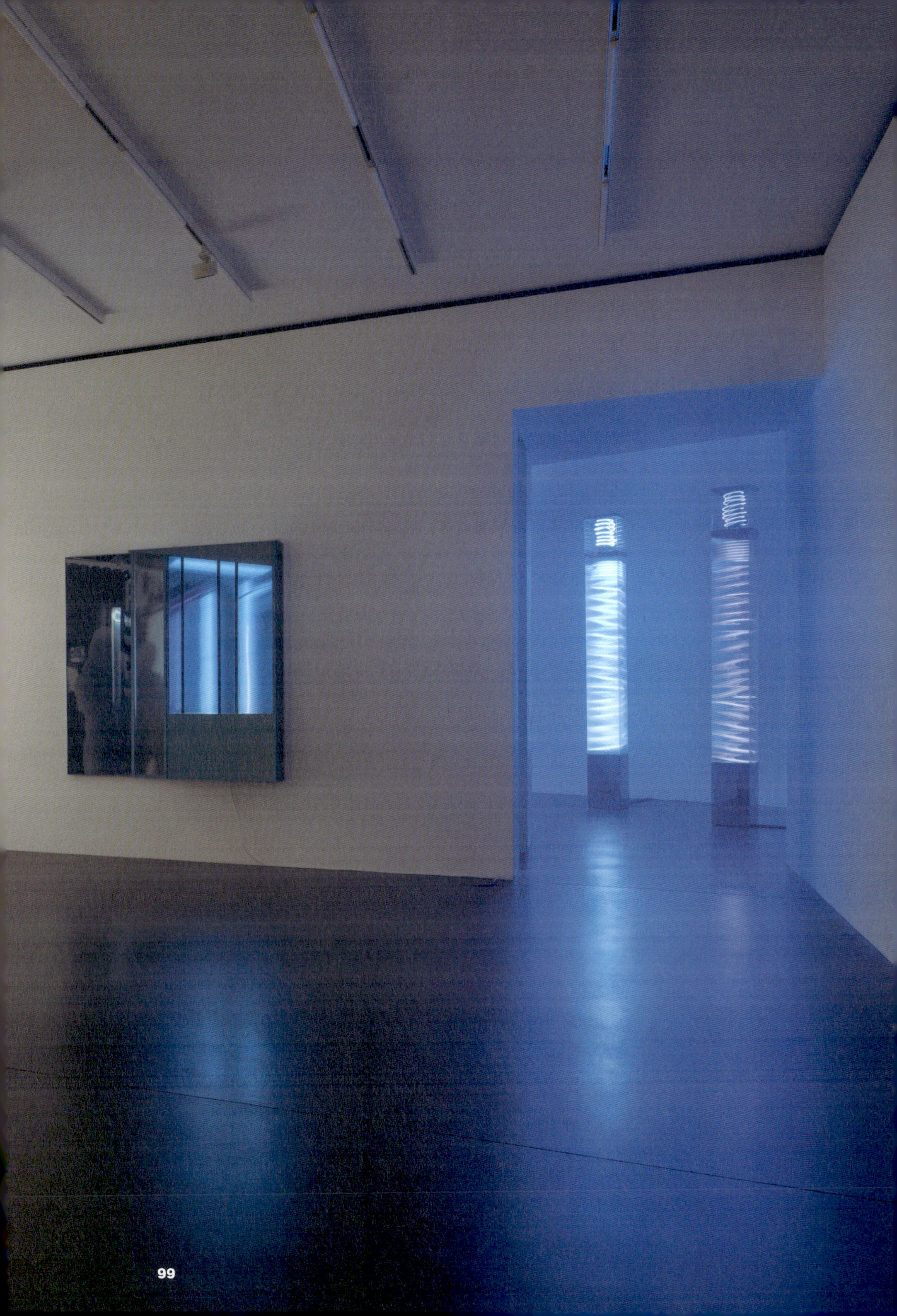

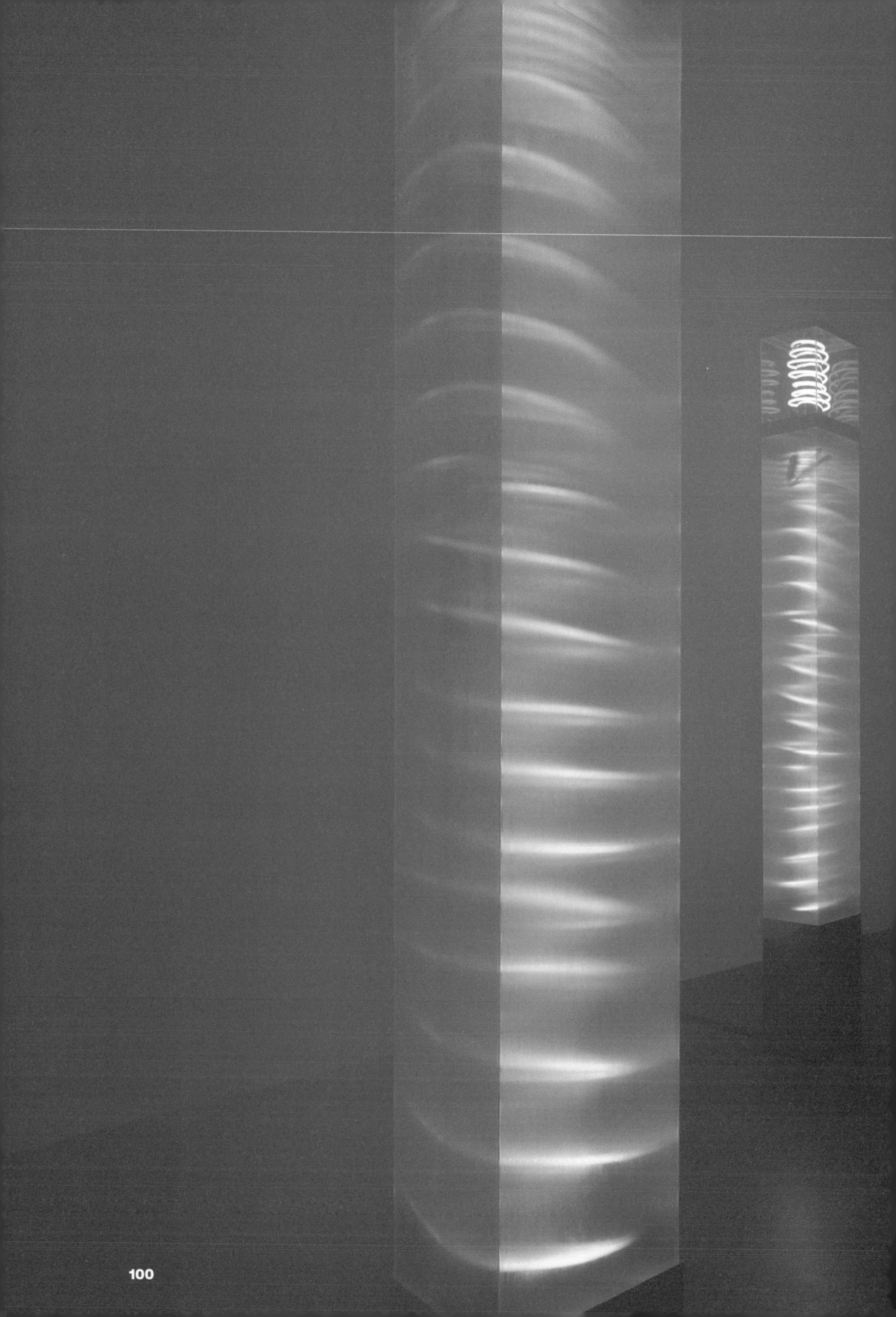

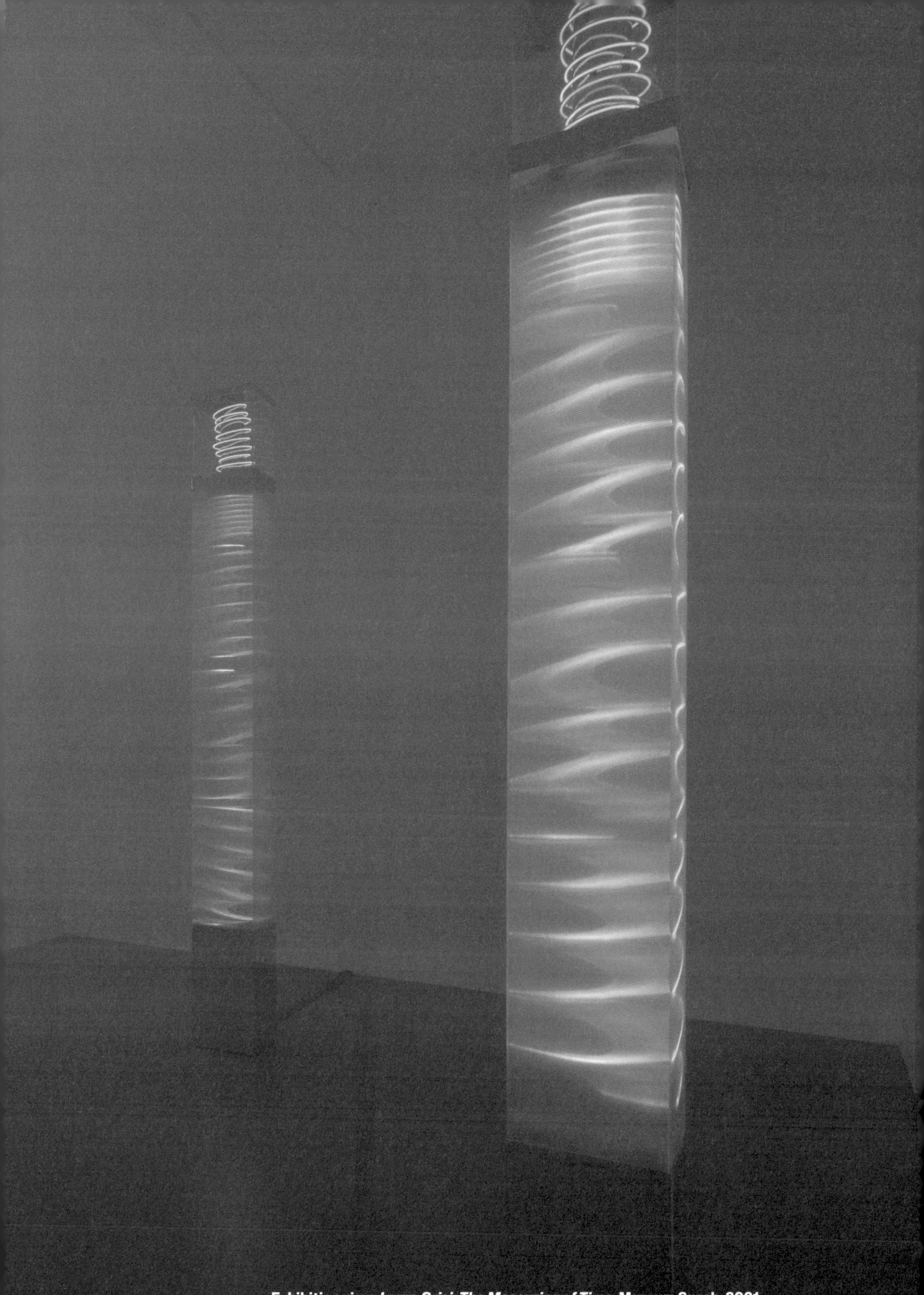

Exhibition view, ***Laura Grisi. The Measuring of Time***, Muzeum Susch, 2021
With ***Un' Area di Nebbia (A Space of Fog)***, 1968

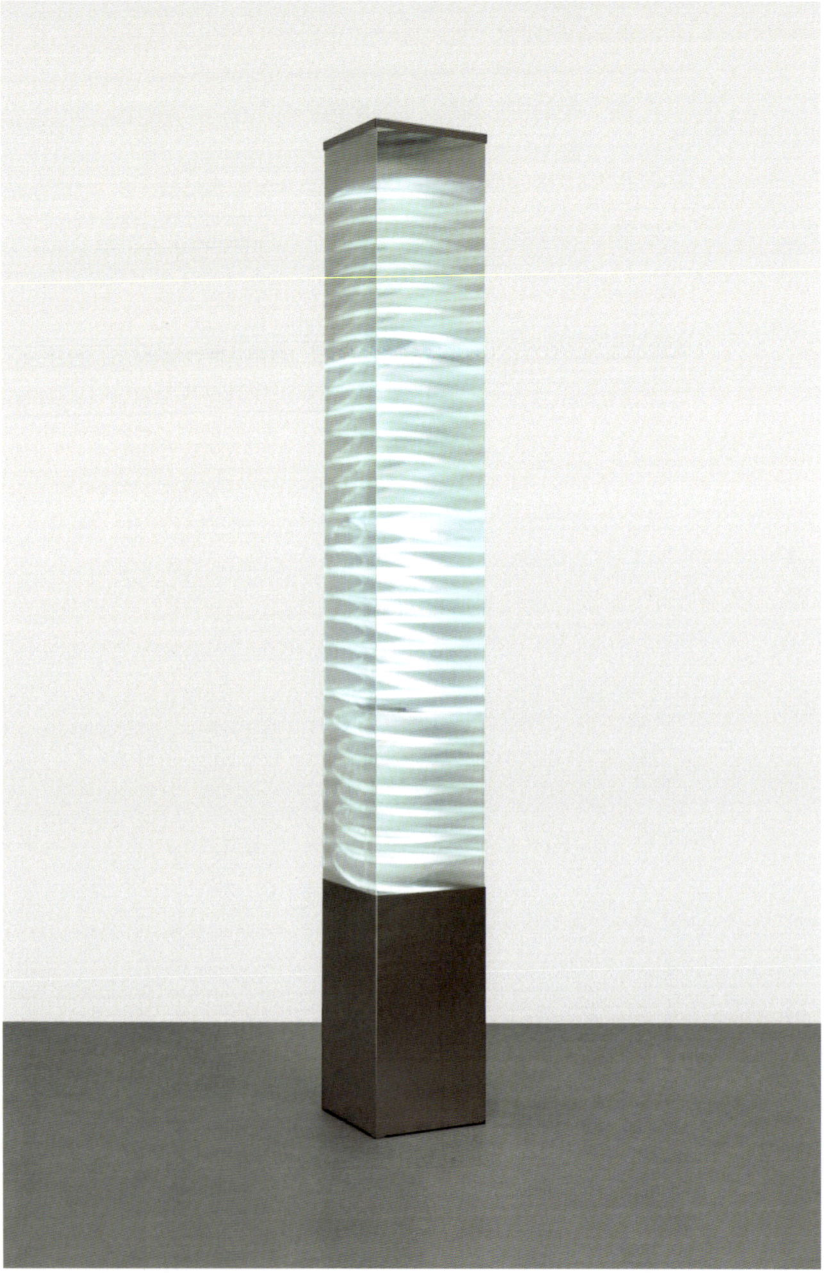

 ***Spiral Light*, 1968**

***Sunset Light*, 1967**

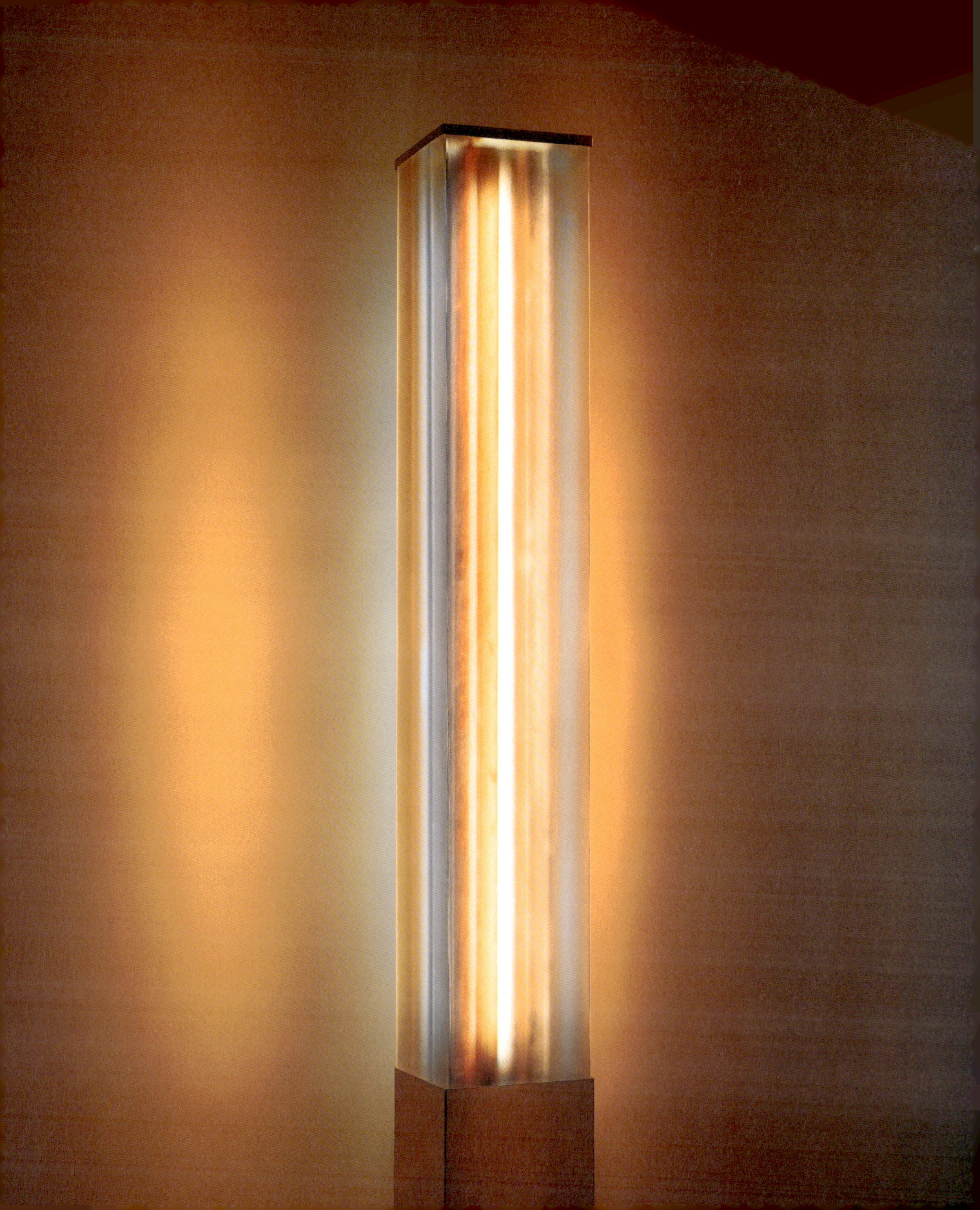

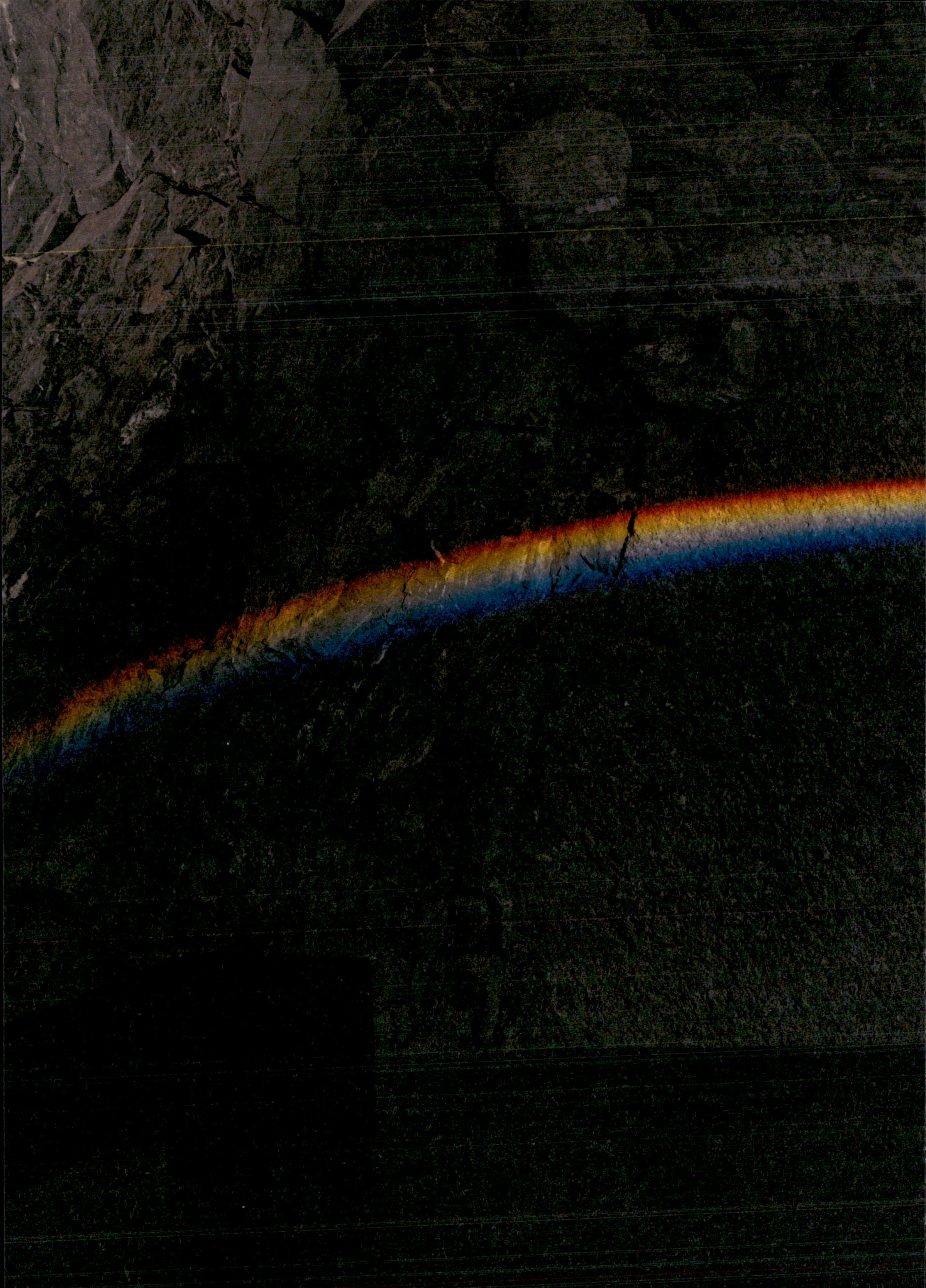

Exhibition view, ***Laura Grisi. The Measuring of Time***, Muzeum Susch, 2021
With ***Rainbow***, 1968

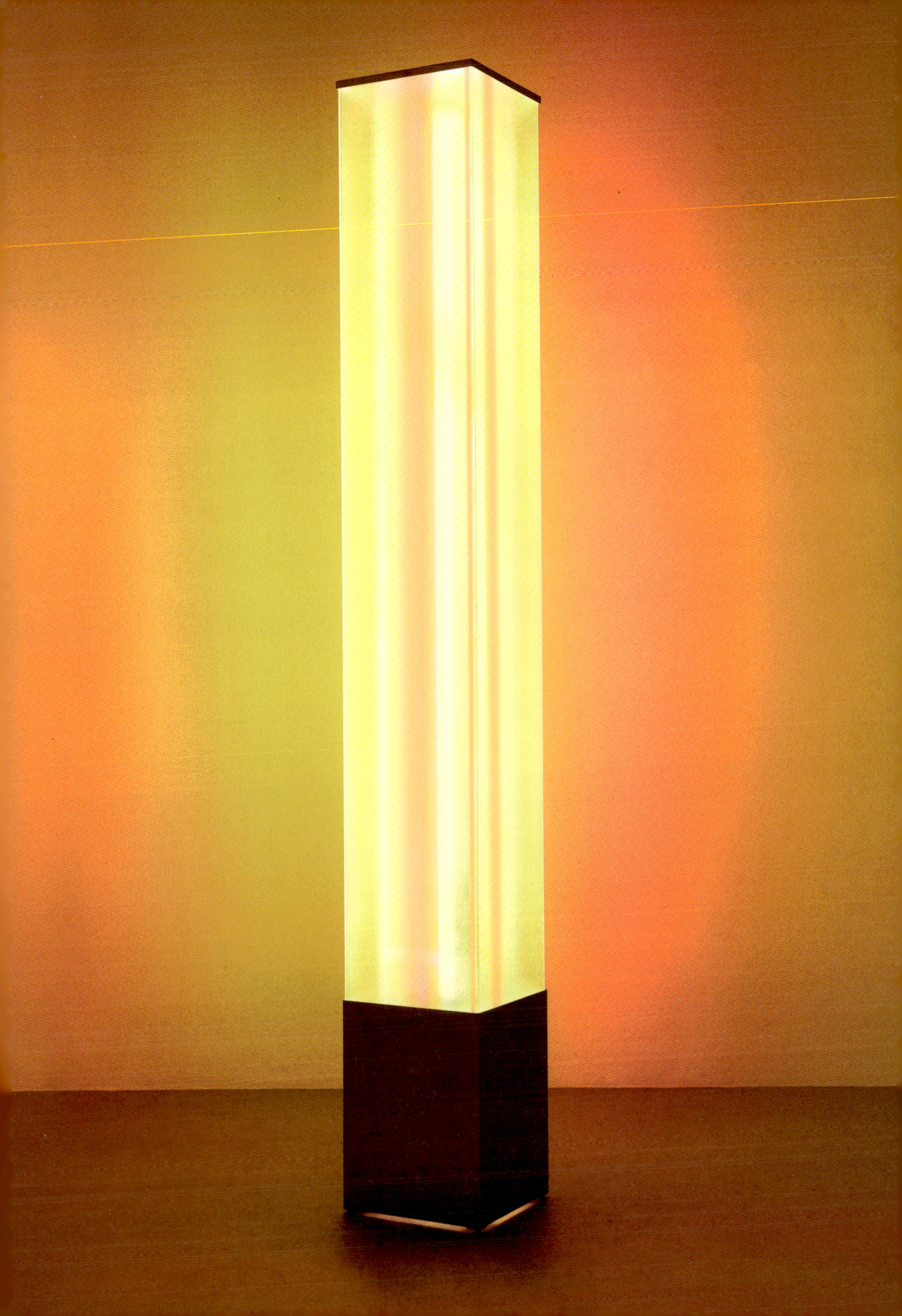

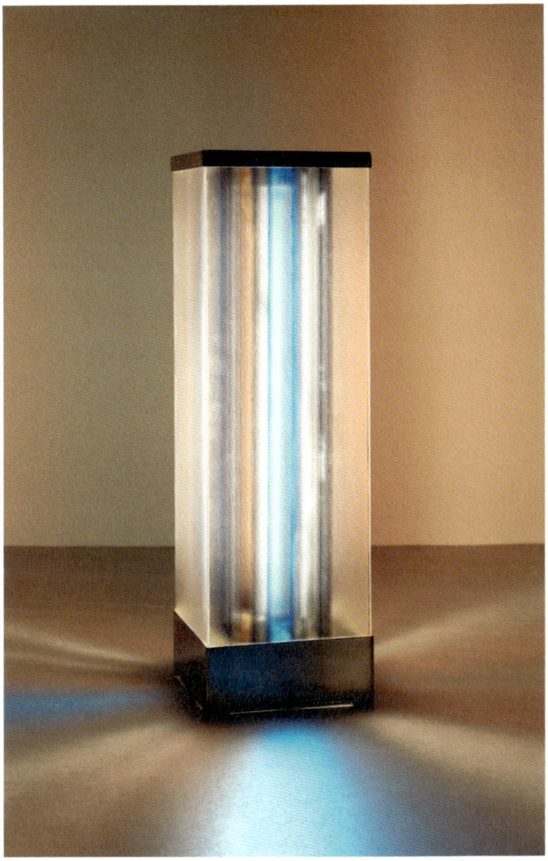

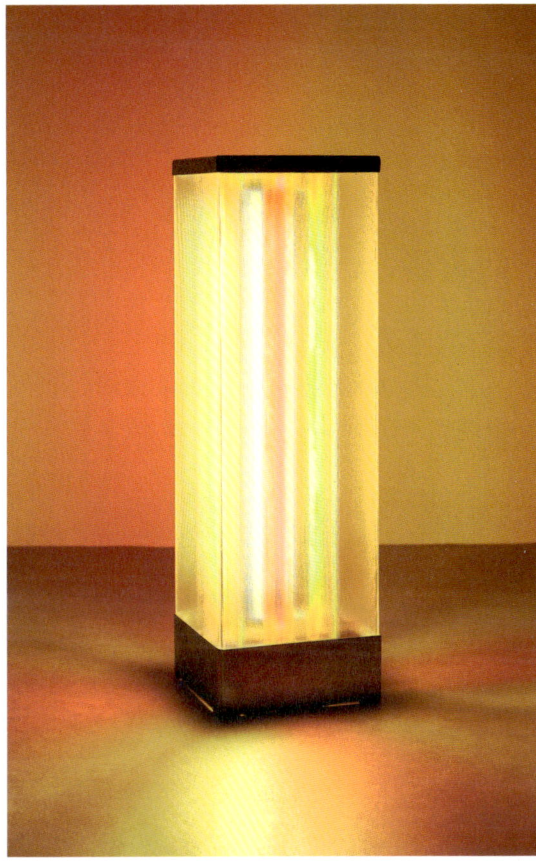

***Sunset Light*, 1967**
***Sunset Light*, 1967**
***Sunset Light*, 1967**

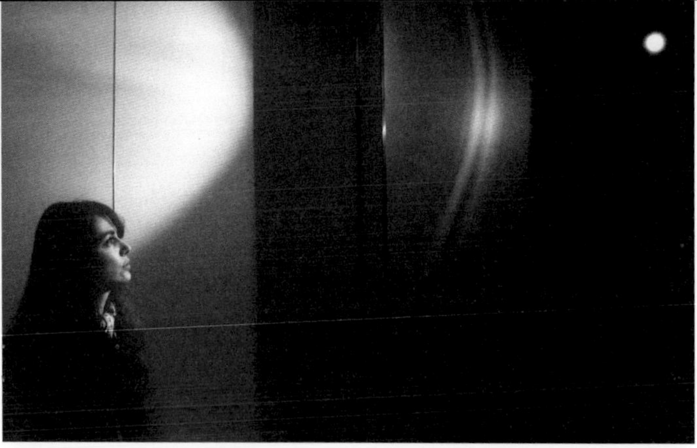

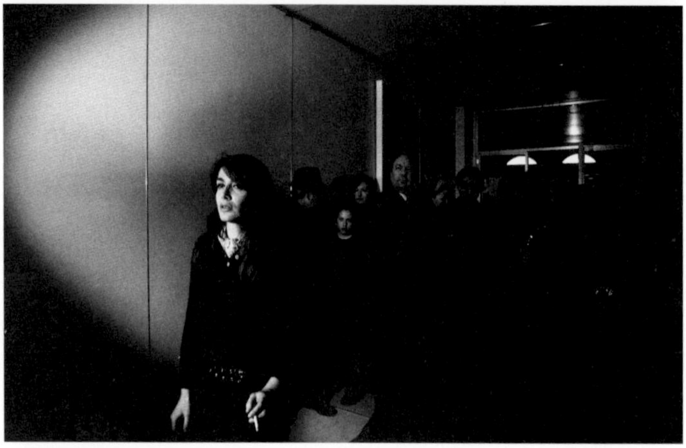

Exhibition views, *Luce + Calore = Tempo di Fusione*, Galleria del Naviglio, Milan, 1970
Laura Grisi in her installation *Light Melting Time*, 1968

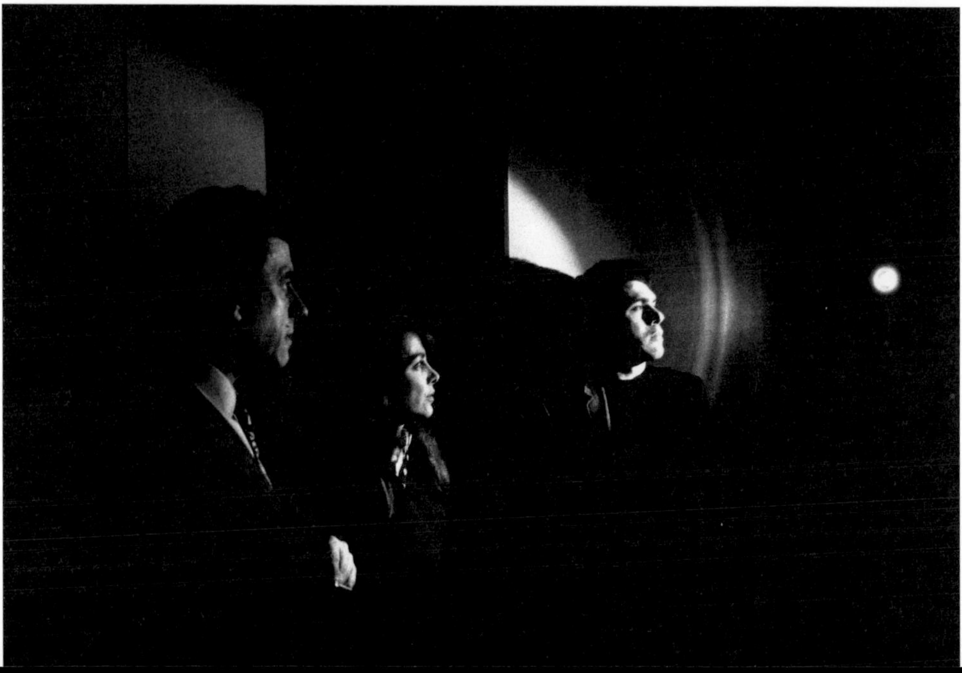

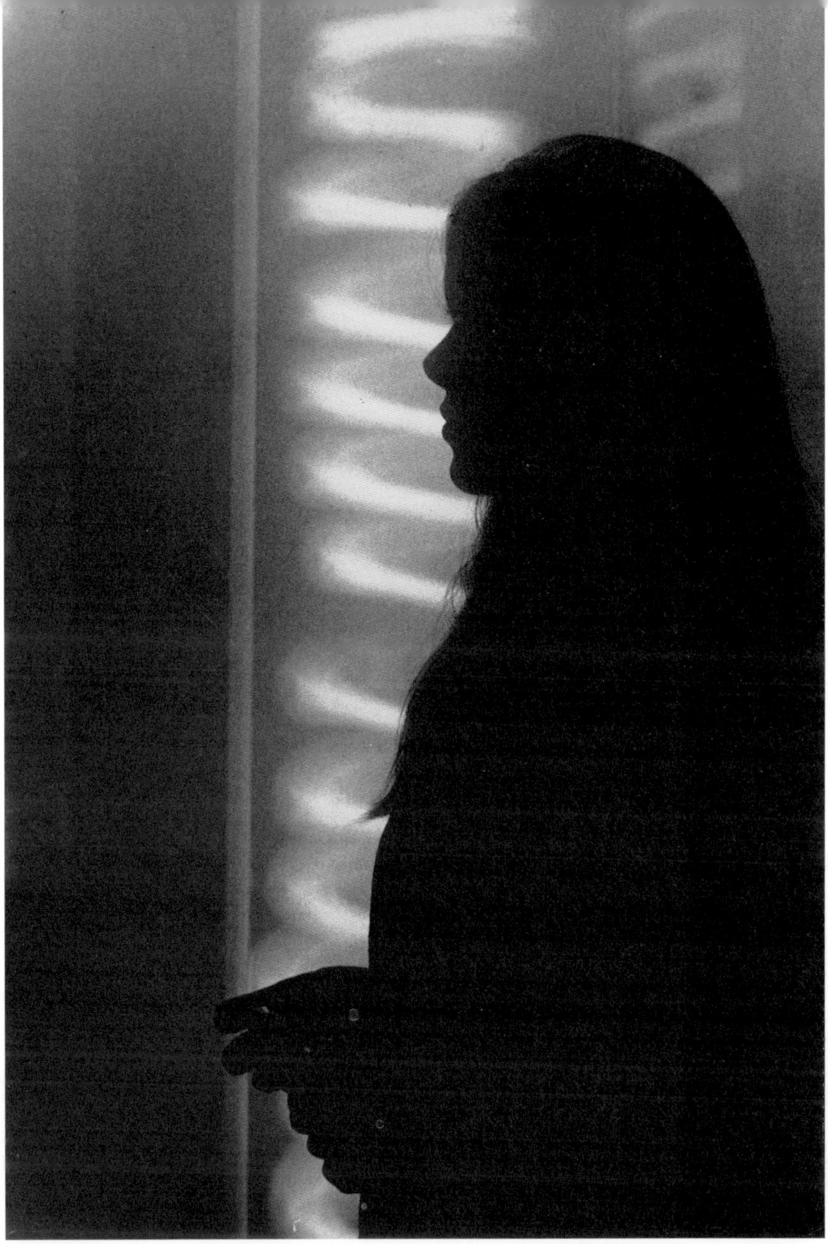

Laura Grisi in her installation *Un' Area di Nebbia (A Space of Fog)*, 1968, Marlborough Gallery, Rome, 1969

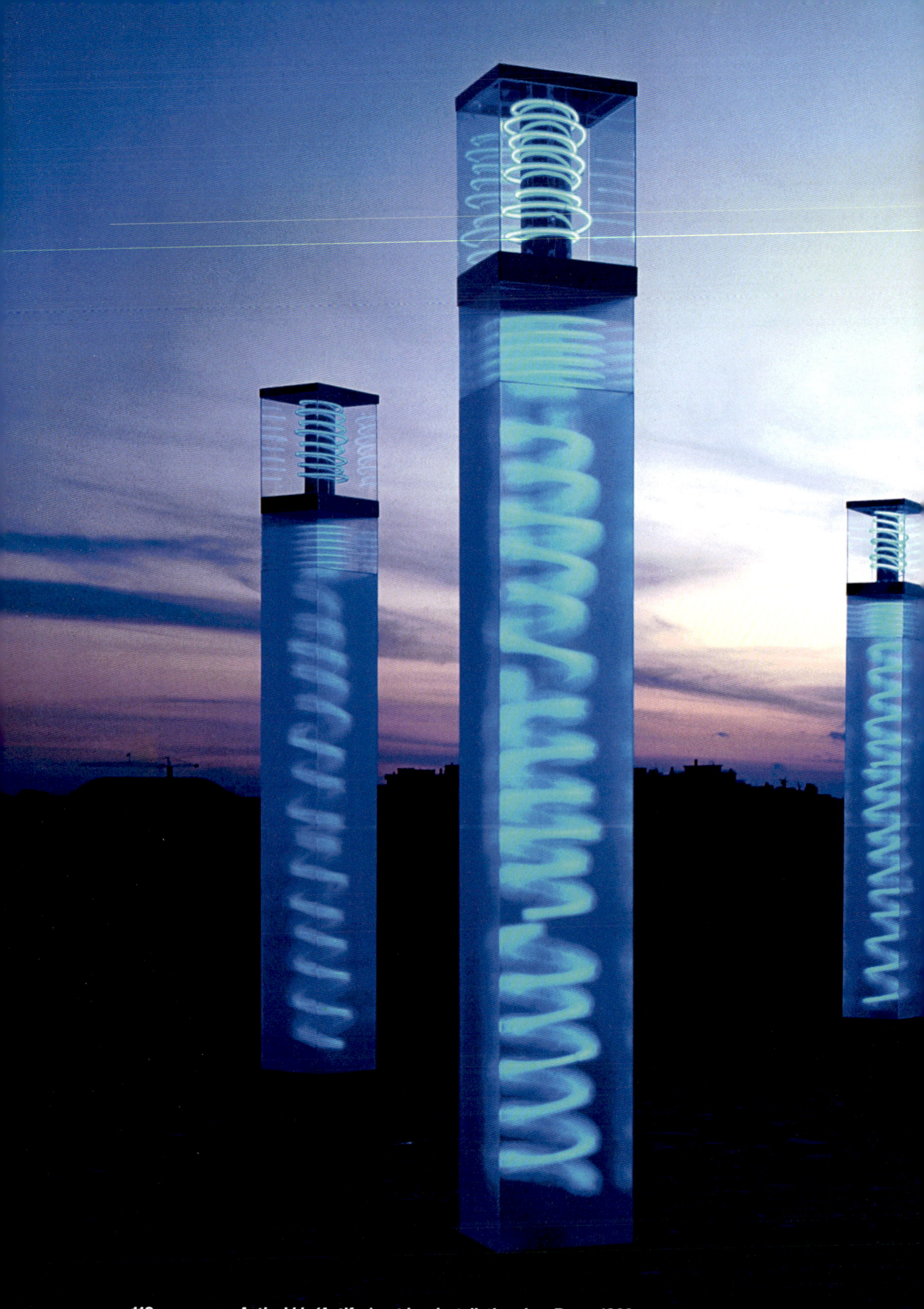

Antinebbia (Antifog), outdoor installation view, Rome, 1968

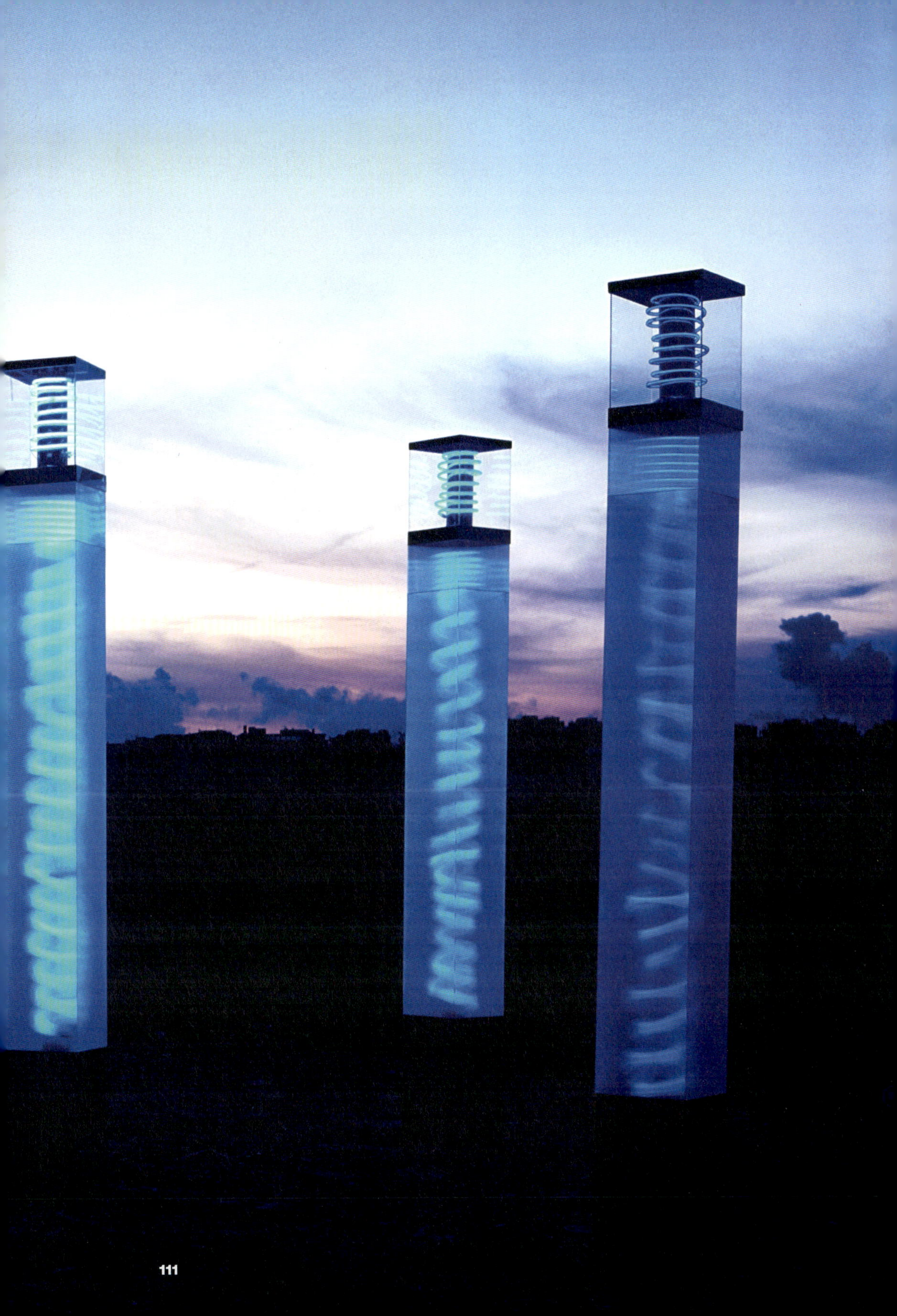

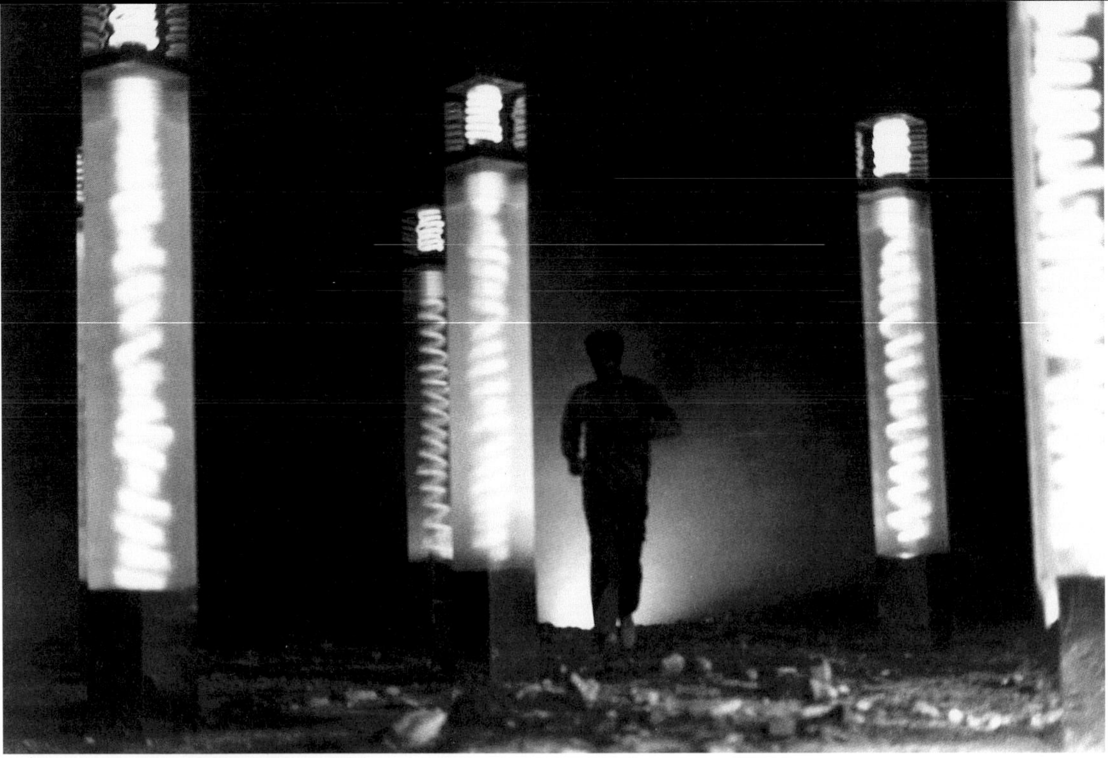

***Antinebbia (Antifog)*, outdoor installation views, 1968**

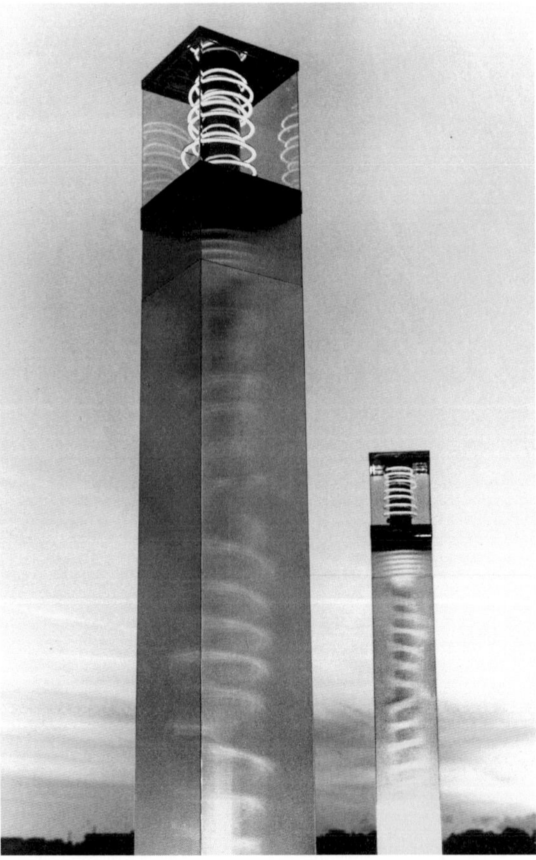

Exhibition view, Marlborough Gallery, Rome, 1969
With *Un' Area di Nebbia (A Space of Fog)*, 1968

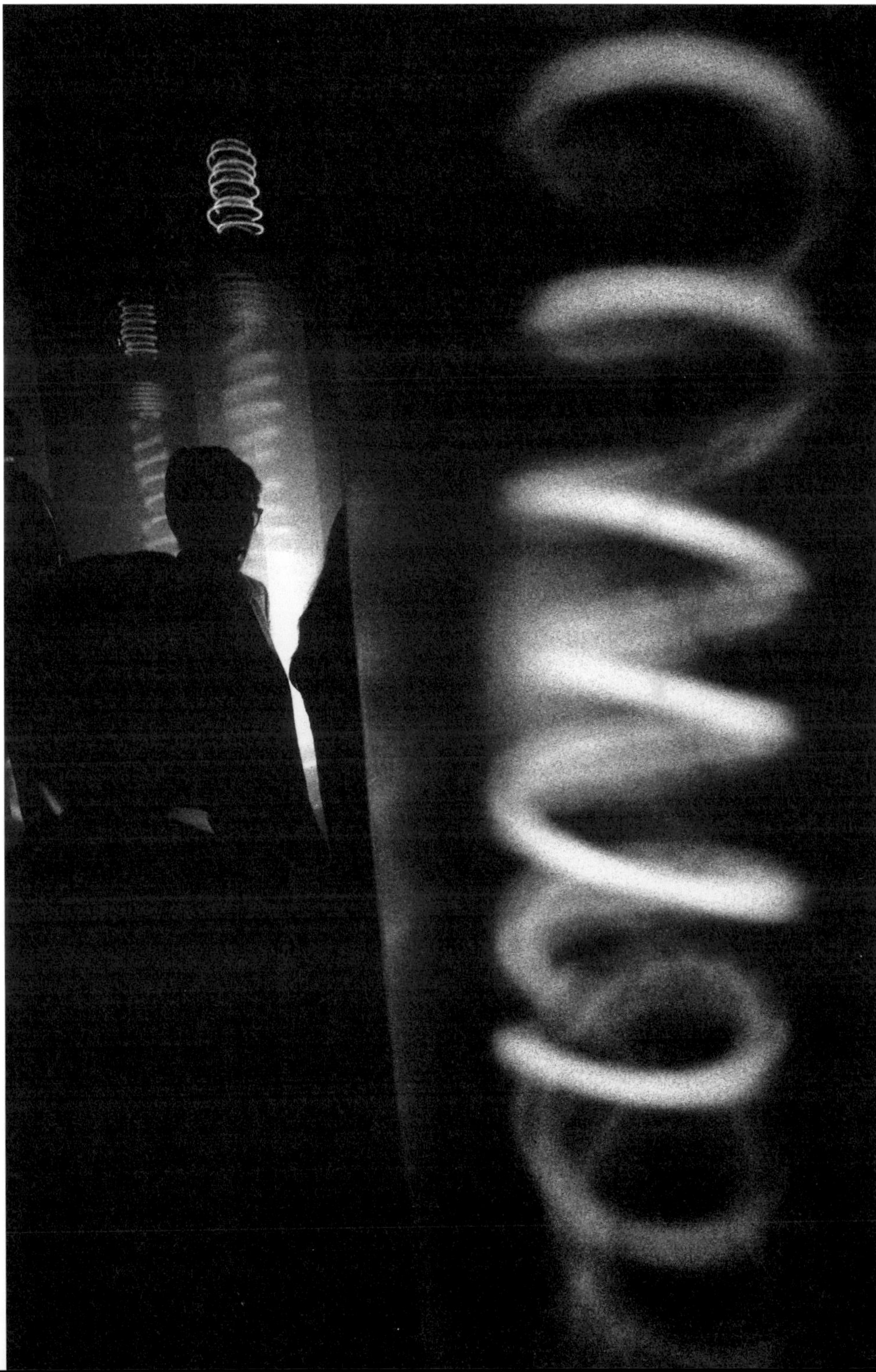

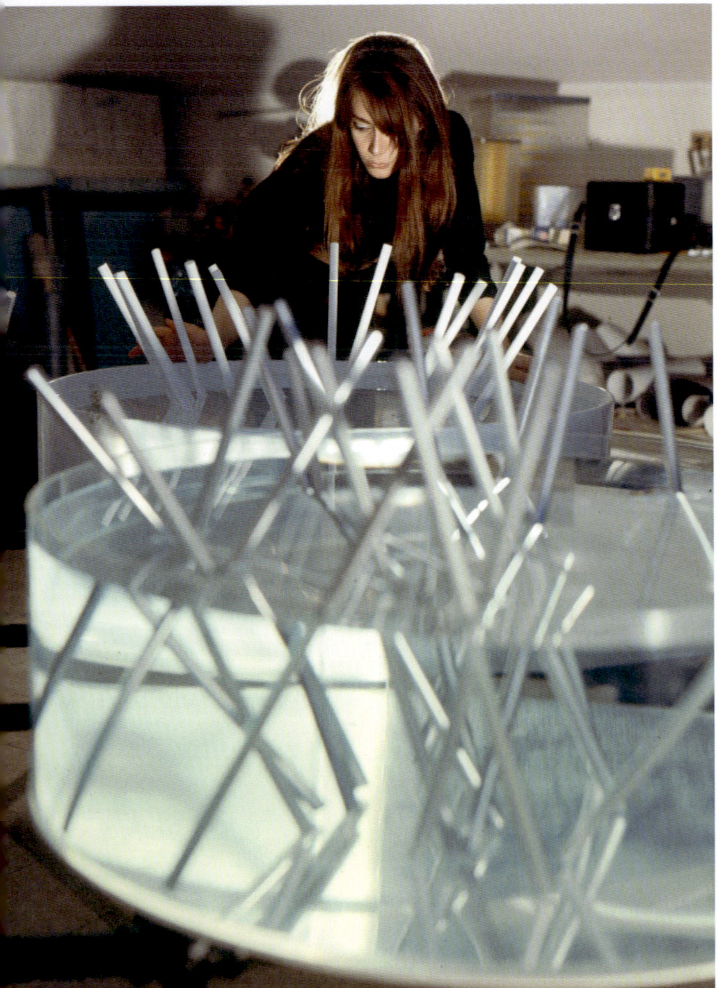

Laura Grisi in her studio working on *Refraction*, Rome, 1968

A practical experiment in refraction, carried out with tree saplings found on the shore of Lake Chad, 1968, **→ p. 40**

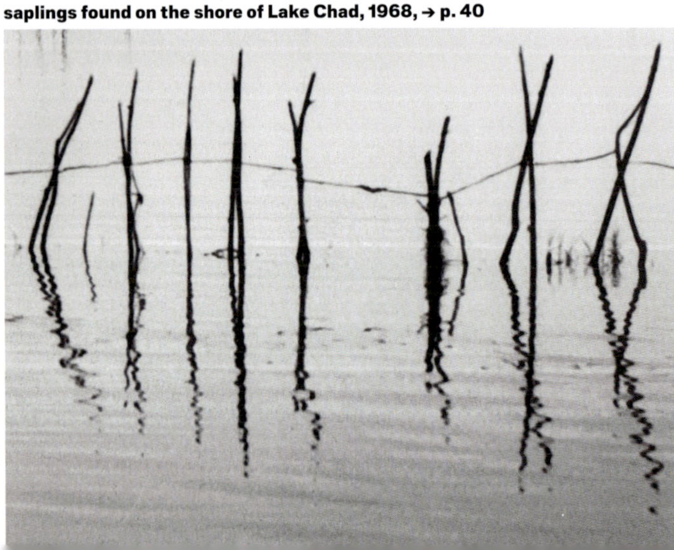

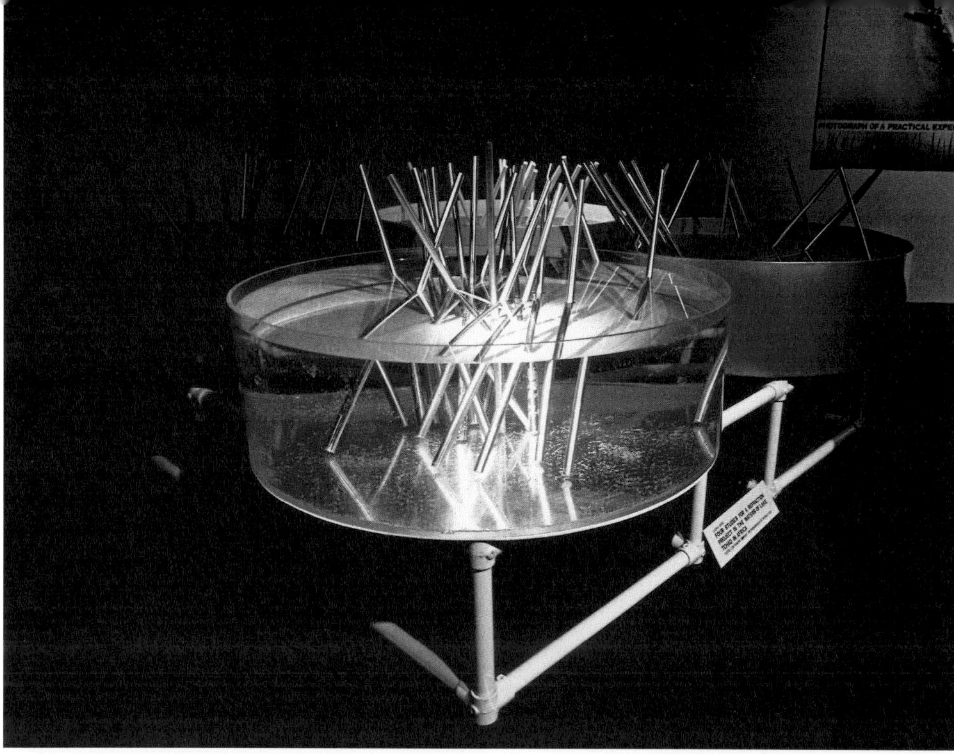

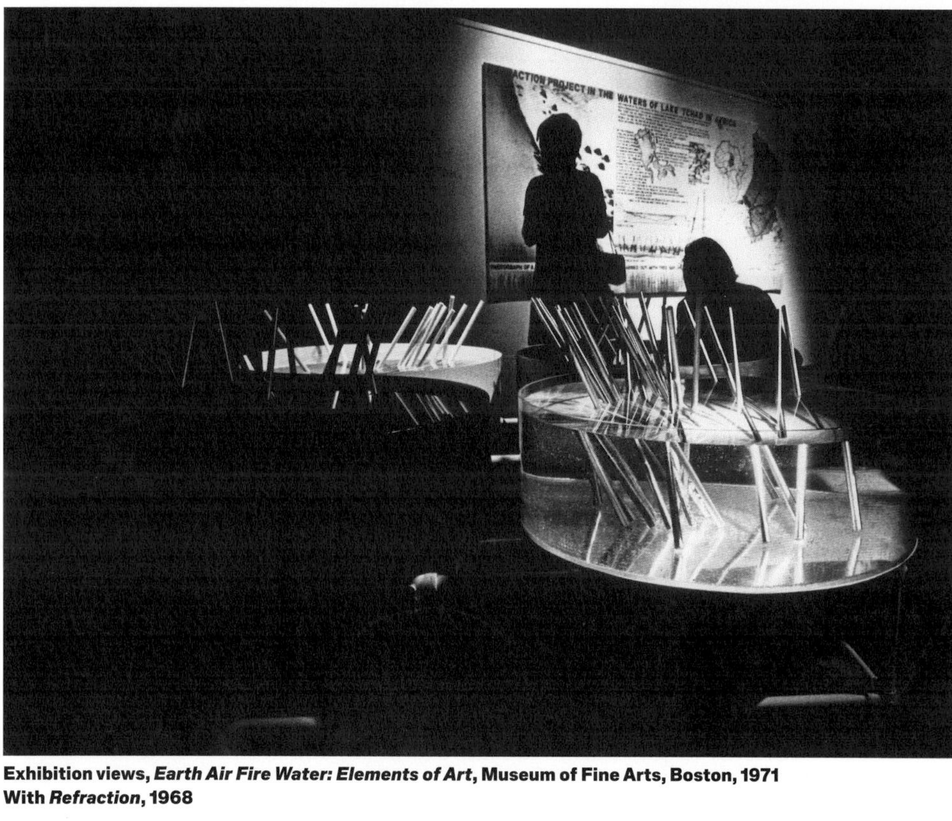

Exhibition views, *Earth Air Fire Water: Elements of Art*, Museum of Fine Arts, Boston, 1971
With *Refraction*, 1968

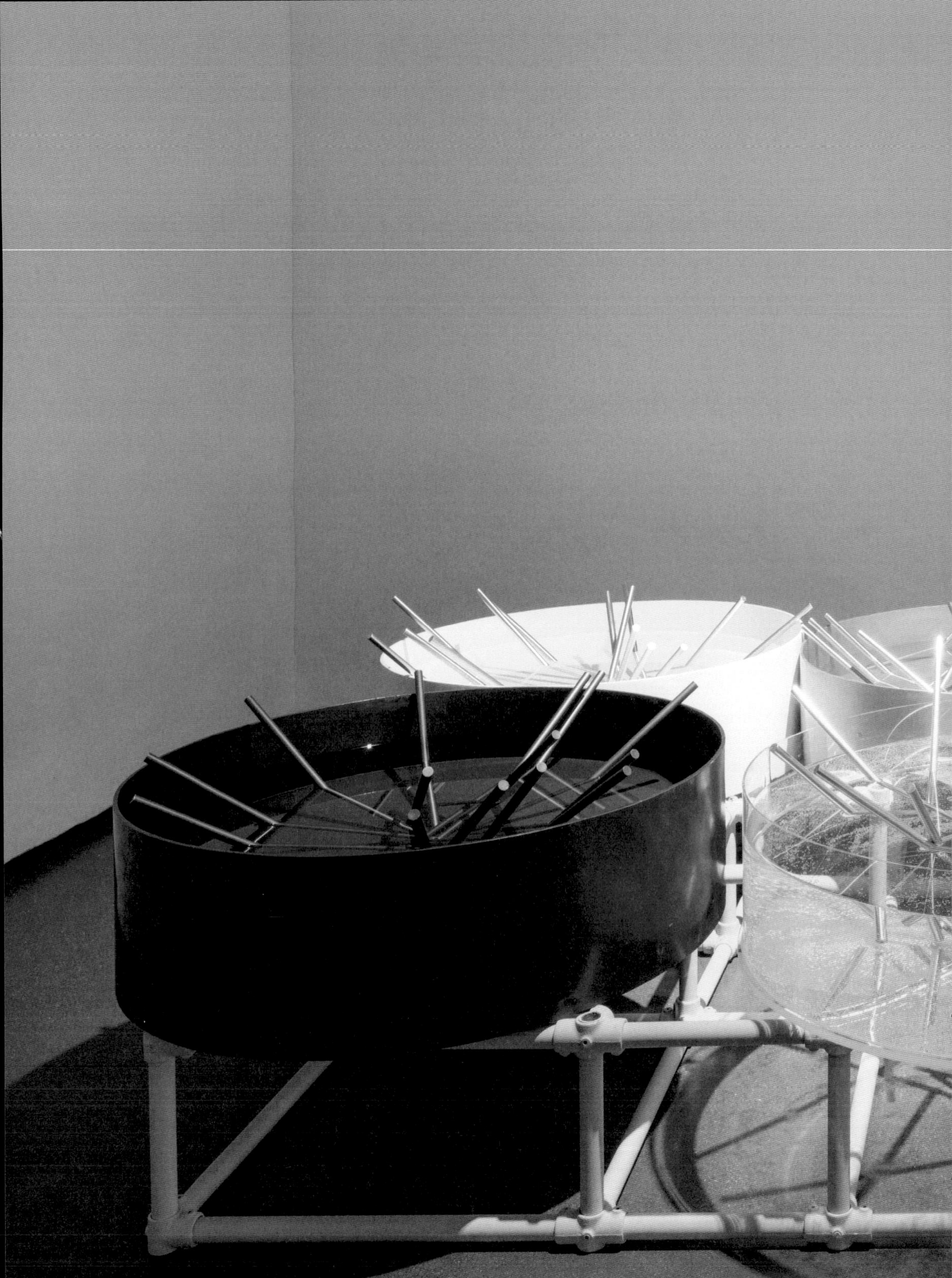

Exhibition view, ***Laura Grisi. The Measuring of Time***, **Muzeum Susch, 2021**
With *Refraction*, 1968

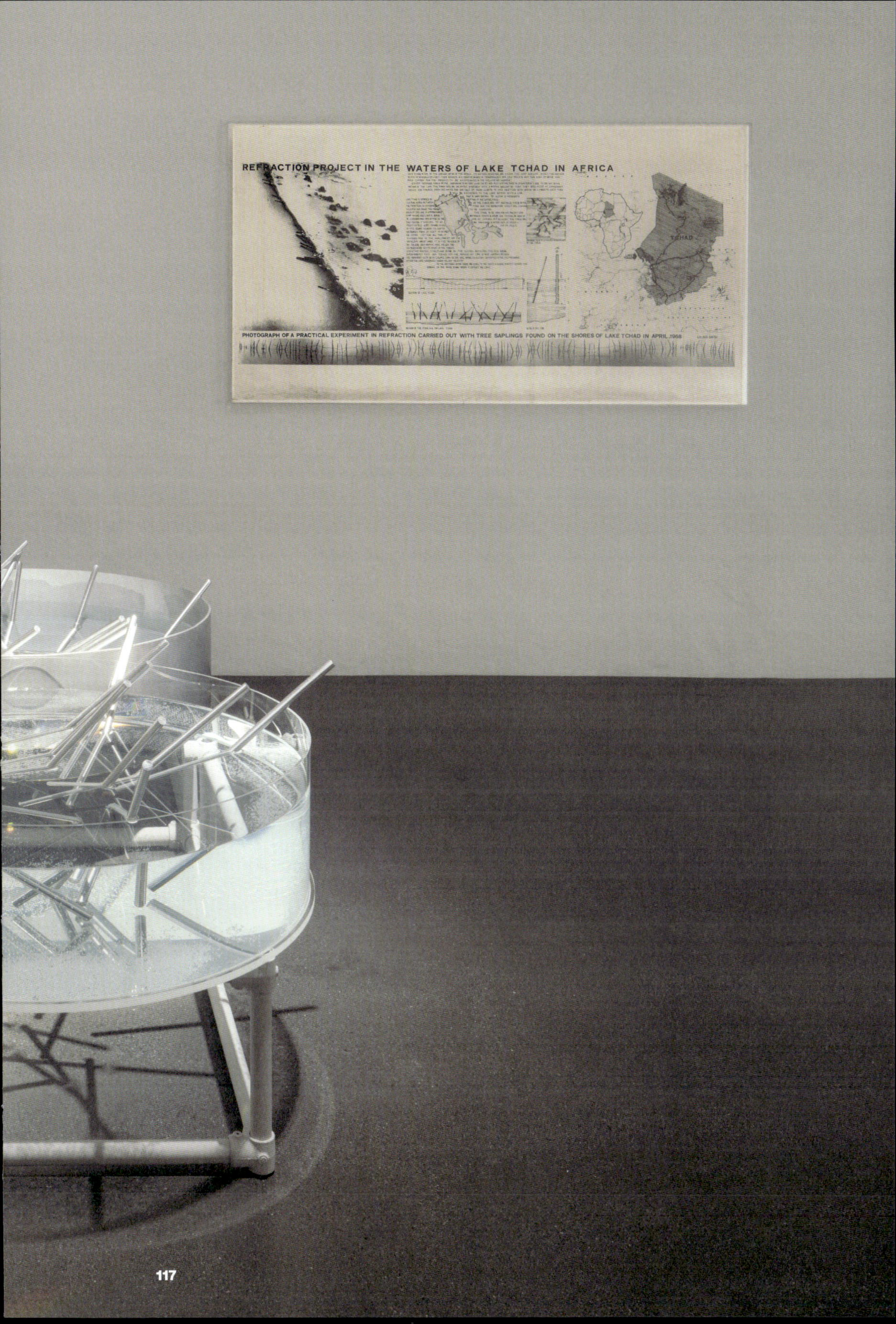
REFRACTION PROJECT IN THE WATERS OF LAKE TCHAD IN AFRICA
TCHAD
PHOTOGRAPH OF A PRACTICAL EXPERIMENT IN REFRACTION CARRIED OUT WITH TREE SAPLINGS FOUND ON THE SHORES OF LAKE TCHAD IN APRIL 1968

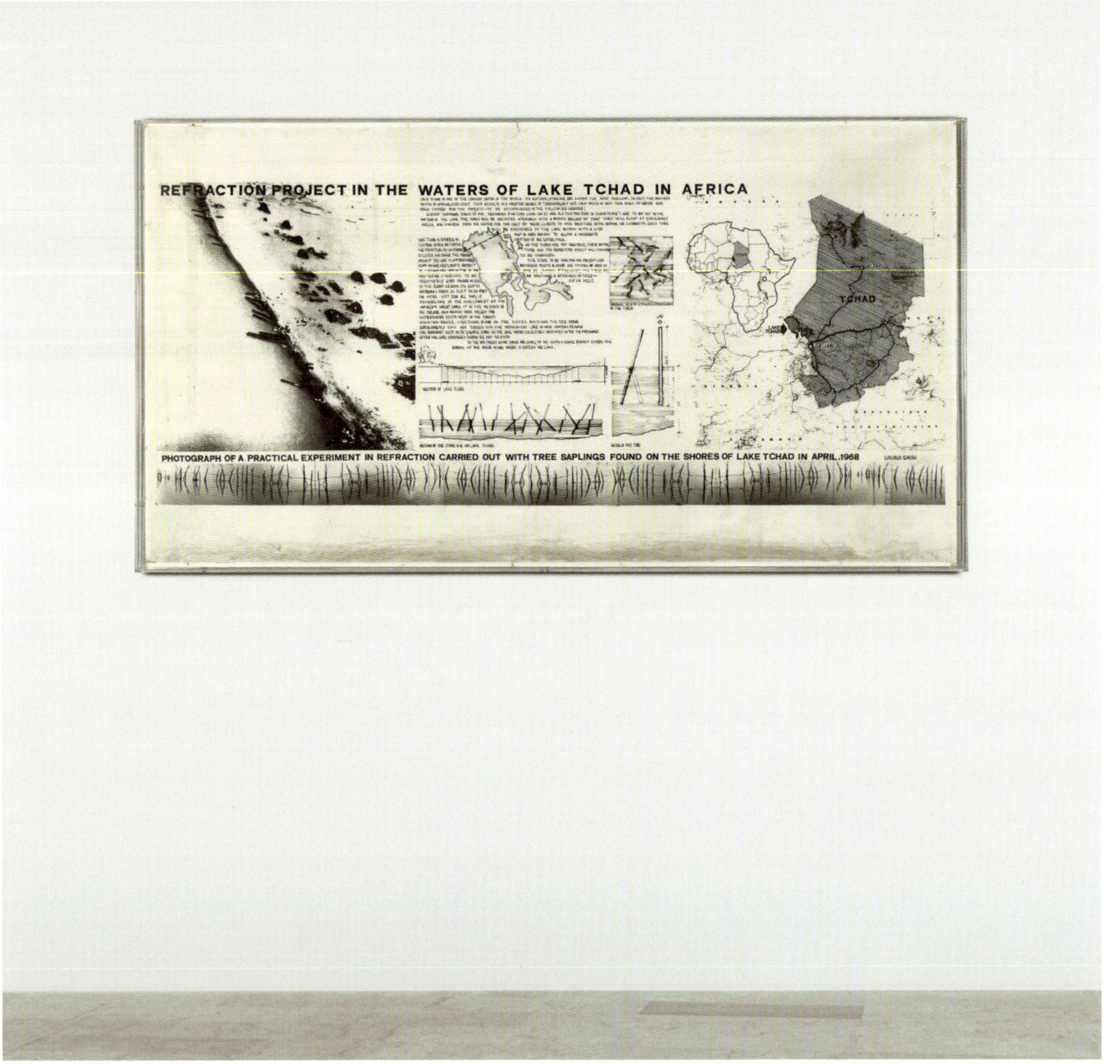

 ***Refraction*, 1968**

WILL BE ANCHORED TO THE LAKE BOTTOM W
THAT IS SLACK ENOUGH TO ALLOW A
DRIFTING OF THE ENTIRE FIELD.
AS THE TUBES ARE NOT INMOB
TIONS AND THE REFRACTIONS EF
TLY BE CHANGING.
THE ZONE TO BE USED FOR TH
BETWEEN POINTS A AND B AND CO
KMQ. 22 (APPROX. 8,5 SQ. MILES
BE POSITIONED A INTERVALS O
2,5 S

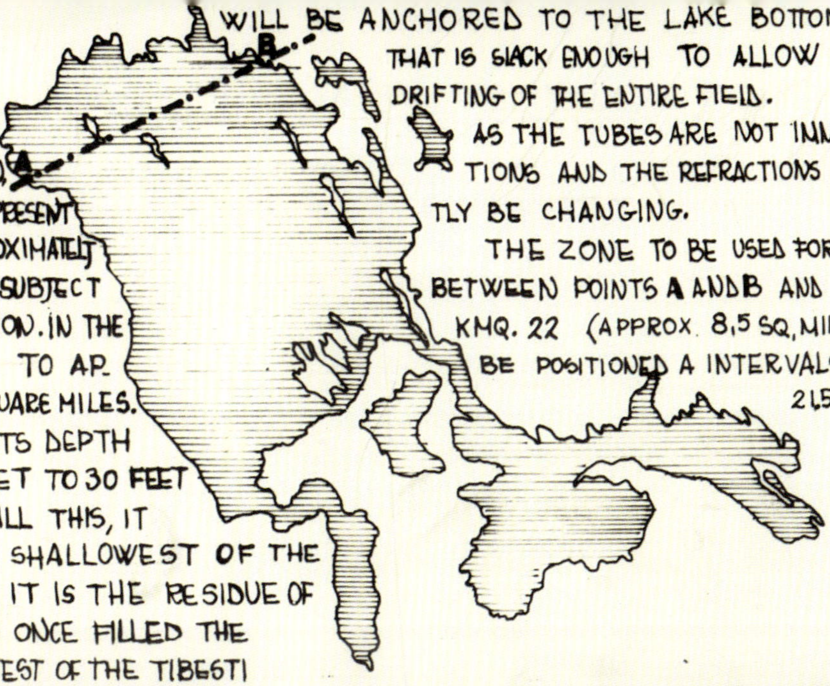

LAKE TCHAD IS SITUATED IN CENTRAL AFRICA BETWEEN THE FRONTIERS OF CAMEROON, NIGERIA AND NIGER. THE PRESENT AREA OF THE LAKE IS APPROXIMATELY 10,000 SQUARE MILES, BUT IS SUBJECT TO CONSIDERABLE VARIACTION. IN THE DRY SEASON IT SHRINKS TO APPROXIMATELY 4.000 SQUARE MILES. IN THE RAINY SEASON ITS DEPTH INCREASES FROM 20 FEET TO 30 FEET OR MORE. YET FOR ALL THIS, IT REMAINS ONE OF THE SHALLOWEST OF THE WORLD'S GREAT LAKES, IT IS THE RESIDUE OF AN INLAND SEA WHICH ONCE FILLED THE DEPRESSIONS SOUTH-WEST OF THE TIBESTI MOUNTAIN-RANGE, STRETCHING AS FAR AS THE SLOPES BOUNDING THE NILE BASIN. SUBSEQUENTLY THIS SEA TURNED INTO THE PRESENT-DAY LAKE WHOSE WATERS REMA
STILL SOMEWHAT SALTY. IN FACT, PEOPLE LIVING ON THE LAKE SHORE COLLECT SALT DEPOSITED IN THE D
AFTER THE LAKE DIMINISHES DURING THE DRY SEASON

ON THE NORTHEAST SHORE THERE ARE DUNES; TO THE SOUTH A DENSE FO
BANKS OF THE RIVER SCIARI WHERE IT ENTERS THE LAKE.

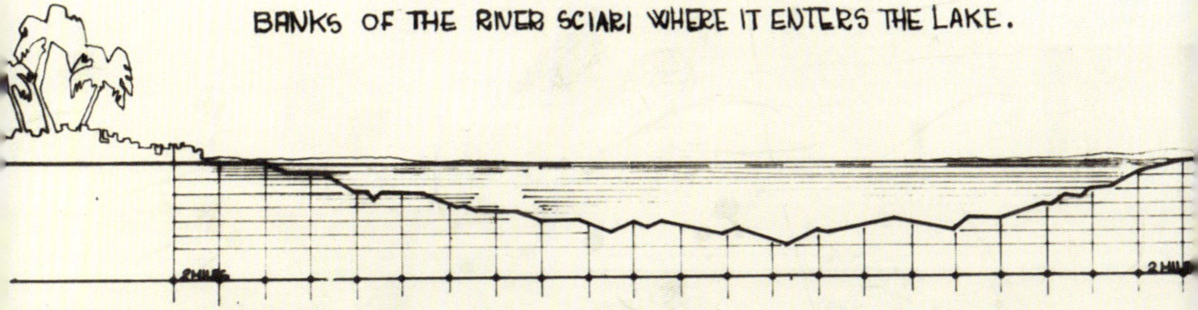

SECTION OF LAKE TCHAD

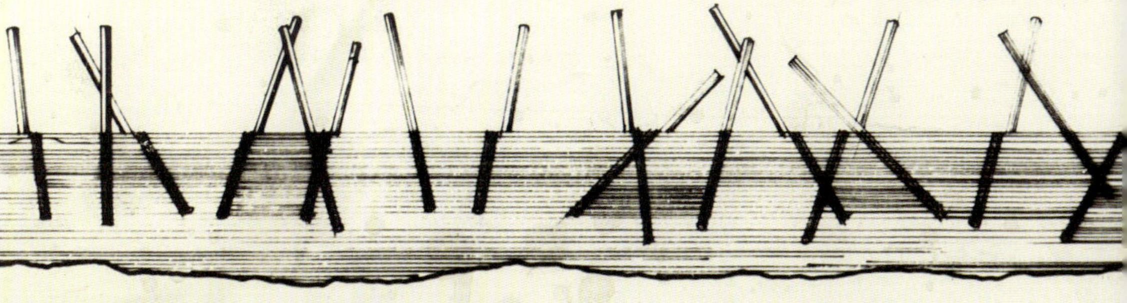

SECTION OF THE ZONE A-B ON LAKE TCHAD

ION CARRIED OUT WITH TREE SAP

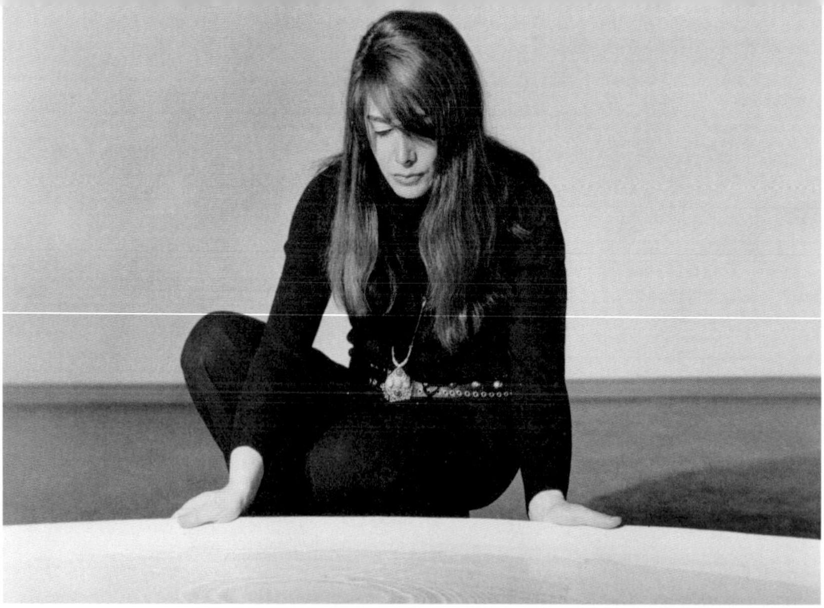

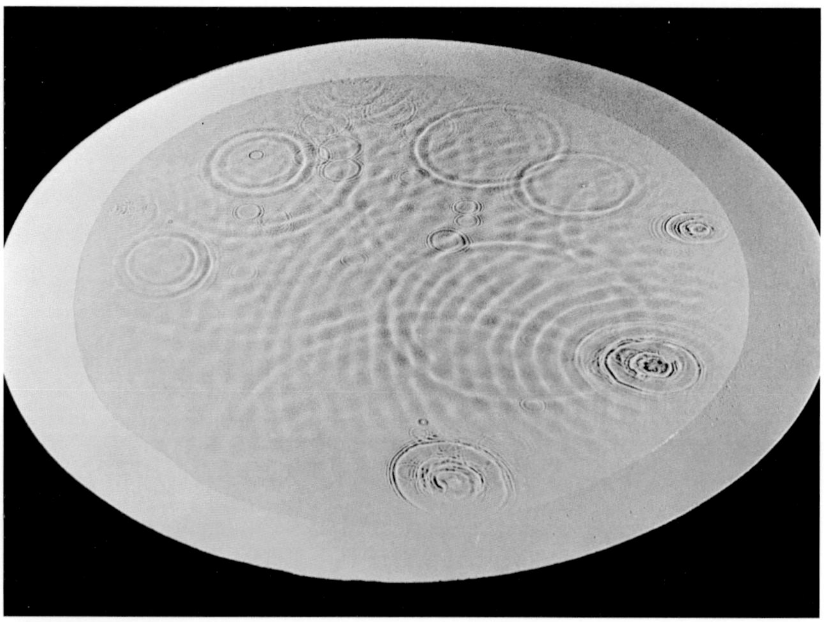

Laura Grisi with her work *Drops of Water*, 1968, in the exhibition
***Earth Air Fire Water: Elements of Art*, Museum of Fine Arts, Boston, 1971**
***Drops of Water*, 1968**

Exhibition view, *Laura Grisi. The Measuring of Time*, Muzeum Susch, 2021
With *Drops of Water*, 1968

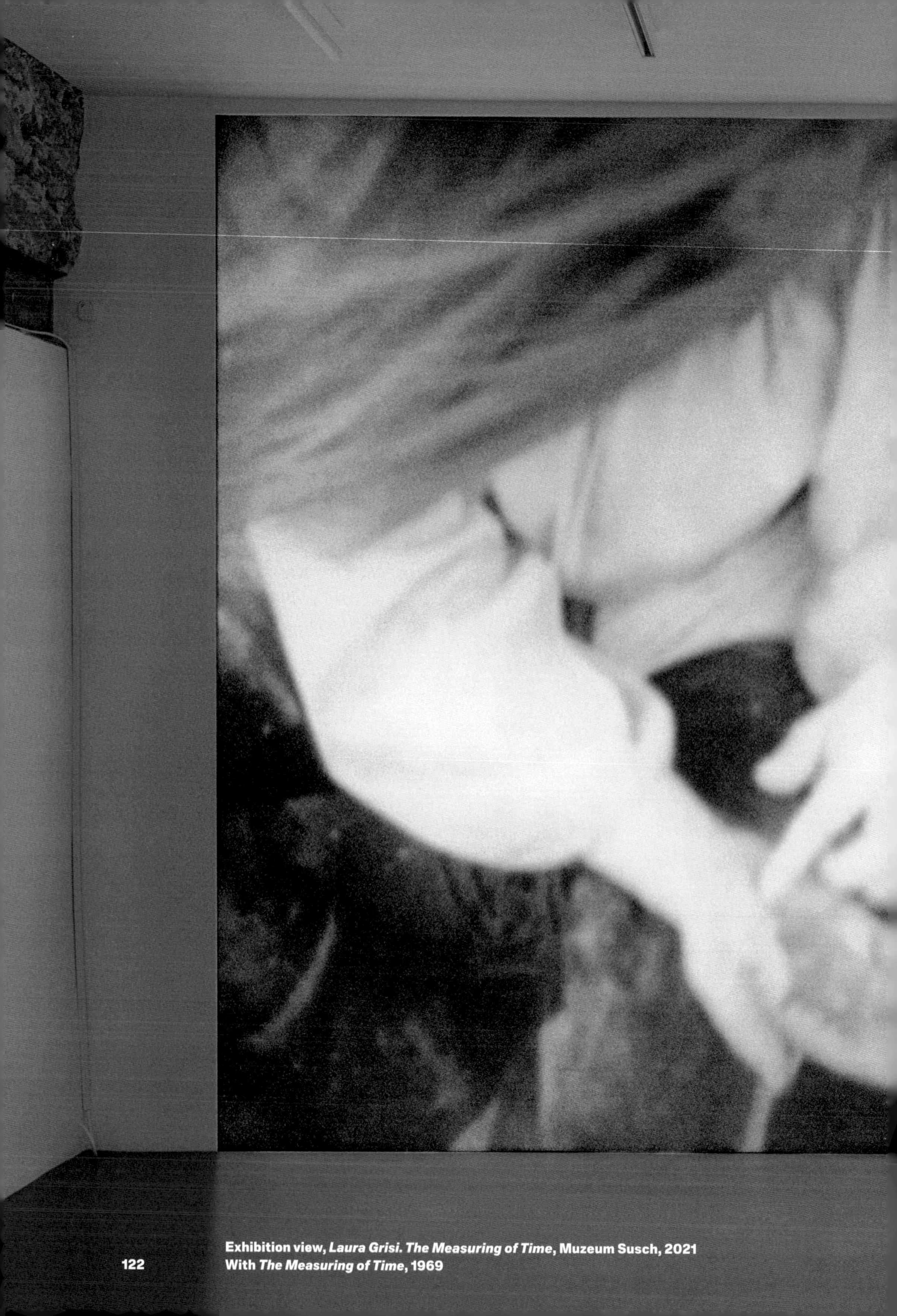

Exhibition view, *Laura Grisi. The Measuring of Time*, Muzeum Susch, 2021
With *The Measuring of Time*, 1969

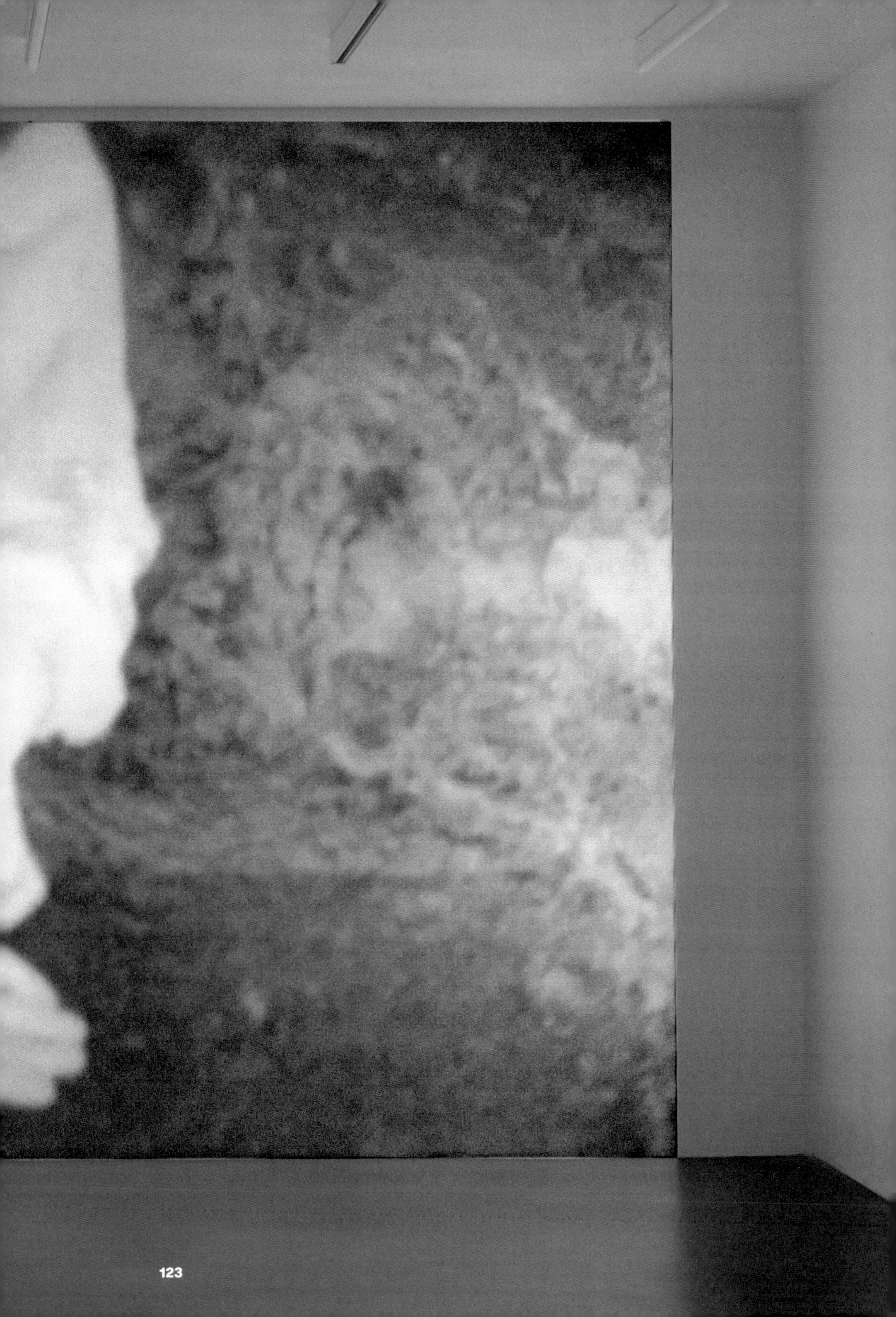

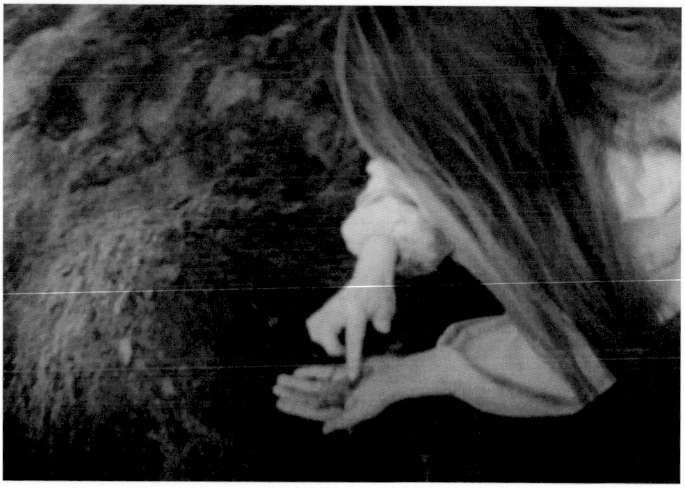

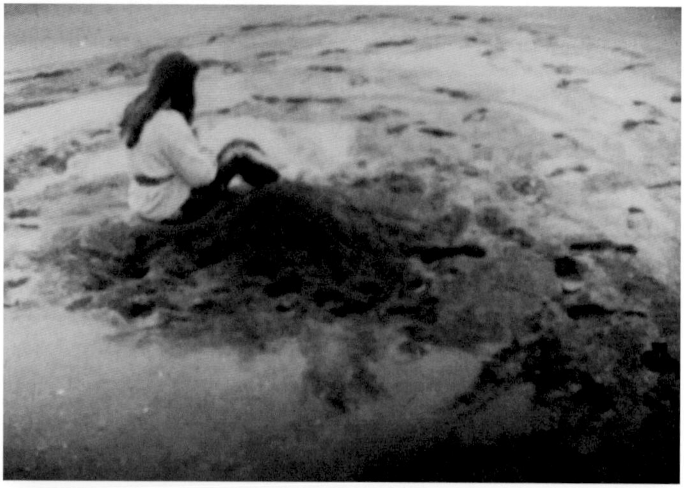

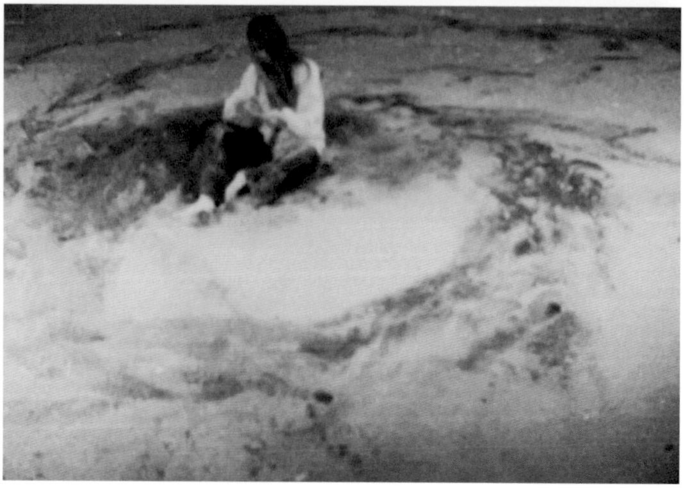

***The Measuring of Time*, 1969**

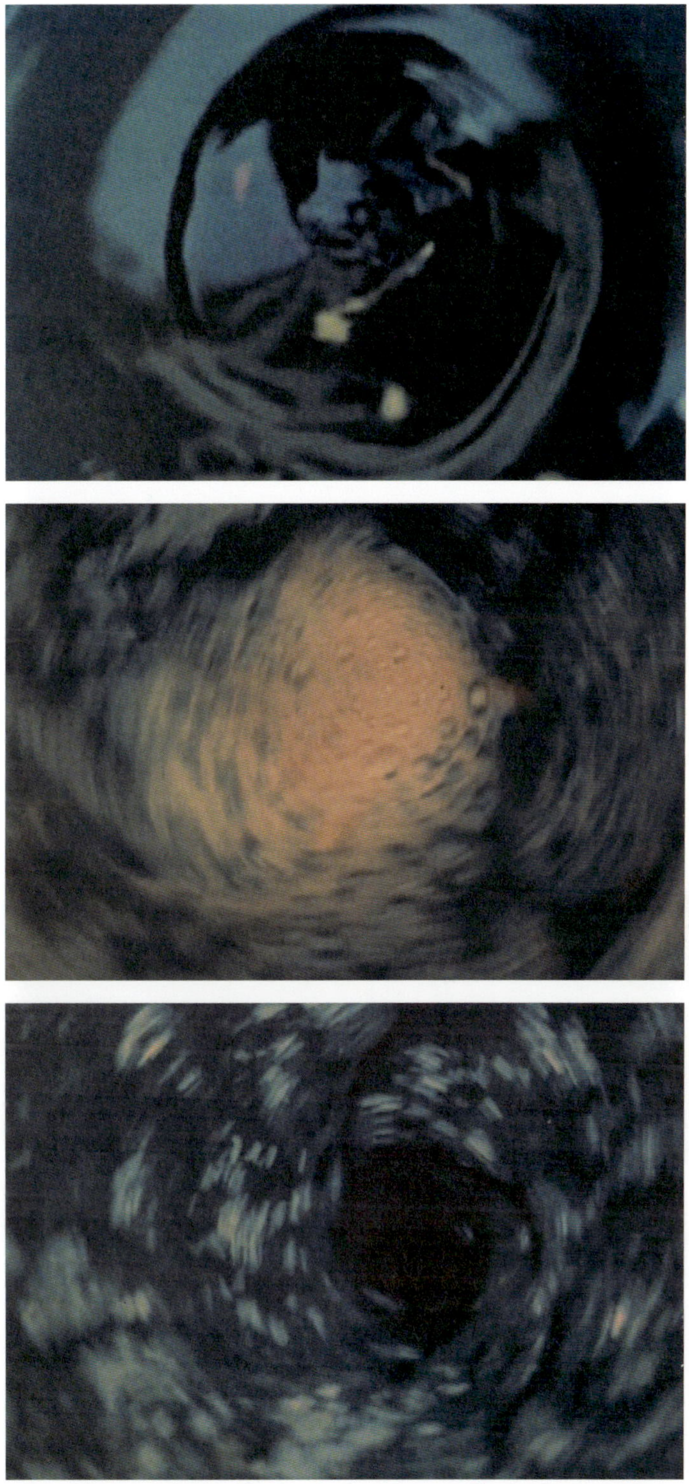

***Whirlpool*, 1969**

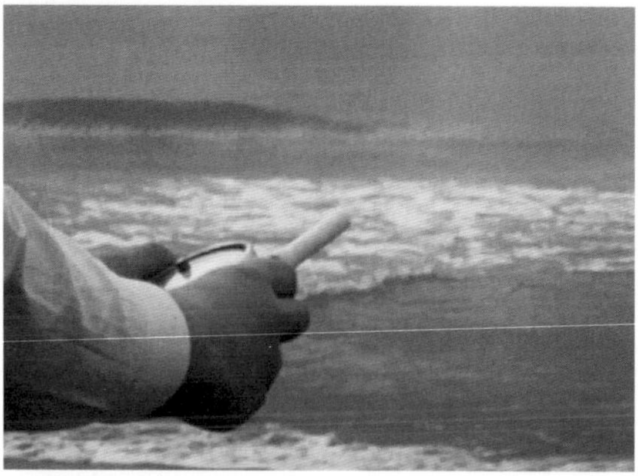
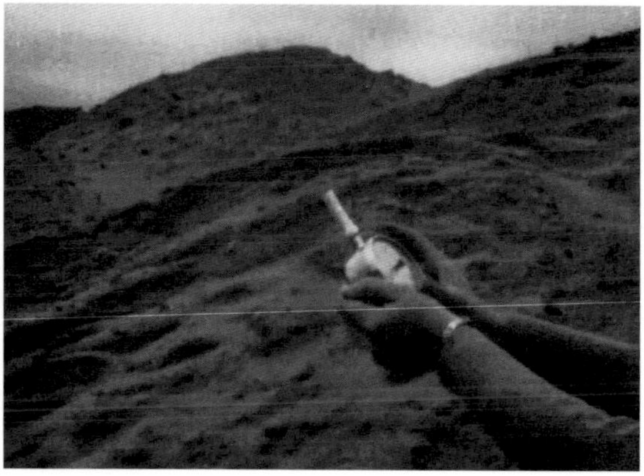
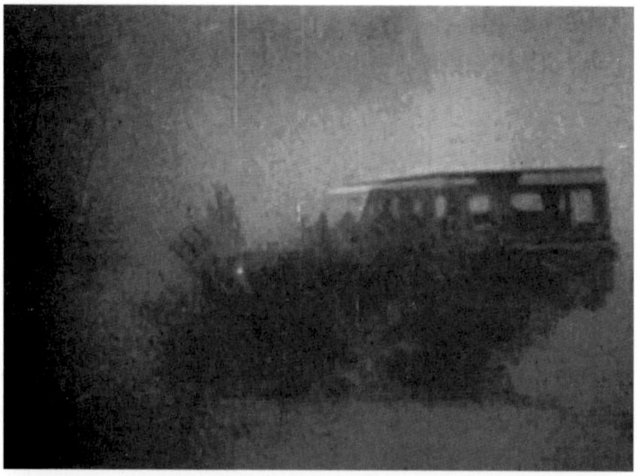
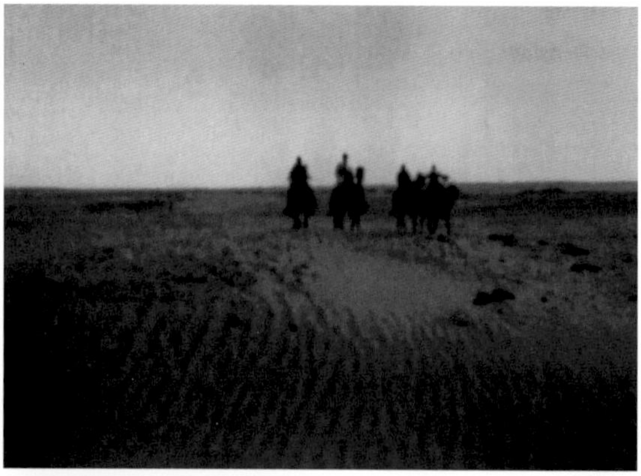
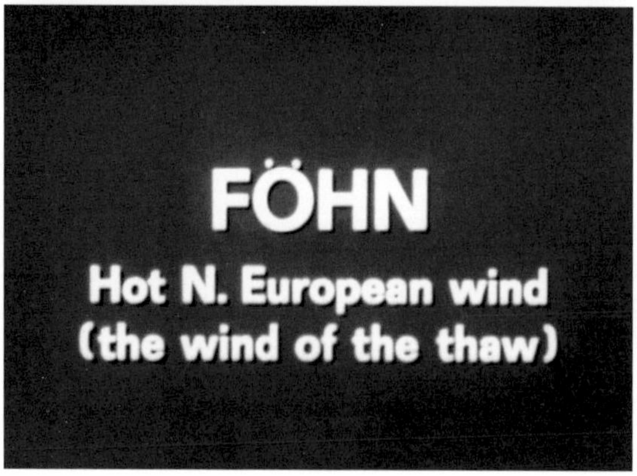
FÖHN
Hot N. European wind
(the wind of the thaw)
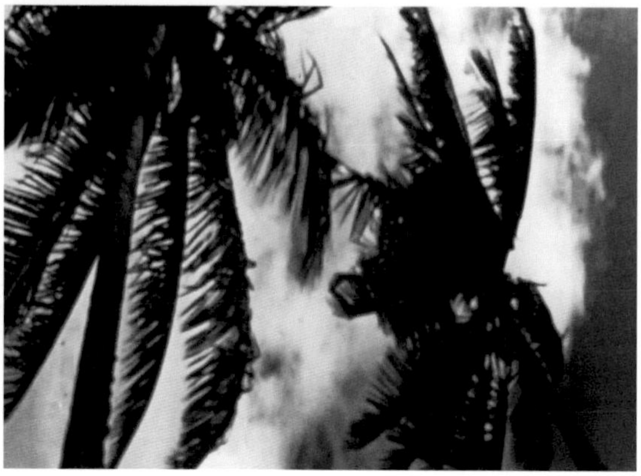

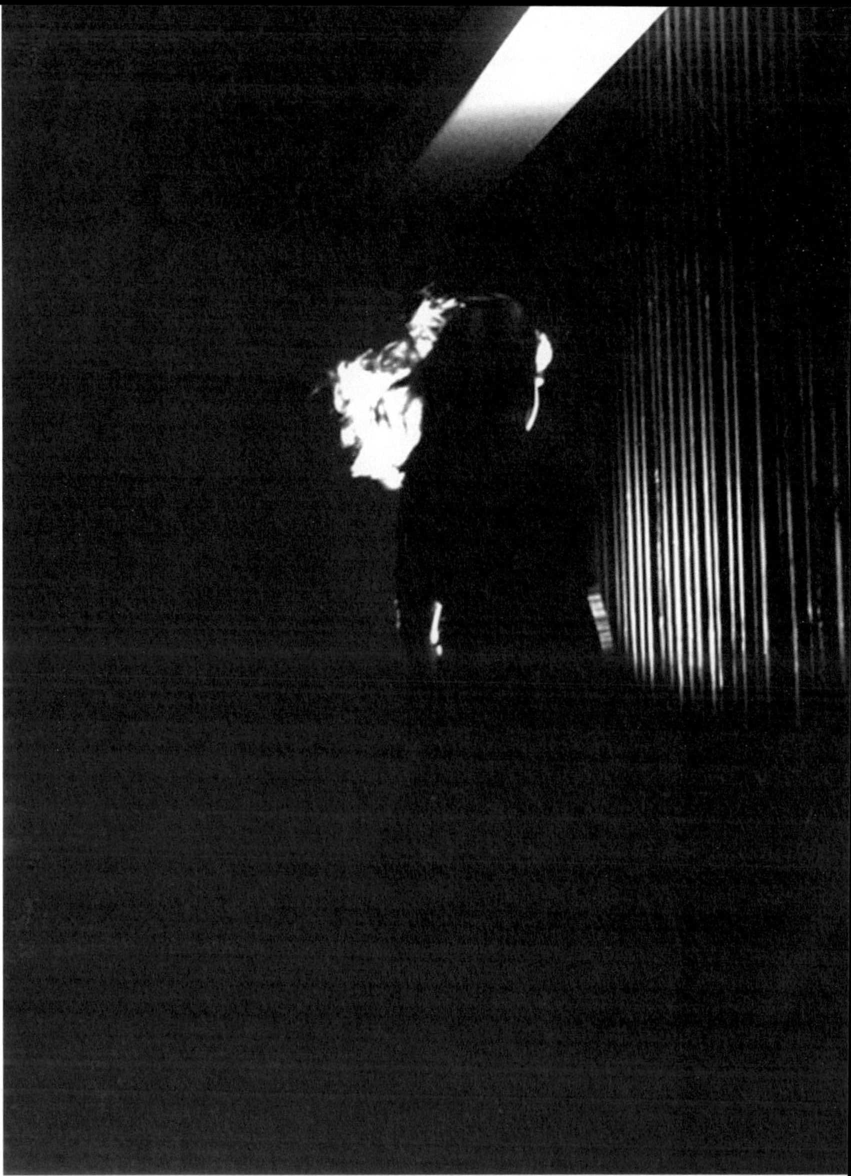

Exhibition views, *Teatro delle mostre*, Galleria La Tartaruga, Rome, 1968
With *Wind Speed 40 Knots*, 1968

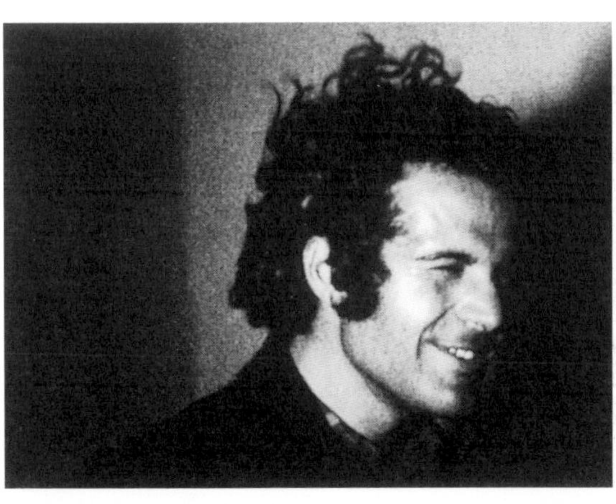

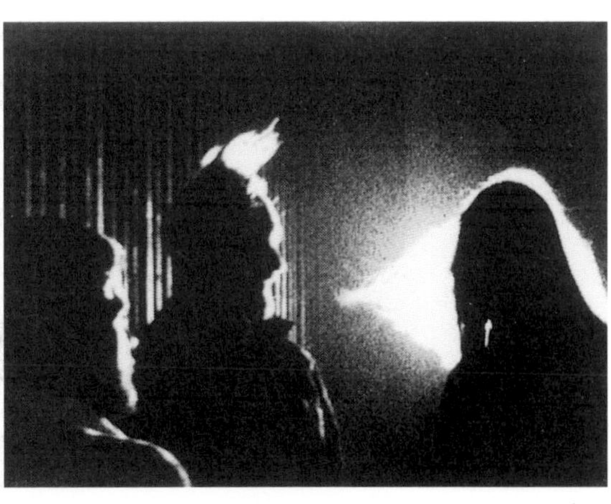

Light and Fog: A Cinema of Environmental Art
Giuliana Bruno

"The whole marvelous panorama of life that spreads over the surface of our globe is, in the last analysis, transformed sunlight."[1]
—Ernst Haeckel

"I speak ... of Colours so far as they arise from Light. For they appear sometimes by other Causes, as when by the power of Phantasy we see Colours in a Dream."[2]
—Isaac Newton

In his elegy to cinema, Roland Barthes famously emphasized the "twilight reverie" one experiences upon "leaving the movie theater" and being "back out on the more or less empty, more or less brightly lit sidewalk ... a little dazed ... a little disjointed."[3] In that opaque space of the film theater, the spectator is immersed in an elaborate play of light and shadow that continues onto the streets. In the theater, there is in fact "one light: the film, the screen," but also "visible and unperceived, that dancing cone" of the light of the projector, "which pierces the darkness like a laser beam" and creates changing figures "according to the rotation of its particles."[4]

In this poetic way, Barthes describes the atmospheric transformation of the space of light by means of technology that is the basis of the art of projection. He arrives at sensing the zero degree of cinema: the luminiferous materiality that constitutes its illuminated, mutable theatrical ambiance. Light reflecting on a surface is indeed the element that makes a projective architecture. As one watches surface reflections change on a plane of vision, a process of "becoming screen" comes to be manifested.[5] A world of moving particles and electromagnetic vibrations is the force that activates screen surface and shapes the atmosphere of projection.

When we approach the work of Laura Grisi, this atmospheric aspect of cinema comes to light. Film culture was an important point of reference and inspiration for this artist, in a way that goes well beyond her extensive, direct acquaintance with the world of cinema.[6] In the presence of her experimental paintings, sculptures, and installations, one senses the vital material base of cinema emerge, and one experiences moving images transformed in new, mediatic ways. Grisi's work goes to the heart of that cinematic situation envisaged by Barthes: it materializes that radiant in-between state, suspended between light and shadow, floating between inside and outside. In her own words, "The panels of my paintings were transparent openings to the outside world through a circle of lights and shadows shaping a geometric landscape ... representing both the instant before movement and the instant after its transformation into another image."[7]

Hovering between conceptual art and diagrammatic thought, Grisi's nonrepresentational practice confounds the difference between two- and three-dimensionality, merging these two forms in works that emphasize ambiance. Overcoming the limits of painting, the artist worked with the spatialization of light and other natural elements to create vibrant environments of projective forms. She experimented with the way in which the subtle effects of light, including the density of fog, can "screen" a space and alter an atmosphere, both physically and emotionally. Her journey through waves of light traversed other natural phenomena of mobility and passage as well, such as the flow of air, the motion of wind, the dripping of rain, and the vital fluids of plants. In such a way, as we will see, Grisi artistically reimagined the vital *atmosphere* that is the zero degree of motion pictures, in artworks that created luminiferous, transitive, transformative environments of energy.

Atmospheric Transformations of Canvas into Screen

In the mid-1960s Grisi made a series of "Variable Paintings" that explored the idea of a variable ambiance, giving the observer the capacity to intervene in and modify the painterly landscape. Each painting has two or three sliding panels of painted canvas and colored Plexiglas that the viewer can move across the surface of the work. Activating these panels that possess different degrees of translucency, one can alter the colors or shades of the images. Acting as both dividers of space and filters of light, the sliding panels effectively function as screens. They can create different superimpositions and sequences, and even construct a montage. The final effect of this screening of surfaces is that the images themselves appear "screened." In such a way, the "Variable Paintings" are capable of producing a variety of ambiances. *Seascape* (1966), for example, provokes an intense atmospheric variation with its effect of filtering light. Its sliding panels contain cast-Plexiglas clouds that can appear or disappear. By opening or closing the panels to screen the light one can make haze and cloud the space, generating a different meteorology of the canvas.

These atmospheric works created a new, luminous effect of painterly projection that, in its novelty, carried the trace of a history. In a way, Grisi's technique feels genealogical because it reminds us that the art of projection came to be invented out of the variable theatrics of light and shadow. The scene recalls in particular the mythical origin of painting, which was conceived as an act of screening by the Corinthian maid Dibutades in the story recounted by Pliny the Elder.[8] According to this landmark tale, the young woman used a lamp to cast a shadow of her lover's figure onto a wall and then drew it, tracing its silhouette. A stream of light was thus effectively "projected," cast upon the wall's surface, producing a new form of representation. In this way, the surface became a canvas, and simultaneously turned into a screen. As if recalling this particular origin of painting, conceived by Dibutades as an act of projection, Grisi realized her own projective cast, for with her "Variable Paintings" she made a canvas-screen, and turned it into cinema.

Grisi's inventive screening technique was further articulated in a series of "Neon Paintings" from 1966–1967, which amplified the transformation of painterly canvas into cinematic screen. The basic elements of the sliding panels of the "Variable Paintings" remained, but neon, wood, and metal were added. The translucency of the panels was combined with internal illumination, which intensified the atmospheric quality of the work. The glow of the neon created a mutable, luminiferous ambiance. Sections of the paintings were furthermore covered with panels of textured plastic, which added a sense of perspectival depth when they were slid over the paintings' surfaces. In the "Neon Paintings," Grisi explained that "the neon lights created the appearance of depth" because "they were seen through the refraction of a Plexiglas veil, transparent but ribbed ... twisted on the diagonal."[9]

Grisi emphasized the spatial sensation of volume in her paintings, calling it a veiling—which is to say, a screening. This effect of concealing, shrouding, and curtaining was environmental in that it revealed the different layers that compose the atmosphere of a site. Furthermore, this spatial canvas was an urban screen. Each of the "Neon Paintings" depicted urban sites in a way that rendered the motion of the city. As the panels slid, they appeared to mobilize the places depicted on the canvas. In the process, the inhabitants of the urban environments also changed their shape. As their position in the space of the painting appeared modified, the figures turned into blurs. Shadows of people seemed to slide through the space of these moving canvas-screens, as if caught in a moment of transition or in a space of transit. Through an actual act of screening, then, a cinema of the city came to light, with figures of passersby turning into moving, filmic silhouettes.

The technique used in the "Neon Paintings" unveiled elements of the architecture of the moving image and its projective atmosphere. The lit-up moving panels created a nocturnal ambiance close to that cinematic "twilight reverie" mentioned earlier. Indeed, the blurry figures on the canvas emerged out of that particular shadow play that, according to Barthes, defines the cinematic condition. As if they were actual shadows projected onto a screen surface, the hazy figures suspended between comings and goings might well be spectators experiencing the sensation of in-betweenness that arises when exiting a movie theater. Grisi pictured that precise mood: the feeling of transition and passage that occurs when the spectator approaches the streets after seeing a film. Her projected urban dwellers, too, encounter a "more or less empty, more or less brightly lit sidewalk" and move dreamily through space, in a state before and after motion, "a little dazed," even "a little disjointed."

The nocturnal streetscape evoked in the "Neon Paintings" belongs to a kinetic metropolis, where one can feel estranged among dazzling neon signs and shimmering advertising reflections. The atmosphere of these paintings clearly reflects a moment in time in the environment of New York City, where Grisi lived for substantial periods of her life. The canvas-screens ask the viewer to take a tour through this city, perusing the *East Village* (1967), attending a *Village Theater* (1966), riding the *Subway* (1967), using a telephone *Booth* (1967), or voyeuristically peeping into a half-lit *Top Floor* (1967). By way of this journey, the "Neon Paintings" materialize the urban energy of Manhattan. One can feel a subway car slide with its rattling sound, and watch flickers of light pulse through its moving windows. A filmic narrative is created as the spectator wanders about the scene of a mysterious, outlined figure calling from the darkness of the phone booth, or decides to follow the silhouette leaving the theater and disappearing into the night. Immersed in this nocturnal environment, one glides through a constellation of mesmerizing atmospheres. The glowing neon assemblages thus render the electric motion of this cinematic city.

The electrical energy of the "Neon Paintings" is magnetic, and it diffuses across the canvas as well as in the space surrounding it. This is not only the effect of the shifting, lit-up frames and the moving montage created by the sliding panels, but also of the movement of the observer. Never static, the "Neon Paintings" change shape depending on where one stands, whether close to or far from the work, or how one moves around it. In the space of the gallery, the projection of silhouettes becomes animated—that is, screened—as the rhythm of light atmospherically changes color and tone with one's motion. Invited to move through this theater of light energy, spectators become an integral part of this emblematic space of projection. Actively, even affectively engaged in this projective ambiance, gallery viewers experience the forms of relationality and sociability that characterize filmic environments of public intimacy.

Environments of Natural Elements

Using the "elements" that characterize a cinematic atmosphere, the "Neon Paintings" initiated an environmental approach that I would term "ambient cinema."[10] This ambient conception of the artistic space was furthered in Grisi's sculptural and installation practice, which fleshed out forms of luminous transmission. Her projective neon sculptures sported significantly atmospheric titles such as *Sunset Light* (1967) and *Spiral Light* (1968). The cinematic effects were especially amplified in a series of environmental works from 1968 that created a veritable ambient cinema. Interestingly termed "Natural Elements," these included the atmospheric installation *Un'Area di Nebbia* (*A Space of Fog*, 1968). Column-like Plexiglas sculptures lit by luminiferous neon tubing that resembled skyscrapers were positioned in an environment made hazy by hidden artificial fog machines. This cloudy and misty space was pierced by the cool light of *antinebbia*, or antifog lights, used to produce an effect similar to the experience of a foggy landscape. In this interior installation, the outdoors was made palpably present, with the effect that inside and outside became porous. Immersed in this nebular environment, the distinction between natural and artificial sites was also confounded. And so, in the process of clouding a space, an art gallery was turned into a natural environment.

In rendering light opaque, the work technologically magnifies the ethereal density of this natural element. As happens in film projection, light, in the process of being filtered and refracted, thickens into matter. The sensation of this shadowed light is so physical that it becomes almost tactile. Inescapable, the palpable fog surrounds the viewers. One cannot simply look at this haze but, most importantly, must experience it with one's body, feeling the immersion in this meteorological environment. As if embracing the gallery viewers, the pervasive mist totally absorbs them in its ambient form, and closes the distance between them. All contours are confounded, and everything becomes a blur in this nebulosity of observation.[11]

In the porous, interstitial ambiance of *Un' Area di Nebbia*, one can become fully aware of the forms of liminality, permeability, and admixture that characterize the experience of atmosphere. "In-betweenness," is, in fact, "the normative condition of the atmospheric," as literary scholar Steven Connor reminds us in his study of haze, because this sphere embodies an inherent "conception of mixed and mutually pervasive bodies."[12] The nebulosity of Grisi's installation thus exposes the conceptual construction of an atmospheric environment by highlighting its elemental, ambient transitivity. In other words, as we observe the effects of *Un' Area di Nebbia*, even a conceptual form of fog emerges from her artistic meteorology.

In this conceptual haze, time itself becomes suspended as an in-between condition, distended in a drift of duration. The perception of natural elements and weather conditions is intensified in this indeterminate environment as their variability and mutability grows over time. And this temporal atmospheric approach to ambiance itself continued to grow as the artist expanded it into a practice that engaged different meteorological conditions. *Un' Area di Nebbia* was in fact the first of many elemental works that Grisi produced in 1968, which encouraged spectators to participate physically in the development of natural phenomena. Her expanded "ambient cinema" experimented in particular with the way in which different effects of light, in addition to the density of fog, could filter and alter the atmosphere—that is, screen a space.

Grisi added more movement to her luminous, projective environments by working with the motion of wind and the flow of water. Stimulated by her travels in various countries and her observation of different air currents and types of wind, she produced a 16mm film titled *Wind Speed 40 Knots* (1968). The process of making this film revealed the precise, scientific modality that characterized Grisi's observation of atmospherics, which in the latter part of her artistic career approached a form of diagrammatic and cartographic thinking. For this film, Grisi attentively measured and recorded the speeds and sounds of various winds as they passed though places ranging from the Sahara to tropical landscapes, whirled through different Mediterranean countries, or blew through South Pacific locations. In this moving way, the motion of natural elements became inscribed in cinematic form, literally and metaphorically becoming "motion pictures."

That same year, with the installation *Wind Speed 40 Knots* (also called *Wind Room*), Grisi brought the wind inside. The breezy atmospheres of moving images she had experienced while traveling were recreated with a hidden wind machine of the kind used in theatrical settings and in cinema. Using this technique, she activated the architectural space of the Roman art gallery La Tartaruga, energizing it with the speed of air flows. As visitors entered this unstable *Wind Room*, they became enveloped in natural elements. A constant wind blew in their faces, creating a variety of physical sensations to which they responded in different ways.

For *Volume of Air* (also called *Air Room*), also part of the 1968 series of "Natural Elements," Grisi intensified her work on the relation between technology and natural environments, producing an "osmosis between a technological medium such as neon light, and a natural element such as air."[13] This airy installation was illuminated by a thin thread of white light, which was drawn along the perimeter and the architectural junctures of the walls, floor, and ceiling of the gallery. In this ethereal way, Grisi joined together the elements of transparency and immaterial density that characterize both light and air. As Germano Celant put it, in this luminiferous airy room, "one is made conscious that the 'void' of our everyday atmosphere is the vehicle of a luminosity and a sensory quality that pass through it constantly."[14] The final effect of *Air Room* was that a transport of light became the medium that gave consistency to air, transforming it into a volume. Ultimately, in an installation that was an ambient cinema, a technological atmosphere of luminosity created a real matter of air.

In the Air: The Climate of 1960s Atmospherics

Rendering the (im)materiality of atmospheric mediums and "air" tangible, Grisi's work ended up even projecting the atmosphere of her time—for at this time, projective light was definitively "in the air." With her creation of ambient spaces of environmental consistency, Grisi offered an original, enlightened contribution to a practice that was emerging internationally as a number of artists began to work with neon lights, and explored the aesthetic potential of elemental materials. In the mid-1960s, Dan Flavin,

Bruce Nauman, Keith Sonnier, Mario Merz, Pier Paolo Calzolari, Joseph Kosuth, and Chryssa, among others, experimented contemporaneously with "neonization." But Grisi's work departed from the practices of others: when she began to use neon in 1966, as we have seen, it was with effects of spatialization and depth that were ambient, and even cinematic. She did not use neon lights or work with elemental materials as sculptural objects, as other artists did. By her own admission, she was "primarily interested in the less material, less tangible quality of the elements," using them "to create feelings and moods rather than objects."[15] Aiming to "exploit light for its possibilities of refraction, to create dimension" in conjunction with the dynamics of other elements, she enhanced the experience of atmospherics in environments that were both natural and artificial constructions.[16]

Because of this attentiveness to the way environments of light can create an "air" and transform an atmosphere, Grisi's environmental practice of an "ambient cinema" might be more closely associated with Lucio Fontana's creation of *Ambienti spaziali*. Known in English as *Spatial Environments*, these works, created between 1949 and 1968, were not just spatial, but "ambient" environments because of the way in which they variously configured and diffused the ambiance of light. Architecturally conceived structures, these *Ambienti* could be physically accessed by viewers, who were invited to sense the atmospheric shifts that occurred in the space due to the play of natural, fluorescent, floating, and other kinds of illumination.[17] One, created in collaboration with the architect and light artist Nanda Vigo, even evoked a cinematic projective atmosphere.[18] It is interesting to note, in this regard, that Fontana was interested in Grisi's work. He owned two of her works in enamel on canvas, went to see her exhibition in 1965, and gave her an oval gouache dotted with his famous holes when she visited his studio.

With respect to the creation of luminous ambiance, Grisi's work also shared the environmental direction taken in the United States by the Southern Californian Light and Space movement. Her creation of luminiferous spatial depth by way of radiant materials resonates with the kind of "ambient cinema" created by artists such as Doug Wheeler and James Turrell, but especially relates to the work of Mary Corse and Helen Pashgian. It is particularly relevant to bring up the practices of Corse and Pashgian in relation to Grisi because these women artists, though less recognized than the male affiliates of the movement, created surfaces that invited acts of screening just as Grisi did in her own way.

Grisi, in fact, used light and air as *mediums*. And she developed these mediums' environmental quality, strength, and impact in a vitalistic way. She used them as mediums of life—forms of transport, substances that transmit a force, dynamic sensations, along with effects of motion. In this sense, air was the perfect medium for Grisi, because, as media theorist Eva Horn emphasizes, it "enables movement and perception (hearing, sight, smell) as well as communication, travel, situatedness, and dislocation."[19] She explored this same force of movement as the medial condition of light. In the radiant *Air Room* and other works discussed, Grisi enhanced this mediality by working with the immaterial density of a cinematic, projective luminosity. Furthermore, in her technologically ethereal installations, light and air not only possess mediatic qualities per se, but also mediate—or, rather, *screen*—the viewers' perception of space. This phenomenological aspect of her ambient cinema informed all the iterations of her "Natural Elements" series, including *Rainbow* (1968) and *Stars* (1968). It is particularly evident in the performative installation *Light Melting Time* (1968), in which brilliant streams of light pierce a wall of lead, and burst through tiny holes to create a dissolution of elements, transmitting the pure energy of the rays to participating audiences.

In Grisi's projective environments, then, light and air were ever-changing mediums of a spatial transformation that, superseding objecthood, communicated via a form of conduction. The energy the work transmitted by waves of light, the flow of air, and the motion of wind was primarily experienced in spectatorial perambulations. As light and air moved, along with spectators, the transmutation of space produced a transduction. This ambient, energetic conversion affected even the psychic dimension of atmosphere. As Grisi synthetically put it: "I wanted to produce natural elements artificially, provoking a psychological metamorphosis that would redefine a space."[20] She indeed imparted a particular sense of ambiance: the idea that atmosphere is a feeling, an affect. In her work, sensing an air ultimately means feeling a pervading tone, absorbing the mood of a place, participating in an energy field. In this atmospheric way, as it recreated weather conditions, her cinematic environmental art constructed an actual climate.

Elemental Thinking, Environ-mentality

As Grisi experimented with nonrepresentational forms that were ambient, she thus projected a way of thinking that I term "environ-mentality."[21] This is because she did not treat the natural elements as mere materials, or containers, but rather engaged them as actual environmental agents, physically affecting mental atmospheres. She explained, "I didn't want a painting or a sculpture containing air, earth, or water; I didn't want air, earth, or water to become objects; I wanted to recreate the experience of natural phenomena."[22] In *Rain Room* (1968), for example, the experience of falling rain was technologically recreated in an interior environment to allow participants to feel a change in climate. Small drops of water fell continuously into a large basin sunk into the floor of the gallery so that it really appeared to rain on the floor. The meteorological sensing of this natural phenomenon was not only visual and tactile, but also aural. Grisi emphasized the rhythmic, sonorous flow of water to generate a contemplative atmosphere. In her own words, the sound effect of dripping water was crucial to "create an environment where one might meditate, listening to the noise of the rain."[23]

This strong environmental aspect of Grisi's work was recognized internationally when she was included in a landmark exhibition produced by Virginia Gunter at the Museum of Fine Arts in Boston in 1971. Entitled *Earth Air Fire Water: Elements of Art*, this show exhibited the "environ-mentality" that pervaded the art of this time. It also made clear reference to elemental philosophy, a form of thinking that, beginning with ancient Greek thought and extending into phenomenology, has treated the four elements of earth, air, fire, and water as both philosophical and scientific environmental ideas.[24] This exhibition of the play of the elements in art was wide-ranging, and featured a variety of artists working in various countries in environmental and material ways.[25] It included a kinetic construction by Otto Piene and his performative event *Charles River Rainbow*, a "Sky Art" piece made of helium-filled polyethylene tubes that, stretching across the river, acted as a strip of rainbow that lit up into the sky. The exhibition also showcased Andy Warhol's venture into nebular space with his famous helium-filled *Silver Clouds*, first shown in 1966. While Warhol's pillow-shaped clouds hovered in the museum space, the film of Robert Smithson's *Spiral Jetty* (1970) was earthbound. In her selections, the curator who had chosen Grisi to be in the company of these, and other prominent artists such as Christo, Michael Heizer, Allan Kaprow, Dennis Oppenheim, and Richard Serra, emphasized the elemental nature that was in the air at that moment. In the catalogue accompanying the exhibition, Gunter stated that "a force is gaining momentum: representation is diminishing" and that "there is no doubt that today's artists are influenced by natural process—or a series of natural processes," which included "the phenomena of nature, the span of time, the life experience."[26]

These kinds of natural processes, and the concepts of elemental philosophy were certainly central to Grisi's practice; her work appeared in the show's catalogue, featured between that of Dan Graham and Hans Haacke.[27] Along with Vera Simons, Grisi was one of a small number of women artists in the exhibition. She was represented by works of her "Natural Elements" series (1968–1969), which were different from many other elemental interventions because of their departure from the large scale of environmental art. Two delicate, contemplative works were shown: *Drops of Water*, which was a remake of *Rain Room*, and a study for her installation project *Refraction* (1968). Conceived during a trip to Africa, where Grisi paused to observe the sand dunes meeting the shores of Lake Chad, this latter work artificially reproduced the sun's light as it glanced off the calm surface of this fluid landscape, refracting in the atmosphere.

This form of contemplation of environmental phenomena was further pursued by Grisi in the guise of "Distillations." This series of works, produced from 1969 to 1971, resulted from the impact of the different cultural and physical landscapes that Grisi encountered in her extensive travels. The *Distillations* were processual interventions. In her practice, distillation was a procedure, a way to condense and distill an experience of ambiance, rendering its visual, aural, mental, and even spiritual base. This process involved a phenomenal analysis of sensations, and engaged a meditative environmental sensibility. A relevant instance of such "Distillations" is the 16mm film *The Measuring of Time* (1969). In this film Grisi, using repetitive gestures, counted grains of sand in the desert as a way to measure the passing of time. The haptic quality of this temporal distillation was clearly expressed by the film, beginning with a close-up of the artist's hands performing this non-action, and then expanding outward to reveal her body and, finally, spiraling back to the hands.

This contemplative process of distilling the nature of elements such as bodies of water or grains of sand extended further to incorporate other environmental materials. Pursuing an even more pensive form of environmentality, in 1972 Grisi made the 16mm film *From One to Four Pebbles*. Here she created a distillation of space that became almost a mapping, with a measured act of arranging pebbles in a series of spatial configurations.[28]

As the film's opening intertitle announces, the idea was that "every possible permutation is the arrangement of four pebbles in the same space." A cartographic procedure was set in motion by way of a cinematic process that arrived at the essence of what constitutes an environment, reducing it to its basic "elements" of combination.

Ambientalismo, Ecological Thought

As an artist attuned to analyzing the environment, Grisi researched the diverse haptic sensations and sounds that pervade and produce a lived space, affecting its experiential transformation. Sound was an important aspect of this elemental practice, and in 1971 she created a specifically aural work. Titled *Sounds*, this was an audio distillation. In this processual piece, Grisi recorded the modulation of sound as a natural element in itself. The sounds of water she captured were both stable and variable, and ranged from a drop of rain all the way to an ocean wave. A number of other material elements were also explored as they produced different vibrations. One could listen attentively to the sound made by asphalt, metal, rubber, glass, wood, mud, gravel, and coal, in addition to the sonorous life of water and sand. Each of these materials was subjected to a careful exploratory process that measured its specific resonance, revealing its constitution as a lively matter. Thus, with *Sounds*, Grisi created a vibrant form of mapping soundscapes, foregrounding the aural alterations that characterize and transform an environment.

These experiments with rhythm and modulation also addressed the cycle of vegetation. In her processual exploration, Grisi attempted to capture the sounds that travel around the soil and inside the earth. The life of plants was brought out in these resounding, tonal voyages into natural elements. Technological recordings made plants come alive as the artist reached for the vital lymph fluid that nourishes them. Grisi went after the most imperceptible vibration that this nutritive fluid makes as it moves through the trunk of a tree or circulates within its branches. With her own conceptual version of "plant-thinking," she strove to listen to the intelligence of plants and apprehend the expansion of fibers in arboreal matter.[29] Incorporating even the noise of pollution in these *Sounds* pieces, the artist created an ambient, environmental soundscape that bordered on ecology.

With a unique perspective, then, Grisi combined ethnographic research with a form of environmentality that merged with ecological thinking. Her particular attention to ecology with a pronounced ambient mentality might reflect the engagement in the health of the environment that was growing around her in Italy, with a specific concern for ambiance. Following the establishment of Italia Nostra in 1955, an organization committed to ecological protection, a wave of *ambientalismo* was established, which expanded the notion of place into a conception of *ambiente*. Italian architecture embraced this form of environmental thinking and promoted different ways of conceiving ecological design, merging architecture with landscape in the construction of ambiance. This *ambientalismo* included a formal exploration of the structure of trees, encapsulating the findings in the form of grids. In 1965, the architect Cesare Leonardi began a photographic project that analyzed trees in this way, and eventually produced *The Architecture of Trees*, a collection of carefully measured drawings that mapped the structure of tree specimens.[30] In this way, as architecture theorist Silvia Lavin concludes in her study of this subject, "framed and made visible by grids, trees became central to environmental thinking in Italy."[31]

It is not surprising that Grisi became interested in the life of plants, given her investment in the many aspects that constitute an *ambiente*. She herself understood ambiance as both a natural and artificial construction, and was fond of measuring the effects of atmospheric phenomena, even in diagrammatic ways. Seen in this light, then, her processual distillations of the vital sound of trees in *Sounds* can be considered part of an expansive ecological exploration of ambiance. Her atmospheric experiments with material phenomena extended their reach into the interior of the land to grasp the inner climate of the earth. With this attention to plant life, Grisi exposed the meteorology of the cosmos as a resounding, connective modality. This is because when one pays attention to the vegetable world, as the philosopher Emanuele Coccia reminds us, climate becomes "the essence of cosmic fluidity, the deepest face of our world," a revelation that enables us to comprehend "how all the elements within a given space" are "at once mixed and identifiable ... through the same 'atmosphere.'"[32]

Thus the vital lymphatic circulation through trees joined the motion of wind, the flow of water, and the transport of light in Grisi's atmospheric artistic practice. In learning from these natural elements, and incorporating the breath of plants in her work, she forged an ecological ambiance for art held together by an organic logic. In this sense, one can interpret Grisi's journey into the natural constitution of vegetation as a way to connect together all the elements of her luminiferous, ambient, moving practice. I would even venture to say that this exploration of plants closes the circle of her cinema of environmental art. Fascinated, as we have seen, by light and motion as the elemental zero degree of the art of projection, Grisi had technologically explored the material base that makes luminous projections possible, progressing from the ambiance of the "Neon Paintings" to the environments of the "Natural Elements" series. Although the investigation of the life of plants appears to diverge from this notion of "ambient cinema," if subjected to our own analytical distillation, it too can be seen to reinforce her "elemental" interest in the materiality of the film medium. After all, celluloid, which is the material of the filmstrip, is derived from cellulose, which is a component of plant cells.[33] As the vibrant substance of vegetable cellulose is transformed into nitrocellulose by a chemical process, it becomes the combined natural and artificial element of cinema. So cellulose, the dietary fiber that makes a plant vital for itself and for us, is also the vital matter of film. In other words, there is a vegetable condition at the root of the material existence of film. A plant stalk makes film stock. Or put differently, the life we see moving on the screen is a form of reanimation of plant life.

Grisi's contemplative practice makes us reflect on these precise conditions of material existence. And it actually goes to the heart of cinema's own environmental life. It even reveals this medium's specific ecology. The work especially invites us to see that plants and film are both materially defined by their receptivity and relation to light. Like a film screen, a plant is also a surface that lives by light. It is itself a *medium* that filters the light, capturing it in order to exist. As a medium of life, a leaf actually *screens* the light as it breathes it, transmuting it in photosynthesis. This alchemy of transmutation is also the chemistry of film. Film's photographic process enacts a moving conversion of "light-writing." The translucent layer of celluloid derived from pulverized cellulose, mixed with a solvent, and overlaid with a crystalline film, basically responds to and transforms light's radiance. When held up to the light, this light-sensitive material can even reveal the luminosity its emulsion base can capture. Moreover, in the space of a film theater, light projected through this material of plant-based elements activates the screen surface, and emanates in an ambiance of darkness. As it occurs in the atmosphere of screening, a vegetable specimen is itself the kind of screen that lives in a delicate balance between light and darkness. And, if deracinated, a plant perishes with all its cellulose, as does a celluloid negative when exposed to light.

In essence, then, these natural and artificial phenomena are atmospheric matters, for, as Grisi intuitively knew, both plant life and film's existence are ambient products of transformed sunlight. Finally, in relation to her ambient cinema, we should emphasize that plants and film are mediums that absorb luminosity not merely for their own vitality, but to circulate it and radiate it in the environment. A plant not only captures, but also converts light into palpable energy. It does so by motioning toward the light, in a system of interconnection with other plants that affects the environment. That is also the case for the moving image, a magnetic product of electricity, which returns artificially mediated sunlight to us in the form of a vibrant ambiance of projected light. One can therefore venture to claim that if a leaf is a screen, the atmosphere is a space of projection. For, ultimately, the natural screening process of light in a plant is as temporal as it is in the art of projection. A leaf not only screens sunlight, but retains its trace. Imprinted on celluloid and on the surface of the screen in the atmosphere of projection, this memory of light also lives in the medium of film. It activates its own luminous, energetic transport, suspended between natural and artificial conditions, bridging the animate with the inanimate. And it is this precise environmental force—the ambient energy of "environ-mentality"—that one ultimately feels in the cinema of Grisi's environmental art, so keen on technological transformations of natural elements. Here, light passing through air in so many forms is an energy that not only creates an ambiance, but transforms its very ecology.

1 Ernst Haeckel, *The Riddle of the Universe at the Close of the Nineteenth Century,* trans. Joseph McCabe, Harper and Brothers, New York and London 1900. Cited in James Nisbet, "Atmospheric Cameras and Ecological Light in the Landscape Photographs of Eadweard Muybridge," *Photography and Culture* 6, no. 2 (2013), p. 139.

2 Isaac Newton, *Opticks, or A Treatise of the Reflections, Refractions, Inflections and Colours of Light* (1730), Dover, New York 1952, p. 160.

3 Roland Barthes, "Leaving the Movie Theater," in *The Rustle of Language,* trans. Richard Howard, Hill and Wang, New York 1986, p. 346, 345.

4 Ibid., p. 347.

5 On the subject of luminous projective surfaces, see Giuliana Bruno, *Surface: Matters of Aesthetics, Materiality, and Media,* University of Chicago Press, Chicago 2014.

6 Born in Rhodes, Greece, in 1939, educated in Paris, and living between Rome and New York, Grisi was the daughter of a film producer. She married the well-known Italian documentary filmmaker and naturalist Folco Quilici, with whom she traveled extensively and spent long periods living in Africa, South America, and Polynesia. She was also friends with many of the Italian film directors of her time.

7 Laura Grisi's statement appears in "Essay–Interview by Germano Celant," in Germano Celant, *Laura Grisi, A Selection of Works and Notes by the Artist*, trans. Marguerite Shore, Rizzoli, New York 1990, p. 19. On Grisi, see also Renato Barilli, *Laura Grisi*, exh. cat., Galleria dell'Ariete, Milan 1965; Udo Kultermann, *Laura Grisi,* exh. cat., Galerie E. M. Thelen, Essen 1968; and Giulio Carlo Argan, *Laura Grisi*, exh. cat., Galerie E. M. Thelen, Cologne 1970.

8 Pliny the Elder recounts this myth in his *Natural History,* circa 77–79 AD. The story of Dibutades' shadow tracing has traveled widely in history, and has been extensively depicted in art. Contrary to the interpretation that sees this scene simply as marking the origin of painting or the birth of drawing, I claim that what is represented in this story is a novel possibility of imaging, and even a future potentiality for representation. This casting of an image by way of light is an act of projection, and the narrative is one that forecasts its origin. This story, in the end, traces the very scene of projection. It presents the material basis of this act and the process of its coming into being: the "becoming space" of projection.

9 Grisi, "Essay–Interview by Germano Celant," p. 12.

10 The subject of atmospherics, projective ambiances, and artistic ecologies treated in this essay is further articulated in Giuliana Bruno, *Atmospheres of Projection: Environmentality in Art and Screen Media*, University of Chicago Press, Chicago, forthcoming 2022).

11 In this nebular sense, *Un'Area di Nebbia* anticipates the spirit with which Diller Scofidio + Renfro made a cloud building in 2002, appropriately called *Blur.* This was an architecture of mist that floated on the banks of Lake Neuchâtel, making an immersive performance of atmospheric phenomena for its visitors.

12 Steven Connor, *A Matter of Air: Science and Art of the Ethereal*, Reaktion, London 2010, p. 191–194.

13 Grisi, "Essay–Interview by Germano Celant," p. 31.

14 Ibid., p. 30.

15 Ibid., p. 24.

16 Ibid., p. 23.

17 See Marina Pugliese, Barbara Ferriani, and Vincente Todolí (eds.), *Lucio Fontana: Ambienti/Environments*, exh. cat., Mousse Publishing, Milan 2018; and Germano Celant (ed.), *Lucio Fontana: Ambienti spaziali; Architecture, Art, Environments*, exh. cat., Skira, Milan 2012.

18 Nanda Vigo collaborated with Fontana on *Ambiente spaziale: Utopie*, conceived for the XIII Milan Triennale in 1964. See Dominique Stella (ed.), *Nanda Vigo: Light is Life*, exh. cat., Johan & Levi, Milan 2006.

19 Eva Horn, "Air as Medium," *Grey Room*, no. 73 (Fall 2018), p. 9.

20 Grisi, "Essay–Interview by Germano Celant," p. 23–24.

21 See Bruno, *Atmospheres of Projection: Environmentality in Art and Screen Media*.

22 Grisi, "Essay–Interview by Germano Celant," p. 24.

23 Ibid., p. 30.

24 For an introduction to elemental ways of thinking, see David Macauley, *Elemental Philosophy: Earth, Air, Fire, and Water as Environmental Ideas*, State University of New York Press, Albany 2010.

25 On this environmental period in art, see James Nisbet, *Ecologies, Environments, and Energy Systems in Art of the 1960s and 1970s*, MIT Press, Cambridge, Massachusetts 2014.

26 Virginia Gunter, "Introduction," in *Earth Air Fire Water: Elements of Art*, exh. cat., Museum of Fine Arts, Boston 1971, p. 7.

27 Ibid., p. 87–88.

28 In 1973, intrigued by her work, Leo Castelli gave Grisi a solo show in his New York gallery, with the title *Pebbles*. The gallery presented other solo exhibitions of her work in 1975, 1976, 1978, 1981, 1986, and 1992.

29 For an introduction to this growing field of philosophical investigations, see Michael Marder, *Plant-Thinking: A Philosophy of Vegetal Life*, Columbia University Press, New York 2013.

30 See Cesare Leonardi and Franca Stagi, *The Architecture of Trees* (1983), trans. Natalie Danford, Princeton Architectural Press, Hudson, New York 2019, originally published in 1983 after 20 years' study of the subject.

31 Silvia Lavin, "Tree Speech," *Log: Observations on Architecture and the Contemporary City*, no. 49 (Summer 2020), p. 118.

32 Emanuele Coccia, *The Life of Plants: A Metaphysics of Mixture,* trans. Dylan J. Montanari, Polity, Cambridge 2019, p. 27.

33 On this subject, see Scott MacDonald, "The Ecocinema Experience," in *Ecocinema Theory and Practice,* ed. Stephen Rust, Salma Monani, and Sean Cubitt, Routledge, New York 2013; and Graig Uhlin, "Plant-Thinking with Film: Reed, Branch, Flower," in *The Green Thread: Dialogues with the Vegetable World,* ed. Patrícia Vieira, Monica Gagliano, and John Ryan, Lexington Books, London 2016.

1970–1979

Laura Grisi working on *From One to Four Pebbles*, 1972

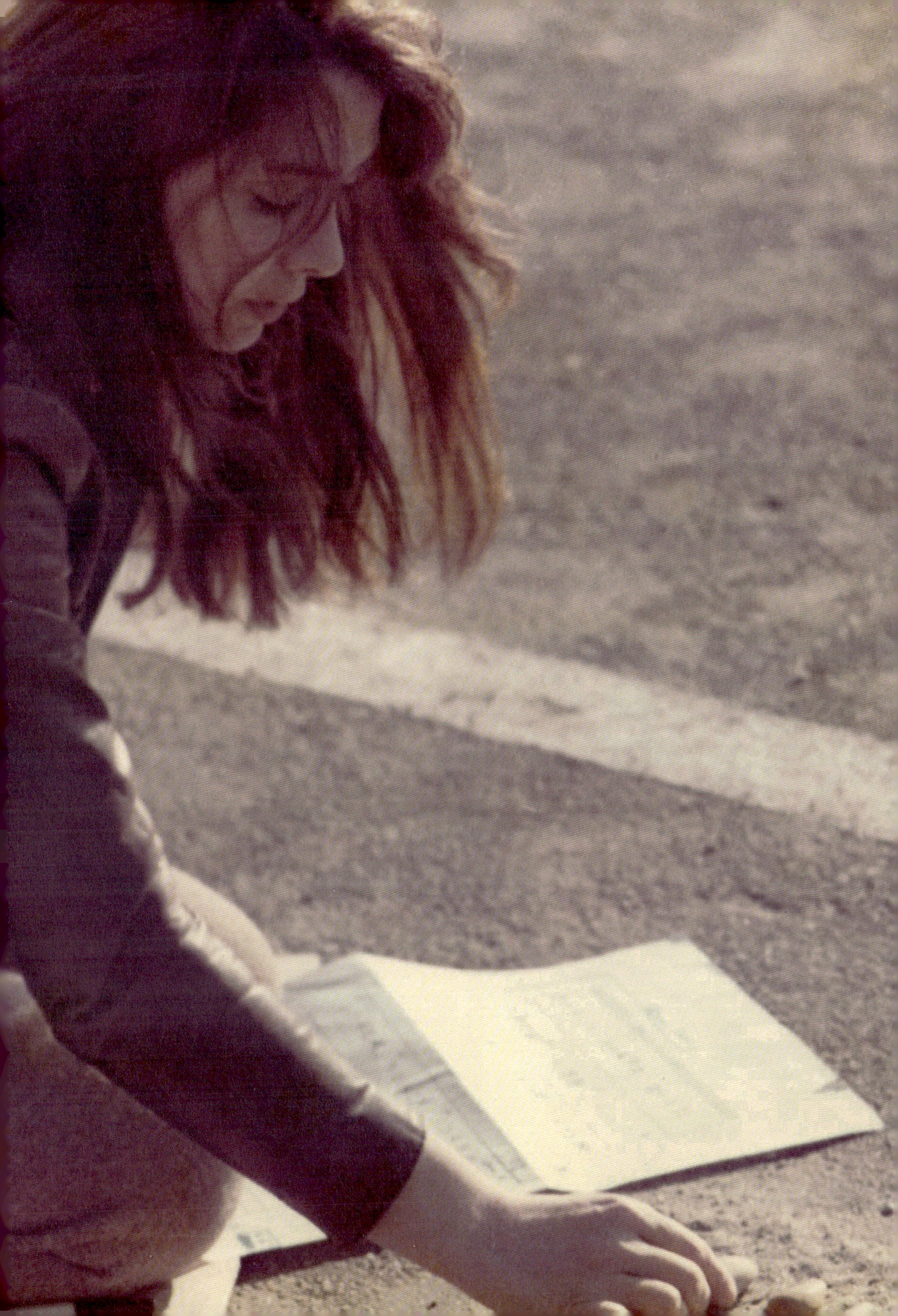

I LOOK AT HOW THE OCEAN MOVES

RAW DATA:

I look at the ocean moving, without time limits, how the waves move, when, which are larger, which are smaller, where and at what intervals big waves form, in which fishes can be seen in transparency, in which only foam, which come further up the sand, which are shortest, at what distance from one another they break, which give the deepest sound, which leave debris on the sand, which seaweed, which fish.

PLACE: Rangiroa
DATE : August 25, 1970
TIME : 5 p. m.

TITLE: Indeterminacy

CONDITIONS FOR THE EXPERIMENT:

1. The ocean, not completely calm
2. Silence
3. Solitude
4. Any day after a storm, when there are algae and debris in the water

INSTRUCTIONS:

1. To look at the ocean until the sunset
2. Not to stand still in one place, but to walk along the edge of the water
3. Not to become distracted by the surrounding scenery

NOTES:

I do not want to establish anything precise: only observe without any time limits.

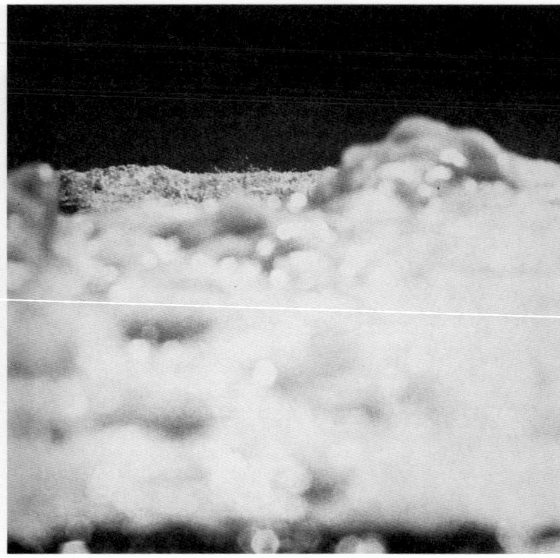

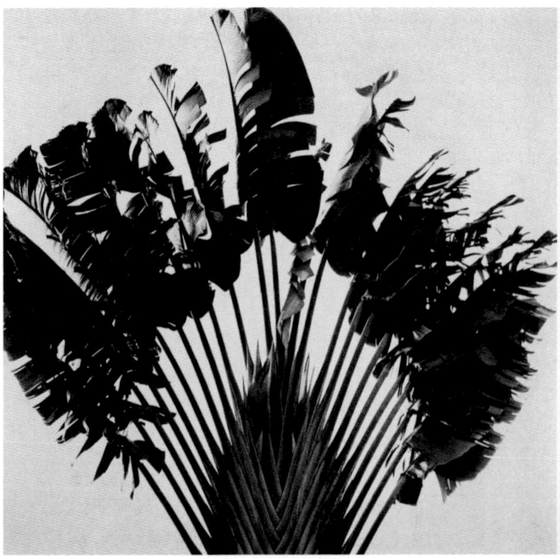

I LOOK AT HOW PALMS MOVE

RAW DATA:

I look at palms and other trees moving, without time limits. Some palms move very slowly, the movement of other trees is different. With the same gust of wind, each tree has a different time of response; the top of each tree is the part that moves more quickly, the leaves on the central branches more slowly. The outside leaves turn in every direction even though the wind blows in only one direction. If leaves and fruit fall down, coconuts fall the most frequently. In some trees the leaves fall first, in the breadfruit tree the flowers fall first, in the banana tree the leaves only move, in the frangipane tree only the small branches at the top (where the flowers are) break and fall. The most rapid movement is that of the palm, and includes also the flexible trunk which bends. After each gust of wind the tree which straightens the soonest is the palm, but that which stops the first is the frangipane; the ones whose leaves continue to move the longest are the breadfruit and the pandanus. Each leaf moves with a different sound. Palm trees give a hissing sound, other trees a drier one; those with smaller leaves a more rapid and metallic sound. The frangipane trees do not have leaves, only branches and flowers, and give a light sound, that of the impact of the wind against the branches, a barely audible sound. The deepest sound is that of the pandanus tree.

PLACE: Maupiti
Leeward Islands
DATE : August 23, 1970
TIME : 3 p. m.

TITLE: Indeterminacy

CONDITIONS FOR THE EXPERIMENT:

1. An area with trees and various kinds of vegetation
2. Silence
3. Solitude
4. Gusts of wind

INSTRUCTIONS:

1. Select a place where it is possible to see more than one kind of tree at the same time
2. Observe the behavior of each tree during and after each gust of wind
3. First watch one tree at a time, note the differences; try to look at all of them together during the same gust
4. Going close to each tree, listen to the sound it makes.

NOTES:

I do not want to establish anything precise: only observe without time limits.

I LOOK AT VARIETY IN PLANTS

RAW DATA:

I walk in an orchid plantation and look at their varieties, qualities and colors.
There are other plants - some mango-trees. I look intently at their leaves and fruit, some over-mature ones have fallen down and broken open.

PLACE: Mindanao
Sulu Islands
DATE : July 13, 1970
TIME : 12 noon

TITLE: Sameness in colors

PROPOSITION:

To find a color similarity in two different plants under the same conditions of light and at the same time of day. The similarity can be found in either the leaves, the flowers or the fruit of the two plants.

CONDITIONS FOR THE EXPERIMENT:

1. Find oneself in an orchid plantation at the time of day when the light is most intense
2. It is necessary to have some mango-trees in the same plantation
3. Be there in the period of the year when the orchids are in flower
4. Be there in the period of the year when the mangos are mature
5. Examine the different plants at the same hour and in the same light

INSTRUCTIONS:

1. Look carefully at the color of the different orchids
2. Select the most intense color
3. Look carefully at the color of the mango-leaves (especially the new ones)
4. Select the lightest green
5. Once the colors are selected, find the equivalent of one in the other plant and vice versa.

NOTED.

A) I found that the orchid with the most intense color has the same color as the pulp of ripe mango.
B) I found that the lightest green of new mango leaves is the same green as that of the veining of the orchid.

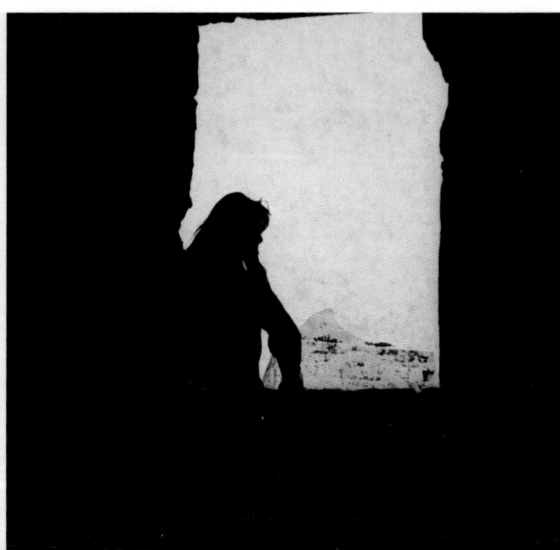

DISTILLATIONS: 3 MONTHS OF LOOKING
July - September, 1970

I look at a fire

I look at the sun

I look at the horizon

I look at a lava flow

I look at water

I look at my skin

I look at how the ocean moves

I look at how palms move

I look at variety in plants

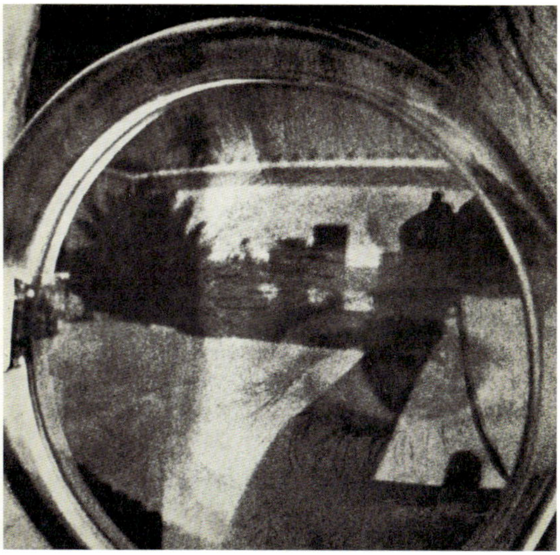

I LOOK AT THE HORIZON

RAW DATA:

I walk in the desert and look at the horizon. There is only sand and no water. I am extremely thirsty. When I find water I attempt to resist drinking it.

PLACE: Niger Desert
DATE : September 12, 1970
TIME : 5 p. m.

TITLE: Thirst in the desert

PROPOSITION:

To isolate and experience directly that very moment when conscious will to resist pain is overcome by the possibility of relieving it.

CONDITIONS FOR THE EXPERIMENT:

1. Be in a desert on a clear day - minimum temperature 98° F.
2. Thirst
3. Water found after walking 5 miles

INSTRUCTIONS:

1. Decide beforehand to resist drinking the water until the discomfort is acute
2. Analyze if thirst can be understood as acute discomfort or as pain
3. Resist drinking to the point in which the overall feeling is sufficiently unpleasant to inhibit self-observation
4. Analyze what the overall body sensation is just before drinking and what the components of this sensation are.

NOTES:

When I found water I tried to resist drinking in order to analyze these sensations but I was able to do it for less than 1 minute.

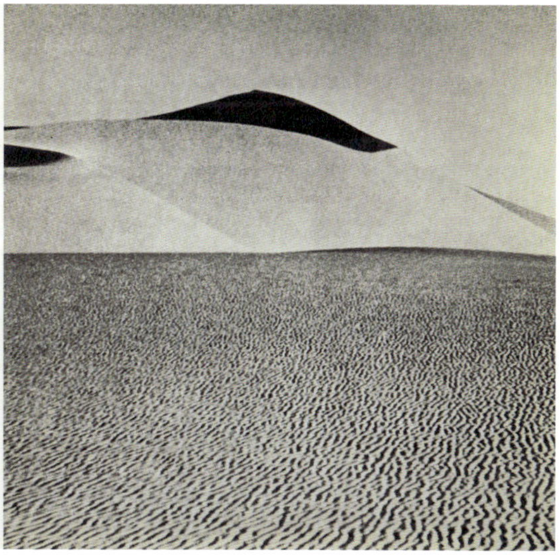

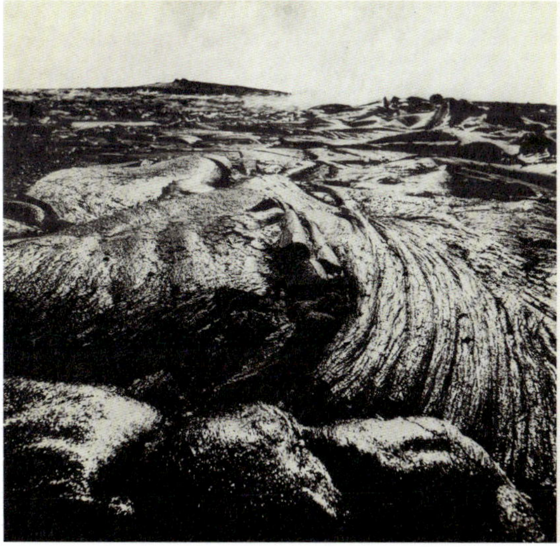

I LOOK AT A LAVA FLOW

RAW DATA:

I walk on the cooled lava of a volcano and suddenly sink 2 feet into the lava. I feel that my life is endangered. I do not know which way to move and be safe, there is the risk of sinking to the bottom. I decide to stay motionless for a while to experience the sensations of danger and fear until the feeling of discomfort at not moving overcomes any further desire to remain still and analyze these sensations.

PLACE: Tanna Volcano
New Hebrides
DATE : July 30, 1970
TIME : 10 a. m.

TITLE: Fear of moving

PROPOSITION:

To consciously delay an act of decision in a personal risk situation in order to analyze which is stronger: the fear of moving in the wrong direction or the anxiety of tolerating the sensation of fear any longer.

CONDITIONS FOR THE EXPERIMENT:

1. Danger
2. Find oneself on the slope of a volcano in a lava flow which appears to have a solid crust (the same experiment can be restructured to be carried out in a swamp or deep mountain snow).

INSTRUCTIONS:

1. Walk until a point where one feels the lava begin to sink under one's feet. At this point it is necessary to: A) choose exactly in what direction to move to avoid sinking in completely B) remain motionless as long as possible to establish the exact sensation of danger
2. Observe very attentively where the fissures of lava are
3. Try to recognize which fissures seem superficial but are, instead, actually deep, and would be dangerous under the weight of a person
4. Observe the color and brilliance of the lava: where it is brighter, it is more crystallized and thus more brittle.

NOTES:

I remained without moving for about 20 minutes. After this time, the fear of choosing the wrong direction was overcome by the anxiety of tolerating these sensations any longer.

Pages from the book published by Artestudio, Macerata

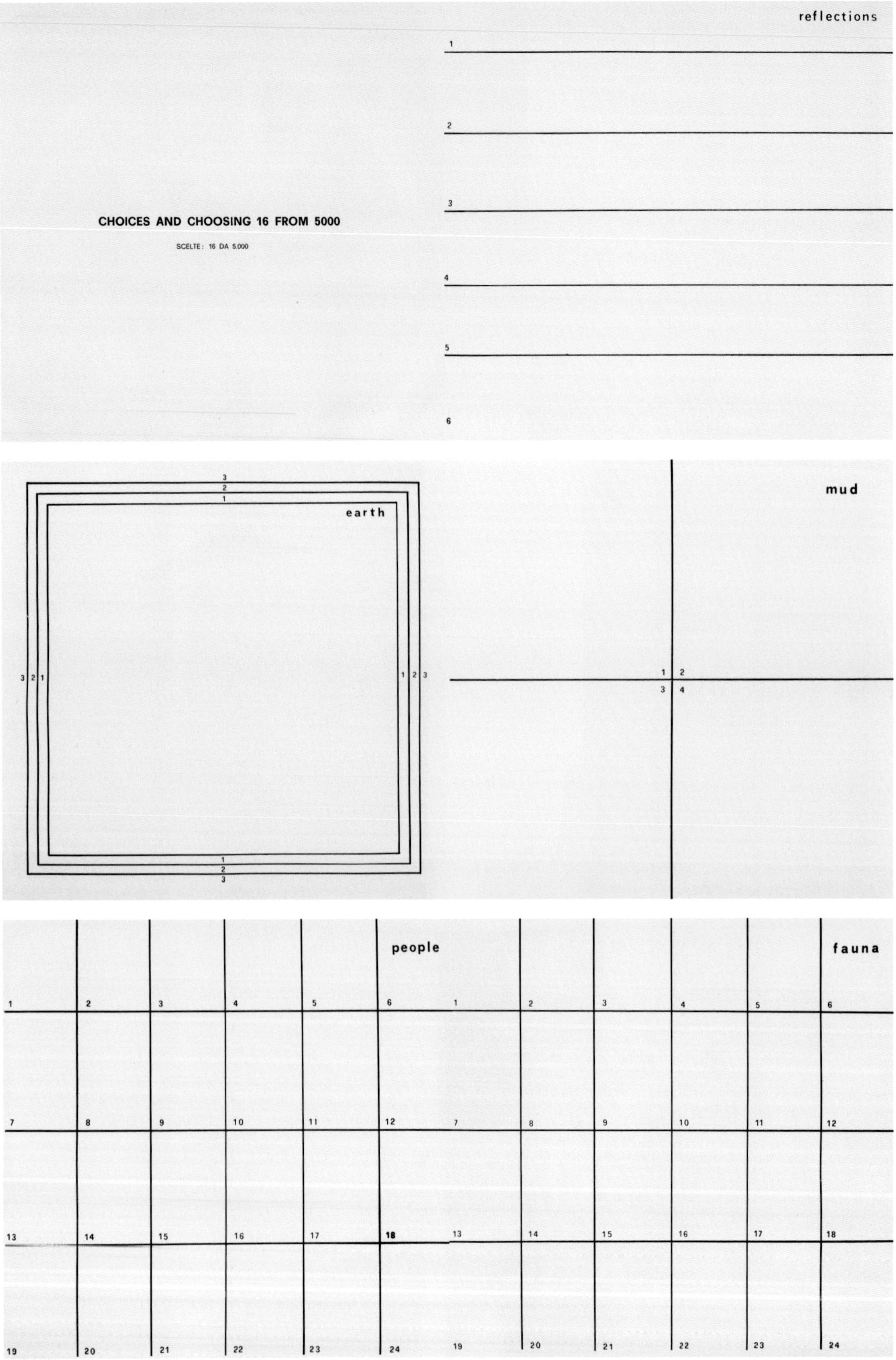

***Distillations: Choice and Choosing 16 from 5000*, 1970**

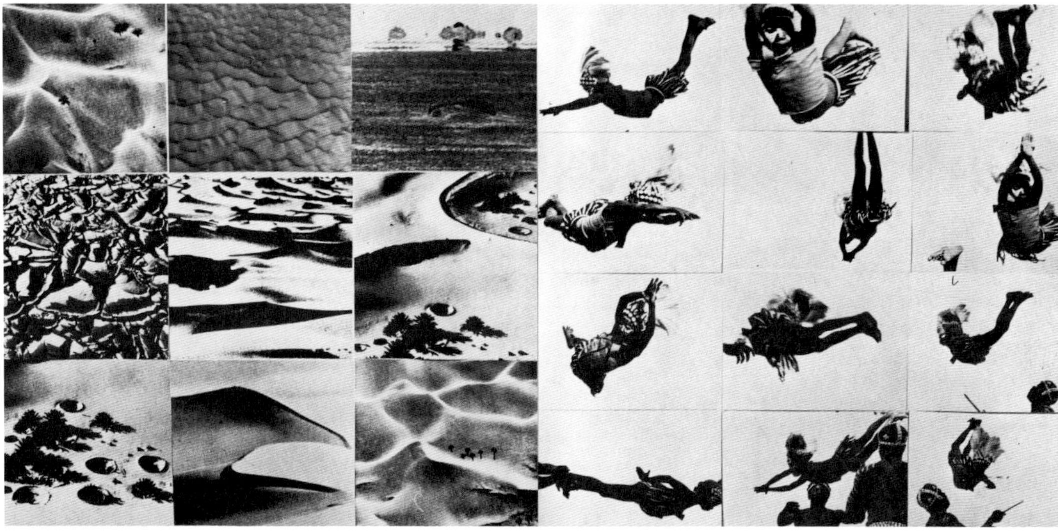

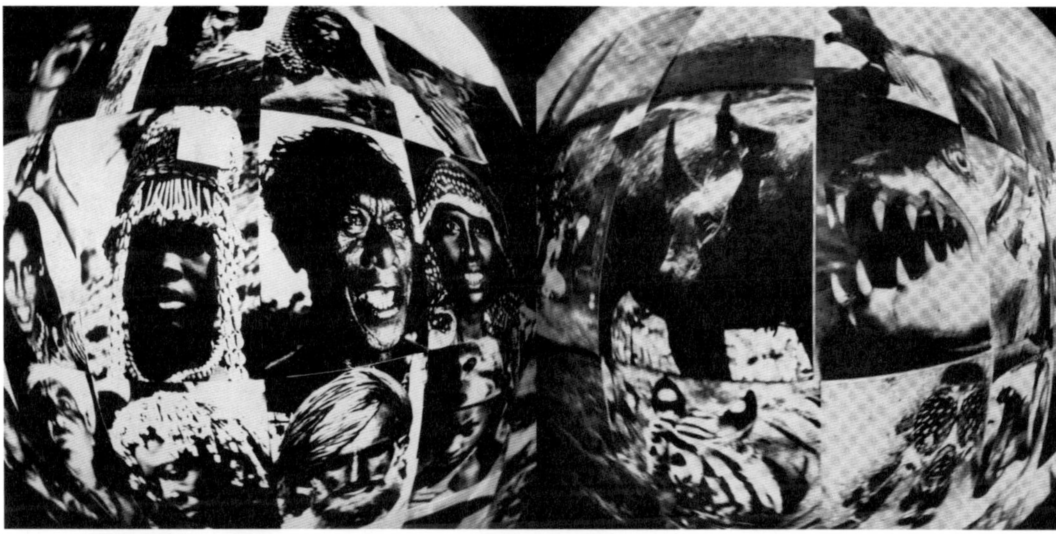

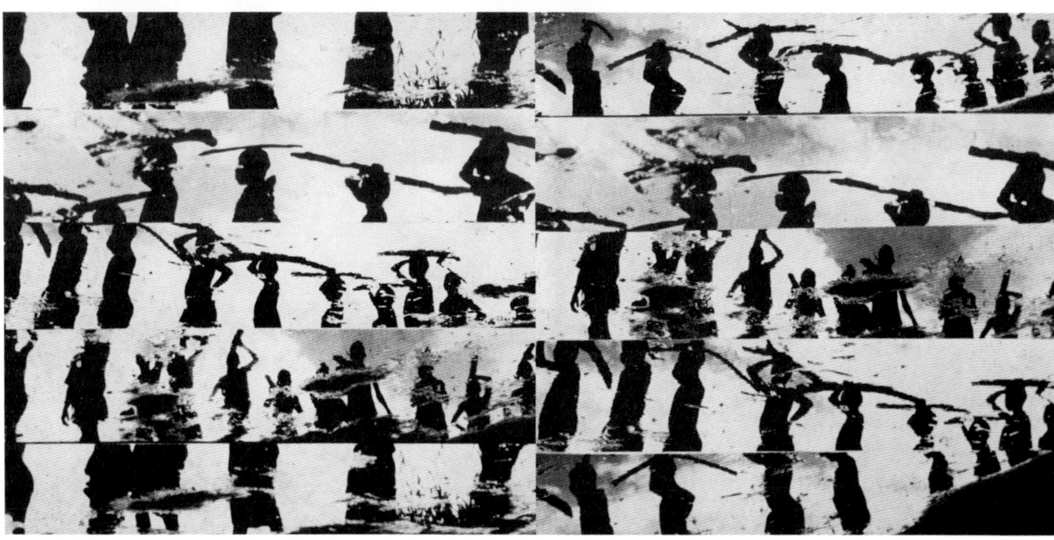

Pages from the book published by Artestudio, Macerata

Sounds (Ten Stones Ten Materials), 1971
Sounds (Ten Stones Ten Materials), 1971
Sounds (Ten Stones Ten Materials), 1971

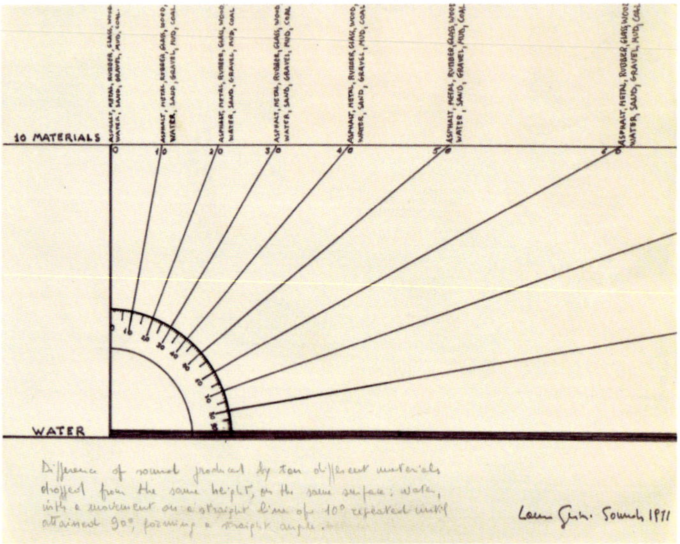

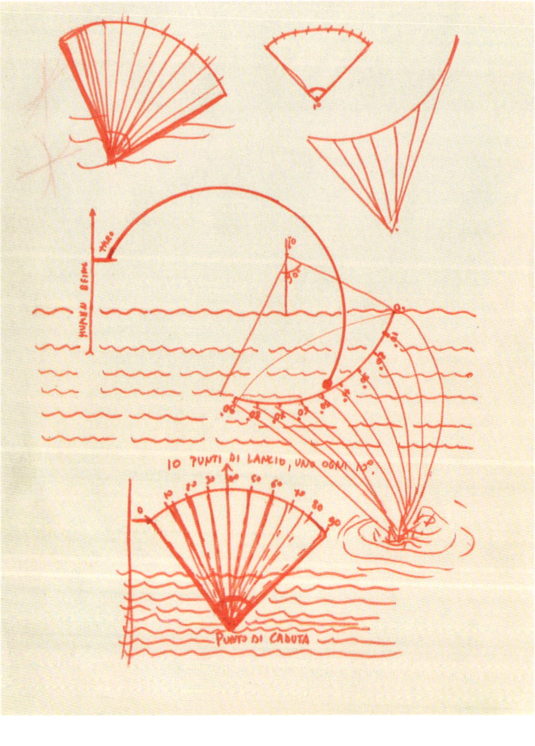

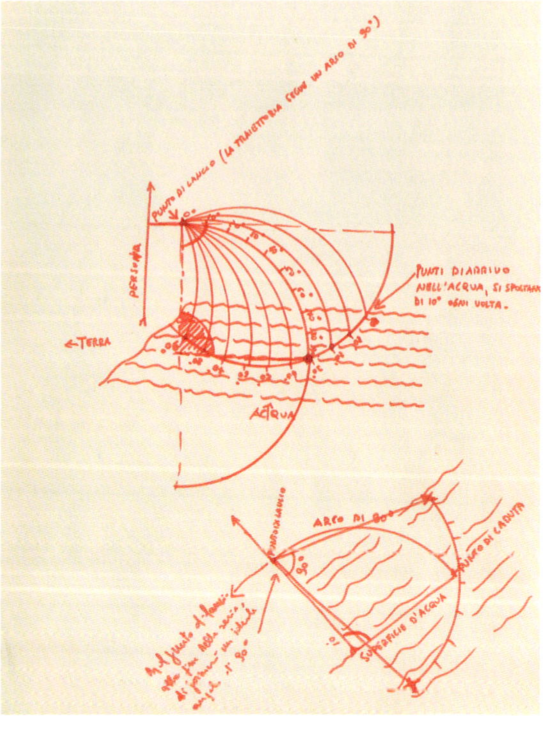

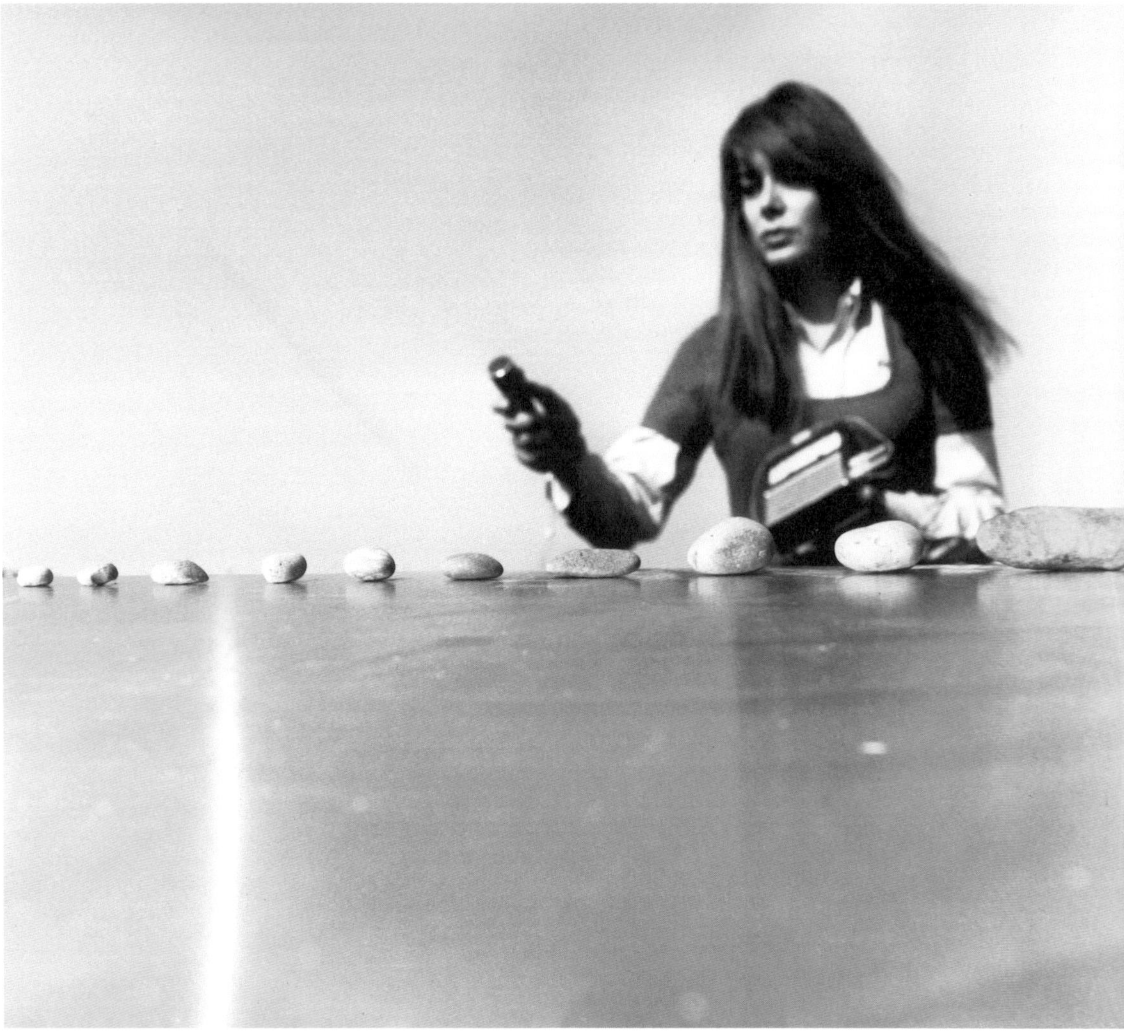

Laura Grisi working on *Sounds*, 1971

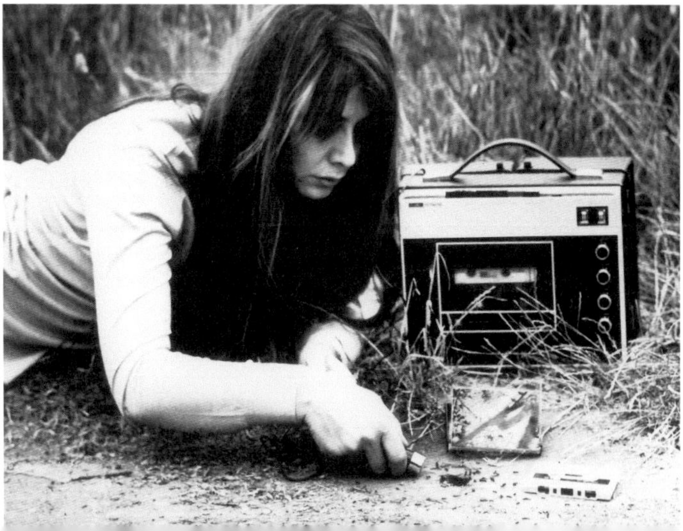

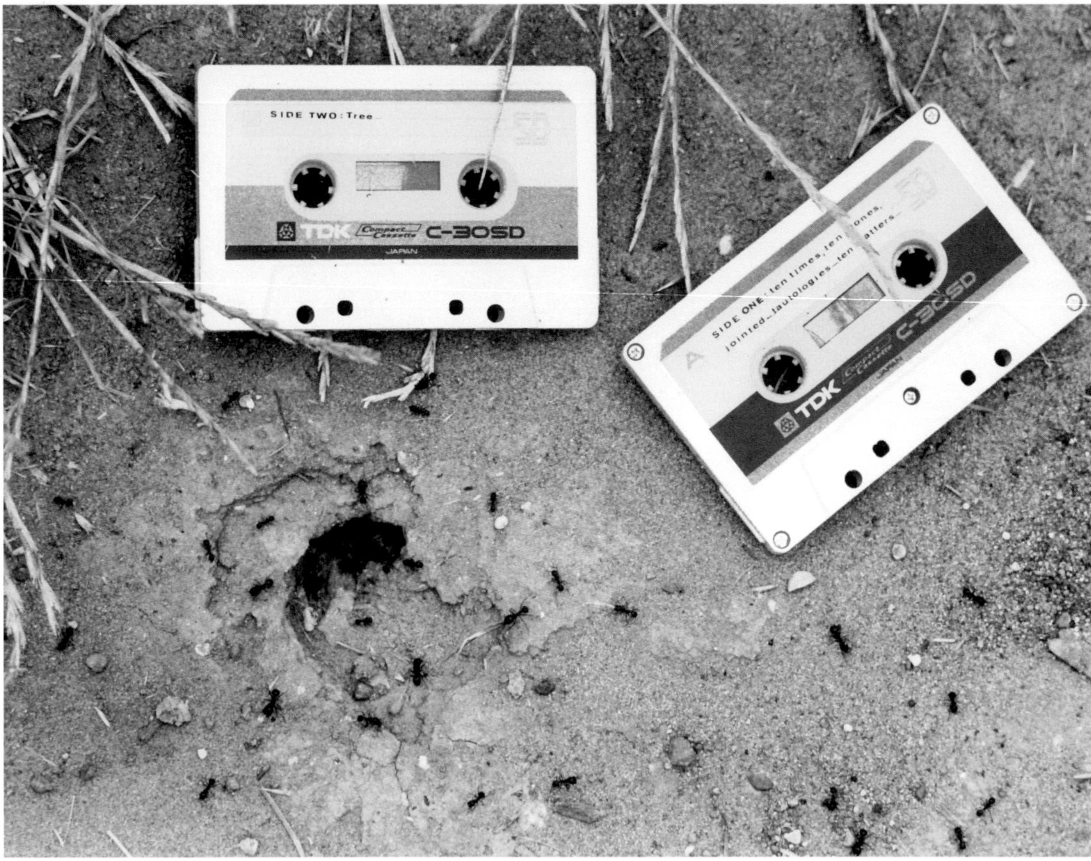
SIDE TWO: Tree_
TDK Compact Cassette C-30SD
JAPAN
SIDE ONE: ten times, ten
jointed_tautologies_ten
TDK Compact Cassette

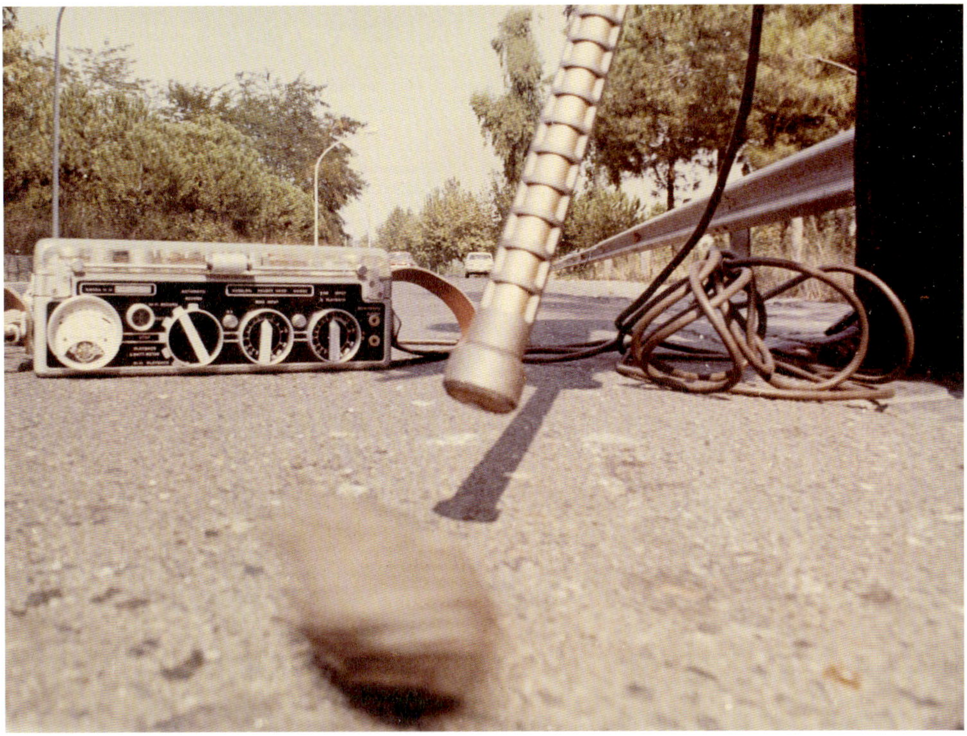

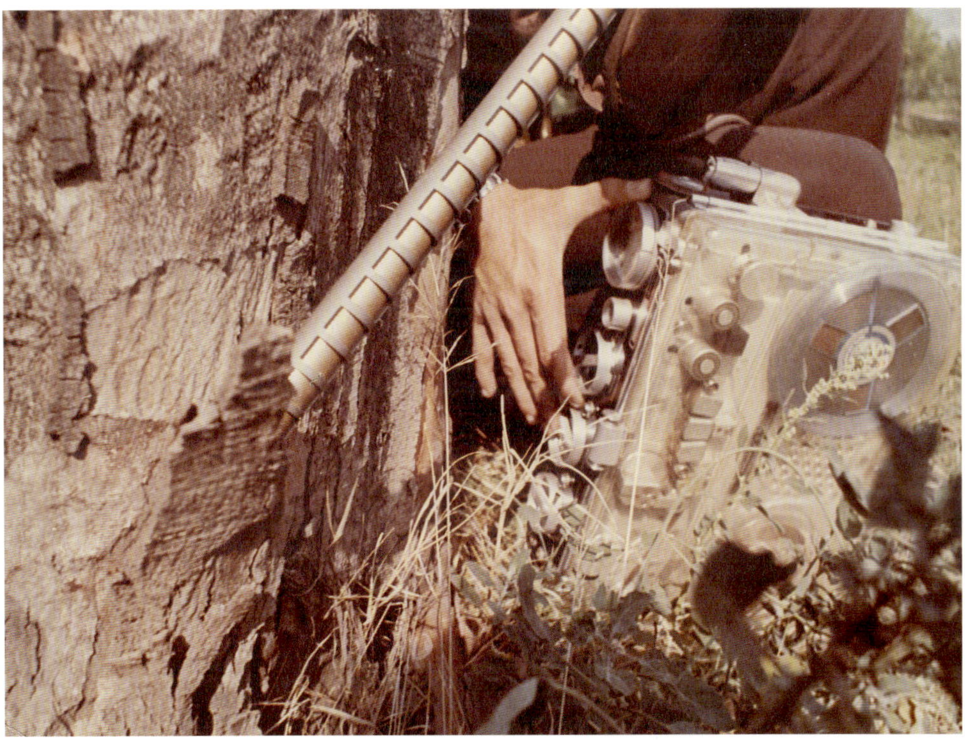

***Sounds (Ten Stones)*, 1971**
***Sounds (Tree)*, 1971**

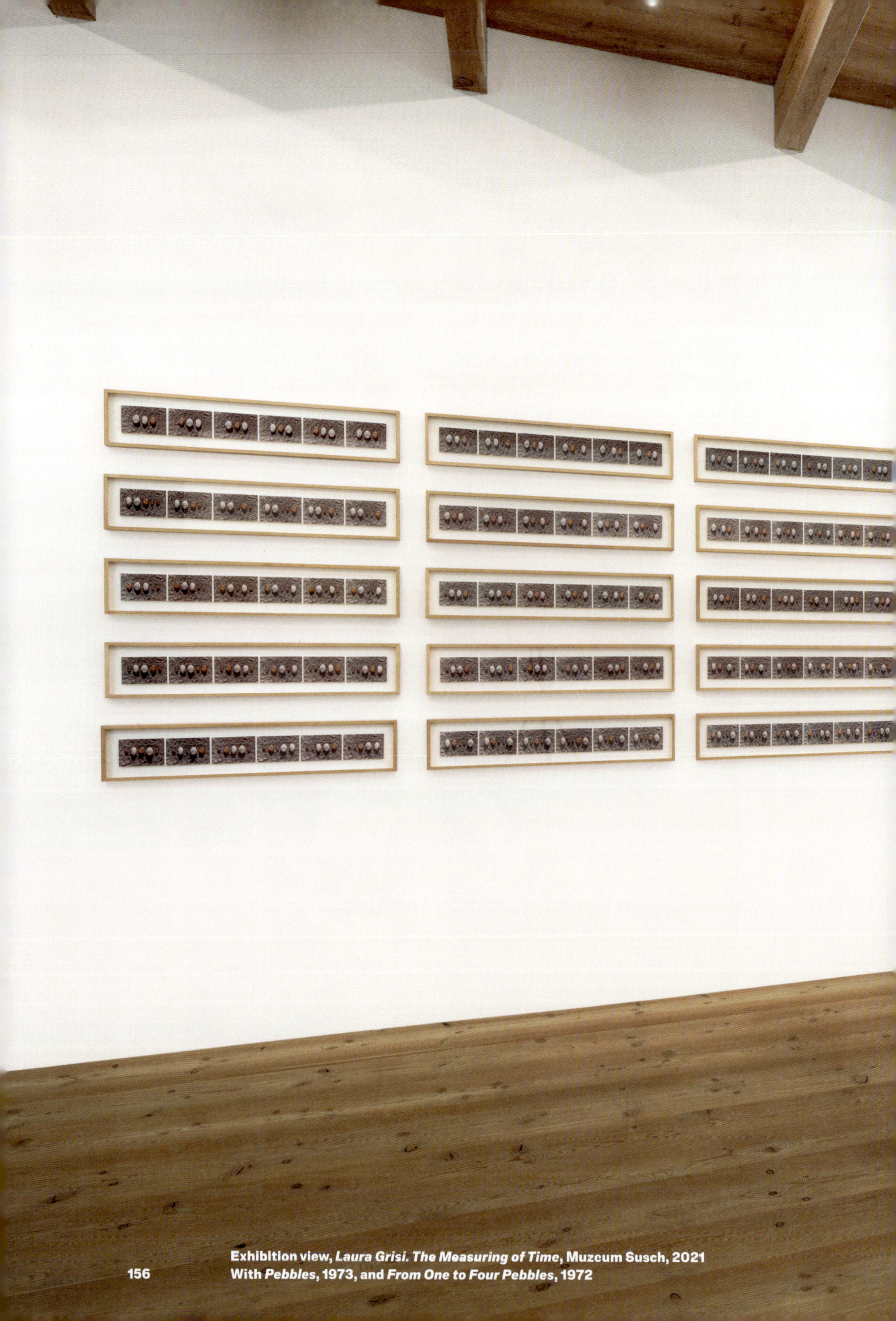

Exhibition view, *Laura Grisi. The Measuring of Time*, Muzeum Susch, 2021
With *Pebbles*, 1973, and *From One to Four Pebbles*, 1972

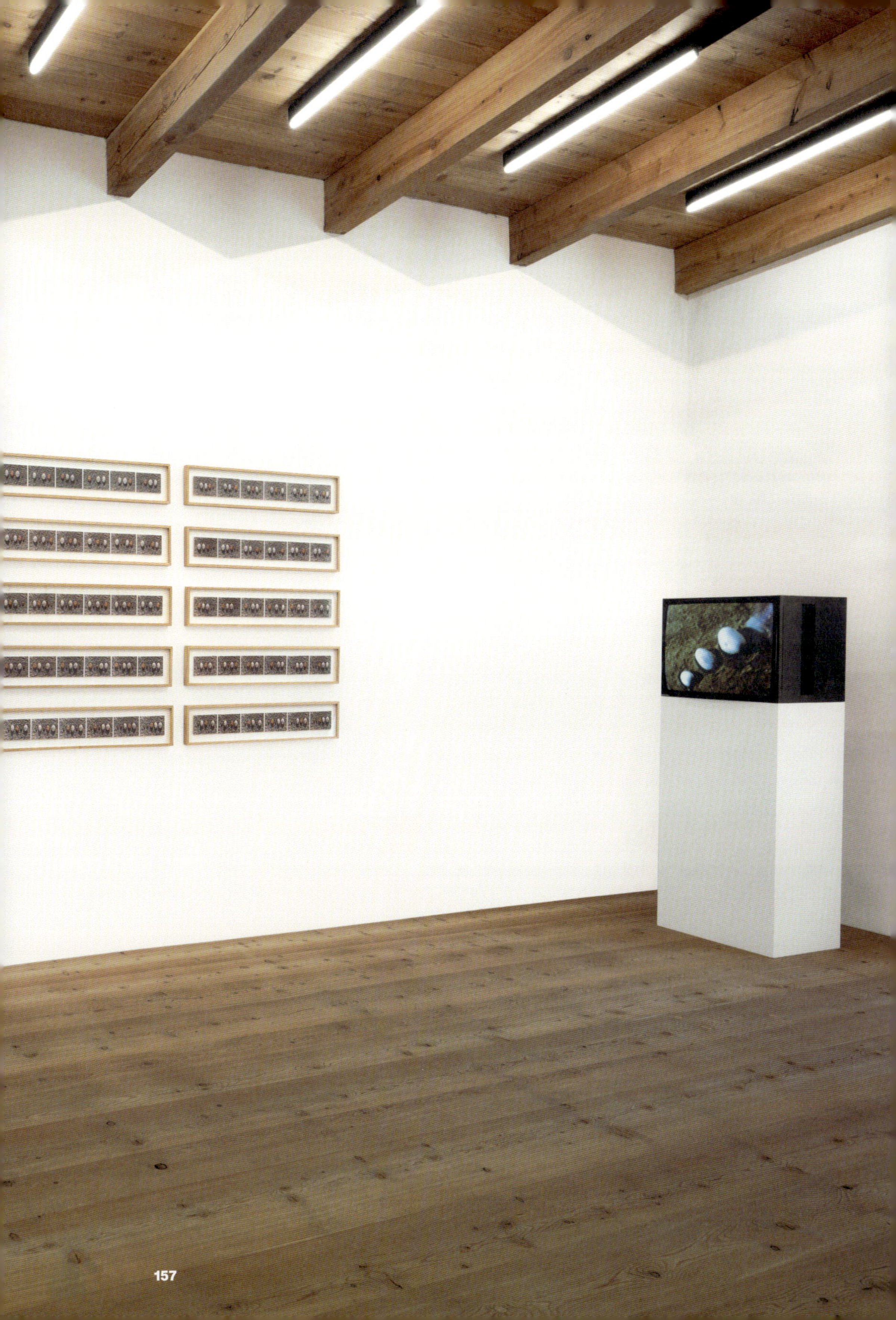

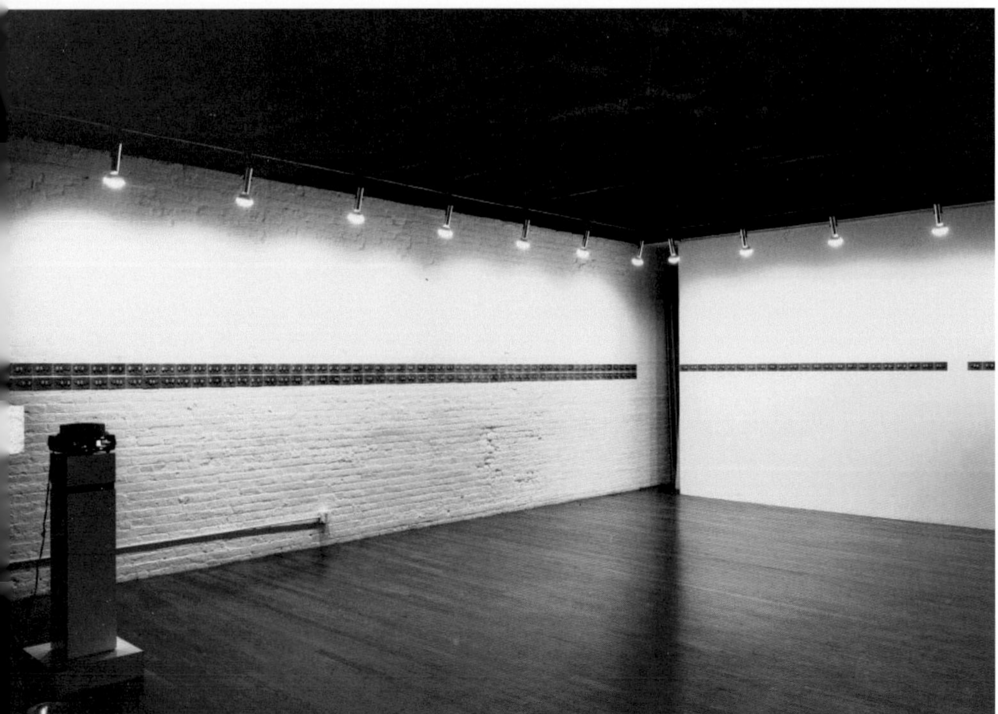

Exhibition views, *Laura Grisi. Pebbles*, Leo Castelli Gallery, New York, 1973

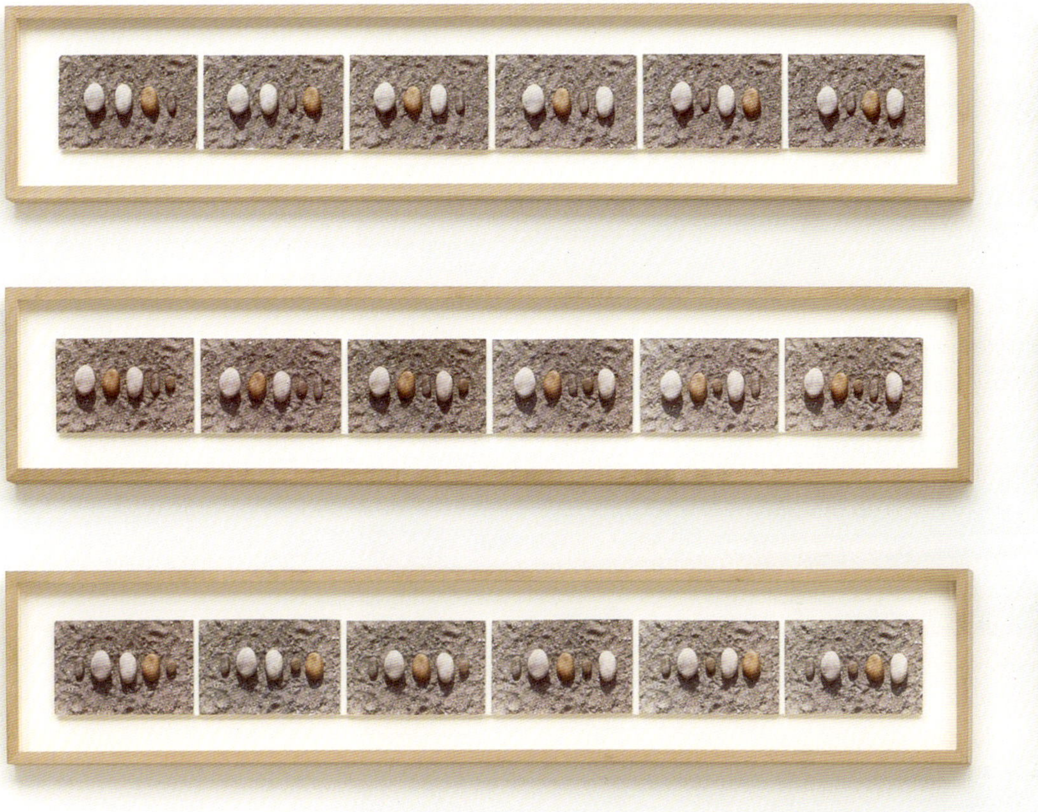

159 *Pebbles*, 1973 (detail)

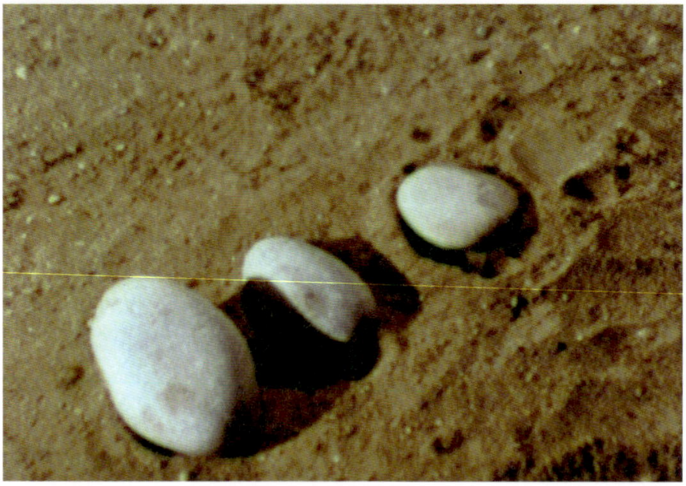

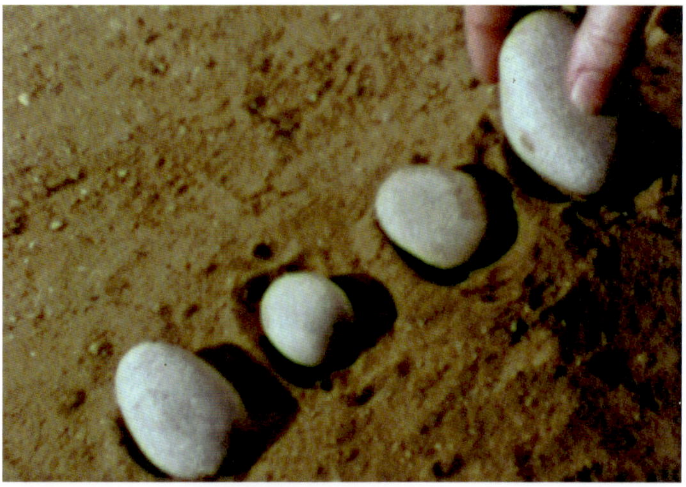

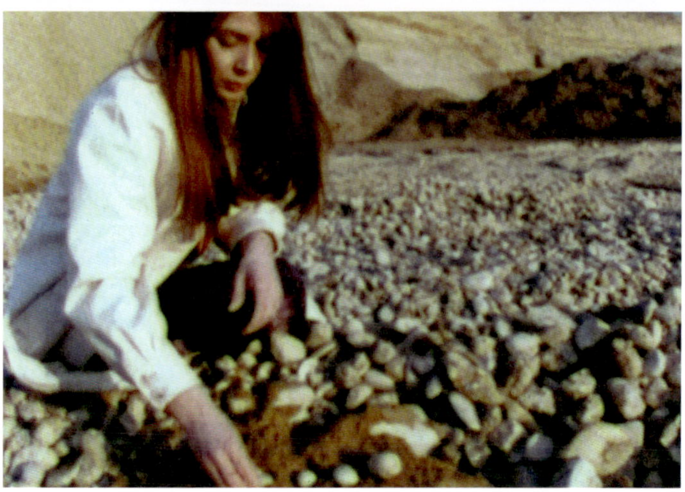

 ***From One to Four Pebbles*, 1972**

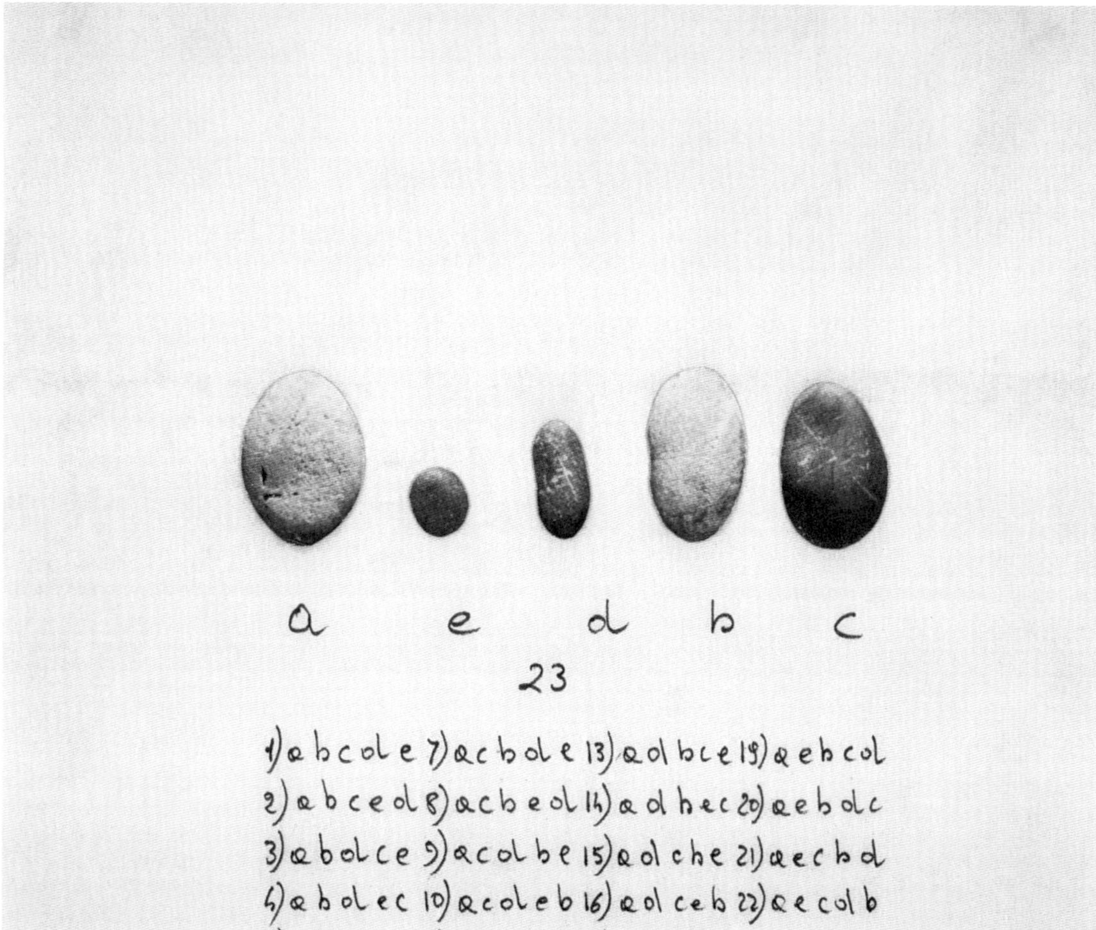

 ***Drawing for Pebbles*, 1973 (detail)**

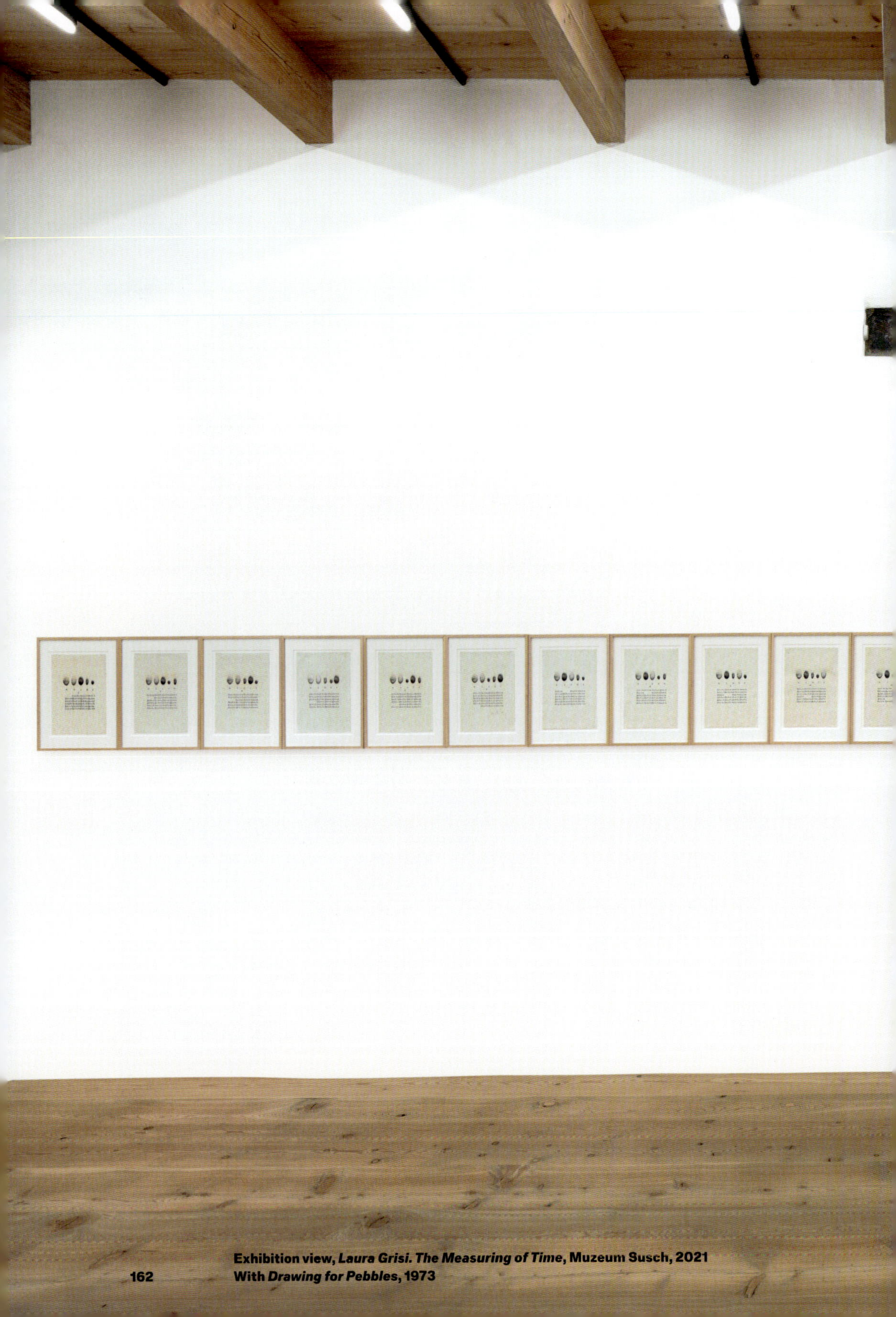

Exhibition view, *Laura Grisi. The Measuring of Time*, Muzeum Susch, 2021
With *Drawing for Pebbles*, 1973

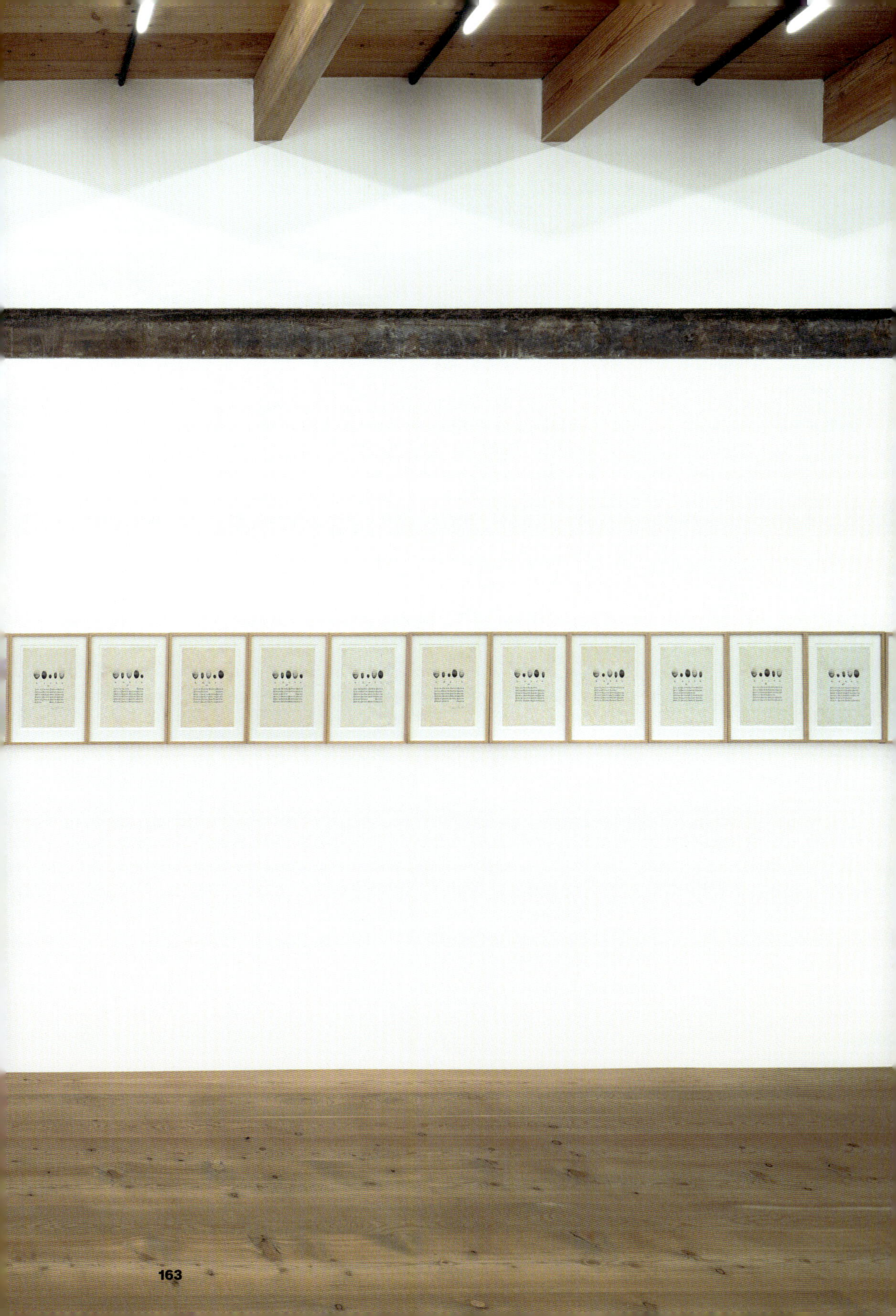

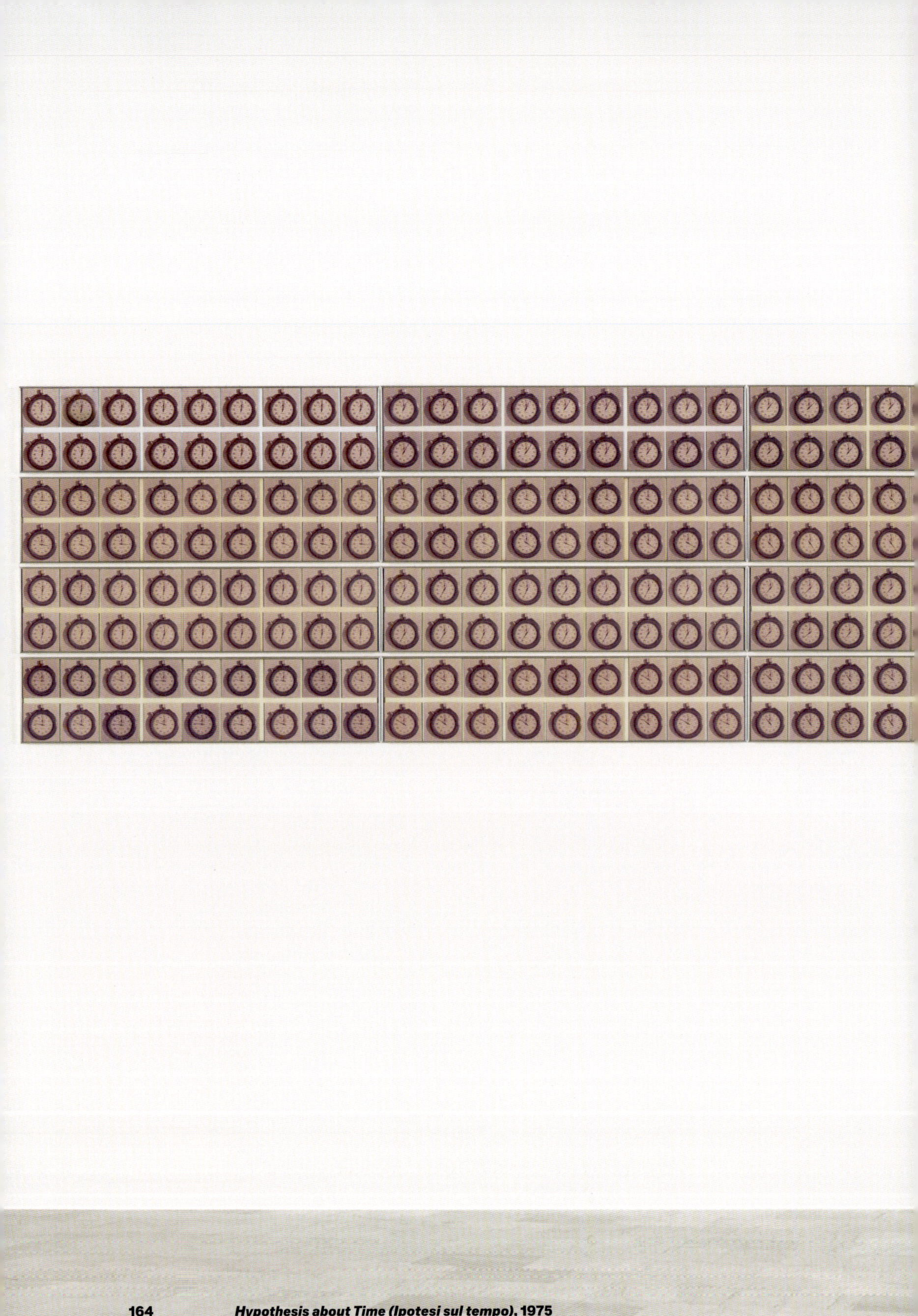

 ***Hypothesis about Time (Ipotesi sul tempo)*, 1975**

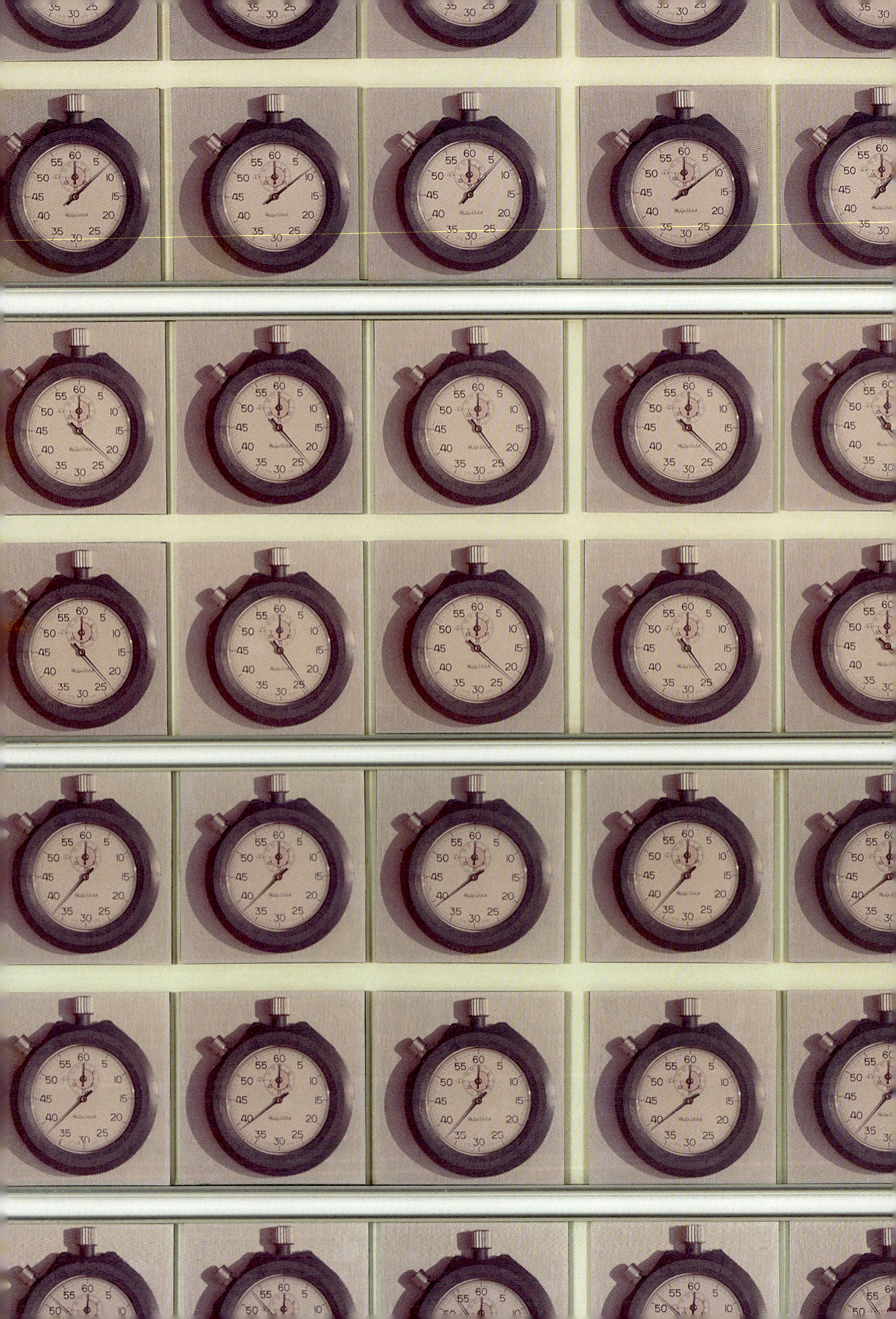

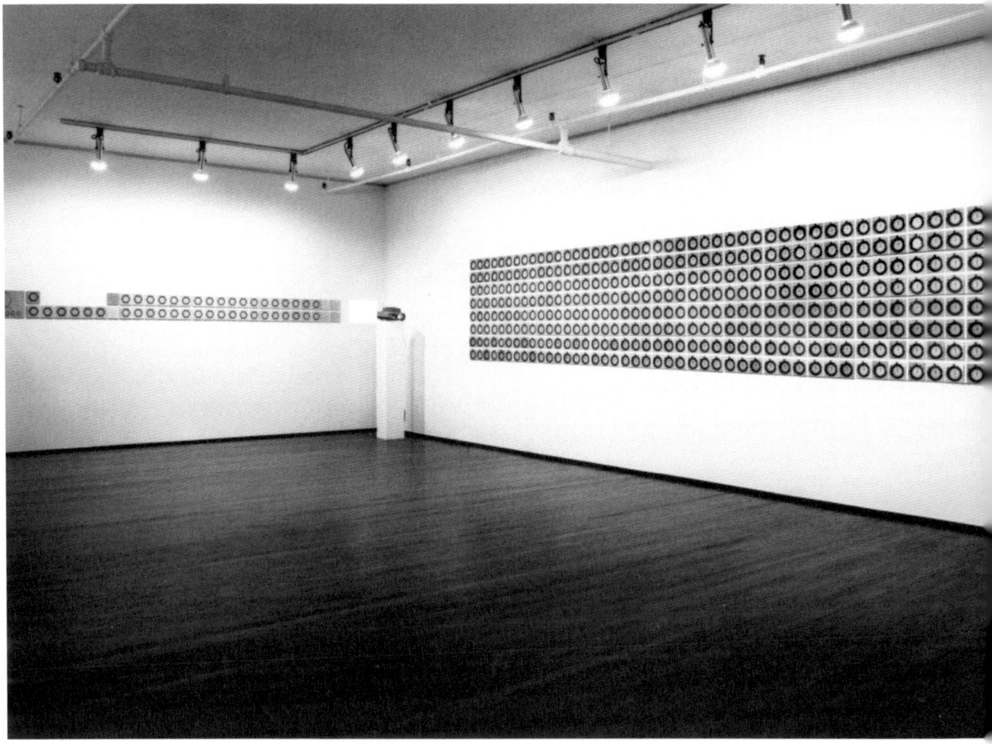

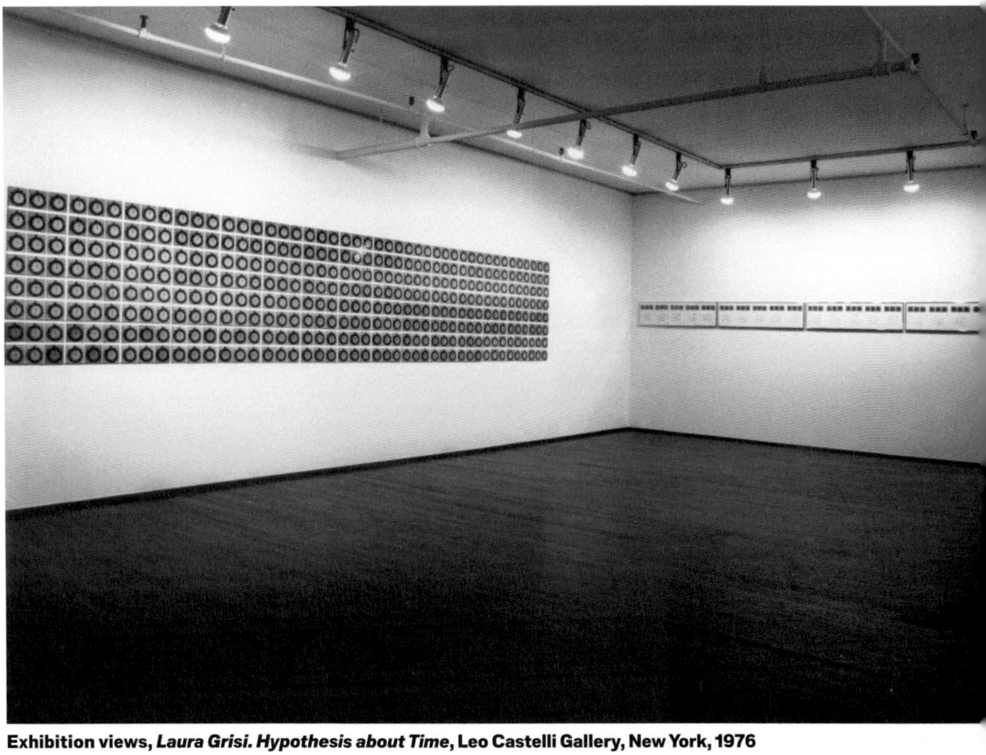

Exhibition views, *Laura Grisi. Hypothesis about Time*, Leo Castelli Gallery, New York, 1976

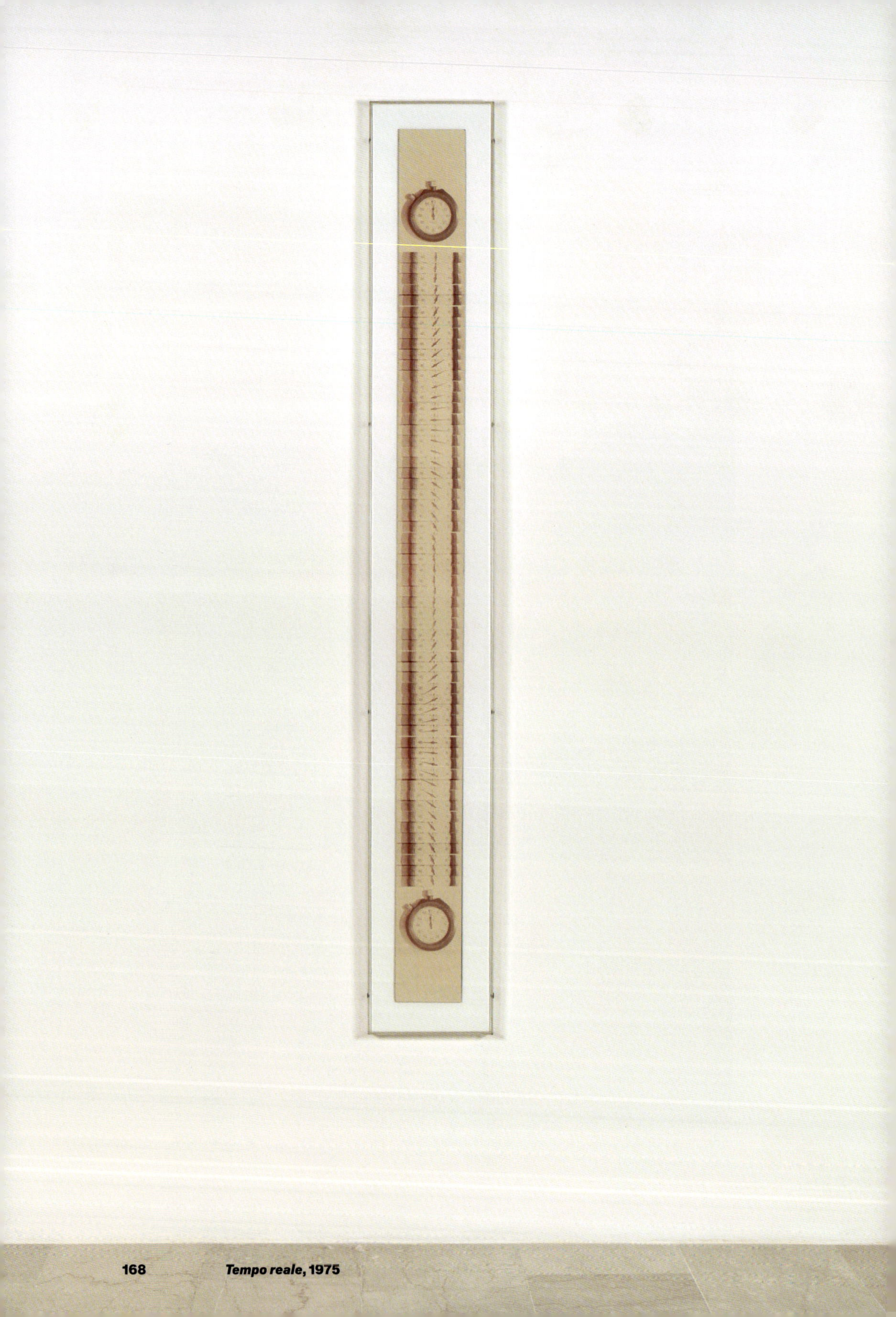

 ***Tempo reale*, 1975**

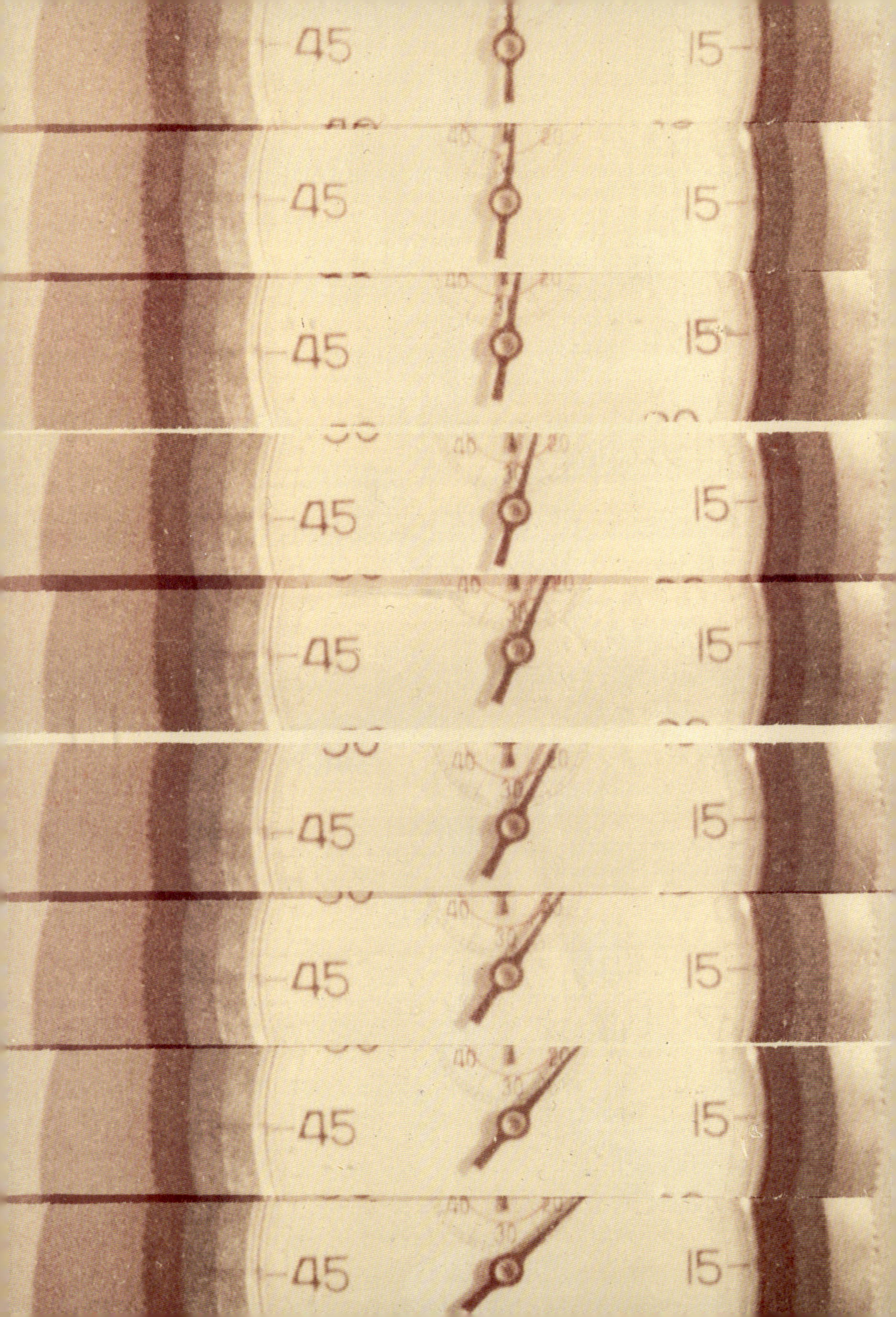

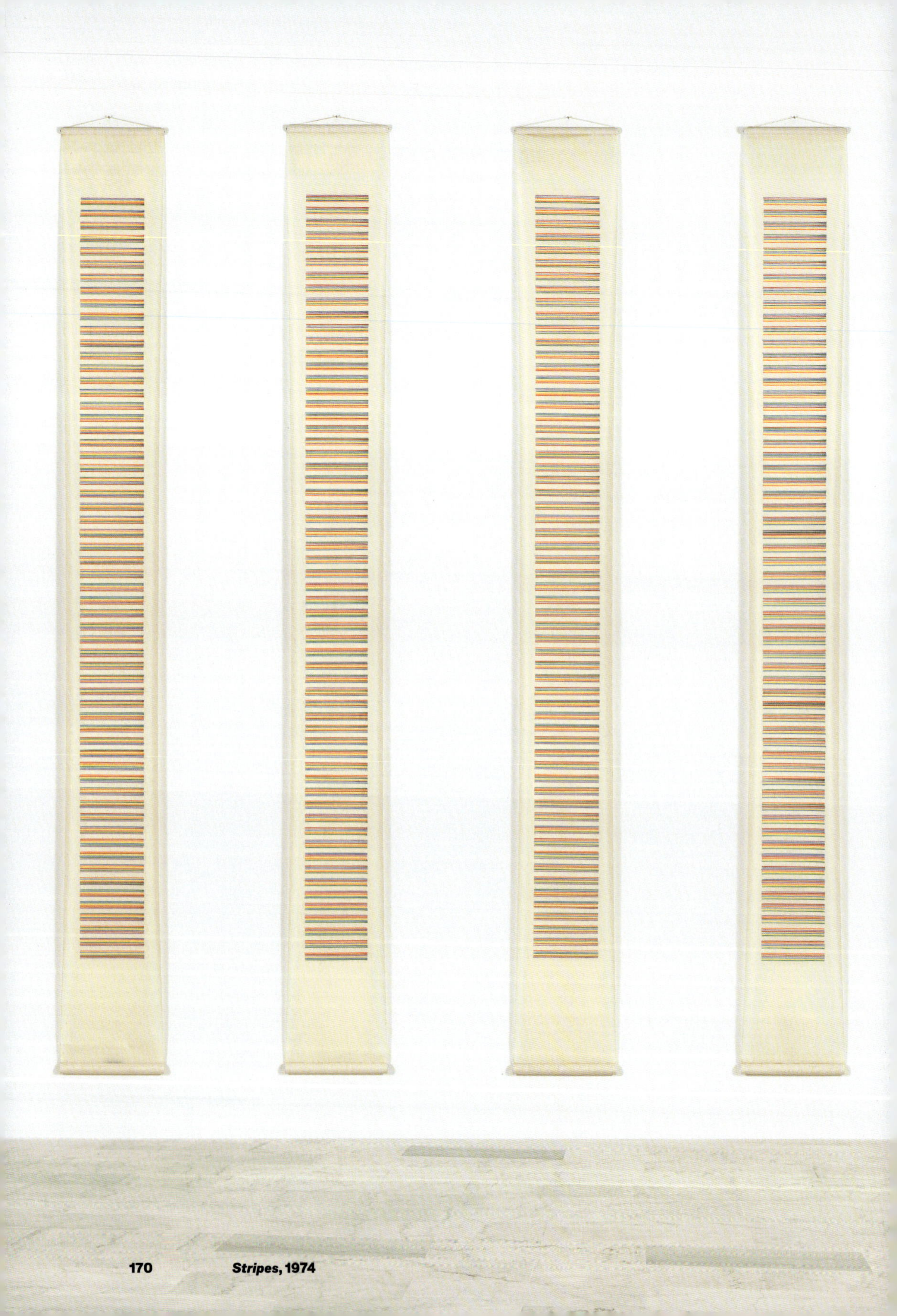

Stripes, 1974

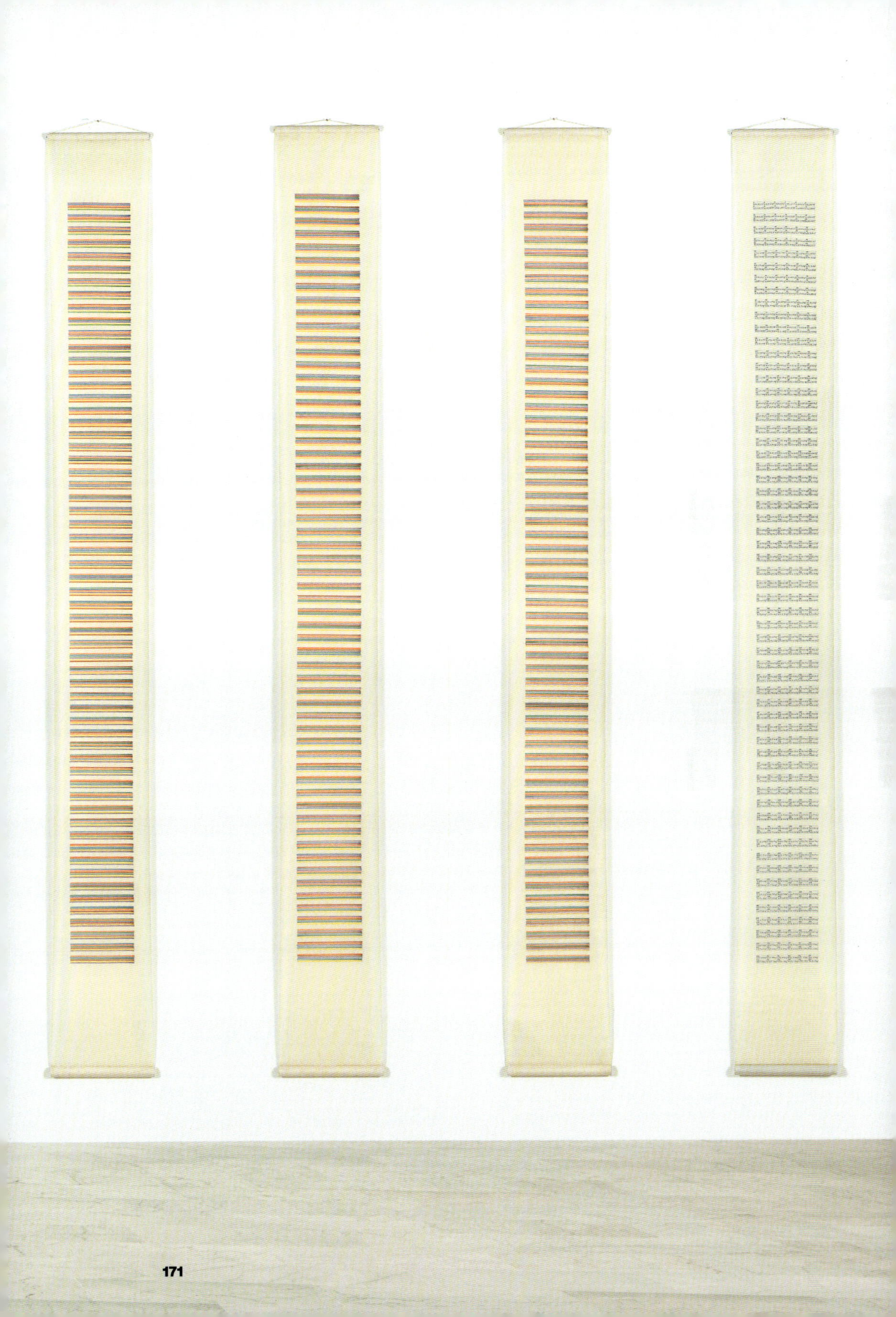

Exhibition views, *Laura Grisi*, Van Abbemuseum, Eindhoven, 1976
With *Stripes*, 1974 (top)

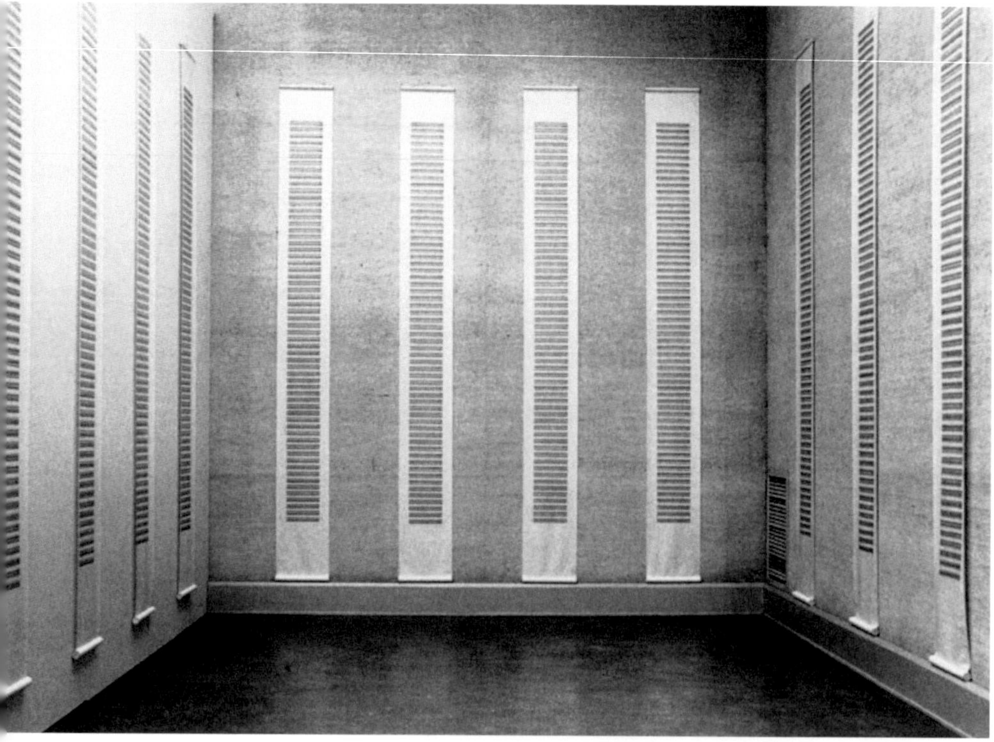

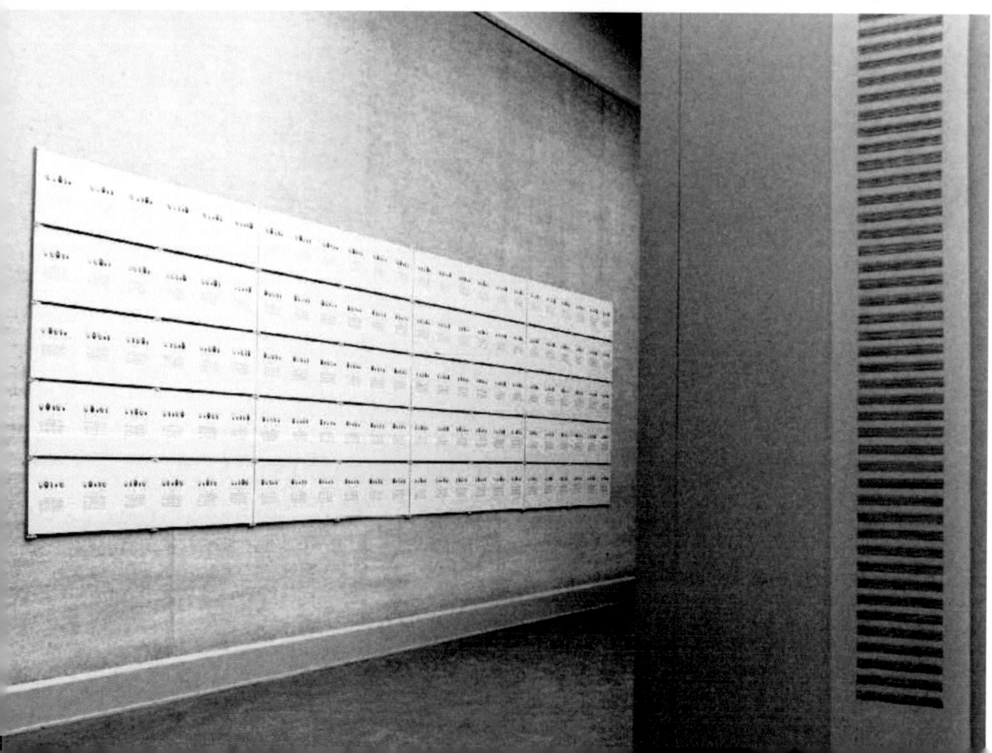

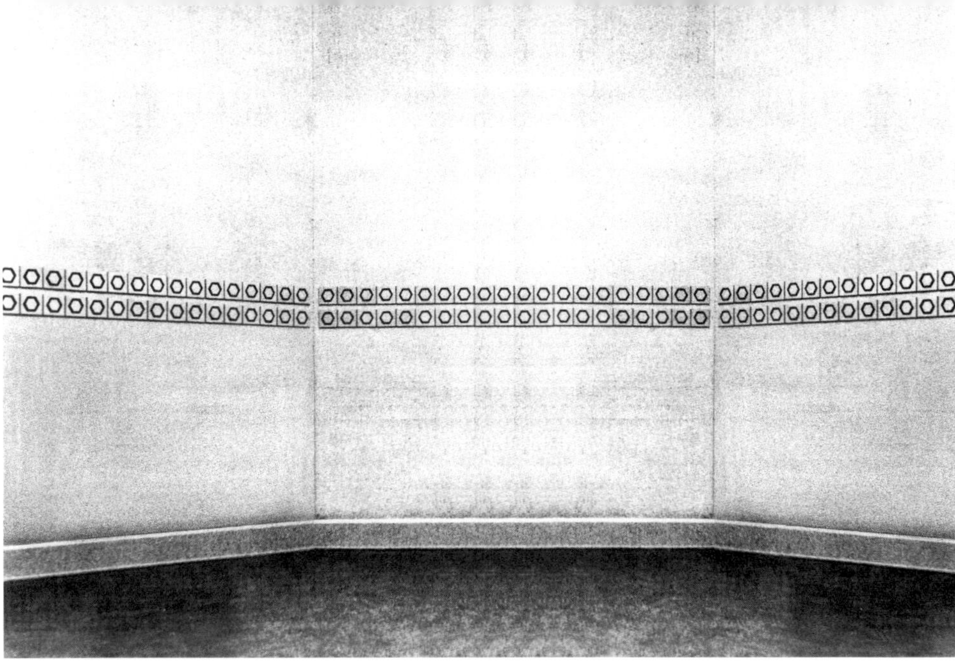

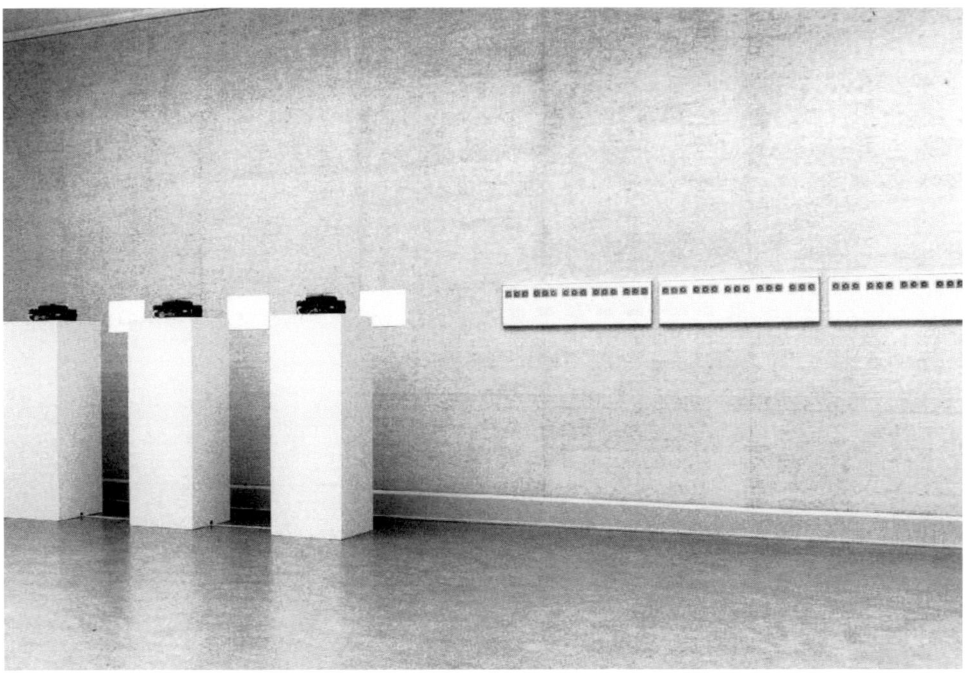

Exhibition views, *Laura Grisi*, Van Abbemuseum, Eindhoven, 1976
With *Hypothesis about Space*, 1975 (top)

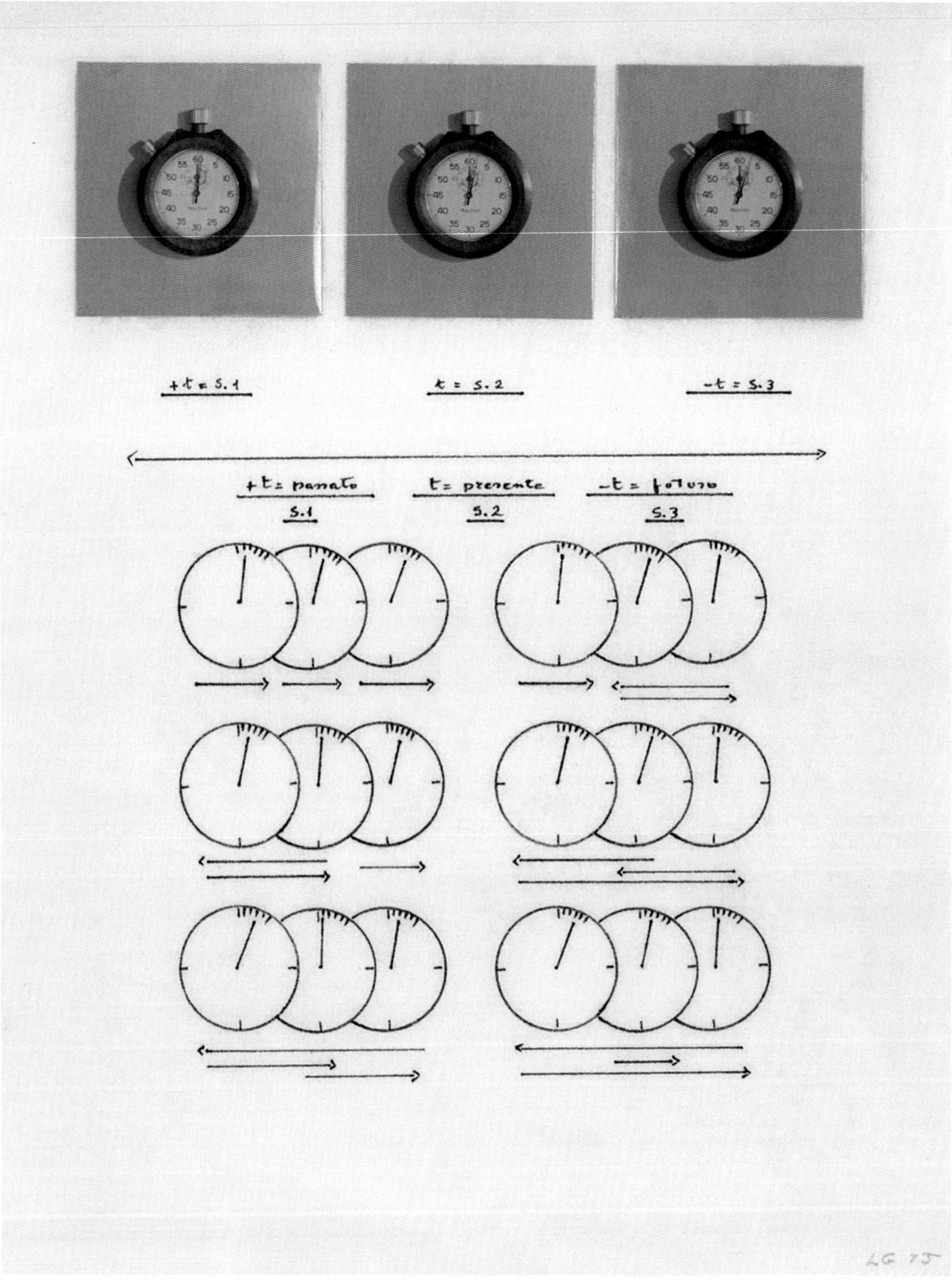

Drawing for Time, 1975 (details)

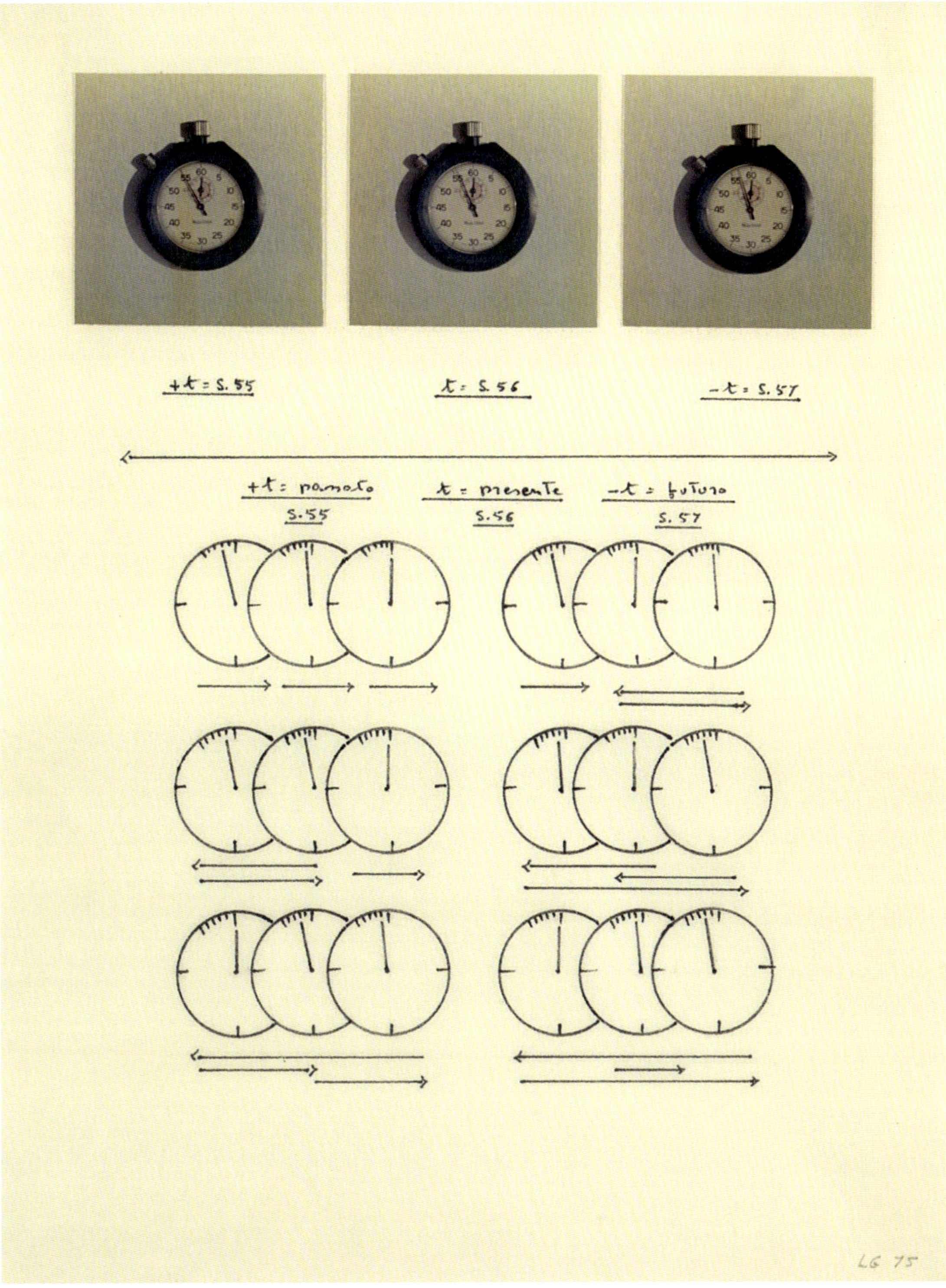
+t = S. 55
t = S. 56
-t = S. 57
+t = passato
S. 55
t = presente
S. 56
-t = futuro
S. 57
LG 75

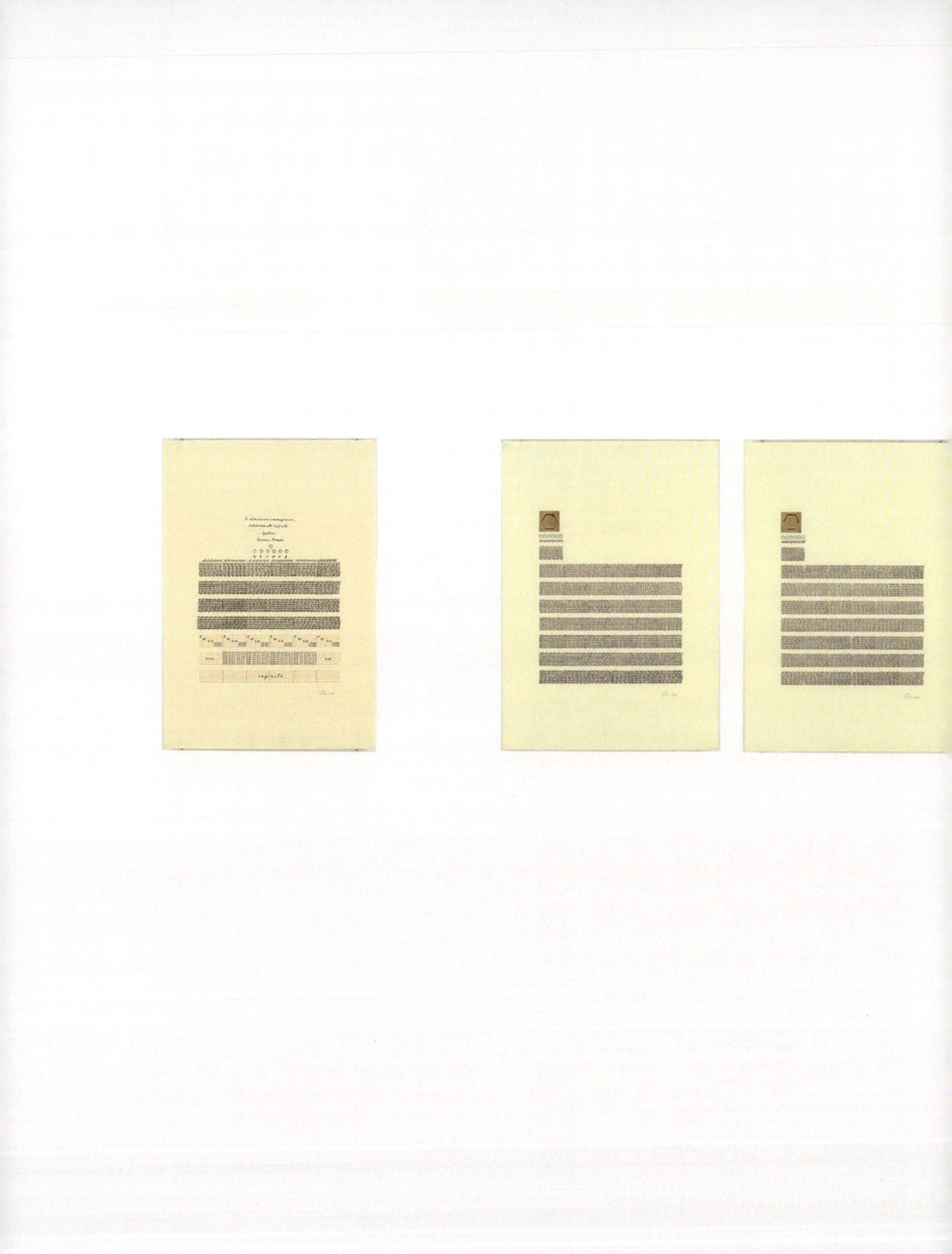

Le dimensioni immaginarie–Rotazione all'infinito/Ipotesi Spazio-Tempo, 1977

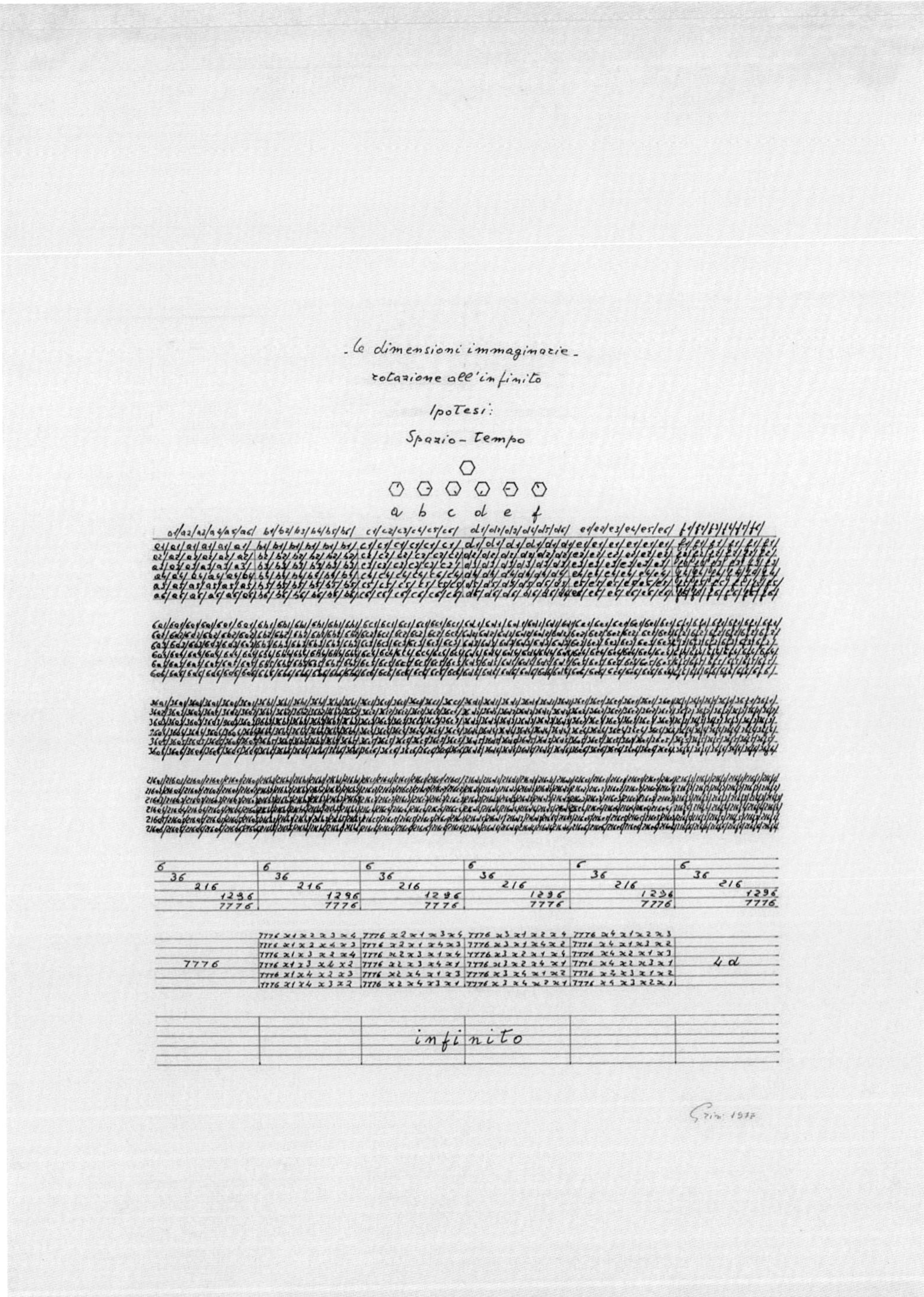

 Le dimensioni immaginarie–Rotazione all'infinito/Ipotesi Spazio-Tempo, 1977 (detail)

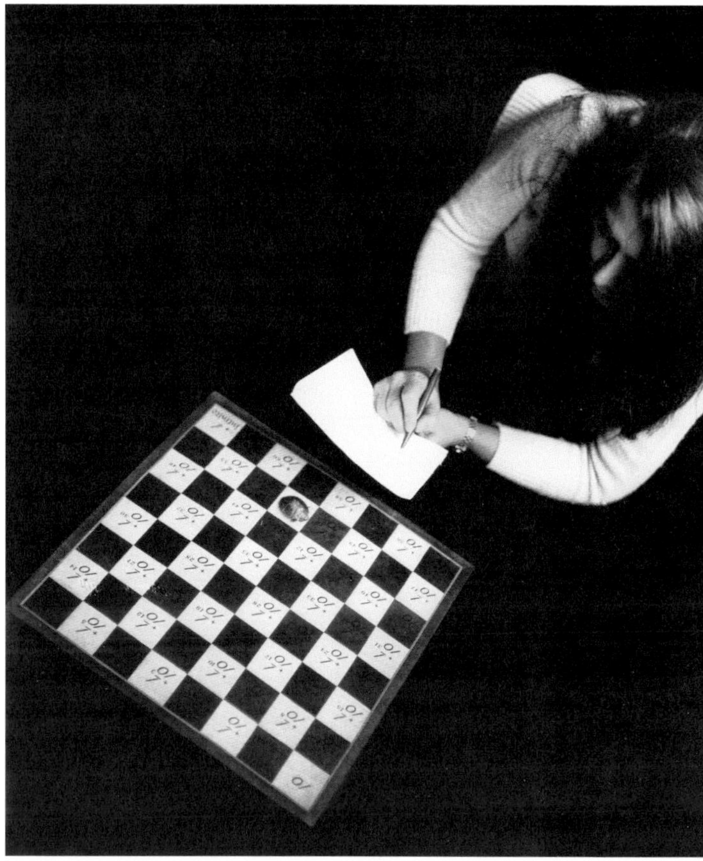

Laura Grisi working on *Endless Dialogue*, 1977

Exhibition view, *Laura Grisi*, Galleria Ugo Ferranti, Rome, 1979
With *Endless Dialogue*, 1977

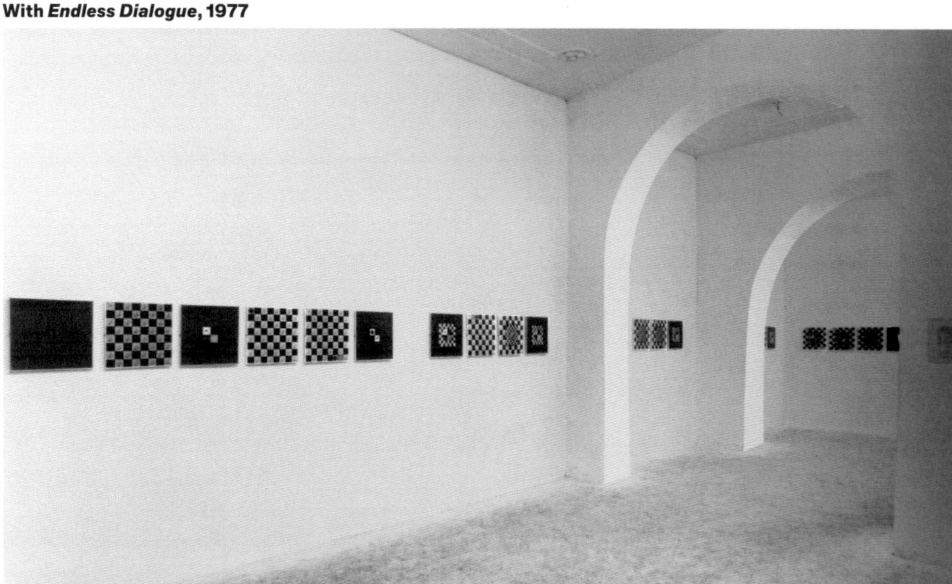

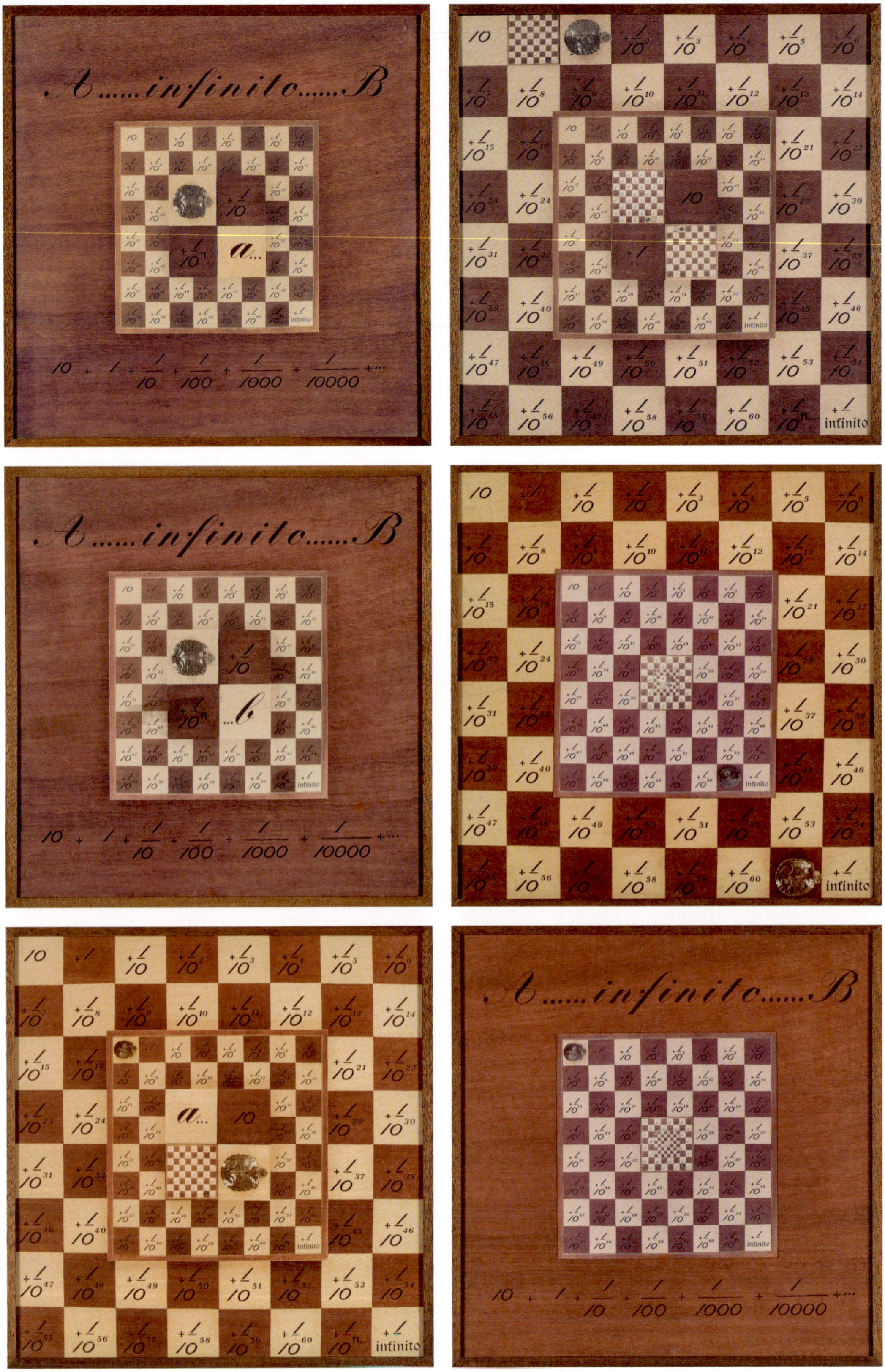

Chessboard, 1977 (details)

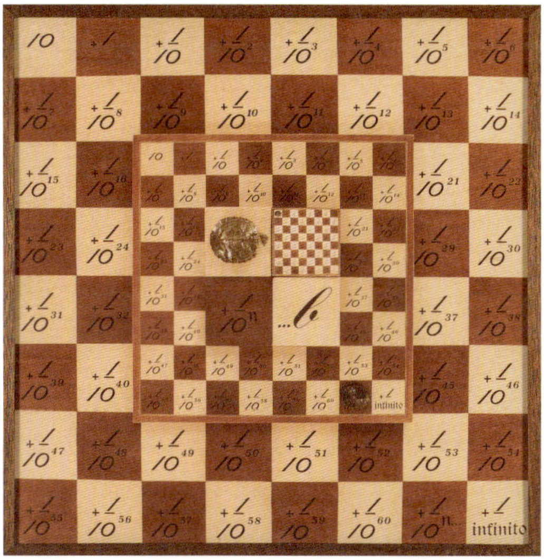
...b
infinito

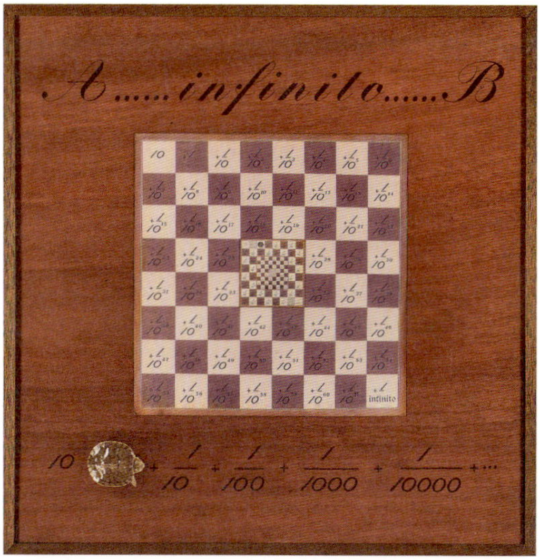
A......infinito......B
10 + 1/10 + 1/100 + 1/1000 + 1/10000 +...

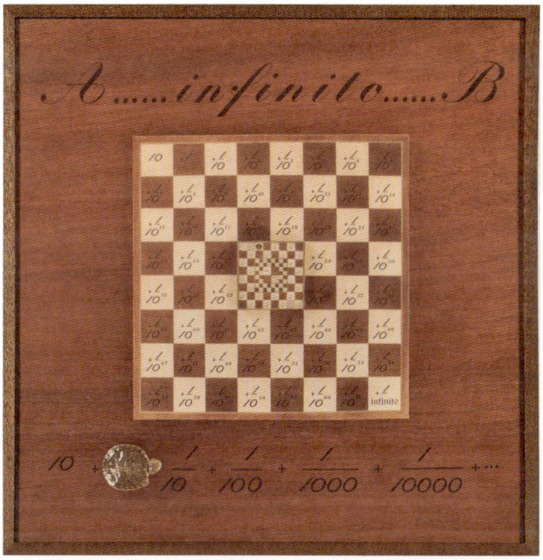
A......infinito......B
10 + 1/10 + 1/100 + 1/1000 + 1/10000 +...

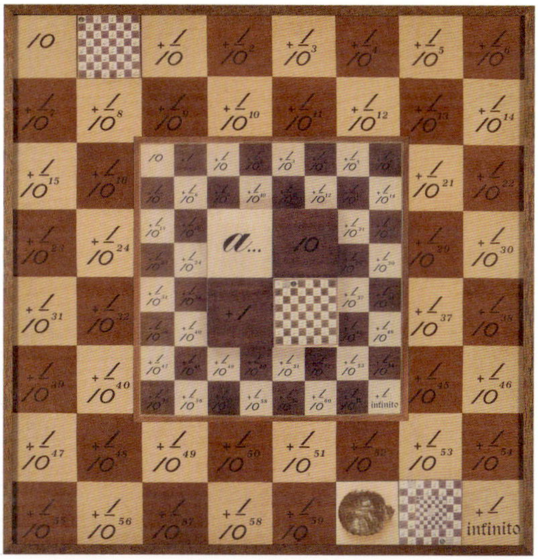
a...
10
+1
infinito

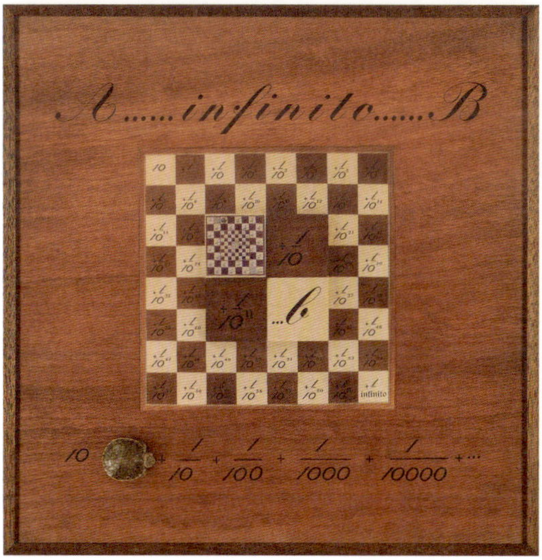
A......infinito......B
...b
10 + 1/10 + 1/100 + 1/1000 + 1/10000 +...

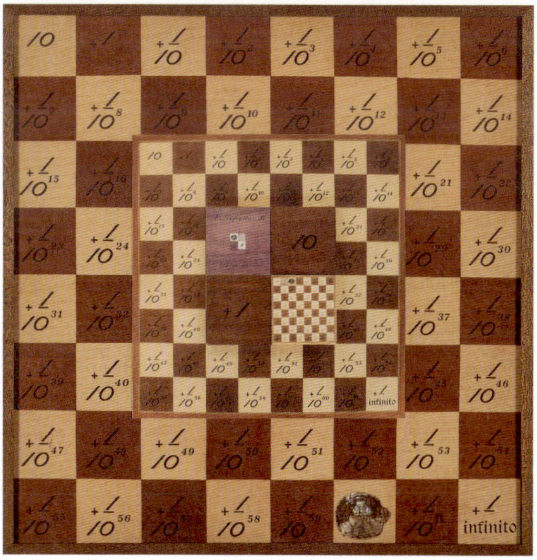
10
+1
infinito

1/10 451
H8/H16/H24/H32/H40/H48/H56/H64/
1/10 n
H8
H16
H24

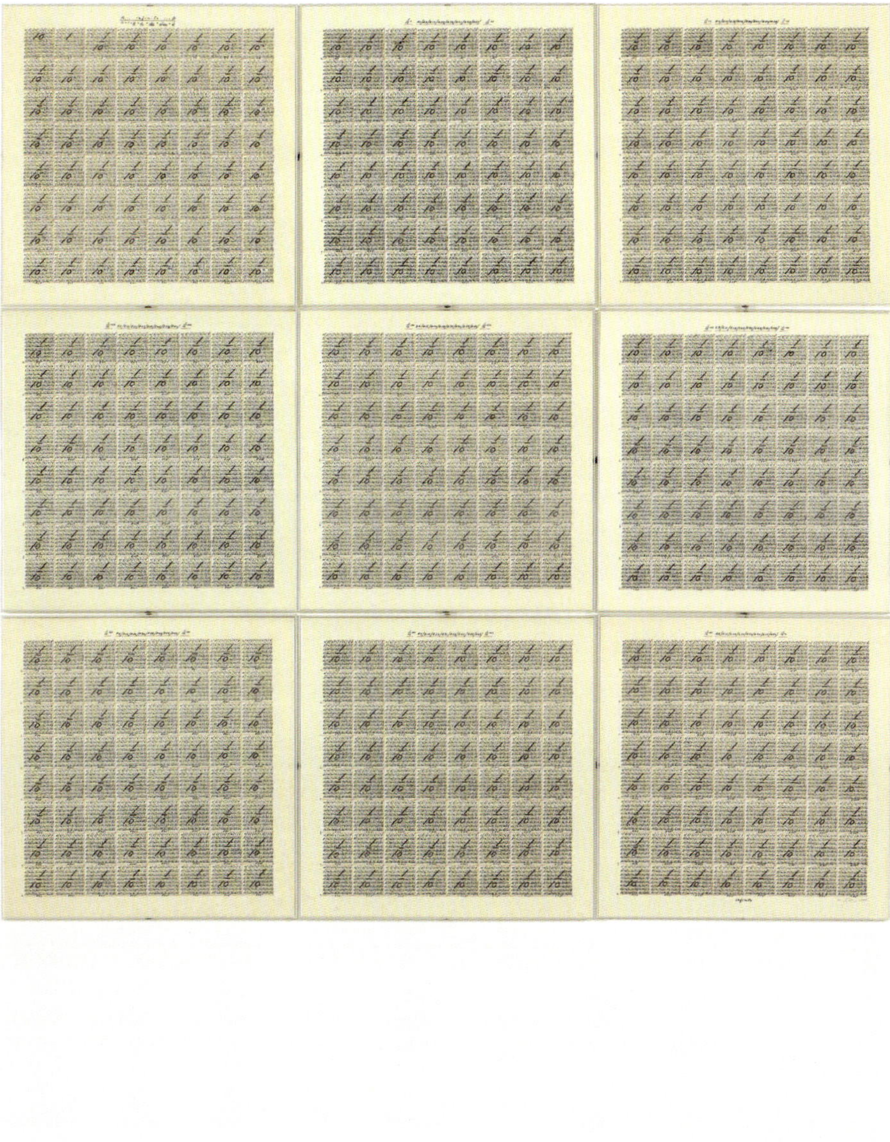

 ***Endless Dialogue–Index I*, 1977**

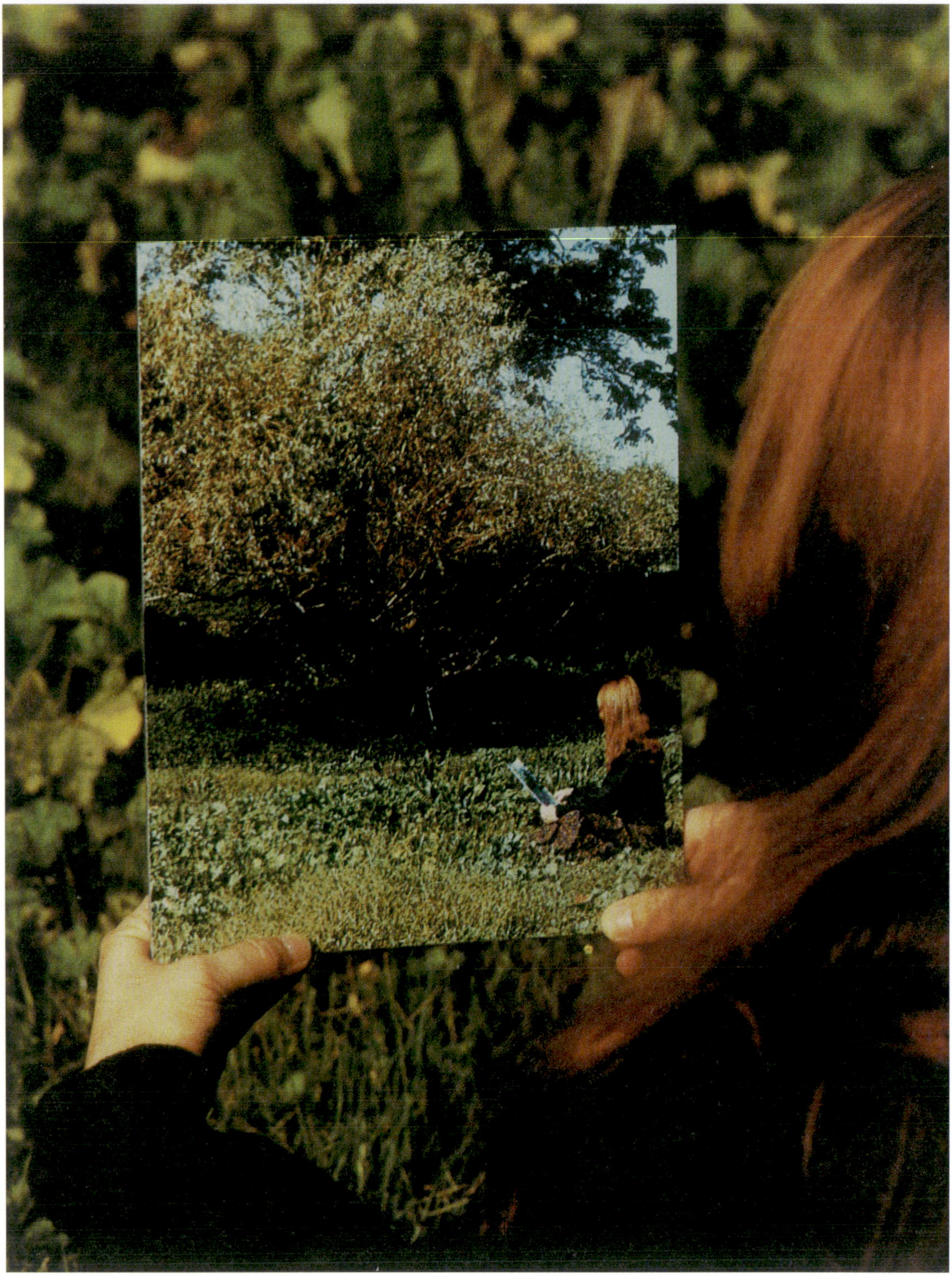

 ***Reflectivity*, 1977 (detail)**

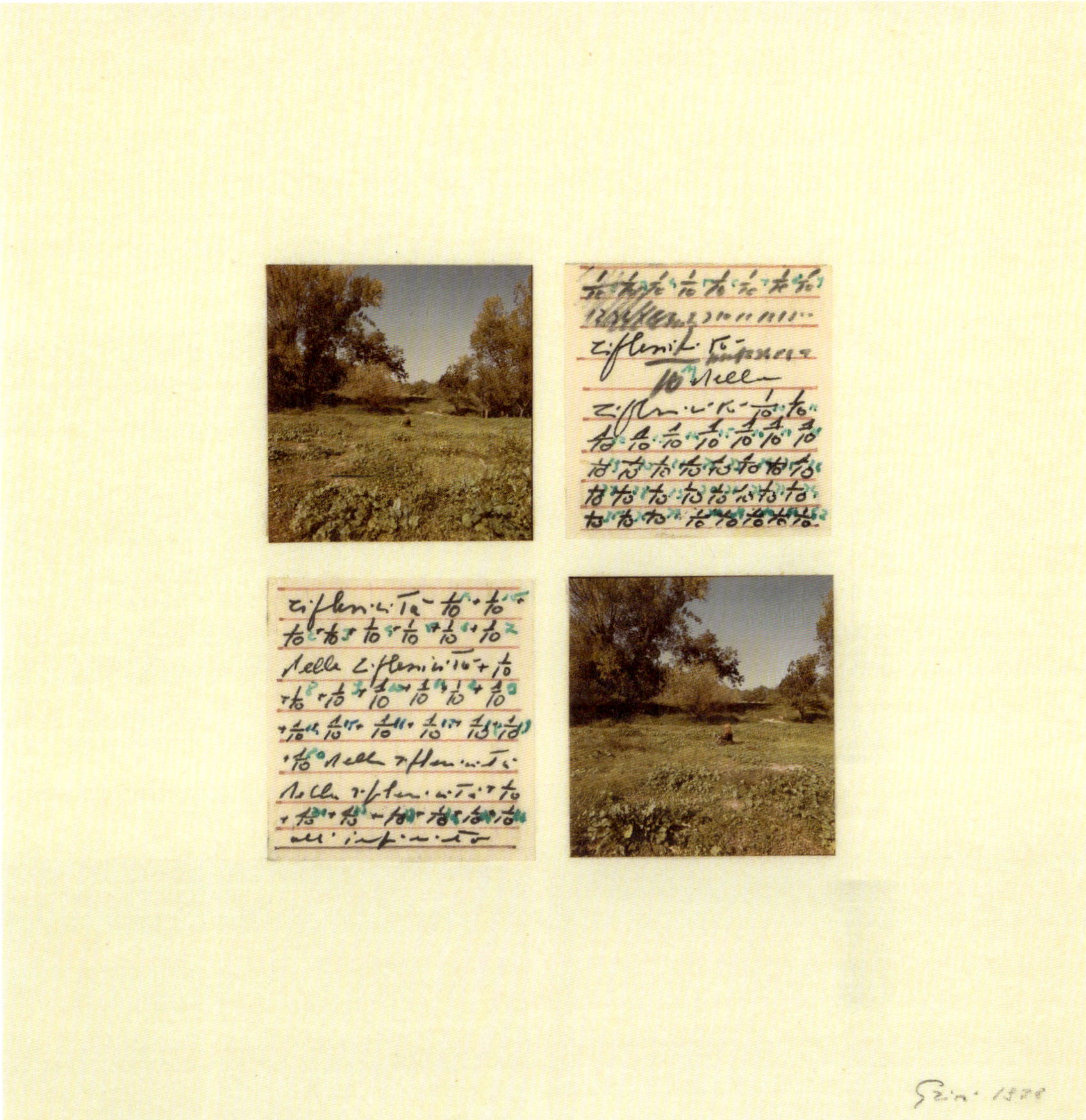

185 ***Riflessività*, 1978**

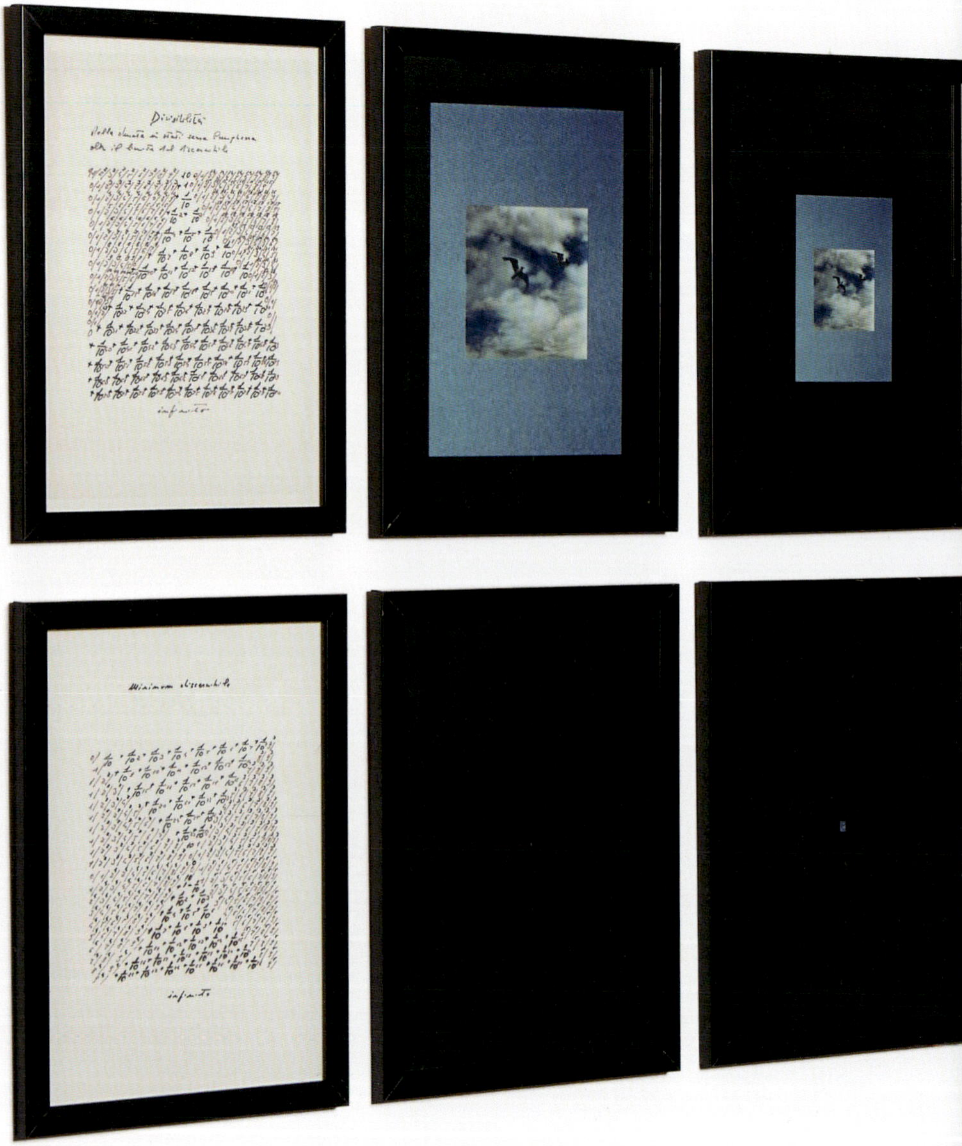

 ***The Minimum Discernible (Double Horizon)*, 1977**

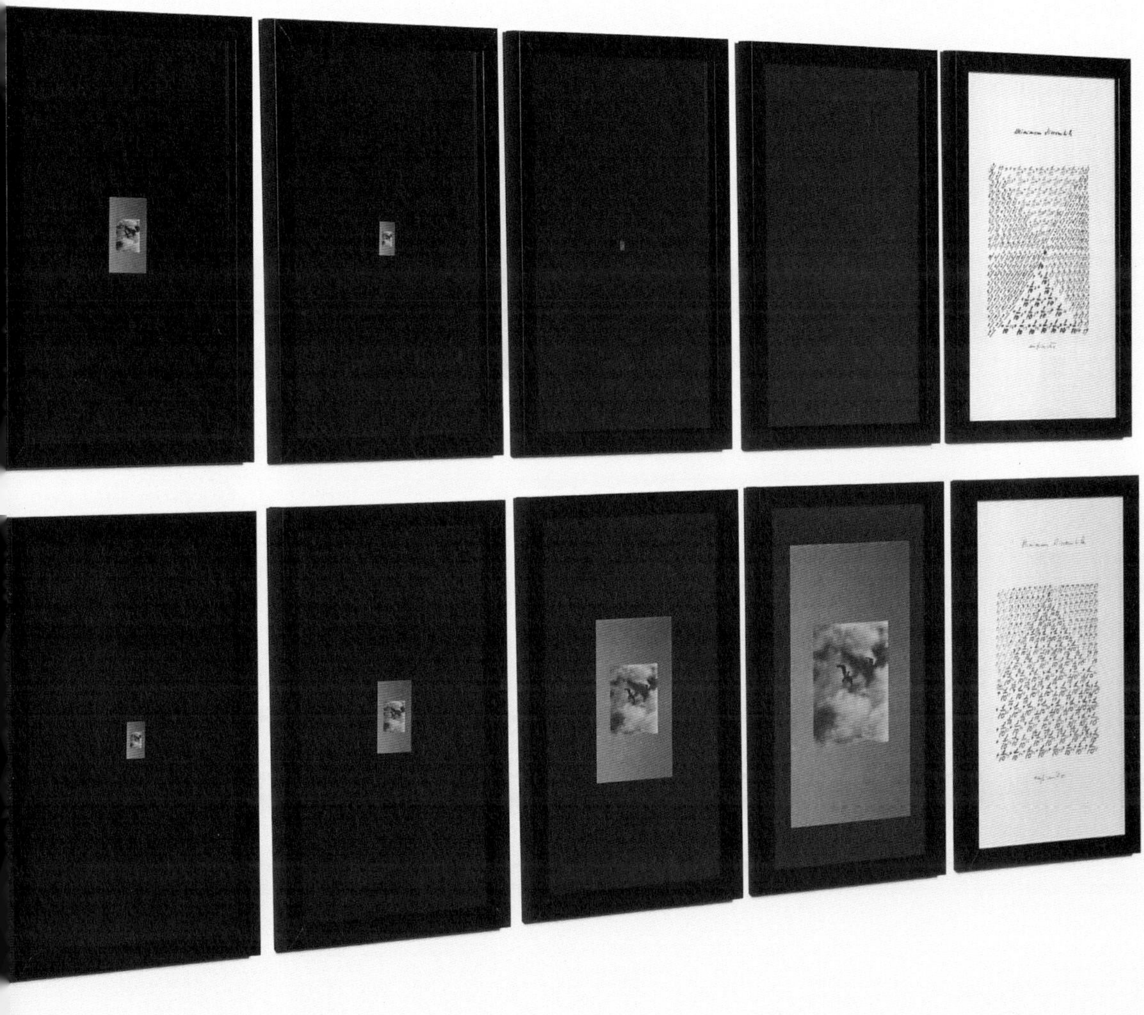

Laura Grisi in Conversation with Germano Celant

Realized in 1989, this conversation with Germano Celant was first published under the title "Essay–Interview by Germano Celant," in *Laura Grisi. A Selection of Works with Notes by the Artist*, trans. Marguerite Shore, Rizzoli, New York 1990, p. 10–42. It has been slightly edited for this publication. We warmly thank Germano Celant's estate for their authorization to reproduce it.

Germano Celant The artist is a person who works both from their own inner depths and as a part of a social and cultural humus. At first artists develop by following their own egos; at first, they have to convince themselves of the need for exterior, public affirmation. Their awareness of this conflict between interior and exterior leads them to interweave periods of personal consciousness and periods of contextual influence in the different phases of their work. The problem of identity begins to make itself felt in the fact that their existence as artists gives rise to works of art, to goods, in which it is possible to recognize a symbolic power or a communicative trace that differs from the content of other goods in the marketplace, for it goes back to an authentic feeling. This feeling can take on the force of an unusual event or of a different experience, small or large, it doesn't matter. Thus the artistic personality arises out of a deep uneasiness, for it is tied both to interior processes and to, for example, personal relationships established with other intellectuals, or to the reading of their work. These are the first mechanisms to transform a person into an artist. Can you tell me about your beginnings as an artist, about the cultural soil out of which you grew?

Laura Grisi I began working in a continuous way between 1964 and 1965. Before that, during what I suppose you would call my formative years, I read a lot, and tried to condense abstract sensations into images. It was at that time that I went to art school in Rome, and also studied drawing, at the Accademia, and etching and engraving in a private studio on the via Babuino. My friend Domenico Gnoli (1933–1970) had introduced me to the studio, where he too was making etchings. We often visited museums together, or went to the Palatine to see the frescoes in the house of the Empress Giulia. Or we looked for unknown ancient fountains or Baroque carved doorways in the old town. When Gnoli went to New York, he wrote me a letter about his impressions while the boat was coming into New York Harbor: when I opened the letter, a blue butterfly sprang out and flew up into the room. It eventually fell to the ground and I realized that it was made of paper with a small rubber band attached, which had remained compressed in the sealed envelope, but suddenly unwound when I opened the letter, making the butterfly seem to fly.

During that period, I often went to buy books from a bookseller near the Trevi Fountain. He specialized in things that you couldn't find in other bookstores—out-of-print editions and antique books. I found Guillaume Apollinaire's *Les Peintres cubistes* (1913) there, and some very small leather-bound volumes printed in the 19th century, works by Virgil and Plato, as well as *Vita Nova* (1294) by Dante. This last volume is now in one of my pieces, the wall sculpture *Apollinaire's Secret* (1985). Resting on a plaster shell, it can be taken out and read, while an identical book, cast in bronze, remains on the shelf. At the same bookseller I also found another rare book, *La Femme 100 têtes* (1929) by Max Ernst, with his engravings telling the story of LopLop and other characters. That book was later stolen.

GC They say that the artist lives in a world of things and images, a forest of signs that are revealed to the glance and thus become known and evident. Yet the corporeality of these sensations grows out of primary realizations almost from adolescence, when one moves about blindly, looking for the path that will become one's life's voyage. At first, the things one sees emerge from one's familiar surroundings. Later on, one ventures on more personal wanderings, searching out buried and hidden moments. In your work I sense that an entire system of images is sanctioned by a constant movement, to the point where your early works, dated 1965–1966 are "variable," that is, they move and slide before the eye of the observer, creating superimpositions and intersections of images and sensations. In addition, many of the figures that enter your iconography reveal what seems like the exotic, sometimes oriental qualities and simple truths of primitive myths. They are often aggregates of a fine dusting of color that forms a desert-like powder that contains the memory of voyages and events from both childhood and maturity. Can you talk about the planets of images in which you have moved?

LG I want to describe the cultural and family context of my childhood. What my father liked best was reading and doing research in physics, mathematics, and geometry. He also studied and carried out experiments with radio and with magnetic fields. This wasn't his real work, but it was what interested him most. Two of his projects—one for the remote control of objects by radio, another dealing with the electrical energy produced through an exchange of magnetics waves—were analyzed by a group of American technicians. They found his work so interesting that they invited him to work with them at the Massachusetts Institute of Technology in Cambridge, but he preferred to continue his experiments on his own. I used to talk to him about geometry, logic, gravity, relativity, and everything else I wanted to know about in these fields, and he gave me books by Bertrand Russell, Albert Einstein, Henri Bergson, and others.

My father had a film production and distribution company. One of his films won first prize at the Venice Film Festival. He was also very interested in automobiles; he bought one of the first Cisitalias, a beautifully designed car, famous in the 1950s, and now exhibited at The Museum of Modern Art in New York. His work brought him into contact with many directors and writers: he knew Alessandro Blasetti, Roberto Rossellini, Augusto Genina (with whom he made two films), Léonide Moguy, Vitaliano Brancati, and Giuseppe Berto. This was the climate and the context in which my brother Fausto and I grew up; he too is involved with film—he has made three, and now has a film and advertising company in Venezuela. In fact, I seem to be the only one in my family who is not a professional filmmaker. As it turned out, my son Brando started his own film production company right after high school, writing and directing his own series of films for television.

My mother was Italian, but was born in Istanbul. She spoke six languages well, and almost always spoke French to us at home. She used to paint watercolors, using images of the Turkish landscape, views of Istanbul, and colorful street scenes. She played the piano very well, especially music by Liszt and Mozart, and she also used to sing classical songs. She had a wonderful voice. She often told us about her childhood in Turkey; her father, my grandfather, had owned construction companies and had built, among other things, a harbor on the Bosporus and roads in Anatolia. When he visited projects in the Turkish interior, my grandmother always wanted to go with him; she loved travel and adventure. They went on horseback, followed by an escort, because the countryside was dangerous, wild and full of gangs and thieves. Then my mother would describe the old city, the souks and mosques, and she would tell me about the Turkish women who at the time never went out into the streets, but had arcades from one house to another, so they could move about without being seen from the outside. Then there was a great rebellion, and foreigners had to leave the country; my grandparents' villa was burned down, and they managed to flee to Rhodes, in Greece (where I was later born). My mother gave me records and books of French poetry—Charles Baudelaire, Arthur Rimbaud, Paul Verlaine, Paul Éluard, Paul Valéry.

GC Among the maps and the itineraries covered, there is one's own city, and the whole world of education and school. Then the places one visits become a form of knowledge; one's encounters with people from foreign countries and cultures come to seem sometimes curious, sometimes different, and what is different offers a crucial perspective on one's familiar environment. To what artistic realities do you owe your formation?

LG I attended the art school in Rome and then took classes on and off at the École des Beaux-Arts in Paris. We were in Paris because my father was producing a film with French partners. When my family returned to Rome, I stayed on in Paris for the entire season, and the people I met and the books I read there were far more important to me than my academic studies. I got to know students and writers and poets at the Galerie du Dragon and at Matta's house in Saint-Germain-des-Prés; I met [art critic] Alain Jouffroy and Jean-Jacques Lebel, a writer and poet who had known André Breton and Tristan Tzara. I had just finished reading Breton's *Nadja* (1928) and the writings of Antonin Artaud. Lebel and I often talked about Surrealist art and literature; I wanted to know more about the "poem objects" and the Exquisite Corpse games, and he knew many anecdotes and interesting stories about that period. One day we went to the Reine Blanche, the café where Breton used to meet with this group in the days of Surrealism. But the Surrealist world was of only relative interest to me. The primitive art that I saw at Lebel's house (his father, Robert Lebel, had a beautiful collection) also seemed interesting, but so distant to me. Later, traveling in Africa and Polynesia, I felt a real love for primitive and ritual objects, and I too began to collect them.

GC To lose oneself in one's early experiences is a fantastic thing: through memory, one can see how certain events and moments have had important formative consequences. The effects of such moments cannot be diminished; they force one to reinterpret what one already knows about oneself. Now it seems to me that your work, from the beginning, has presented a certain "theatricality," connected to its often large scale and to its awareness of the fictious illusion of the spectacle. Even if you have been on real voyages throughout the world, the places discovered by your works are more like expeditions into the artificial, into fiction, as if into the industrial culture of reproduction and repetition. They pertain to territories unknown to the human eye, but tied rather to the technological and mediated glance. Where does this fascination with fiction and with the labyrinth of artificial images come from?

LG A lot of it comes from my reading and from my early experiences with art and with the theater. My favorite artist when I was growing up was Jackson Pollock; though I had seen only one painting in the flesh, I knew his work well in reproduction. I also liked Wols, and especially Constantin Brâncuși. I was interested in photography, and took a lot of photographs that I developed and printed myself. I read a lot—I particularly remember Jean-Paul Sartre, André Gide, Goethe, Voltaire, Marcel Proust, the Comte de Lautréamont, and Thomas Mann—and I liked plays, because of the structure of the dialogue. I'm thinking of Miguel de Unamuno, Samuel Beckett, Alfred Jarry, and Bertolt Brecht. Then, in Paris, I got to know two Russian set and costume designers, the Dobuzhinskys, a couple who had been in the theater world forever. They had an atelier near Montmartre where ten people worked, all Russians, and at the time they were making sets and costumes for Jean-Baptiste Lully's *Armide*. They were making plaster casts from which they could model large masks to be part of the costumes. I immediately offered to help, and I worked with them for three months, during which time I learned a great deal about Russian culture, from music to theater, from poetry to painting, from Konstantin Stanislavski to Sergei Eisenstein, from Sergei Prokofiev to El Lissitzky and Vladimir Mayakovsky. It all seemed to come alive, because when they were young, they had worked with Stanislavski, they had known Mayakovsky, and their stories were fascinating. I wasn't even 18 yet, and it all seemed so extraordinary to me. We went together to the movies to see Eisenstein's films—*The Battleship Potemkin* and *Que Viva Mexico* (1925 and 1931). I also remember Jacques Feyder's *La Kermesse héroique* (1935).

One thing that was very important for me at the Dobuzhinskys' was the immediate contact with pictorial techniques and with materials. In their atelier everyone was always "inventing" materials to make objects that, on the set, had to seem completely real, but that were really composed of so-called "fake" stuff. We had to manipulate the "fiction" of the stage, for example, by using a plastic that would seem transparent and light under the theater lights, or a tulle or silk, maybe chosen only for its color, that could be rigidified with a special glue that they knew how to prepare, and that then would seem like a polished metal surface. All this was useful to me later. My "Neon Paintings" (1966–1967), for example, were made out of many different materials, from metal and wood to fabric and rubber; and the neon lights created the appearance of a depth that was actually nonexistent, because they were seen through the refraction of a Plexiglas veil, transparent but ribbed, which I twisted on the diagonal.

GC Your early interest in art dates from the beginning of the 1960s, when the climate in Rome and Milan favored finding a way out of *art informel* and American Action painting. I remember the artistic scene in Rome around the Piazza di Spagna and the atmosphere defined by Galleria La Tartaruga, which showed the work of Franz Kline, Mark Rothko, and Cy Twombly, as well as young artists like Jannis Kounellis, Mario Schifano, Franco Angeli, and Tano Festa very well. There was a clear focus on popular icons, and on the theme of the city as a system of sign structures. But I must point out that while Schifano and Kounellis integrated objective data in the form of street signs or advertising directly into their work, your discourse turned more in the direction of a self-reflexive image, as if the subjective had to prevail over the industrial objecthood. In fact, your "Variable Paintings" (1965–1966) include your profile, or I should say your shadow, interlaced in an almost metaphysical manner with details that would have been appreciated by Giorgio de Chirico, like the square rule, the arc, the target, and the circle. But what was the artistic situation in which you found yourself when you began your visual journey?

LG When I got back to Rome from Paris, I began to frequent galleries like La Tartaruga, Marlborough Gallery, and L'Attico, and I met many artists there. I also went to Milan, where I knew Piero Manzoni, Vincenzo Agnetti, Gastone Novelli, and Lucio Fontana. I had painted two small works in enamel on canvas, and Fontana looked at them and bought them. He often bought work from young artists. When I had my first show in Milan, in 1965, he came to see it. I visited his studio and he gave me a gouache, an oval with holes.

In Rome, at La Tartaruga, I saw a show of Twombly's work that impressed me. Marlborough was showing the work of Toti Scialoja, Achille Perilli, Piero Dorazio, Carla Accardi, Giulio Turcato, and the sculptor Nino Franchina. I knew these artists well, and saw them often at the Herlitzkas' house, or at Rosati's in the Piazza del Popolo. Franchina's wife, Gina, was also there often; she was Gino Severini's daughter. All this went on, however, for only a short period, because I stayed in Rome just a few months. During that period, I met Folco Quilici, the film director and writer who had made *The Sixth Continent* (1954) and *The Last Paradise* (1956); just a month later we got married and left for South America, where he was shooting a film in the Andes. From that time on I traveled for long periods with him, which was an extraordinary experience. Because of the type of films he made, we were always looking for places where tribal cultures still existed, to document the last traces of cultures, practices, customs, and rituals that were disappearing.

This is how I came into contact with so many peoples and cultures that were distant from my own cultural context, an experience that strongly influenced my way of thinking and of visualizing life. During those years I read Claude Lévi-Strauss, James Joyce, Robert Musil, Dylan Thomas, and Pier Paolo Pasolini. I discovered Jorge Luis Borges while I was living for some months in Buenos Aires and he impressed me deeply. While I was traveling, I could only make easily portable pieces like gouaches and drawings, and so I concentrated on photography and writing. I published a photographic book, *Pasos por Buenos Aires* (1959), and during a year when we were in Polynesia I wrote another book, *I Denti del Tigre* (1964), set on the atolls of Tuamotu.

After a year I had spent traveling between the Andes, the pampas, Bolivia, Terra di Missiones, and Buenos Aires, my son, Brando Quilici, was born in Buenos Aires. We spent another year in Polynesia, and many months in Africa, and then returned to Rome, where I started my first paintings.

GC I'm interested in what you knew about art outside Italy. Alongside the system of galleries and museums, there is the circulation of books and art magazines. There weren't many of these in Italy at the time, however, and all the information about what was going on internationally was carried in only a few publications.

LG I remember contemporary art magazines like *Art International*, *Domus*, *Le Arti, Marcatre*, and *Collage*. American publications such as *Artforum*, *ARTnews*, and *Art in America* were available only by subscription. The galleries used to make catalogues for every show, with an essay by a critic, and other catalogues were published by the Galleria d'Arte Moderna, which was directed by Palma Bucarelli.

GC To continue with my interpretation of the dimension of movement, it seems clear to me that your work with variability, in framing devices, and in the mobility demanded of the observer, is tied to cinema. Your first paintings progress from perception to action: to "read" the work involves moving sliding panels, almost like movie frames inserted one upon the other, to define a new image emerging from the "montage." Your panels thus establish a communication among variable wholes that refer to each other. They imply a slice of space and of image that changes its particular meaning when one panel is superimposed upon or flanked by another. The presence of the human figure is also a memory of movements of characters, almost like the fixed stage of Chinese shadow theater, which, as we know, is a matrix for cinematography. But let's go back to the places and the artistic readings of the time.

LG During that period we were also friends with many of the Italian film directors and with writers such as Italo Calvino, who had written the story for the film shot in Polynesia, *Tikoyo and the Shark* (1962), which told the tale of a friendship between a shark and a Polynesian child. The film was produced by Titanus, which at the time was producing the most interesting films by Federico Fellini, Michelangelo Antonioni, Francesco Maselli, Luchino Visconti, Francesco Rosi, Valerio Zurlini, and Gillo Pontecorvo. It was the era of the films of Antonioni and Monica Vitti, and of the books of Alain Robbe-Grillet; this was when *Last Year at Marienbad* (1961) was made, when François Truffaut, Jean-Luc Godard, Alain Resnais, and the other members of the Nouvelle Vague were working. These filmmakers often seemed to be addressing difficulties and problems in communication, and their mood influenced the way in which we were beginning to visualize reality in a different dimension, detached and cool. At the Venice film festival, a journalist asked René Clair about the euphoria and general enthusiasm for the Nouvelle Vague, and he answered only, "Chaque vague, c'est une nouvelle vague."

GC Your attention to the Nouvelle Vague leads me to talk about visual perception, of the phenomenology that is the source of much 1960s cinema. This was based on an antinaturalism of the glance, which turned itself over to the glass eye of the movie camera. What mattered was the registration of things and appearances, slowly canceling out the human presence. There was an attempt to avoid all psychological interpretation and every visceral dimension, to turn oneself over to a gnoseology of writing and of images. Every entity was seen through a lens that distanced and negated the romantic spirit of the work. Did your art reflect the presence of this Nouveau Roman attitude?

LG For a while I was painting large canvases (1964–1965) with a center similar to a camera lens: a circle or square containing an image. These works represent a character within the universe of appearances. They are like a world seen through a camera lens, a medium that emphasizes the reproduction of reality. Reality was revealed in the paintings, but was transformed by a hypothetical lens to become a symbol of representation. The central image in the lens was out of focus, more an impression than a real image. This was a world seen through a lens with an altered focal distance. The rest of the canvas, on the other hand, was filled with precise, meticulous diagrams and descriptions of all kinds of lenses, photographic calculations, times of exposure, aperture widths, and so on, all the media and methods that could eventually help to give focus to objects and forms. These large canvases were divided into two or three parts, with the stretcher frames fixed to the wall, one next to the other. I did this to give the sense of sequences of images.

GC Through the connection and concatenation of images, your "Variable Paintings" are also about time and the organic organization of painting. Personally, I see them as a discourse on the relative dimensions of figures and representations, but also as a representation that carries with it the totality, the whole, and its parts. It's almost as if there was a quest for an active montage in which the immensity of the narrative implicit in a painting or other image could be understood. In this sense, the images mixed and filtered by a circular lens create a spiral of perspectives and accelerated communications, based on the dialectic of parts. What are the linguistic and philosophical principles, in addition to the mathematical ones, that govern these variable compositions?

LG At the core of my "Variable Paintings" lies the desire to use the image over successive periods of time, to imbue the same image with different meanings. They are an attempt to move beyond the static structure of the canvas, making it mutable. Historically, the Futurist representation of the object in motion and the sequential images of Eadweard Muybridge's photographs can be seen as a common root for the "Variable Paintings." But I think of them as more related to the Bergsonian concept or "duration," to the idea of the interpretation of the image in a determined instant of time, which becomes the current instant, *the time of the work*. Also, I wanted to allow the spectator to participate in the work according to their own personal choice, to provide the opportunity to see the images of the painting in different "moments," with a variety of possible readings. Many levels of interpretation arise, depending on the movement created by spectators as they shift the sliding panels.

GC You refer to Bergson and to his idea of movement as a passage from one moment to another, a sort of dance between object and spectator. The prehistory of cinema is also based on this mechanism of exchange and transfer between two entities, active and passive, which is why you point out Muybridge and Étienne-Jules Marey. Is art, then, an activity focused on a "moment" that is part of a larger sequence, or a series of the notable small "instants" of an artificial movement in which time is not represented but implied?

LG In the "Variable Paintings" the work process was a dialogue that involved the viewer; it was a reaction to the accepted historical way of reading an artwork. I was looking for a way to have the work convey many different moments of perception, escaping the static condition of a univocal image. Culturally and conceptually, I was trying to reach another dimension, which the static surface of the canvas was unable to provide: a simultaneity of perceptions and images that achieved even greater shifts of meaning, depending on time and movement. Setting in motion figures and objects that represented a static moment, I wanted to erase the absence of time from my paintings, and give them a temporal dimension.

GC Because of this open dimension of the work, your research tends to go beyond traditional linguistic frontiers, moving away from painting and arriving at installation and environmental art, with incursions into materials like Plexiglas and artificial fog. In the end, you have moved toward the creation of a "field" of variable and indeterminate configurations. It is no accident that you tend to emphasize the movement internal to your work, both through the iteration of the same figure or sign, and through the modification of the structure of the work to give it a kinetic dimension, a dissolution of its usual stasis. All this occurs a few years after the publication of Umberto Eco's *The Open Work (Opera Aperta)* in 1962, a book that deals with mobility, with ambiguity, and with the multiperspectival nature of meaning. What is your relationship with these theories, which informed an entire generation of poets like the Gruppo 63, and artists like Pino Pascali?

LG I only got to know those people in 1965, at a Gruppo 63 conference in Palermo. We were all together for a week, for meetings, meals, trips to the seaside, exhibitions, and concerts. I remember music by Sylvano Bussotti and Cathy Berberian. Inge Feltrinelli was there with the entire Gruppo 63, and I met Umberto Eco, Alberto Arbasino, Angelo Guglielmi, Furio Colombo, and the others. I had already read Arbasino's and Eco's books, Edoardo Sanguineti's poetry, and their writings in general. After that I saw them often in Rome (where many of them lived) at the house of Luisa Spagnoli, who was more or less at the center of things, a friend of artists and writers; or in Milan, at the houses of Ottiero Ottieri, Camilla Cederna, and the Feltrinellis, where I used to go with Beatrice Monti, who had shown my paintings at her gallery (Galleria dell'Ariete) a few months earlier. Eco often came to our house and to my studio. I gave him a gouache that he called his portrait; it represented a pair of broken eyeglasses in a stylized geometric landscape (it was a sort of joke, to remind him how he had slipped in a puddle of water in Palermo, breaking his glasses, which he wore that way during the days that followed). In response and in thanks, Umberto sent me a strange letter of four pages filled with adverbs, written in rows one below the other.

In Palermo, at the same conference, I got to know Pino Pascali. He sometimes came to visit me at home, where I had a large zebra skin on the floor, which I had brought back from Africa. One day he looked at it carefully, then made a gesture, tracing its outline in the air. Seeing that he was drawing it mentally, I gave him a pencil and a sheet of paper, but he once again repeated the outline in the air, answering that he didn't need paper and pencil, the form was now imprinted in his mind and he would remember it. Sometime later he made a piece, representing an animal skin with thick fur, that hung on the wall. I always wondered whether it was my zebra.

During that period I read *V* (1963) by Thomas Pynchon, *Le Degré zéro de l'écriture* (1953) by Roland Barthes (which impressed me deeply), and Herbert Marcuse. I also liked the theater pieces of Carmelo Bene; I particularly remember his *Pinocchio* (1965).

GC Working with the movement of bodies on a painted surface, you present the enigma between evidence and shadow, to the point where, in your work, the body remains silent and lets its reflection speak, a reflection that appears like an unknown, I would even say metaphysical force, which is also found in the superimposition of transparent surfaces and clouds. It is almost a moment of alienation from the physicality of the image, a quest for an unknown place that seems to come out of darkness, in the shadow, or out of light, in the clouds or the transparent surfaces. It is as if there were an artificial awakening where you seem to have put things in order, establishing the walls, the furniture, the landscape where you project yourself, and where your existence now has an unnatural rather than a natural appearance. This attitude obviously implies a cold, "immaterial" feeling. These are objects suspended between dream and waking, in the movement of thought and time.

LG We can represent the same image in many different ways. It can be read on different levels depending on the surrounding circumstances. Each difference creates its own diversity of mental responses and perceptions. The shadow is used as an abstract representation of a human reality, and the hidden parts of the painting are used as different moments of the same reality, revealed and changed through the movement of the panels and through the presence and superimposition of the shadows.

GC Your world—half internal self, half external reality—moves between a vision of your own being and the transparency of the context, and your technique is controlled and cool. It is as if you had renounced the corporeality of the hand to entrust yourself increasingly to a plan. This feeling is reinforced by the geometric and linear elements in your work, which are consistent with a controlled, programmed, almost "geometric" existence.

LG The panels of my paintings were transparent openings to the outside world through a circle of lights and shadows shaping a geometric landscape. In this personal territory I was playing a game of opposites: an image of myself was seen by the outside world, but at the same time the situation was reversed, and my image became the spectator. The painting was the stage for this dialectic, a cool description of a motionless figure that had an abstract presence, in a changeable configuration. The work had two levels of communication. It was a bidimensional world seen through a kaleidoscope, representing both the instant before movement and the instant after its transformation into another image.

GC When and where did you show your first pieces from 1964?

LG I exhibited these works in 1965 at the Galleria dell'Ariete in Milan, with an essay by Renato Barilli in the accompanying catalogue, and then in group shows in Rome and at the Rome Quadriennale, where I was chosen for the Young Artists section of the 1966 Venice Biennale. That same year I started the "Variable Paintings."

GC At the previous Biennale, in 1964, the Grand Prize had gone to Robert Rauschenberg, and that year also marked the beginning of a widespread diffusion of American Pop art, with which many Italian artists sought a relationship. At first, this tendency led to the proposal of banal images, but later it was distinguished by recourse to a more historical, less current iconography. Furthermore, if one thinks about the situation in Turin, with the presence of Michelangelo Pistoletto and Giulio Paolini, or of Luciano Fabro in Milan, one understands that Italian art at that time was engaging in a broad reflection on systems of making art and of confronting reality. Through terms of linguistic motivation and connection it dealt with a transformation of the exterior situation at hand. What mattered was to keep oneself from being distracted by the outside appearance of everyday life and mass consumption; instead, one had to focus on what lay behind this, and on its analysis and deconstruction. This was the beginning of the philosophy of art that was to develop in the mid-1960s. What is your relationship to the Pop generation in Rome and in Turin?

LG The impressive exhibition of American Pop art at the 1964 Venice Biennale, curated by Alan Solomon, was the first I had seen of the work of those artists. I learned more about them when I went to New York two years later. Pistoletto, Enrico Castellani, Mario Ceroli, and I had been included in the Biennale in 1966, where I showed my first "Variable Paintings." There I met Leo Castelli—with his wife, Toiny—and Ileana Sonnabend for the first time. Leo liked the idea that the sliding panels of my paintings were movable. Through that exhibition I had my first group show in New York, in October of that year. Organized by the Galeria Bonino, the show was called *Italy: New Tendencies*. I had never been to New York before. Many important artists came to the opening—I remember Barnett Newman there with Frank Stella and Larry Poons, as well as Alan Solomon, who then decided to organize a larger American show of young Italian artists. The following year he came to Italy and chose the pieces for a group show at the Institute of Contemporary Art in Boston—works by Kounellis, Pistoletto, Valerio Adami, Getulio Alviani, Pascali, Ceroli, and my "Neon Paintings." The show later traveled to the Jewish Museum in New York, and there I met Castelli again, looking at my neon works. The next time I met him was in Boston, in 1971, at the *Earth Air Fire Water* exhibition at the Museum of Fine Arts, in which I showed my water pieces. Two years later Castelli gave me my first exhibition at his gallery.

During my 1966 visit I went to see Roy Lichtenstein, who showed me some of the work in his studio. I visited Jim Rosenquist, who was painting a huge piece, and I went to Andy Warhol's Factory, which was crowded with his friends. I remember that the walls were entirely covered in a brilliant silver material. I also saw an extraordinary series of events at the Armory Show, in which Rauschenberg and other artists each performed for an evening. To see these performances was a really amazing experience.

In Rome, La Tartaruga, which was located above Rosati's in the Piazza del Popolo, showed the work of young Italian artists. Plinio De Martiis and his wife, Nini Pirandello, owned the gallery, and it was the center around which the Roman intellectual world revolved during that period. Every evening artists and writers met there, including Alberto Moravia, Goffredo Parise, Arbasino, Schifano, Kounellis, Ceroli, and Pascali. I remember that I saw Festa's *Persiane* (Wooden Shutters), Angeli's *Quarto di dollaro* (Quarter Piece), and Schifano's *Il Futurismo rivisitato* (Futurism Revisited) there. Soon after this Pascali left the gallery to show his "cannons" at Gian Enzo Sperone's space in Turin. Arte povera was born, with artists from Turin, Milan, and Rome—and the center shifted.

Plinio closed his gallery during the summer of 1968 after a final series of shows entitled *Teatro delle mostre* (Theater of Exhibitions), in which I showed my *Wind Room* [also called *Wind Speed 40 Knots*]. It was a time of worldwide student protests—a period of illusion, as it turned out—and there was an atmosphere of confrontation everywhere. A group of Roman students loved the poet Giuseppe Ungaretti; one of the newspapers named four of them "the birds," because every day they climbed a tree facing his house and roosted there until evening, rhythmically chanting "Giuseppe! Giuseppe!" When Plinio closed his gallery he opened a bar behind the Piazza del Popolo, and the same crowd that had frequented his gallery went there every evening. Ungaretti also dropped in occasionally, and he came to my studio with Dorazio to see my "Antinebbia" (Antifog) pieces, which he called "colonne luminose a pareti" (luminous walled columns). He came back to see them surrounded by artificial fog in the installation at the Marlborough Gallery.

GC From 1966 on you began to incorporate fluorescent tubing in your work, evoking advertising culture and commercial display. I am sure that you were aware of Chryssa's and Dan Flavin's use of the same material around 1963–1964, the former manipulating it as writing, the latter as a tautological entity. Both were interested in this technological and informational totem. Chryssa used it to construct a sequence of paginations, while Flavin was more struck by the possibility of aniconic, primary combinations. From about 1966 other artists like Mario Merz and Bruce Nauman also began to make use of neon. Were you aware of these developments, and how did you perceive them?

LG Flavin's use of industrially produced fluorescent tubing is part of a discourse that pertains to Minimalism. Chryssa's neon is more monumental, a large technological sign. Nauman drew with neon, writing out his own name, for example. I remember seeing his work for the first time, in New York in 1968. Merz also wrote an ideological phrase on an igloo piece, which I saw in a show in Rome that same year; then, with his series of Fibonacci numbers, he too was writing and drawing with these luminous signs.

When I began to use neon, in 1966, I wanted a material that was technologically defined but that I could still use in a craftsman-like way. With neon I wanted to obtain different gradations of the same color, disturbing the gas and curving the tube in which it was sealed according to the result that I wanted to achieve. I wanted to create effects of depth, to exploit light for its possibilities of refraction, to create dimension and an artificial perspective, a three-dimensional painting in neon.

GC It seems to me that your explorations led you toward a certain "pictorialism," that is, you worked with the visual metamorphosis of colors and of the environment that fluorescent tubing creates. It is, again, a discourse on the passage between day and night, in which the city, with its shop windows and its signs, continues to dominate.

LG My "Neon Paintings" reflect the impact of the nighttime environment of the city, the constellations of hundreds of luminous signs, the striped and colored Plexiglas, the advertising, the fluorescent light, the steel and aluminum, the illuminated windows with backlit shadows through the glass. The figures in the works are closed off in that world of neon signs and lights.

Representing the psychological oppression of the urban environment, they see landscape as an artificial universe, in which reality is only an illusionary duplicate. The works define the boundary of that open arena. The life-sized figures appear and disappear, opaque and mysterious, subjects and objects seen through transparencies and lights, framed in a three-dimensional space of simultaneous flatness and depth.

GC In *Racing Car Room* (1967), you use the silhouettes of racing cars, as you had used your own and others' silhouettes and shadows in previous works. It is as if the theme of the velocity of communication, or of the passage of shadows, were connected to the speed of the automobile. This is clearly a continuation of your recourse—almost a Futurist recourse—to Italian art history, seen, however, from the perspective of contemporary culture.

LG The challenge of the laws of mechanics, dynamics, and gravity was what interested me—the power, the speed, the design of Formula One cars. I wanted to imprison an image of movement in a transparent box, to block it and transform it into a static object. I wanted to see a lot of these cars together in one room, a silent competition of immobile racing cars in a delimited space, closed off by the wall.

GC From 1968 on, a certain artificial "naturalism" works its way into your art. I am thinking of your "Antinebbia" series, the "antifog" columns of neon conceived to be installed in a natural context such as a meadow. They are extraneous to the context, yet they add an element to nature, are a further replication of it, although they are urban in tone. If I look carefully at them, these tall towers surrounded by fog end up seeming like skyscrapers on a reduced scale. But they are also the departure point for your experiments with natural elements, where contrasts and elisions between parts are used to discover a dualistic view between the extremes of the natural and the unnatural.

LG I wanted to produce natural elements artificially, provoking a psychological metamorphosis that would redefine a space. This was due in part to my experiences in nature during my travels, almost a rediscovery for me of natural phenomena, with monsoons in Asia, rain on the atolls, refraction in the desert. I made several works using fog, wind, air, and rain, and I called them the "Natural Elements" series.

I had just finished the "Neon Paintings" series, in which I transmitted signs of the urban environment, figures imprisoned as if in glass booths, malaise, incommunicability, capturing the ambiguity between the backlit figure and the spectator. Then I wanted to use natural elements, liberated from structure, to bring the same spectator into a more human, more free condition, to give them the possibility, within a cultural context, to hear once again the sound of the rain, isolated, presented as a new experience, or to feel the wind, or to see that the air is a presence, that there are stars and rainbows as well as the noise of the city and the lights of advertising. This is why I "artificially" recreated phenomena as naturally as possible, not contained inside a painting or three-dimensional object. I wanted to involve the visitor and to experiment with the elements in a physical way, letting the spectator participate in the physical quality of the element itself, which was made provocative by its reproduction in a context as different from the space of nature as the space of a gallery. I didn't want a painting or a sculpture containing air, earth, or water; I didn't want air, earth, or water to become objects; I wanted to recreate the experience of natural phenomena.

GC In 1967, L'Attico in Rome held an exhibition entitled *Fuoco Immagine Acqua Terra* (Fire Image Water Earth), in which Kounellis and Pascali celebrated primordial elements like earth, fire, and water. Did you see the show, and what was your position with respect to its naturalistic representations, its puddles and its daisies of fire?

LG I remember that show. I was primarily interested in the less material, less tangible quality of the elements, how they were used to create feelings and moods rather than objects. I was using fog, wind, air, rainbows, stars, refractions, whirlpools, and rain.

GC What is surprising and unusual is your use of fog or wind in an enclosed space, as if you wanted to charge the traditional territory of art, the gallery, and the museum, with the immaterial effects of a natural phenomenon.

LG They are interventions to modify the structure of a space with the presence of a natural element. The "fog" becomes form, participating in the definition of the space, modifying it with its presence. The "wind" is unexpected in a closed space, as is the "rain" that drips from a pipe in a room, and the sound of its drops, and the volume of water into which it falls, stirring the surface with circles of ripples. To experience the dizzying depth and concentric velocity of a whirlpool in a closed environment alters that environment's prerogative. Likewise, air, colorless and transparent, isn't usually noticed as a presence, though it is omnipresent, so I wanted to define it visually, through a perimeter of light.

GC A visual vertigo comes out of putting fog and fluorescent tubing together; there is a perceptual similarity between the two, both operating on a principle of "fine dust," of particles that reflect or radiate light. What lies behind the interweaving of the immaterial and the imperceptible? Does your use of these effects in an interior space also imply an alteration of the architectural container? What is the analogy between the concrete, realized objects and their existence as images?

LG In the "Antinebbia" pieces, the last neon pieces that I made in January 1968, I added artificial fog to create a further effect of refraction, through which the light filtered—broken, refracted, visible, and invisible at the same time. The neon was in different gradations of color, from a blue violet to a near white that was absorbed by the white of the fog. I was working at reproducing natural elements in an enclosed space, to alter the space's structure with something extraneous to it. The fog was the first of these outdoor elements that I transferred indoors.

GC Together with the experience of the nontactile, you present an experience of the world as an infinite production of images, as aggregates of fragile, changeable states—a forest or a landscape in which the human being is "reflected." In 1968, the same year that you began your investigations into the passages of nature, you embarked on another series of travels, which triggered profound reactions in your work. It seems to me that the most important of these was your journey to Africa. How did this come about, and why? What were the consequences of your exposure to Africa's almost invincible, intangible sort of nature, as opposed to the relatively domesticated European landscape?

LG We went to Africa to find locations for part of a film that Folco was shooting on the continent's history. We visited Nigeria, the Sahara, Niger, Upper Volta [Burkina Faso] Dahomey [Benin], and then we went to Chad.

There was a piece that I wanted to do at the time, recreating the effect of refraction in water, but I didn't know where or how to do it. I imagined it in a large expanse of water, which couldn't, however, be very deep. Then I arrived at Lake Chad. With the sunlight reflecting on the water, the lake seemed like an infinite flat surface. Dazzling, immobile, it stretched as far as the horizon. I didn't know it yet, but Lake Chad, one of the largest lakes in the world, is also the shallowest of any approaching its size. I had found the place I was looking for to make my *Refraction* piece.

One afternoon in the Sahara, about two hours before sunset, the sun's rays were shining in a kind of diagonal light, and we saw a mirage. On the horizon, the sand dunes appeared to be reflected in a water surface on which a man and two camels were slowly walking. The sand dunes were reflected upside down, reversed. I took a picture of the mirage, and was surprised later when I saw it exactly reproduced in my color photograph; in a way, I had expected that this immaterial, nonexistent image could not be recorded on film.

A few hours later we arrived at an oasis, with nomads and camels, and I understood that this was where the images I had seen before had come from. The oblique rays of the sun had created the effect of a mirrored surface on the sand, producing a refraction effect, and the image had appeared some miles away from where the real scene actually was.

Making a work on Lake Chad, using the effects of the sunlight's refraction on the water, I remembered its refraction on the sand dunes. They were both optical illusions, and I wanted to recreate them both in an indoor space.

GC The use of these properties of the desert and water implies an attempt to reappropriate the mobility of the material. Placed indoors, they create a "false" reality. If I connect this to the "Variable Paintings," I notice that shadow and reality seem to change roles: there, the shadow haunts reality, almost as something external to it, and here the shadow moves in "spirit" and matter, light and water. But the spectator remains the subject, remains at the center of the interpretation. In the "Variable Paintings" the spectator is inside the action; in the environment, they are literally surrounded by the artistic event. The spectacle is no longer sustained through sliding, alterable "sets," but through the force and energy of natural effects.

In *Rain Room* (1968), we again find ourselves faced with an operation of the "void," a further metaphysical turn in which there is an emphasis on nature's will to exist.

LG I wanted to create the natural effect of the sound of water falling into water, to create an environment where one might meditate, listening to the noise of the rain. Above, there was a pipe from which water dripped constantly; below, there was a large shallow basin. The level of the water in the basin was flush with the floor of the rest of the environment, like a small lake in a room where one could sit and hear only the sound of a natural element, closed off from the rest of the world. When I remade *Rain Room* with my piece *Drops of Water* at the Boston Museum of Fine Arts, in 1971, I saw young people seated on the floor around the basin in a circle, listening to the falling drops and looking at the ripples that ruffled the water's surface in a continuous, always changing pattern.

My travels in Africa were also an opportunity to work on a wind piece for which I explored a selection of air currents—different types of wind, at different velocities, in different situations. During a storm in the Sahara, the blowing of the wind and the swirling of the sand had created such a compact material effect that it made me consider wind in a completely objective way. I decided to compare this element in a variety of environments, with many different winds blowing at many different speeds. I started documenting their effects on camera, and also recorded their sounds. I collected a number of images of different winds in several countries and in a variety of types of location—in the ocean, in fields, in the trees of the forest, in the city. That same year, 1968, I decided to reproduce a particular wind speed—40 knots—with a wind machine in the closed environment of a gallery, altering the usual connotations of its space. In this *Wind Room* I again brought the feeling of an element of exterior space into an architectural interior.

GC In *Air Room* (1968, also called *Volume of Air*), one is made conscious that the "void" of our everyday atmosphere is the vehicle of a luminosity and a sensory quality that pass through it constantly. Here there is a quest for the minimal, imperceptible presence of the vibrations of the air. It is almost an experience without stimuli, where one is pushed to listen to oneself, to be aware of oneself. Reducing image references as much as possible, and polarizing one's structure and context, sound and light, you seem to push the body from the perception of external objects to that of internal processes, so that one's responses exalt one's inner senses and their modes of association.

LG *Air Room* is the spatial and volumetric reflection of a thin thread of light that gives an imaginary, almost visually perceived consistency to a volume of air. It is an osmosis between a technological medium such as neon light and a natural element such as air, whose specific characteristics are colorlessness, transparency, and immateriality. Yet air can acquire a volumetric visual texture by being focused through artificial light, which defines its form and solidifies its shape.

GC At times you create a dialectic between day and night, light and dark, body and shadow through the use of other symbolic materials, for example the lead and light of *Star Room* (1968, also called *Light Melting Time*). Since ancient times, lead has been the material that emerges from and represents darkness, blackness, night. In addition, its malleability symbolizes a motility of materials. In this piece the lead is melted by the heat of the light, which slowly moves beyond its two-dimensional boundary and makes the space fecund, giving birth to a system of "stars."

LG At first I wasn't sure whether to use a wall of lead or of tin to create my wall of stars in *Star Room*. I decided I liked lead better. It's more interesting, because it's a contradictory material: soft and extremely malleable, which usually suggests lightness, but dark and heavy.

Behind the wall of lead there were special tiny high-intensity light bulbs, partly laminated in gold on the inside. These lamps melted small holes at different points in the lead, a few at a time, over the entire wall, letting rays of light filter into the rest of the space. These beams took the form of stars, because of the diffraction effect. In the end, the entire room was full of stars.

GC In *Rainbow* (1968), another strong image enters your work. It is a sign of the mediation between high and low, between one world and another. It also represents an example of transference from one attribute to another, a path between two entities. As in the other rooms, the path or passage that you intend or that you seem to want to communicate is the transformation of technological mechanisms into natural ones. You first create stars, then a rainbow, both with artificial light. In the final analysis, the aspiration is for the union of opposites, of the natural and the artificial. I see the same impulse in your alliance between fog and neon. This was a pressing subject in the early 1960s, when the traditional humanist culture of the West realized that it was being inundated with the effects of the mass media. It attempted a renewal and an integration, with art trying to function as the bridge.

LG My purpose in *Rainbow* was to create a horizon at eye level, traversing the four walls of a room, and making visible all the colors of the spectrum that the air, which is colorless, lets pass through. I obtained this effect by shining a light through a prism, which is the simplest, most elementary way to decompose the colors of the spectrum. What I wanted was to have a rainbow inside a room.

GC The transit or the transition between one element and another is also represented in your use of photography, which mediates between the photographer and what is photographed, establishing more relationships between natural states and artificial ones—the photographing subject and its camera, the photographed subject and what appears in the frame. Once again we have a dual situation, an attempt at osmosis. In the book *Distillations: Choice and Choosing 16 from 5000* (1970) there is also a passage from a naturalistic aspect to an anthropological one. The images are those you gathered during your travels, and a recourse to another artificial language, that of representation, of simulation. In addition, I see another dialectic established within the visual result. To present the photographs and their subjects, you create a very precise grid that visually "structures" this explosion of images, which are rich in magnificent visual elements and information. Is this another intermediary moment?

LG Distillation as procedure: an extract of visual, mental, spiritual experiences. These photographs were the result of the impact on me of many different cultures, with their various rituals and modes of behavior in various cultural contexts and traditions. They were also the sum of my personal reactions to a wide range of environmental situations. I was interested in finding affinities between ethnic groups that were both very different from each other and also often alike, with similar mythologies, rituals, customs, and habits, although occurring in countries quite distant from each other. In the cordillera of the Andes, for example, I saw the last surviving symbols of the Inca culture mixed with symbols introduced by the infiltration of Catholic missionaries: the *hombre pájaro*, the birdman, is an Indian who represents a bird symbol and is covered with colored feathers, but he carries a cross, and leads the Easter procession to Tilcara, 13,000 feet up in the Andes. Likewise, animist rituals along the Atlantic coast of Dahomey [Benin] include symbols found on the other shore of the Atlantic, in the *Macumba* rites of Brazil. The initiation rites and the masks occur in different cultures, but have the same matrix. Then there's the covered face: from the blue litham veil of the Tuareg chiefs to the mud masks that cover the faces of the "Mudmen" in New Guinea, or to the silver mask that covers only the nose of the king of Abomey [city in south Benin; capital of the Kingdom of Dahomey]. This latter example has a mystical purpose, since the king's subjects believe they are hearing from his mouth the voices of their ancestors, venerated as divinities. I also found a system of oral traditions present in both Asiatic and Polynesian culture, with the shaman and the *Warepo*, both having the task of keeping alive the memory of their history and mythology, from the Tiki to the oceanic transmigrations.

Distillation as a selection among a large number of images, provoking personal reactions and meditations. The present of the present, the present of the past, the present of the future, which is discussed by Saint Augustine. Distillation as a meditative quality: the counting of grains of sand as a measurement of time, sand and spiral a suggestion of infinity, the spiral as unending circular motion, representing endless time. This work, *The Measuring of Time* (1969), was the first of my three "Distillations" pieces, inspired by travels through several deserts. The second, *Distillations: 3 Months of Looking* (1970), was a piece I made while traveling in places like the Leeward Islands, Malaysia, the Philippines, the Sulu Islands, and the New Hebrides; it was an analysis of my personal visual and physical sensations. The third piece, *Distillations: Choice and Choosing 16 from 5000*, was a collection and selection of images from earlier trips, like a grid of different realities restructured in a single image.

GC The reconciliation between different and opposite interlocutors is a recurring notion in the history of Western metaphysics; the condition of something midway between beautiful and ugly, nocturnal and diurnal, is the attempt to fill the gap. *Distillations: Choice and Choosing 16 from 5000* takes what were first photographic "remains," a body of around 5,000 images, and makes them into a book. It is almost as though you wanted to communicate to the reader another, different approach to your experience. As in the "Variable Paintings," the idea is to circulate the image, leaving the spectator free to travel within it. Is this another passage?

LG It was almost a necessary linguistic choice. I really wanted an object to leaf through, one image after another, to be perceived in successive moments, in the dimension of the page. *Distillations: 3 Months of Looking* was about sensations and experiences I had had on different physical and psychological levels that I wanted to describe, making them available to be repeated by those who might find themselves in similar conditions of place, time, and environmental circumstance. It was almost an analysis that could be repeated as an experiment. The same criterion holds for *Distillations: Choice and Choosing 16 from 5000*. Photography was necessary here in two ways: first, as a technical means for gathering images and materials during numerous voyages; secondly, to create the assemblage of images, to restructure them successively as a single photograph, providing a unity of place and of time that is, precisely, the purpose of the work.

GC The selection is made from 5,000 images; how did the associations and juxtapositions come about? What visual analogies did you want to establish in the structure of the individual groups?

LG The 16 groups of photographs that are the subject of the work were selected from around 5,000 photographs taken during several years of travel. I chose them using various different criteria, including size, location, subject matter, time of year, number of objects, similarities in shape, affinities in content, and so on. For each of the 16 groups I used a different method of choosing, introducing a variety that forces the viewer to read the photographs comparatively rather than out of the more habitual kind of visual response. Because I made my selection on the basis of a variety of formal and other affinities, each of the 16 groups became an assemblage apparently having the same linguistic value. In reality, however, the differences between and within them are enormous, because the photographs belong to different countries and different cultures, and were taken with different cameras and lenses at different times in different years. I decided to create a unique image-symbol that could unify each group, by rephotographing it with a single lens, at a single time, in a single place. As Claude-Lévi Strauss said, "I believe that content never has a meaning in itself—it is only the way in which the different elements are combined together that gives them a meaning."

GC You're interested in dance, which is also a way of organizing an explosive subject, the body, in sequences and in combinations of almost mathematical order. Dance is a classical manifestation of movement. It represents rhythm and establishes a harmony of gestures, regulating the organic magma, causing one image to slide into another.

LG Classical dance is a sequence of calculated movements regulated by very precise, perhaps mathematical, harmonious laws. Clearly, gravity and equilibrium are among the elements of dance, among the components to be analyzed; for me, they constitute its essential value. This is true for both classical and modern dance, although in the latter realm I have seen completely antigravitational performances. Music is also tied to mathematics, especially contemporary music. I remember a page that Philip Glass gave me from the score of *Changing Parts*. It was a true page of mathematics, with precise repetitions and variations of the same alphabetical letter, numbered and repeated according to his theme.

GC In *Equilibrium: To Carlotta Grisi* (1971), why were you interested in reducing the movements of the body to lines and arcs?

LG Because I wanted a synthesis of the movements of dance, their image no longer organic but abstract.

GC Why did you choose an image from a ballet of 1843?

LG I chose this image because it represented a new movement in dance, Carlotta Grisi's *pas de quatre*. One of the most interesting steps in the history of classical ballet, the *pas de quatre* coordinated four dancers in a single movement; it is almost an abstract concept. Théophile Gautier was so taken with Grisi's *pas de quatre* that he wrote a poem for her.

GC The traces of dance movements led you to define a series of right angles and diagonals—why?

LG This is my interpretation of dance. I wanted to imagine successive movements as diagonal lines. In my drawings for *Equilibrium* (1971), the lines that form acute angles, right angles, arches, and semicircles, and the spheres suspended from these lines, are all imagined as being in motion. Then they stop, in positions that challenge gravity; and then they return to their movement. It is a calculated alternation of motion and stasis, according to a measured rhythm, like dance steps.

GC After the presentation of definite outlines in your early work, you moved onto elements characterized by indeterminacy and indistinctness, like sound and the ocean. These are entities without form, again a condition between extremes, like transparency and darkness.

LG Living for some months on Rangiroa, a Polynesian atoll, during the rainy season, I developed a new sensitivity to the rain, to the rhythmic sound of drops falling constantly on the flat surface of the lagoon, in the center of the atoll, mixed with the sound of the Pacific waves breaking on the reef. My work *Drops and Ocean* derived from that experience. Later, I decided to incorporate that work into the piece *Sounds* (1971), which attempted to capture the effects of sounds by presenting them in the form of a commercial product: an object like a cassette tape, to be used as artwork/entertainment.

GC You move from the diffuse, unplaceable sound of the water and the ocean to the positioning of stones. This is a passage toward another dialectical condition. The falling stones, one after another, symbolize sedimentation and construction. It is no wonder that you combine them, setting up interrelationships among them, almost as if they formed a cyclical crystallization. Furthermore, stone is passive, yet another reason for manipulating them and for organizing them according to intellectual and numerical variations. In ancient times the stone was a symbol of consciousness, a dynamic instrument of conceptual activity, always in terms of the interweaving between the artificial, what is built with the mind, and the natural.

LG After *Sounds* I actually did a series of works, "Variations in Space," some of which were based on pebbles. I devised a mental and visual system for arranging a small number of pebbles in a vast number of different combinations. I also used coins and other objects. The pebbles were used as part of a codification that gave a different linguistic value to a natural material. The pebble became an abstract object, a numerical entity. There are 120 different possible combinations in the same space if five pebbles are arranged in every mathematical permutation of their sequence. The piece is a reflection on the data of reality applied to a finite number of pebbles, to give a different order to natural objects. It reminds me of Galileo's description of nature: "Nature is like a book of infinite pages; the language in which it is written is mathematics, and its letters are geometrical figures."

GC Photographic sequences, cinema, and dance all deal with "nonfixed" values, movements, distributed in space and in time. It is, then, a self-evident step for you to move into film and video work. This evolution bears witness to the reciprocal action between parts, your hand, and its organic movement affecting the "static" movement of the stones.

LG I made the video/film piece about a year earlier, in 1972 *(From One to Four Pebbles)*. It was a way for me to have direct contact with action in nature: working in a stone quarry, I chose four stones from the multitude, and used them as an arithmetic symbol, methodically giving them an order, a different code from the one they had had before.

GC From the rainbow to the sequenced bands of color in *Stripes* (1974), from the natural element (although artificially recreated) to the drawing of individual, colored stripes, almost like the creation of an infinite chromatic score, a two-dimensional rainbow. The colors also represent the element and space, and therefore a further transportation from one territory to another. It is as if the metamorphosis and the encounter between two truths or two souls of our culture were meant to bring about the new "subject." In the process from one to the other, through abstract formalizations or through concrete realizations, your work aspires to point out a reciprocal tension, a creation of images of thought, which are the "new" reality.

LG With *Stripes* I returned to the rainbow, this time not as a natural phenomenon but as an analysis of color and of all the possible different juxtapositions that six colors can have, alternating in the same space, which was a scroll of Japanese canvas. Why this scroll? Because the work has a meditative quality that I associate with the spirit of Zen. The abstract indifference of the work's method also reminds me of Zen. I arranged stripes of the three primary and three complementary colors in their 720 different possible combinations, examining and drawing them all. I ascertained that there were that many possibilities, no more, no less.

GC This phase of your work is tied to the slipping by of the moments, to the constellations, and the imperceptible nature of time. One piece, *Hypothesis about Time* (1975), makes the theme explicitly visual in the watch face, which is photographed so as to document segments of time, a temporal sequence of time. You make visible the mental and visual experience of the passing moments, giving physicality to an immaterial condition.

LG As physical objects, the clocks serve the purpose, in their stasis (because fixed in a photographic image), of visualizing a different measure of time. Each of them records a different second, motionless, as a negation of the movement of time—they are the fantasy, the duplicate, of the real unit of temporal measure. Together they embody a hypothesis of time in which the past, the present, and the future switch their usual serial order into a new cycle of repetition: the future anticipates the past, altering time's supposedly unidirectional flow. As Marshall McLuhan says, "The future is a thing of the past." The enigmatic nature of time has fascinated artists and thinkers from ancient Greece to Bergson and his theory of duration: "The only real dimension of time is its duration as an instantaneous fact of knowledge." Borges too wrote, "Time doesn't exist except as time perceived by someone."

GC And how does the interaction between past and present, before and after, manifest itself in this work?

LG I applied a mathematical system of permutation to groups of three different seconds, obtaining a variation of the unidirectional serial order in which time goes. The images of the seconds of the clock move backward as well as forward, in a passage of time in which future and past switch order and direction.

GC Time and its linearity are not iconic, so that they can be put down in "abstract" images or figures—geometrical figures such as the hexagon or the triangle.

LG The hexagon is a geometric figure with multiple equivalencies. I have always imagined labyrinths as hexagons placed one next to the other, forming figures in which every intersection is like a corridor impossible to exit. To multiply the lines of a hexagon by the addition of other hexagons is to multiply it each time by six squared. The shape is the geometric figure that is closest to the *aleph*, the number to which one can add or subtract any number and its value doesn't change. I used the hexagon in my *Hypothesis about Space* (1975) a continuous rotation of the form from one to infinity, always identically repeated, in a perspective in which the continuity of space and the movement in time provide the possibility of infinite repetition. For me, the hexagon rotation also has a symbolic relationship with the continuity of the melodic structure of the rondo, which is an unending, circular melodic rhythm, repeating itself continuously. I also used hexagons in *Scheherazade* (1972), which is a materialization of the dream of Chuang Tzu, from an ancient Chinese text. One night he dreamed he was a yellow butterfly, and as a butterfly he could see himself as Chuang Tzu, sleeping. Yet at the same time, Chuang Tzu was flying about as the butterfly. It was a mirrored dream in which he was his own double. My butterfly in *Scheherazade* is enclosed in a hexagonal space that is repeated, doubled, and multiplied, and that the prismatic vision of the butterfly makes even more labyrinthine and infinite.

GC Your works always seem directed toward a "control" of the possible permutations of mental or physical data, almost like an infinite outline of moves that, however, must remain open. Examined in reverse, this suggests an inner control of the self, a theater of "interior" organization in which one must accept the alternation of parts. In *Endless Dialogue* (1977), you make use of the chessboard, the richest, most open symbol of this mobile duality: it has white and black (like day and night), velocity and control, linear and diagonal progress, but it always remains a coherent, controlled system. The chessboard fascinated Marcel Duchamp because it is an instrument of infinite significances, all of which can be found in a single element. I am also thinking here of the permutations of the I Ching, which has been used in contemporary art by John Cage among others.

LG I think of "De More Geometrico" (the group of my works that includes *Endless Dialogue*) as a world of geometric forms in a continuity of space that is always divisible into smaller spaces. The movement becomes a progression though distances that withdraw into infinitely divisible extensions. As Zeno said, "If everything that exists is in space, space itself must be in space, and so on ad infinitum."

I used the surface of a chessboard as a territory in which to extend my working process. The chessboard as an image has always interested me for its linguistic significance, which is related to its great number of possibilities of arrangement and movement. I used it as an object, in actual size, with a small green tortoise. My chessboard is a surface divisible into forever smaller spaces; it is crossed by a tortoise, which, before reaching the last square, faces another infinitely divisible square: another chessboard. The last border will never be reached. It is an idea of a route that has a clear beginning but no end.

I don't play chess, but I am fascinated by the process of the game, with all its possibilities and its permutability of movement. It is a structure in which two people confront each other philosophically and intellectually. I know that Cage played chess with Duchamp. I cannot imagine a greater confrontation, Duchamp's world and Cage's world facing each other. Both have extended the boundary of what can be understood as art. And Cage introduced the idea of using random occurrences and random sounds as the basis for artistic and musical composition.

GC Organizing a show and exhibiting your work means bringing about a structural transformation of time and space, of both individual and cultural experience. In other words, it implies a setting in motion of relationships that are internal and external to your pieces, which are in themselves relationships and transmissions. What does it mean to you to set up an exhibition, to utilize a space or a sequence of works, to place a progression of figures or groupings within an architectural space?

LG Each work needs its own psychological space, on which its physical space depends. I am talking about environmental installations. I always thought that my hexagon works should be installed in a hexagonal space, as they finally were. An installation can be created depending on the way a work needs to be perceived. Some works can be read in different ways: my chessboard piece has been installed in a line around the entire length of the walls of the space, but it could also be installed as a big square composed of all the square chessboards, becoming an enormous chessboard itself. A work can fill the space entirely, can become part of the space, or can even give an illusionistic quality to the space itself.

I have planned three installations that would deal with space in this last sense. The first from 1971, the most physical of the three, would consist of a perfectly level floor divided into two halves, one covered in wood painted with a bright enamel, the other covered in water dyed the same color. A perfect place, an identical color. Under the lights, the two different materials would look the same, giving the illusion of a unique surface entirely filling the space.

I'm also interested in perspectives that give space a different viewpoint from that of classical perspective. The second installation, from 1977, was related to this idea. It was designed as a space to be viewed from a focal point related to the movement of visitors, and located somewhere in a unidirectional line that would go around the entire room, traversing the wall at eye level. There would be two real clocks, one at the beginning and one at the end of the line. It was called *Time-Perspective Room*.

The third installation was suggested by Alexius Meinong's writings. I was fascinated by his theory of objects: "Objects remain objects and have a definitive character and definite property even if they have no existence: a gilded mountain is gilded and is a mountain, even if such an object does not exist." So I started thinking about images that, no matter how realistic, are actually only mental objects. In the planned installation *Nonexistent Objects Room* of 1978, there would be images such as Alice's looking glass, from Lewis Carroll, and Étienne de Condillac's sentient statue, Meinong's gilded mountain, Zhuang Tzu's yellow butterfly, Rudolf Hermann Lotze's hypothetical animal, Lao Tze's infinite stick, the fourth dimension, and so on. The description of each of these abstract objects was to be printed on almost immaterial surfaces—transparent sheets of glass, and a progression of glass cubes, which were to fill the entire space as pedestals for imaginary, "nonexistent" objects.

GC In *Blue Triangle* (1980), from "De More Geometrico," the Bergsonian spirit of time is united with the atomized path of the bird and with the infinite divisibility of space and of the moment. Beside the formal and mathematical aspects of the infinitesimal, I am interested, again, in the bird's role as an image relating sky and earth, while the triangle (the form that multiplies and governs the work, as the element of fragmentations) is an indicator of harmony and of proportion. The use of the bird seems to refer both to Marey and to Giacomo Balla, and thus to Futurism, just as the triangle of light can refer to Rosicrucian symbolism. How do you see the commingling of these figures?

LG As an artist I have never been concerned with Rosicrucian philosophy, or with the other spiritualist philosophies of the late 19th and early 20th centuries that attribute special spiritual or mystical qualities to the triangle. Instinctively, however, I can feel the purity of that perfect geometric shape. I used it as a reflective form—"reflectivity as definition of the infinite," as George Cantor said—and I looked at it from the point of view of the divisibility of a space. Each triangle can be divided into others, which can themselves be divided into still more, always smaller triangles. And the original triangle can itself be considered a fragment of an infinite triangular form. For Balla and the Futurists, and for Marey, movement was visualized through the representation of a sequence of images succeeding in time. My triangle subdivides and multiplies its geometric form in space as in a perspective of mirrors, a progression in which the triangular images become smaller and smaller in each succeeding reflection.

In *Minimum Discernible* (1977), the flight of birds is used to investigate the limits of visual perception as they relate to the dynamic of time. It shows the division of movement applied to an instant of visual duration that becomes progressively shorter. The flight of birds is subjected to a continuous process of division until it reaches the "minimum discernible," the limit of our visual perception of an image.

GC One could also read these pieces as mosaics, as an aggregate of tesserae recounting a visual and rational investigation into movement and duration.

LG I have used the concept of mosaic to capture and break the flow of light, and to reflect and illuminate the mystery of specularity. The tesserae of the mosaic create a fragmented vision. Through their subdivision of the image, they create an effect of temporary immobility—the hieratic quality of silence and stillness. The colored tesserae, with all of their different shapes, divide the image, break and multiply the effects of light.

GC The measure of time is the measure of light in your "Sundials" works.

LG Many of my works are related to the concept of time. A static object blocks time and space. The absence of movement annuls the instant of time. The sundials are static objects, but they are also instruments that measure the movement of light. Their shadows create a measure of time relative to the length of the day, to the season, to the weather. Their relativity interested me as a boundary in the continuous flow of time, in which the present, the past, and the future become simultaneous in a continuous present related to the light of day.

GC Since 1983, your research has shifted from the use of photography and linear or sequential, always two-dimensional montage (from *Endless Dialogue* through *Blue Triangle*) to complex constructions and assemblage structures that present themselves as wall sculptures. Here too there is the choice of the labyrinth, but a labyrinth in which the objects determine the voyage and the route, the analogies and the oppositions. The memory of Futurism has been left behind, and the passage seems to be toward a "metaphysical" objectification, toward a concrete memory of your history or of your culture.

LG The "Wall Sculptures" embody a plurality of linguistic means, through the use of a large number of different media and objects. This continuous variation of materials creates a flow of images based on a matrix of the European past—a cultural link with different historical concepts and territories, passing from one to the next through the same basic notion as in my preceding works, as if in a labyrinth of memories and objects.

In the "Wall Sculptures" of 1985, the process is a mental approach in which objects become instruments of tools to clarify a concept. The work assumes a dialectical quality; it is a dialogue between objects and forms, and among a variety of different materials, each with its own linguistic meaning. Some works are painted in gold, which reflects light and increases the sense of three-dimensionality. Others contain mosaic or marble, with all their art-historical associations. They represent different art-historical meanings and periods, taken out of their usual context to be focused in a new one. Many references coexist in the same piece: *Apollinaire's Secret*, for example, contains a little *stile nuovo* volume of Dante and a bronze egg that refers to Piero della Francesca's Urbino fresco, but the structure that holds these objects is a Cubist *tondo*. A representation of the "one and his double" and the "one and the many" is found in *Parmenides's Moon* (1985).

In *Classical Symmetry* (1985) I wanted to represent the law of symmetry and the classical, single-viewpoint, Renaissance perspective in opposition to the fourth-dimensional perspective that is a stratification of different levels of time and variable viewpoints in space. Some of the objects within these wall sculptures are usable, such as the hourglass that can be turned over, or a little volume that can be taken out and read. The concept of reflectivity is represented in *Borromini's Violin*, which contains a bronze violin—an object Baroque in form—and its double, an identical but tiny violin hidden in the central oval. A Bach rondo, a Baroque, repetitive mathematical structure, is etched in a bronze tablet in the same work.

GC To conclude. In 1989, the date of this interview, your work and your life revolve around New York. What relationships do you see between the landscape in which you initially moved, the city of Rome, and your new panorama? The question specifically concerns your most recent work, which has a strong Baroque component, almost a plastic compensation for American linearity.

LG In opposition to the univocal character of contemporary art, I wanted to explore the Baroque world of diversity and its elaborated form. Though Baroque forms appear in the wall sculptures (which I called "The Baroque Series"), Cubist and classical forms do as well. The wall sculptures, taken together, are a kind of diary of multiple interests and influences. They represent a plurality of meanings through an elaboration of many different forms. In the latter sense, I consider these works connected to the Baroque visual experience. They are signals transmitted by a culture of the past, of another place and time, to create confrontation and reaction. They are an arena in which different elements coexist in a relationship based on mimesis and conflict. I like to recycle art objects and meanings—different things become the same thing. The Baroque cupola of a Roman church or the spire of a New York skyscraper can be seen as similar symbols in different contexts and cultures. I am interested in a changing process through which a unity of concepts can be achieved.

1980–1999

Laura Grisi, 1981

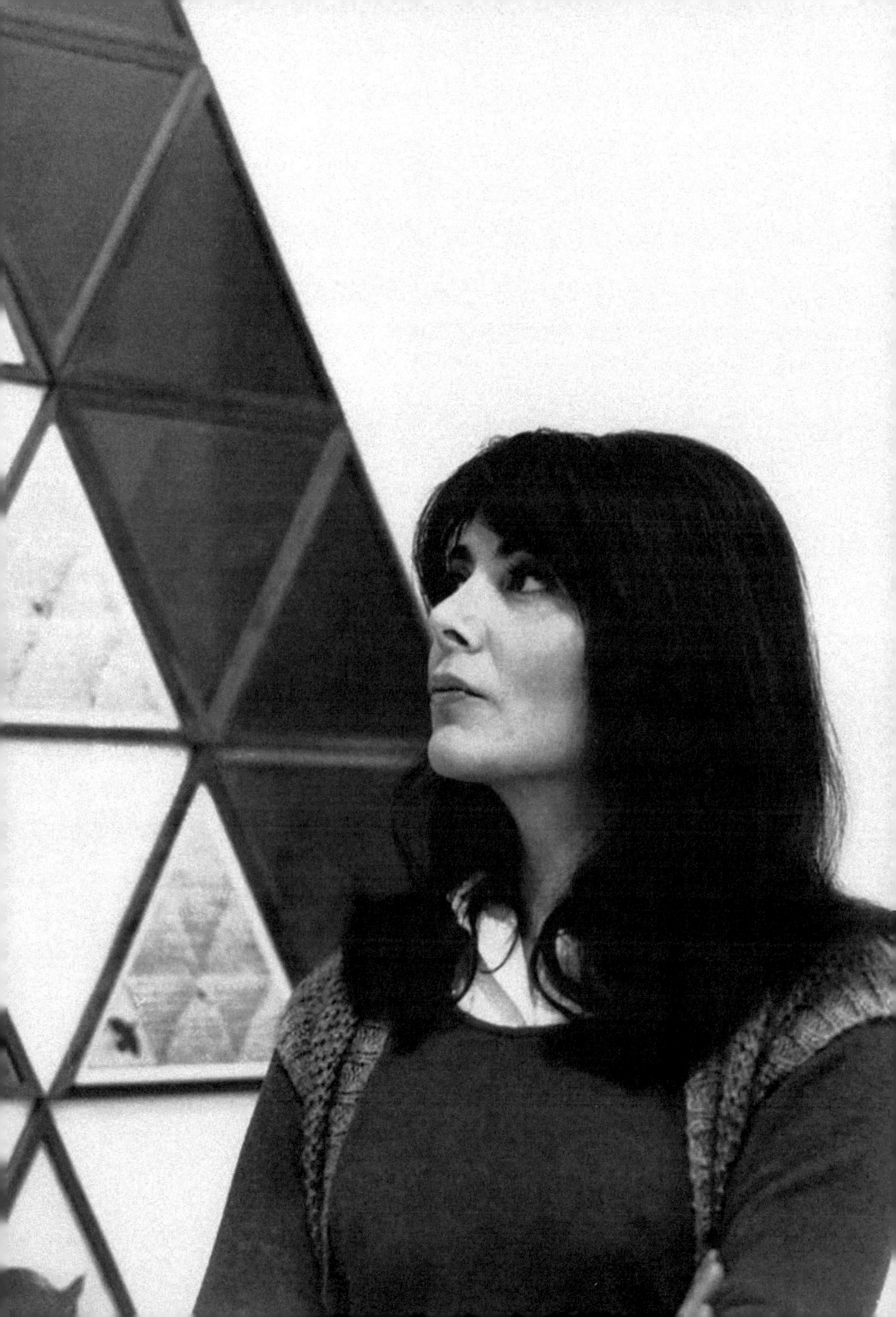

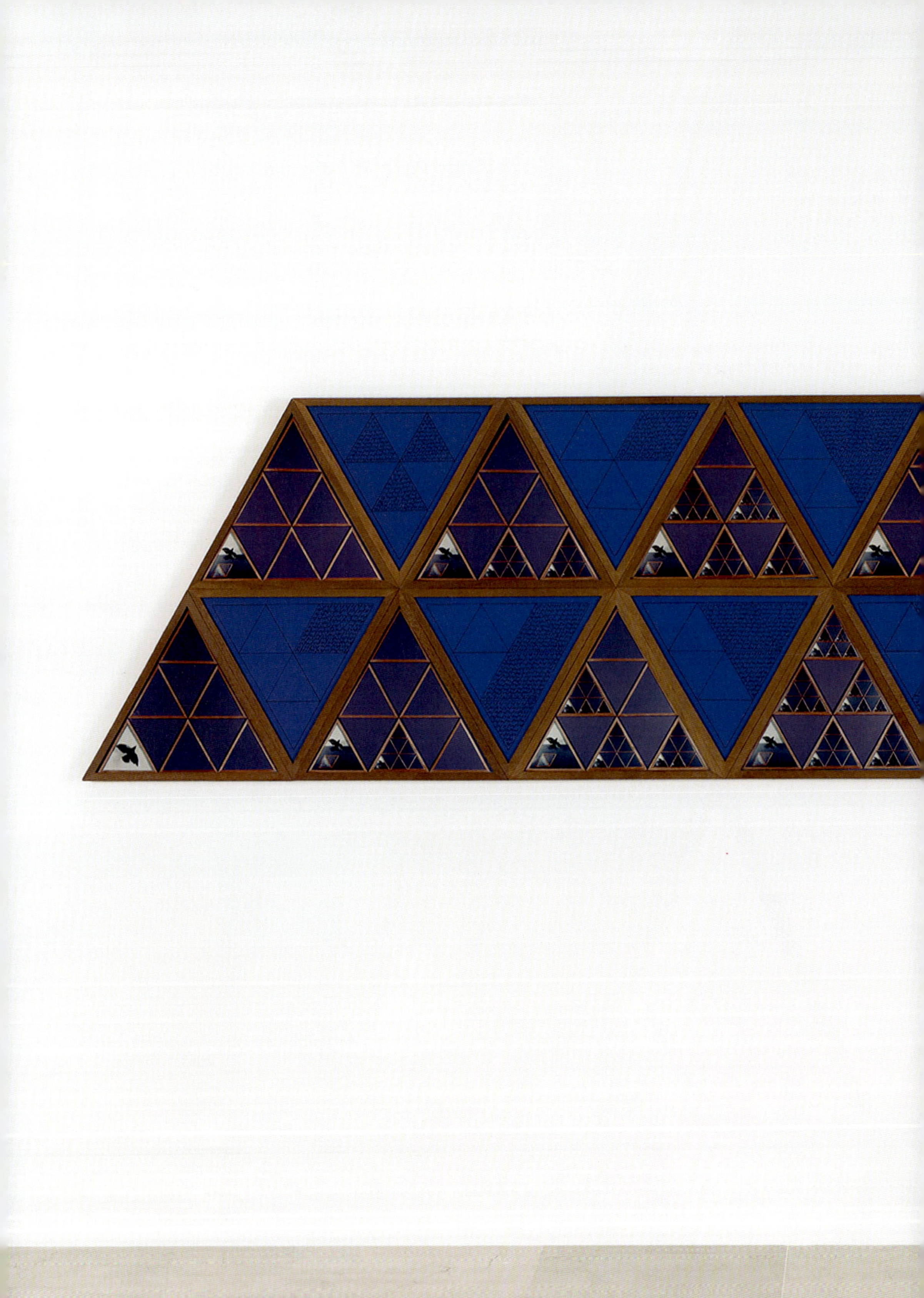

 Blue Triangles, 1981

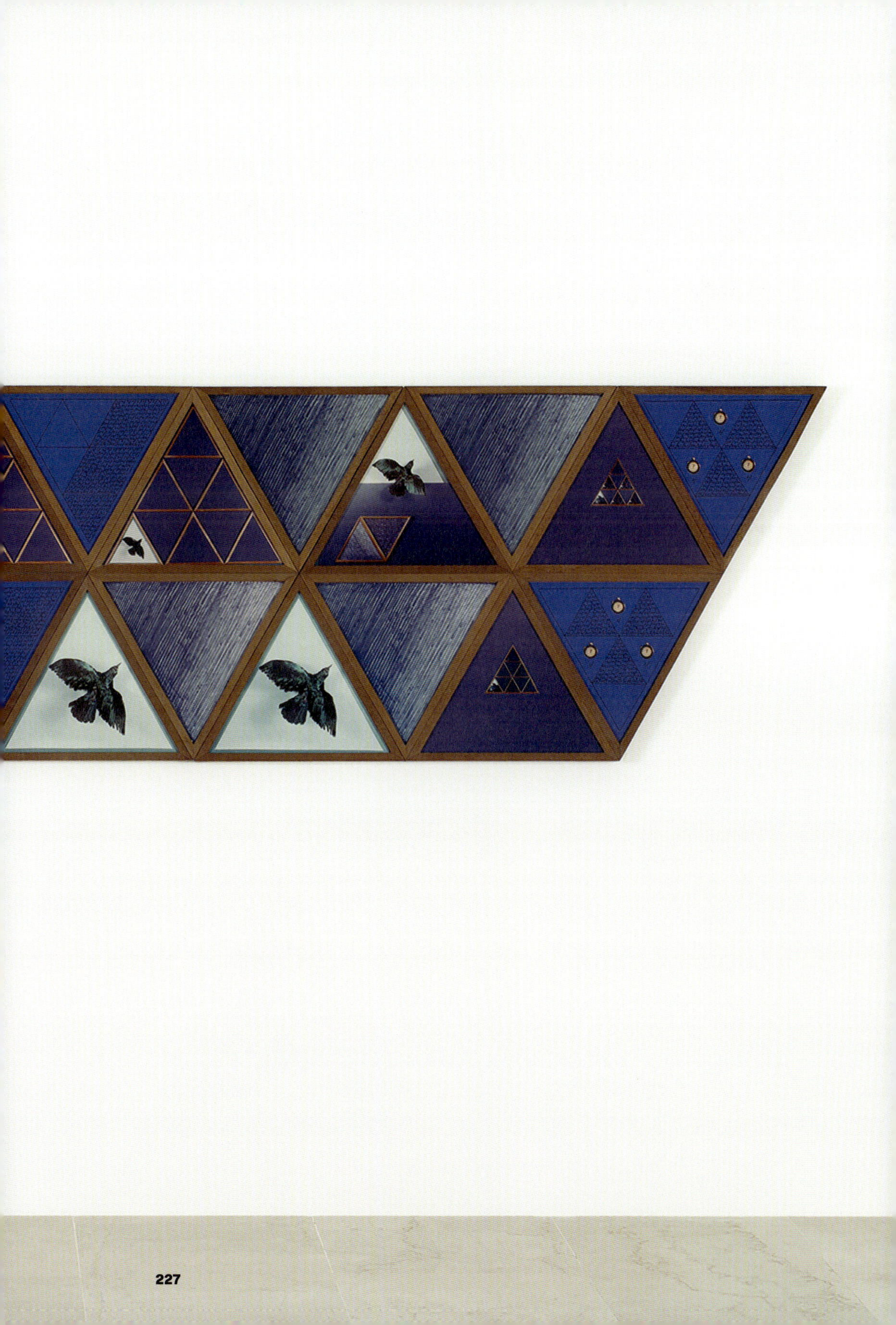

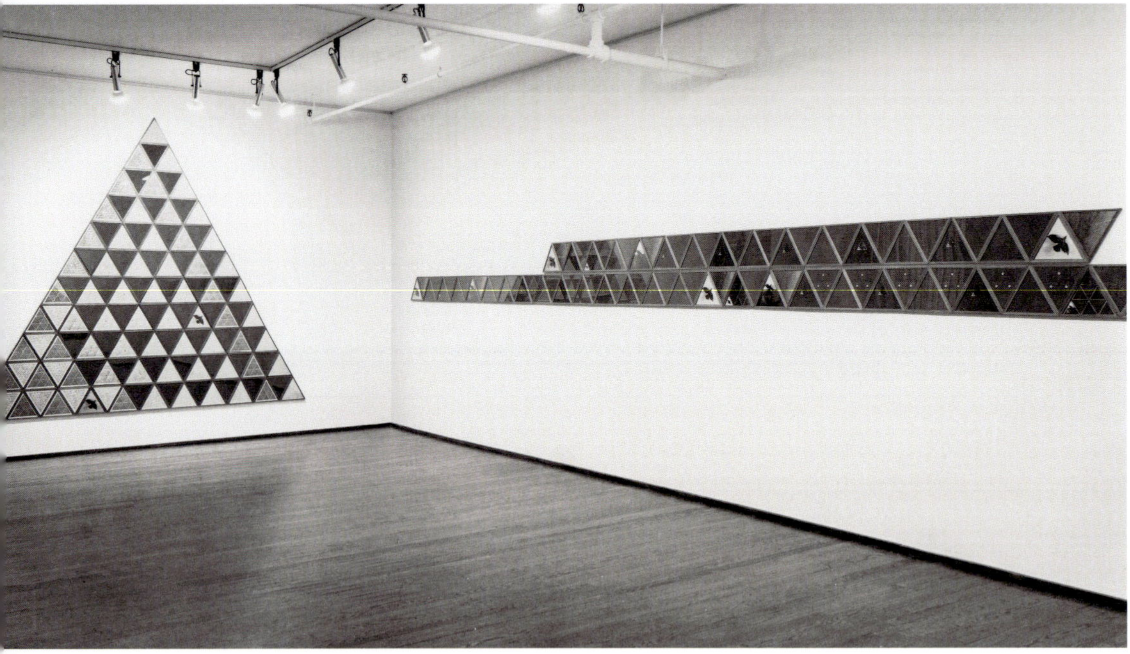

Exhibition view, *Laura Grisi*, Leo Castelli Gallery, New York, 1981

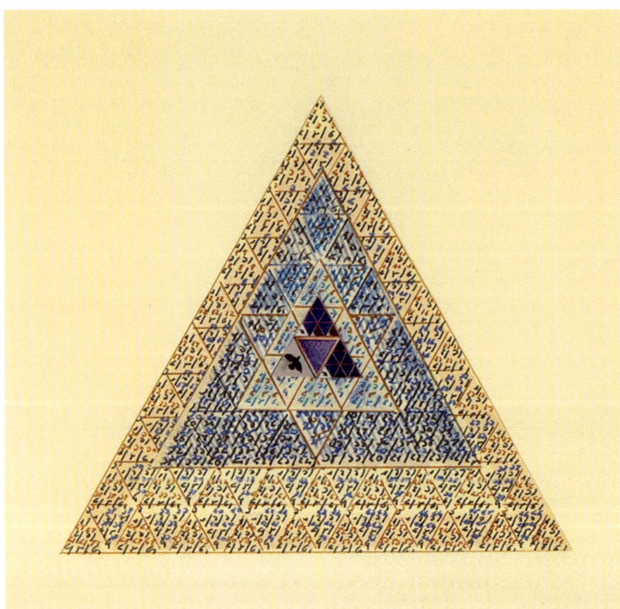

***Untitled*, 1980**

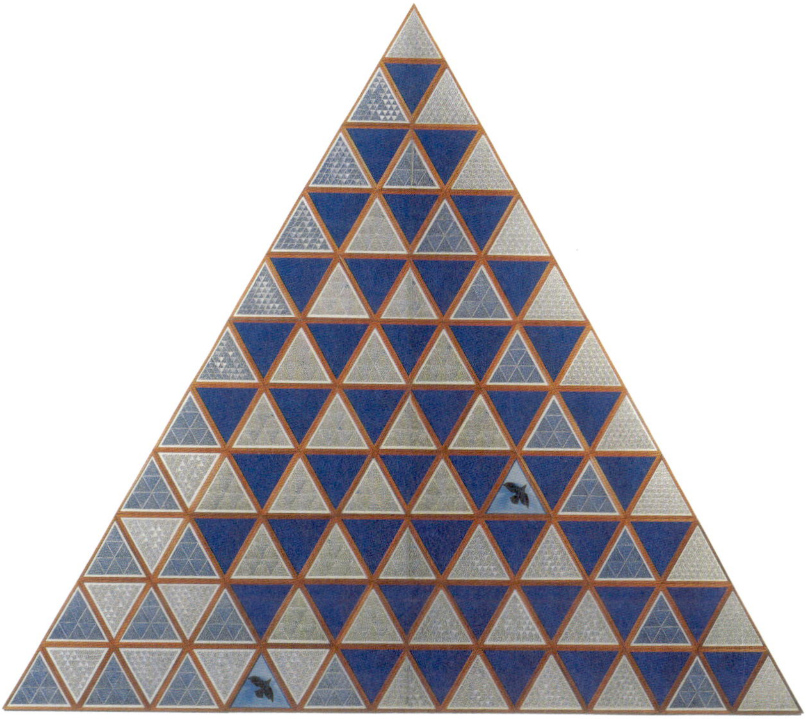

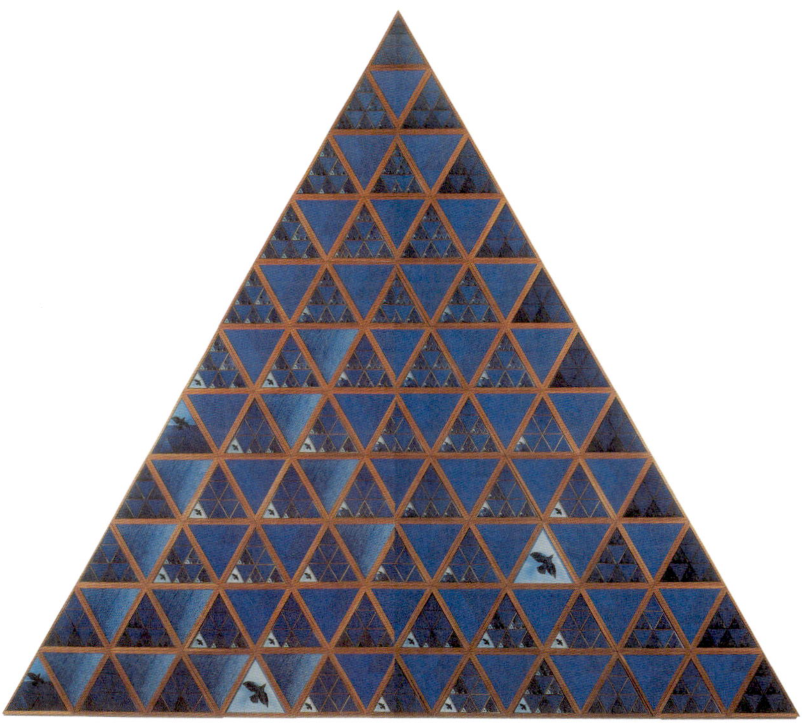

Triangle with Two Birds, 1980

Blue Triangle, 1980

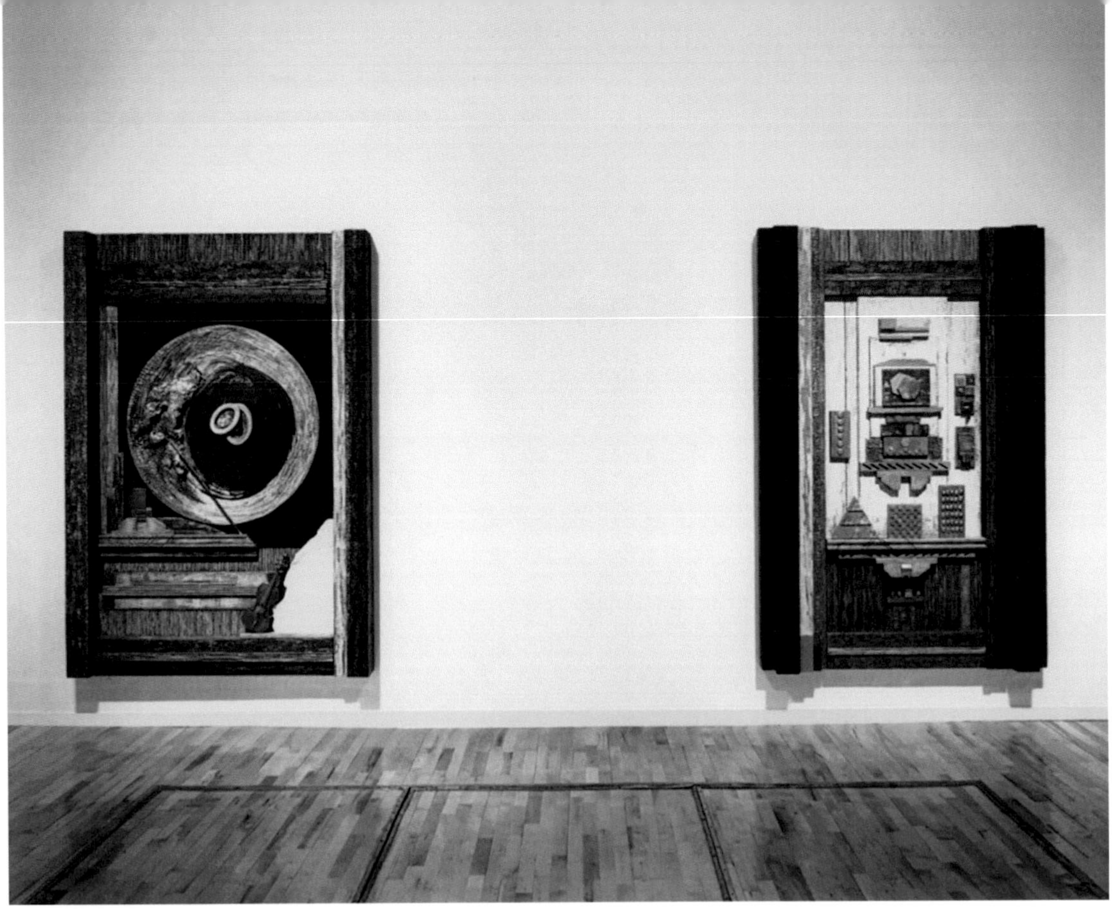

Exhibition view, *Laura Grisi*, Leo Castelli Greene Street Gallery, New York, 1986
With *Borromini's Violin* and *Diary*, both 1985

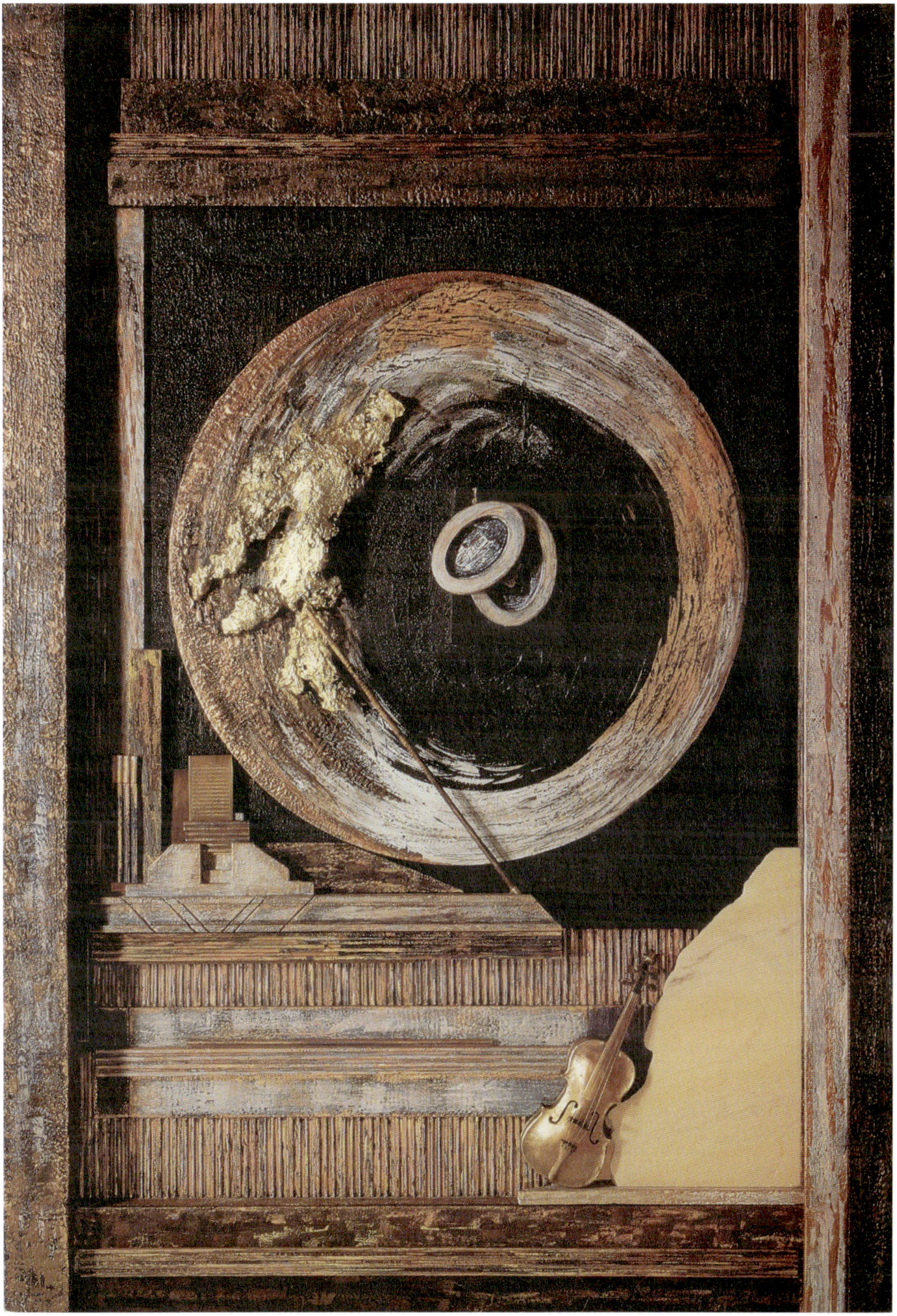

***Borromini's Violin*, 1985**

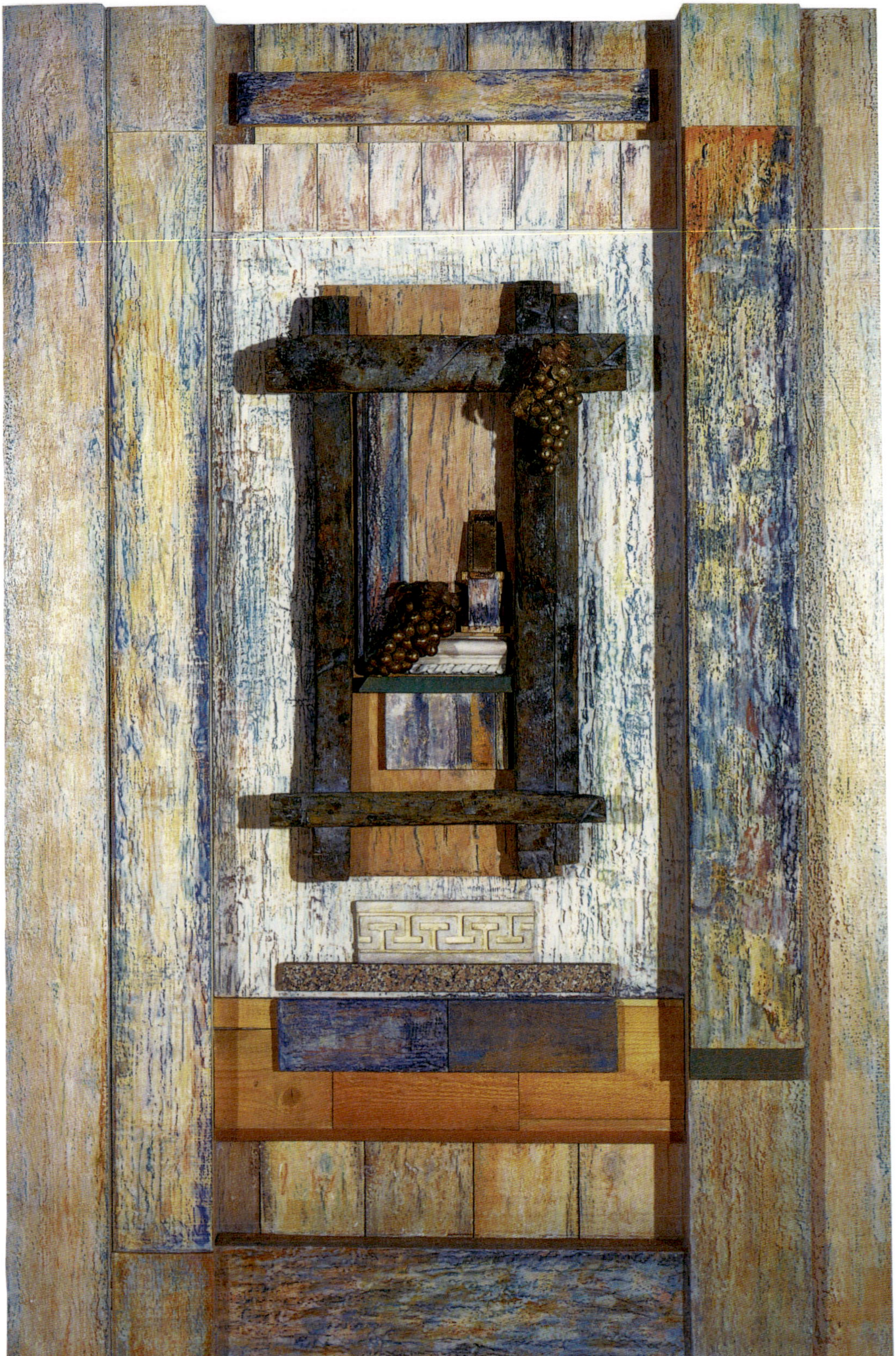

Classical Symmetry, 1985

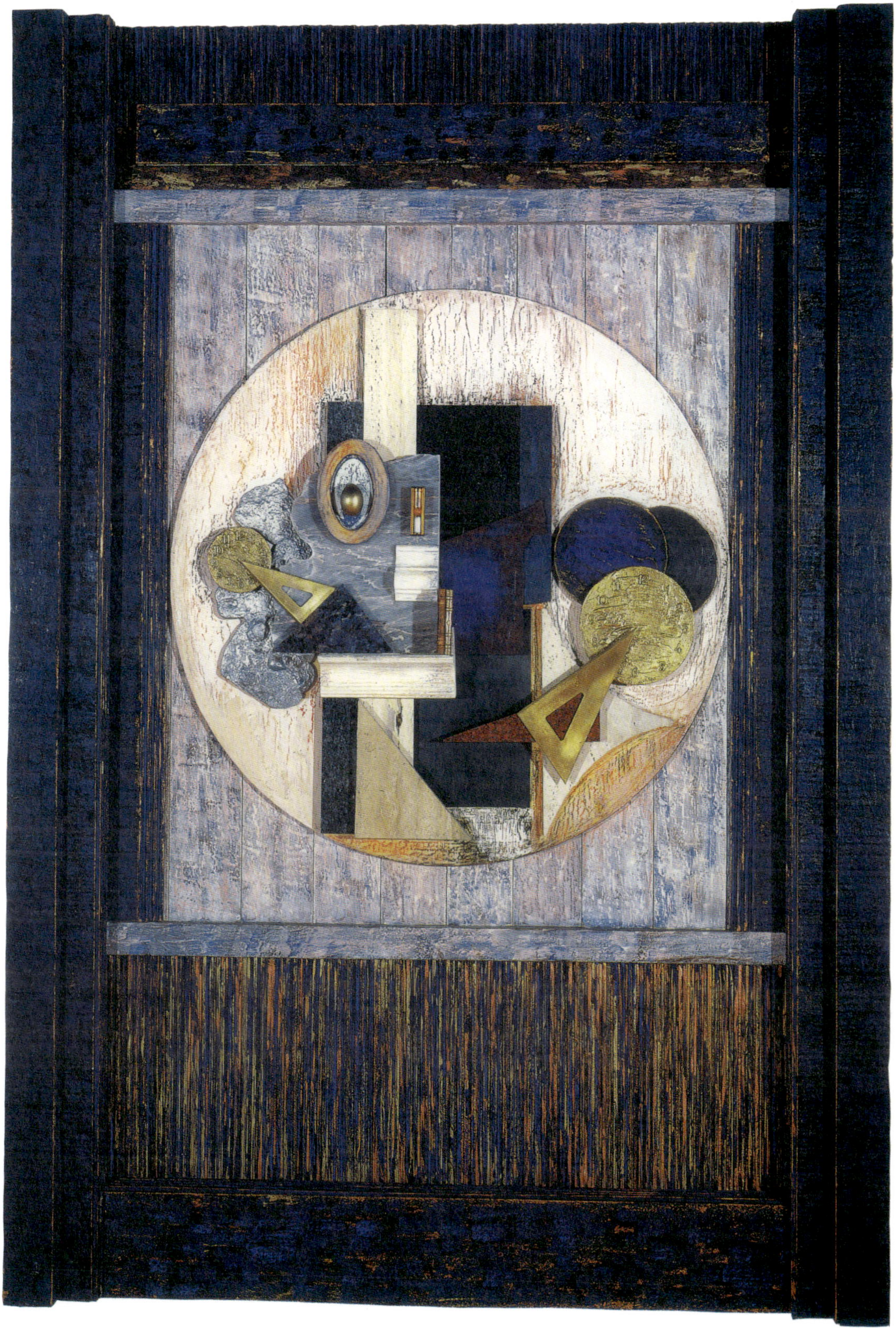

233 *Apollinaire's Secret*, 1985

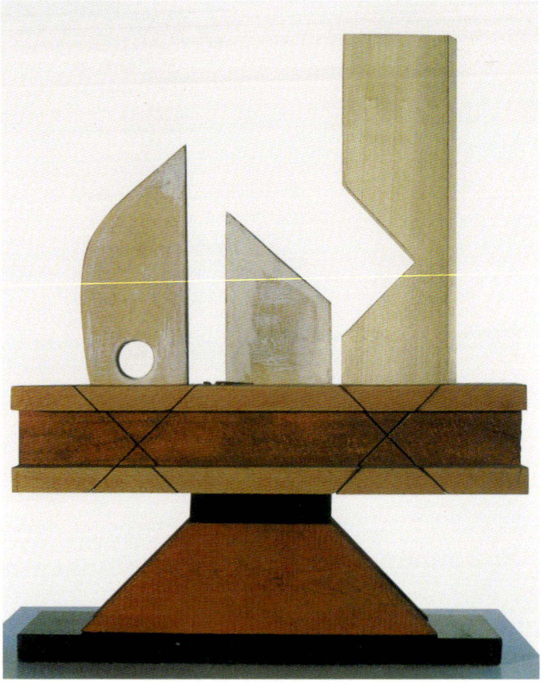

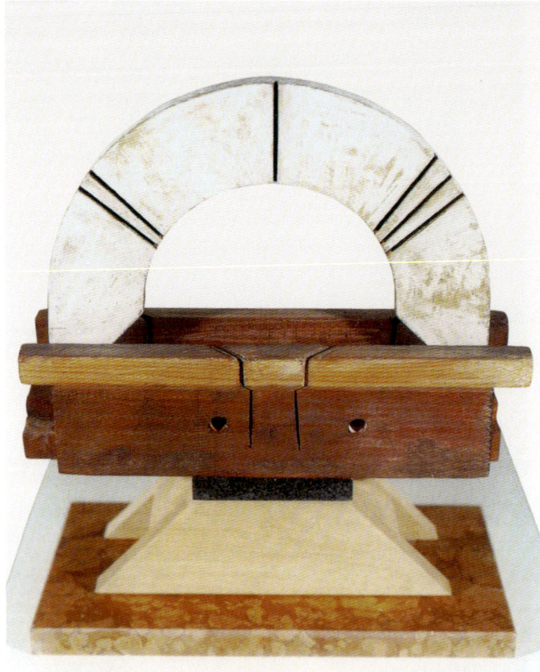

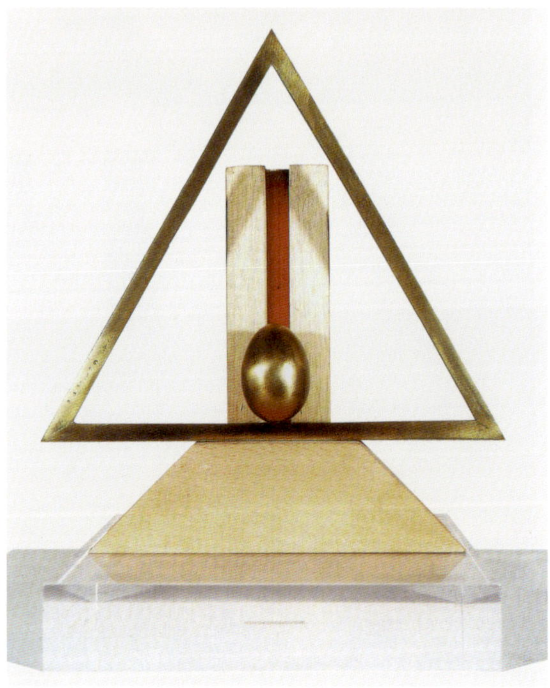

Time Geometry, 1985
Moondial, 1985
Urbino, 1985

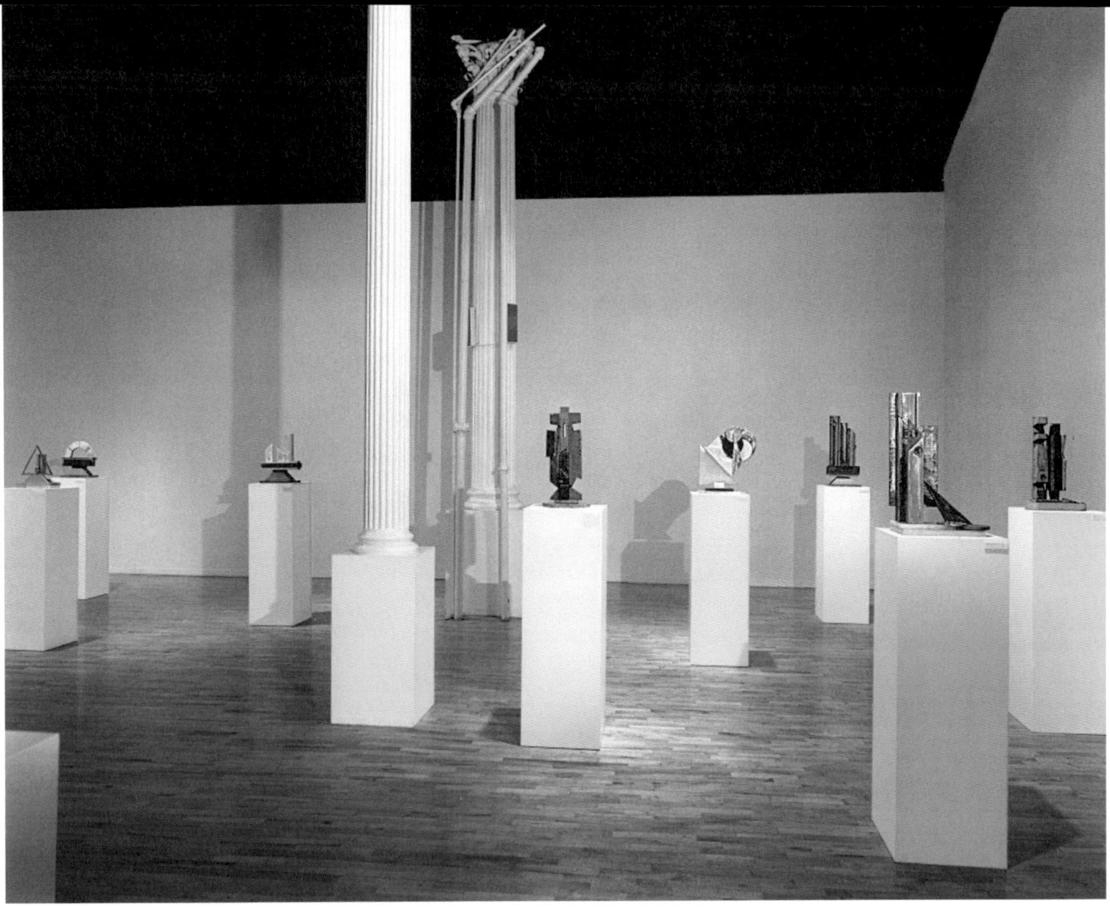

Exhibition view, *Laura Grisi*, Leo Castelli Greene Street Gallery, New York, 1986
With works from the "Sundials" series, 1985

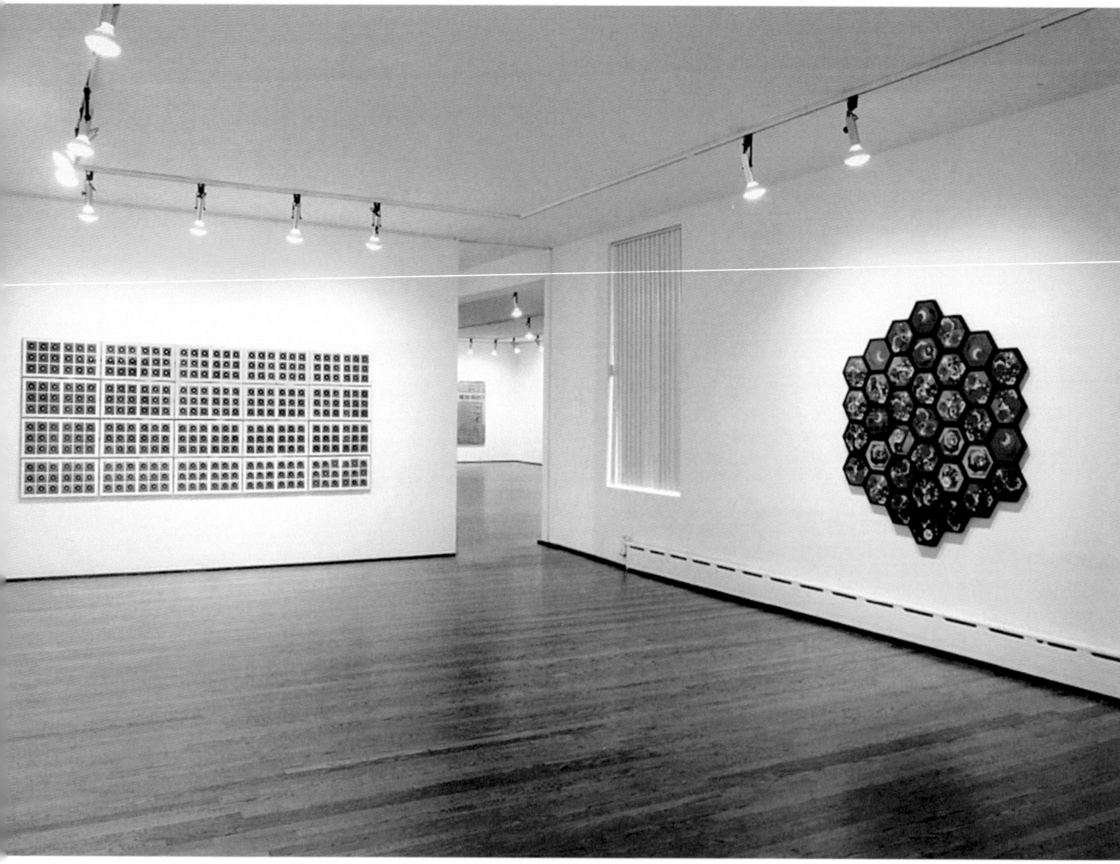

Exhibition view, *Laura Grisi. The Mirrored Series*, Leo Castelli Gallery, New York, 1992

Laura Grisi and Leo Castelli, 1990

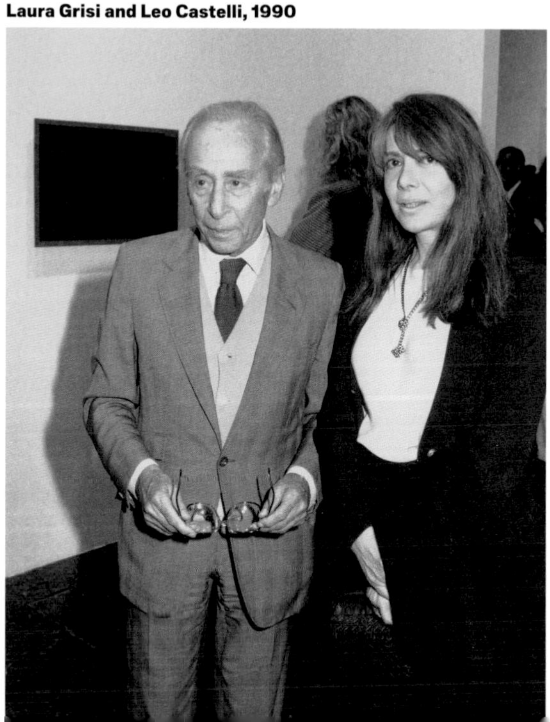

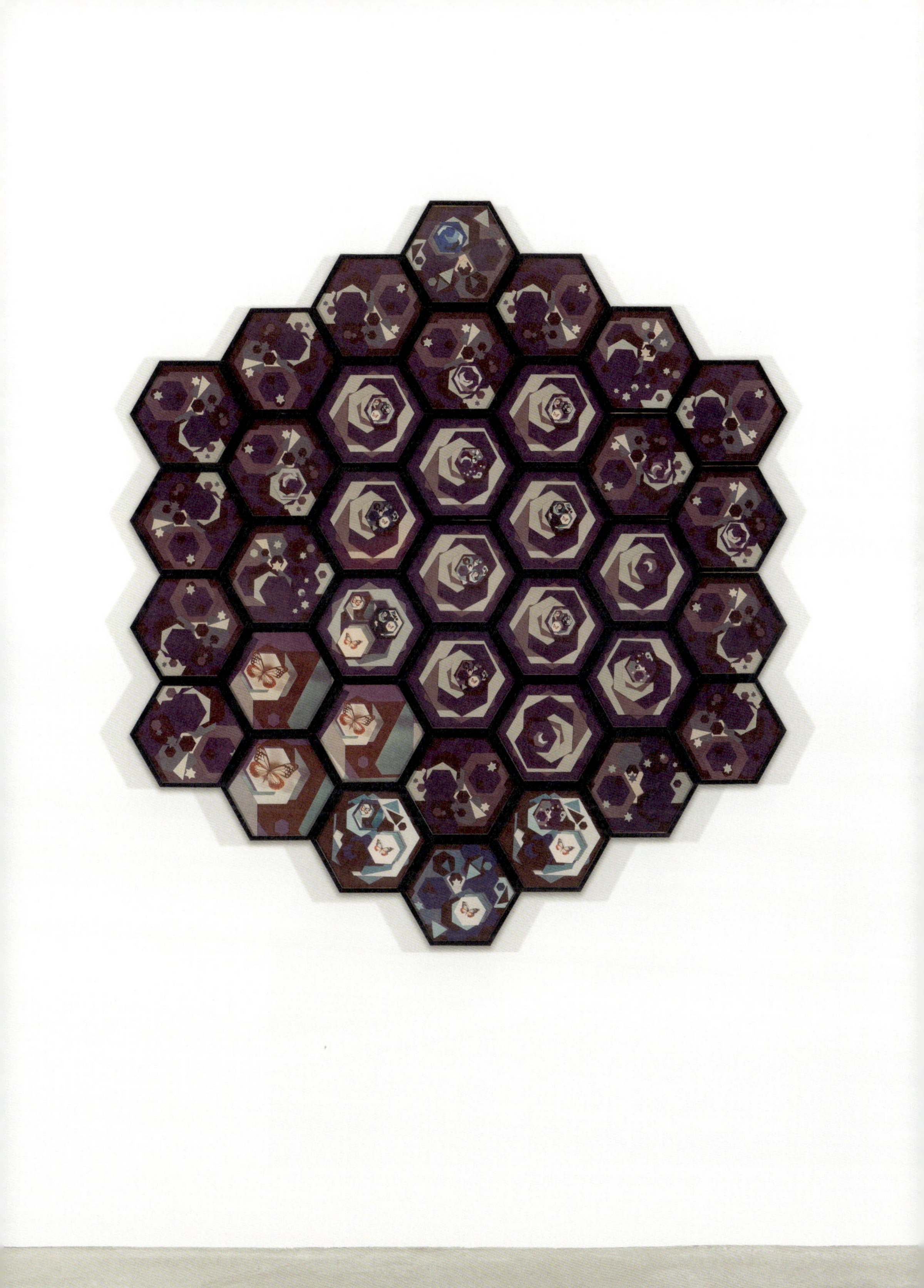

***Scheherazade Part 1*, 1982**

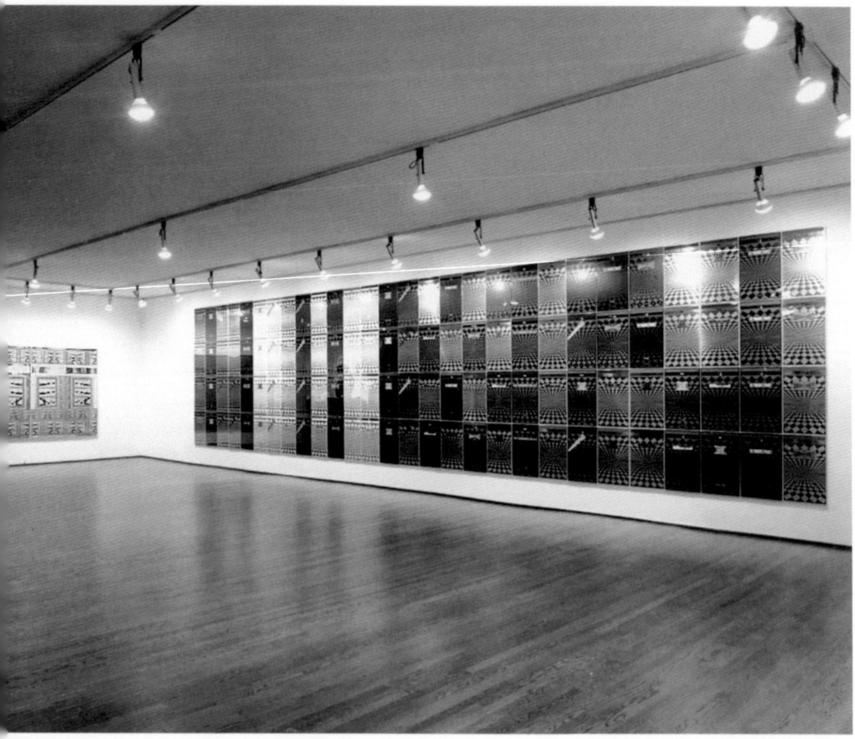

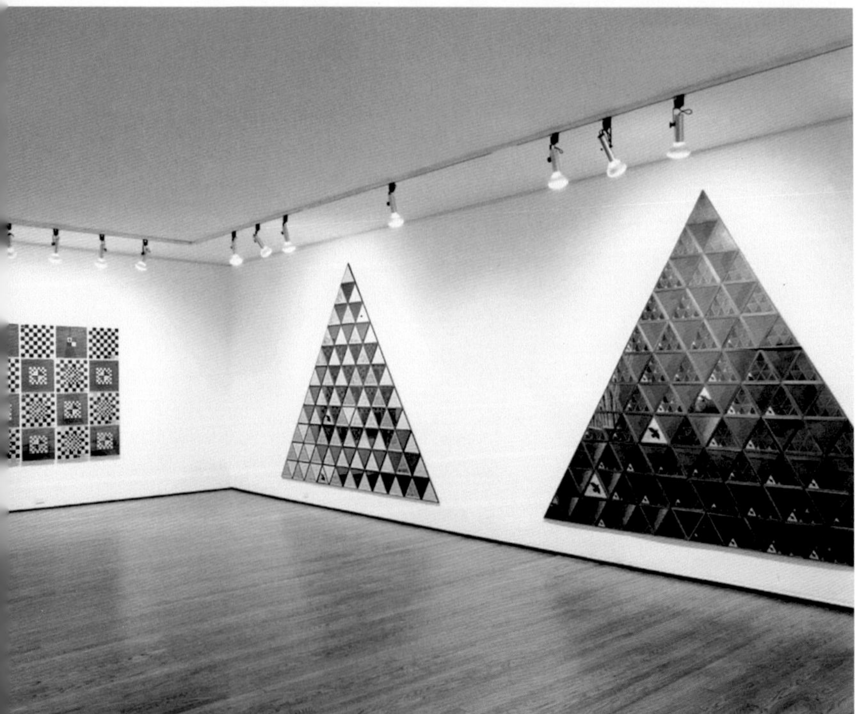

Exhibition views, *Laura Grisi. The Mirrored Series*, Leo Castelli Gallery, New York, 1992

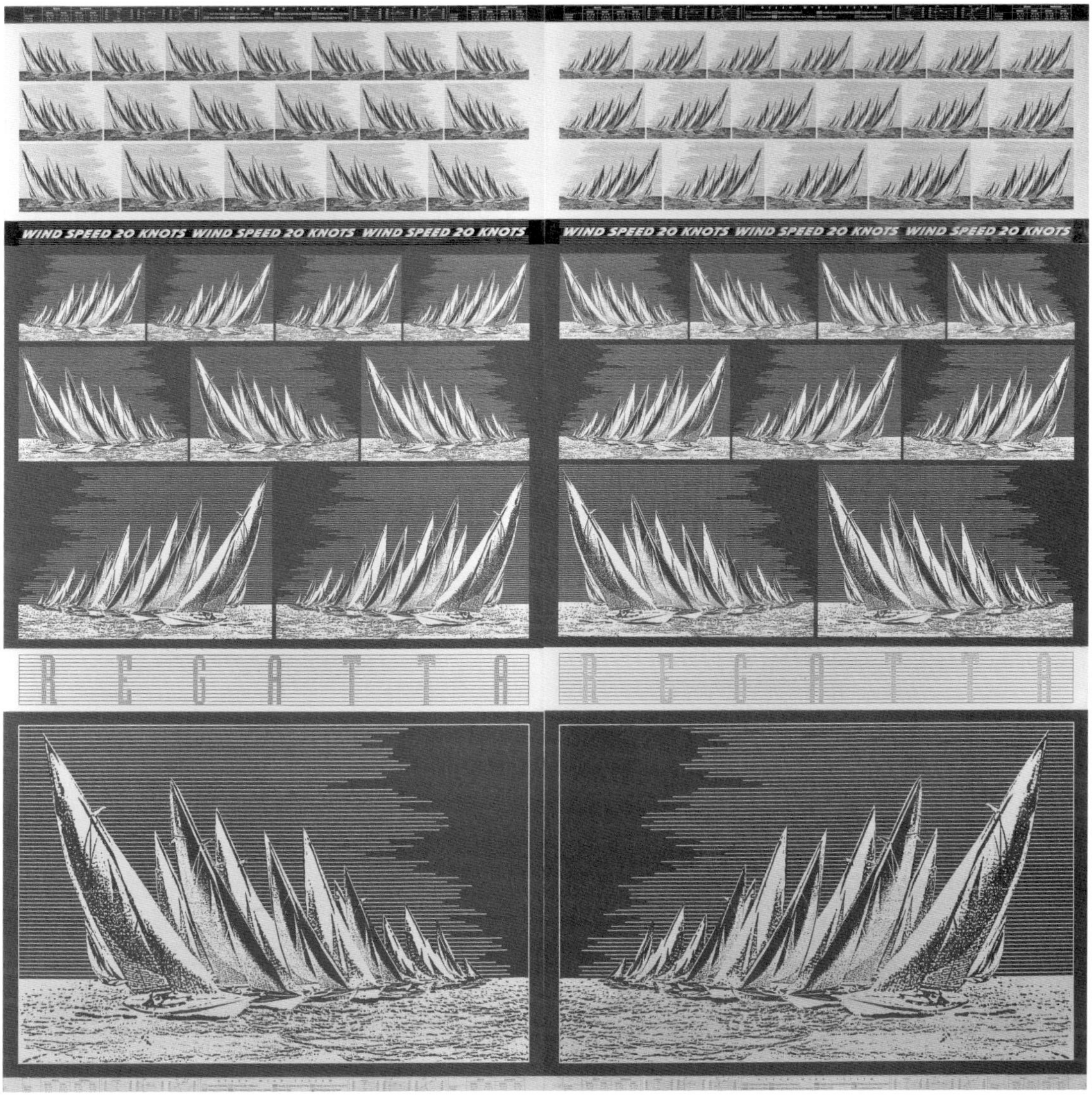

 Regatta, 1999

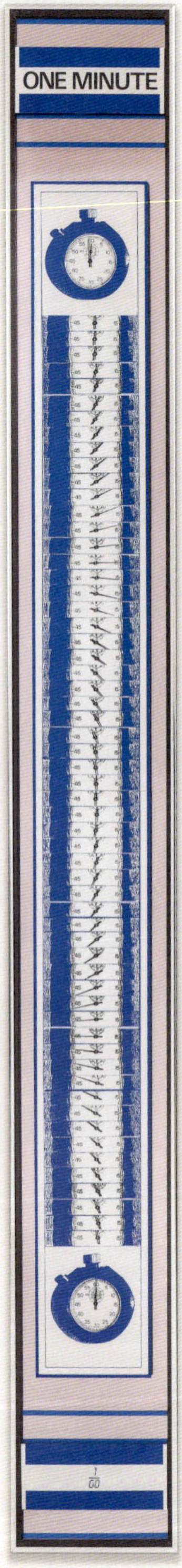

 ***One Minute*, 1975–1994**

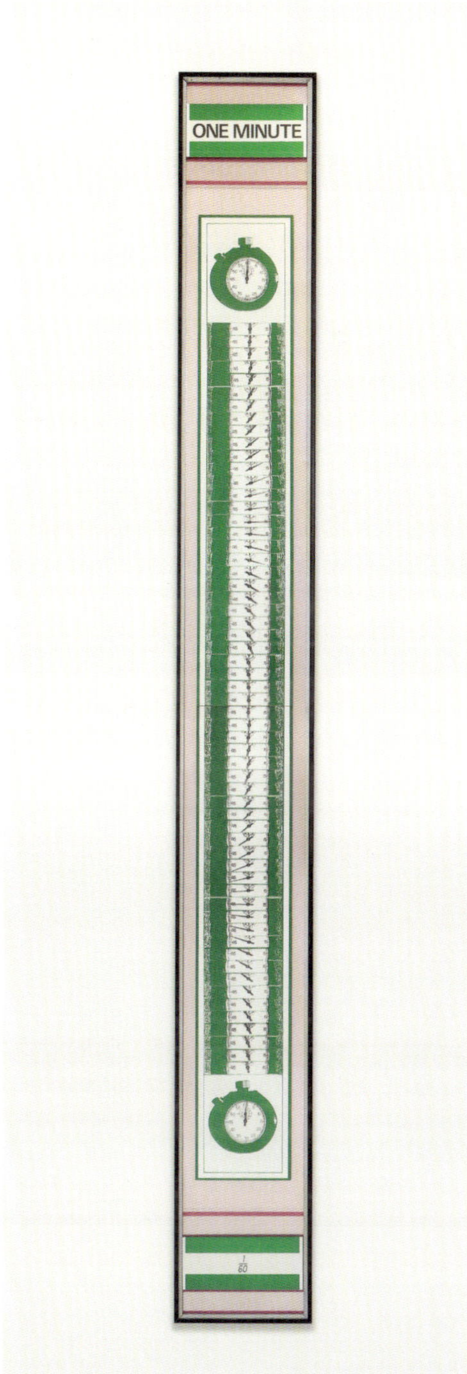

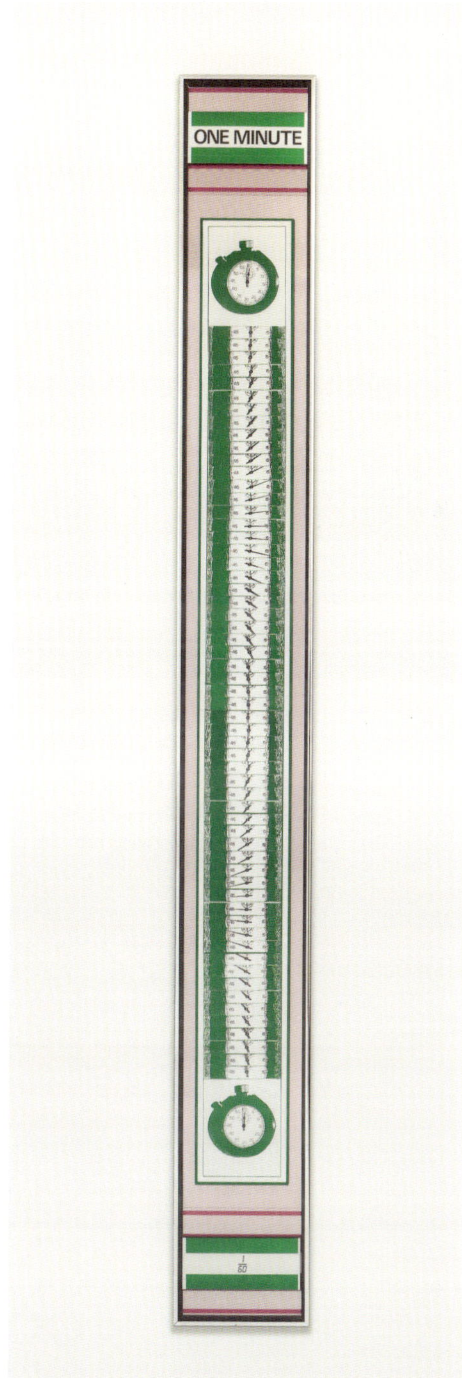

***One Minute*, 1975–1994**
***One Minute*, 1975–1994**

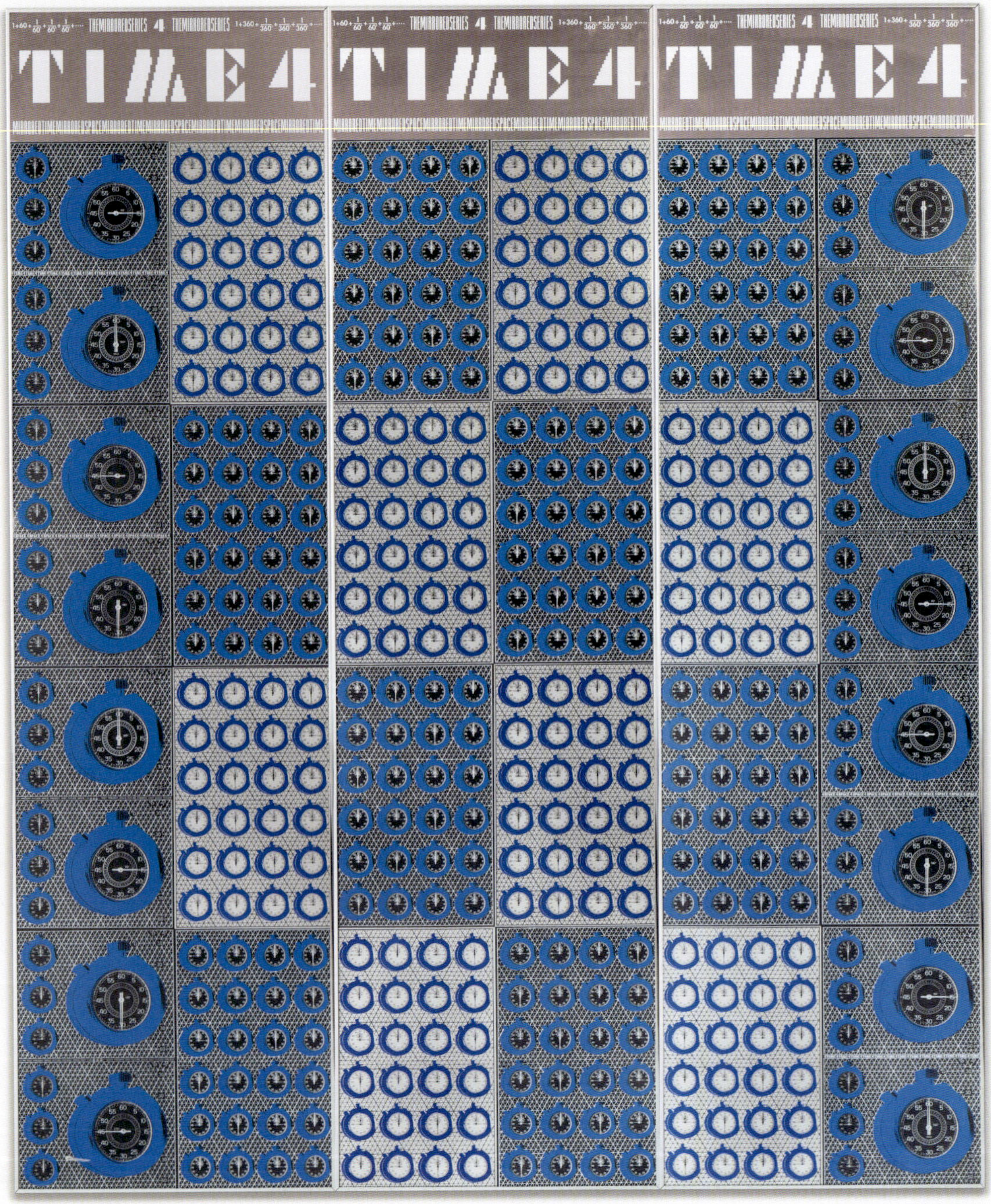

 Time4Time, 1994

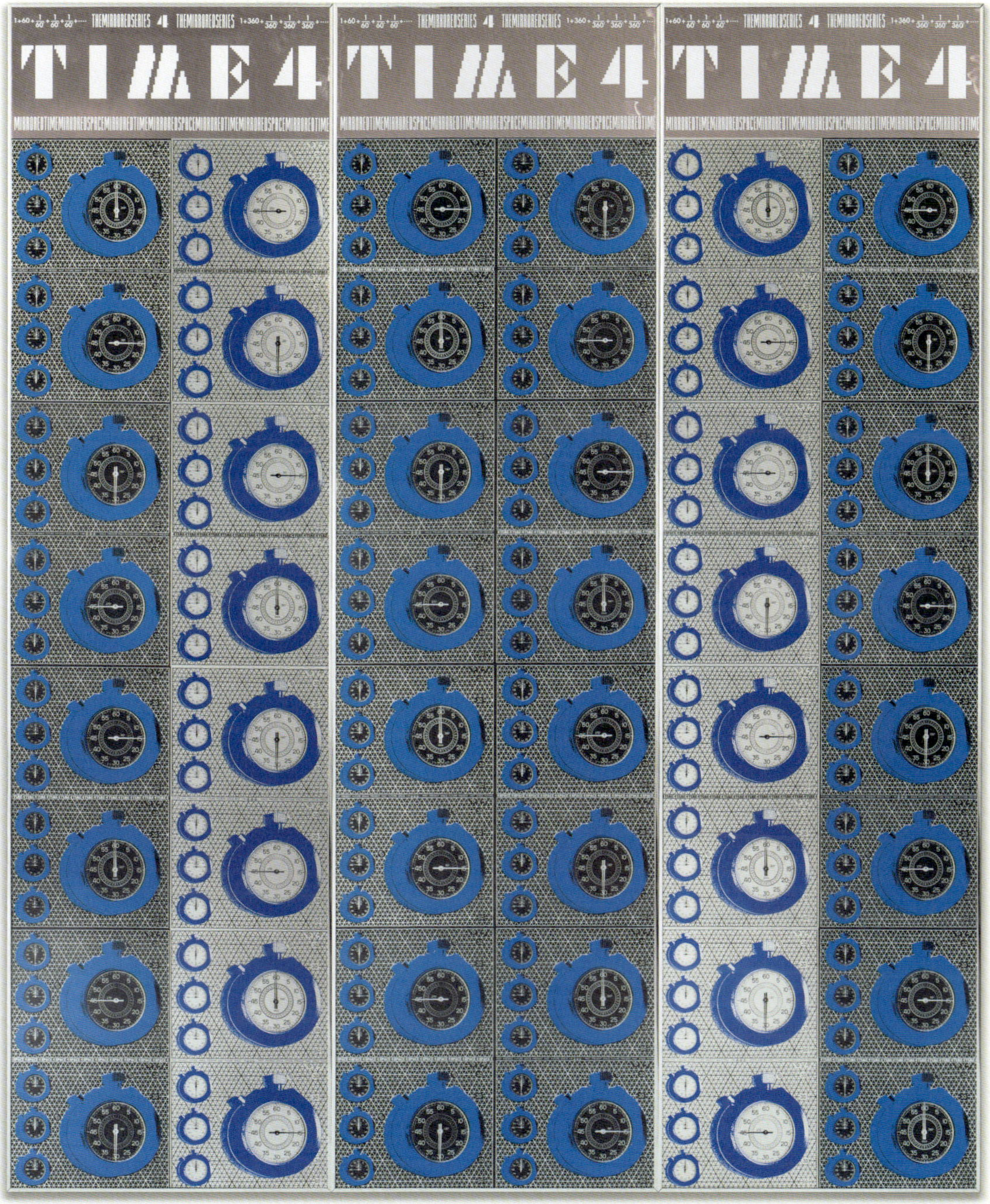

 Time4Time, 1994

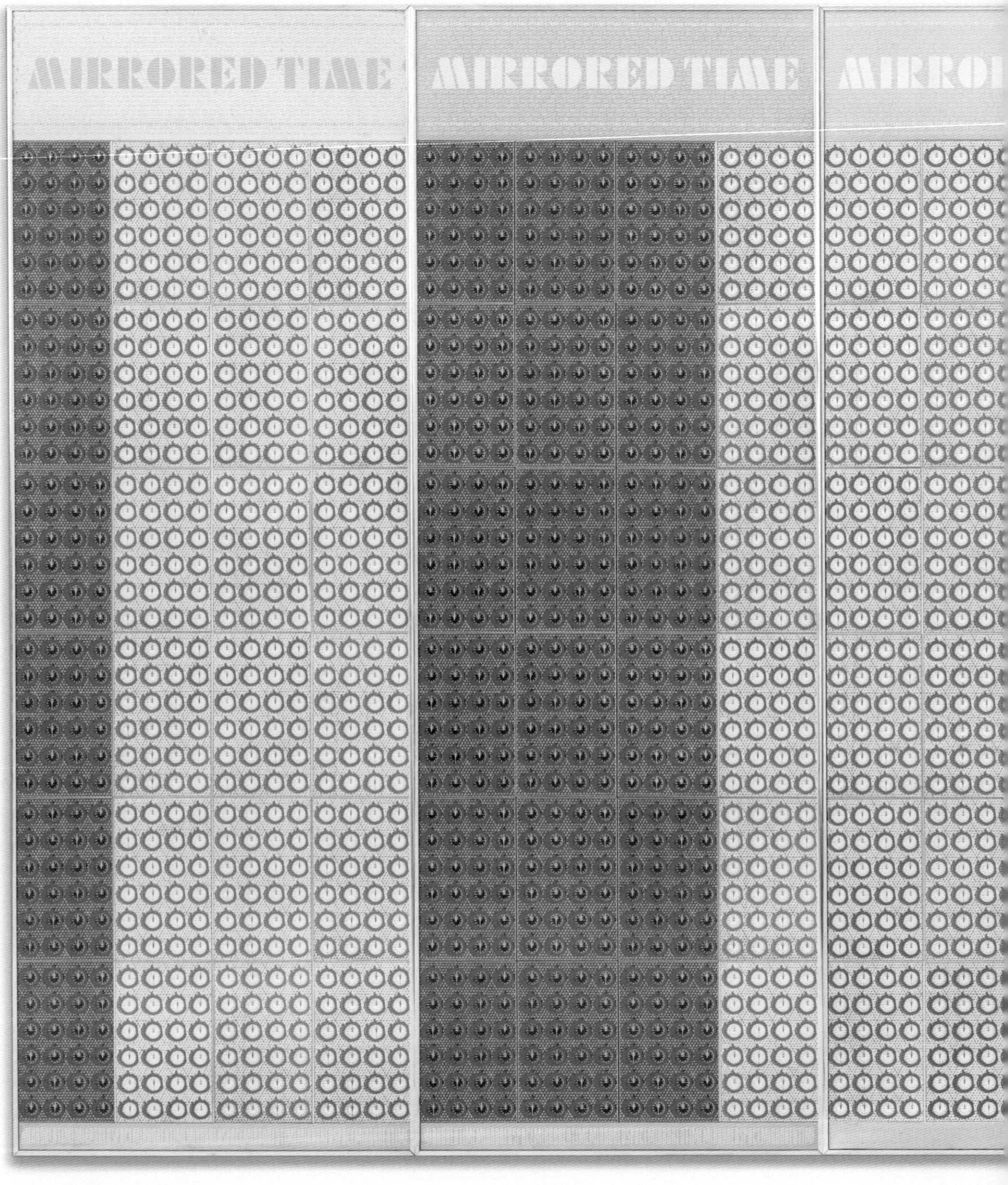
MIRRORED TIME
MIRRORED TIME

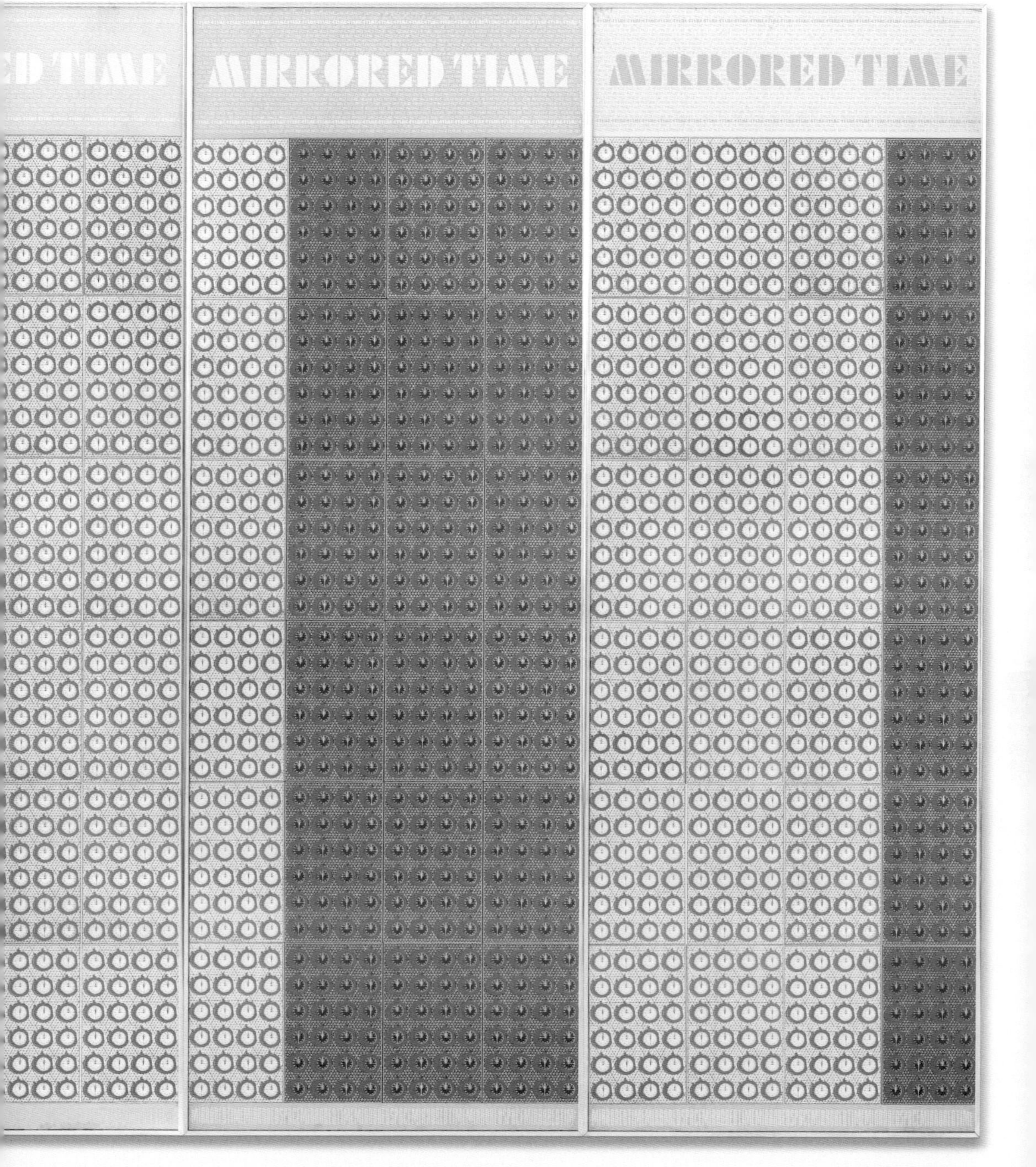
ED TIME
MIRRORED TIME
MIRRORED TIME

Eternity in an Hour
Martin Herbert

In her 1969 film *The Measuring of Time,* Laura Grisi sits on the seashore, counting grains of sand from her left hand and adding them to a sizable heap on her right. It is as if she had already begun this endless task—scientists continue to wrangle over whether there are more sand grains on Earth than stars in the universe or vice versa—an unconscionably long time ago, and will continue it for centuries after the 16mm camera shuts off. Redoubling the conceptual dimensions of the act via symbolic geometry, the film begins with a close-up of Grisi's hand manipulating these tiny objects created over geologic measures of time, spirals outward to take in the whole scene, then spirals in again, like breathing. The artwork cannot fully encircle the infinite—there is not enough film, nor human life—but it can point emphatically toward it as a graspable concept, as in William Blake's famous poetic injunction to "see a world in a grain of sand / And a heaven in a wild flower / Hold infinity in the palm of your hand / And eternity in an hour." At the point where the work stops, the wider world begins, somehow accounted for.

In her art, Laura Grisi wanted it all, while yieldingly marking the limits of the possible. Her practice, from the mid-1960s onward, enacts this in formal terms, too, alighting on stylistic approaches only to move on: Grisi's work harmonizes, at various points, with Pop, Minimalism, Kinetic art, Conceptualism, Systems art, Performance, and more, its restlessness indivisible from the artist's own peripatetic geographic motion and thematic preoccupations with movement, time, the natural world, and how those aspects might be represented via the typically static media of art. Already by 1966 with her "Variable Paintings" she had introduced dynamism and open-endedness into the usually immobile format of the canvas, incorporating sliding Plexiglas panels so that the compositions—fusing the natural (seascapes, clouds, birds, grapes) and the geometric—could be manipulated by the viewer. This was a redistribution of authorship in tune with the times (consider Charlotte Posenenske's subsequent sculptures circa 1967–1968, which could be modularly modified or rotated by gallerists or the public), but it also reflects Grisi's determination to infuse her art with bounded mobility, pointing wryly away from itself toward real limitlessness.

An art like that might get closer than most to the reigning spirit of the universe, in which everything is in perpetual, Heraclitean flux: the billion cubic light years' worth of matter released by the Big Bang has—we believe—only changed form over the millennia, not increased or reduced. But to be an artist is to be slightly removed from nature; you are a maker of fixed, generally static *things.* A way around this is to point to naturalistic qualities by their conspicuous absence, or create systemic microcosms of the larger reality you want to gesture toward (this, indeed, is the only way to deal with the boundlessness of infinity, no matter how big your gallery is). So a good deal of Grisi's art engages with nature while remaining emphatically cultural, and in doing so makes us mindful, respectful, and even awestruck in the same way that the famous 1968 *Earthrise* photograph taken during the Apollo 8 mission—the first image of our whole planet—was considered to have a galvanic effect on ecological consciousness. Grisi's 1967 *Racing Car Room* and *Model Car Racing* pieces, inspired by her love of Lotus cars—a pointedly cultural, technologized form of movement, of battling with time and space—cannot trap the barreling velocity of Formula One racing in art objects, so it alludes to the blur of movement via Perspex cutouts, neon light, and a reflecting floor. The following year's *Un'Area di Nebbia (A Space of Fog)* and *Antinebbia (Antifog)*—which anticipate, by decades, related perceptual experiments by Olafur Eliasson and Antony Gormley—with neon spirals sealed in Plexiglas towers, their light diffused by artificial fog, present, again, natural phenomena in technological translation.

One way of looking at Grisi's art, then, is as an elegant mobilizing of limit conditions and, at the same time, an illumination of things we might not otherwise remember to see as special, often using the white cube as a focusing device. In her 2019 book *How to Do Nothing,* the artist and writer Jenny Odell describes a progressive process of re-enchantment by nature triggered by various methods of heightening attention (deep listening to city sounds after a John Cage concert; learning the names of plants; communing with crows, etc). Grisi, in the late 1960s, would propose something similar through controlled environments that replicate elemental phenomena: her *Volume of Air* (1968), in which a white neon filament marking out the dimensions of the room makes the air within it a speculative sculpture; her *Drops of Water* of the same year, which—again, long before Random International's tech-heavy simulacrum *Rain Room* (2012)—brought the weather (and the meditative sound of rainfall) inside.

There is a cumulative logic to this restive oeuvre, a gradual revealing of the possibilities released by connecting deliberately with what surrounds us (and what is within us). *Distillations: 3 Months of Looking* (1970) is comparable to contemporaneous works such as Lee Lozano's text pieces recounting her social (and antisocial) experiments, but much less urban. An outcrop of Grisi's wanderlust, it finds her alchemizing art during a multi-month, global tour—spending extended periods of time in places where "primitive" cultures still persisted—observing (for example) the movement of palms or the ocean or the material specifics of fire. This is generous work, with an applicable and adaptable takeaway: it reminds us that seeing, as a prelude to understanding, is a skill that can always be honed, intensified (even if you are already an artist); that there is always something new to see. You can, if you like, have this work symbolically in your pocket the next time you leave the house, which is to say that it exists weightlessly in the present.

It is hard to say exactly at what point Grisi's art expands from the material world into the speculative and theoretic—perhaps on the beach in 1969, or when she began using combinatory systems of pebbles (e.g. the exhaustive photo series *Pebbles,* 1973) as metonymic for the set of all pebbles, all *things* in their myriad variations and iterations—or whether there is really any dividing line at all. Her practice does move, though, from phenomena that we might, in an increasingly technocratic society, be progressively isolated from (hence her spending time in decidedly converse societies), to surrounding conditions that in themselves are hard to grasp or make visual. *Hypothesis about Time* (1975) elegantly condenses the Einsteinian concept of space-time—the three dimensions of space plus a fourth, time—in which all moments of the past, present, and future "exist"; we just have not visited some of them yet. Grisi's 360 frontal photographs of a blue stopwatch show its hands moving progressively forward and backward, time pivoting on its axis. She coupled this work with a *Hypothesis about Space* (1975), 266 images of rotating hexagons signaling the artist's brainiac thesis that, after six rotations, the hexagon does not return to its original position, but, thanks to the added dimension of the time taken for the process to transpire, the original hexagon is gone and this is now a *new* hexagon. It is part of the understated humor of Grisi's art—think, again, of that huge mound of sand that she had supposedly counted out before the camera was switched on—that none of this is visible in the work; it is pure, if science-backed, conjecture.

Time leads her naturally back to infinity, and to the conundrum of its representation. In his 1979 treatise *Gödel, Escher, Bach: An Eternal Golden Braid*, Douglas Hofstadter makes repeated reference to the tortoise in Zeno's Paradox (via Lewis Carroll, who nestled it into his own writing), in which the tortoise proves to

Achilles through logic that the former would win a race across a room if given a ten-meter head start, because Achilles would have to first cross half that distance, and then half of that, and so on in continually smaller halves, which are never-ending, such that he could never traverse the room. Grisi's *Endless Dialogue* (1977) finds form for such mental gymnastics, in a 22-part series of photographs in which a tortoise travels along a chessboard marked with subdivisions to increasing powers of ten, only to be confronted, at the penultimate square, with a recursion—the same chessboard miniaturized, in which the shell-toting beast is back at the first square; and so on, in various permutations. Something similar happens in her *Blue Triangle* (1980), a work made up of latticework of framed ink-on-cardboard panels, in which a triangle is subdivided into smaller triangles in which the bird's flight—across the "big" triangle—is continually thwarted by further subdivisions, which we are given to see could be endless.

In subsequent works, both playful and hermetic, drawing on and giving form to concepts by Parmenides and Isaac Newton, among others, and musical structures by Bach, Grisi prowled around notions that would seem resistant to visuality, to being seen. You cannot picture infinity, count every grain of sand, bring the natural world wholly into a gallery, or fully convey what it means to be enraptured by reality, by anti-intuitive scientific conjecture, by a sense of our place in the universe. What you can generate, though—and she does, with the highest ambitions—is wonder, and Grisi makes wonder contagious. In a sense, though she traveled far from the "Variable Paintings," she never stopped inviting viewers to intervene in her works. We pick up where they leave off: where they say, as it were, this cannot be shown, this grandeur; you can only think about it, try and hold this sense of nature, of the infinite, of the infinite variety of the natural world, in your mind. And, inevitably, we do. It hurts, but beautifully.

Not Even the Choice of Having to Choose
Krzysztof Kosciuczuk

* All quotes are from Laura Grisi's conversation with Germano Celant (1989), see p. 188–222 in this volume.

"He took the biscuits carefully out of the packet and laid them face upward on the grass, in order as he felt of edibility. They were the same as always, a Ginger, an Osborne, a Digestive, a Petit Beurre and one anonymous. He always ate the first-named last, because he liked it the best, and the anonymous first, because he thought it very likely the least palatable. The order in which he ate the remaining three was indifferent to him and varied irregularly from day to day. On his knees now before the five it struck him for the first time that these prepossessions reduced to a paltry six the number of ways in which he could make his meal. But this was to violate the very essence of the assortment, this was red permanganate on the Rima of variety. Even if he conquered his prejudice against the anonymous, still there would be only twenty-four ways in which the biscuits could be eaten. But were he to take the final step and overcome his infatuation with the Ginger, then the assortment would spring to life before him, dancing the radiant measure of its total permutability, edible in a hundred and twenty ways!"

This is a passage in Samuel Beckett's early novel, *Murphy* (1938), in which the protagonist sits down to a daily frugal meal of biscuits in London's Hyde Park. Shortly before, Murphy witnesses a defaced statue of Rima—a bas-relief by Jacob Epstein erected in 1925 to commemorate the writer and naturalist William H. Hudson, which became hugely controversial, both in real life and in the novel, due to its nudity—splattered with red paint and being cleaned up. Having realized the limited array of choices he has left himself to consume what little food he has, Murphy, frustrated, compares it to the vandalizing of the statue—an attack on art itself. The solution, it seems, is yielding to one's preferences and dislikes for the sake of mathematical permutation.

From the late 1950s and into the 2000s, the multifarious practice of Laura Grisi aligned with a number of genres and stylistic idioms. One might dissect and examine her biography to come up with what will seem to be perfectly convincing explanations for the presence of the different aspects and approaches: the mise-en-scènes in Grisi's work can be connected with her stint at the Dobuzhinskys' workshop of set and costume design in Paris. "In their atelier everyone was always 'inventing' materials to make objects that, on the set, had to seem completely real, but that were really composed of so-called 'fake' stuff. We had to manipulate the 'fiction' of the stage."* Scientific mind and individual regime are due to the influence of her father: "What my father liked best was reading and doing research in physics, mathematics, and geometry [...] Two of his projects [...] were analyzed by a group of American technicians. They found his work so interesting that they invited him to work with them at the Massachusetts Institute of Technology in Cambridge, but he preferred to continue his experiments on his own." Photographs are the result of pure necessity—lengthy and distant travels do not allow much time for studio work: "While I was traveling, I could only make easily portable pieces like gouaches and drawings, and so I concentrated on photography and writing." Film had always been present for her: Grisi's father had a film production and distribution company, her brother Fausto also made films and opened an advertising company for cinematic productions in Venezuela. "In fact, I seem to be the only one in my family who is not a professional filmmaker." Then came the Nouvelle Vague which, one might argue, made a lasting impression on Grisi's questioning of the gaze of both the cinematic lens as well as the human eye. So, in all of the novelty of her practice, there is, in fact, little new. But, "Chaque vague, c'est une nouvelle vague," (Each wave is a new wave) she concluded, mockingly quoting René Clair while speaking with Germano Celant in 1989.

To trace the individual influences, ascribe stylistic criteria, and ultimately argue for a belated recognition in constellations that did not allow the artist to be present, would be less productive and rewarding (for both Grisi and contemporary audiences I dare to say) than to turn our attention to what emerge as inconsistencies, rifts, if not patent paradoxes, in her work in art historical categories.

Among Grisi's abundant drawings made between 1964 and 1966 are studies of perception, of how the photographic and camera lens capture and, in essence, distort the captured object. These come close to scientific diagrams—analytical renderings tracing the field of view, and how it is affected by the conditions of the device meant to convey it. They question the objectivity and fidelity of the photographic image in a scientific way. In 1966 Grisi created *Sphere with Grass Field*, one of her more intriguing works in which an acrylic painting of a meadow, encased in Plexiglas, is fronted by a large hovering sphere of blue plastic sheltering a fragment of the same landscape. Here the lens is more of a metaphor: it is, perhaps, the human eye, or the Earth as the blue planet. From a mathematical calculation to a poetic rendering, Grisi's practice is arguably most compelling if we see it as one straddling two extremes.

There are constant tensions at play between the open-ended nature of her "Variable Paintings" (1965–1966), and the closedness of the works involving permutations, such as *Pebbles* (1973) and *Stripes* (1974); between the complexly layered, structured "Neon Paintings" (1966–1967) and the works deploying natural elements and casting their physical sensations in the foreground, such as *Wind Speed 40 Knots*, *Drops of Water*, and *Refraction* (all 1968). But even then, Grisi does not move far away from meticulous observation and a reflection on it: if her drawings from the mid-1960s questioned the mechanical gaze, *Refraction* is a set of four containers filled with water in which the artist submerged several dozen thin metal rods, which demonstrates that the human eye is no better; it can be easily tricked into believing that things appear different than they are. Then, again, comes the moment of what can almost be called self-mockery and driving the stubborn scientific method into the wall: *The Measuring of Time* (1969), a film that has lent its title to the exhibition at Muzeum Susch, is a visually captivating recording of about six minutes that questions the very ambition to arrive at and deliver hard results of methodical thinking. As Martin Herbert wrote in his essay for this publication: "It is part of the understated humor of Grisi's art—think, again, of that huge mound of sand that she had supposedly counted out before the camera was switched on—that none of this is visible in the work; it is pure, if science-backed, conjecture." One can count, measure, calculate, but the job is supposedly never finished. Perhaps it is truly not the task of an artist to deliver hard facts, but to question them instead. This is what makes Grisi's position distinct among many conceptual artists. There is hardly an ambition to make a definite statement. Rather, these are statements garnered from observation and filtered through personal experience. They are statements about what seems to be accessible to us, not about what we can claim.

The exhibition's curator Marco Scotini has chosen to conclude it with a sequence of works concerning time: *Tempo Reale*, *Drawing for Time*, and *Hypothesis about Time* (all 1975). In so doing he has come full circle, from the photographic works of the earlier decade to a moment in which Grisi seems to challenge the very way we relate to each other. *Hypothesis about Time* features photographs of a permutation of a single minute, and calls into question the nature of the flow of time.

This is the first publication about the artist in almost two decades, and the flow of time, at least in the way we measure it between ourselves, still seems relevant. I would like to thank Grażyna Kulczyk, the Founder of Muzeum Susch and the Chairwoman of the Board of Art Stations Foundation CH; Marco Scotini, the curator of the exhibition; the Laura Grisi Estate in Rome; Gallery P420 in Bologna; Anke Kempkes, Director of Instituto Susch; and Clément Dirié of JRP|Editions for having an unwavering trust in this ambitious project and making it possible.

Laura never gave up the curiosity of observing, nor the opportunity to be surprised. "One afternoon in the Sahara, about two hours before sunset, the sun's rays were shining in a kind of diagonal light, and we saw a mirage. On the horizon, the sand dunes appeared to be reflected in a water surface on which a man and two camels were slowly walking. The sand dunes were reflected upside down, reversed. I took a picture of the mirage, and was surprised later when I saw it exactly reproduced in my color photograph; in a way, I had expected that this immaterial, nonexistent image could not be recorded on film."

What she stood to prove as one of the early ones to do it, was that perception based on visual or mathematical rationality was lacking when speaking about our experience of the world. Other methods, based on the bodily or the speculative, but not on vision itself, are just as adequate. The choices that are there to be made are hardly fully informed. As Scotini aptly pointed out in his essay in this publication, "Permutation is effectively the opposite of selection."

"Overcome by these perspectives Murphy fell forward on his face on the grass, beside those biscuits of which it could be said as truly as of the stars, that one differed from another, but of which he could not partake in their fullness until he had learnt not to prefer any one to any other."

Laura Grisi
Rhodes, 1939–Rome, 2017

Laura Grisi, 1960s

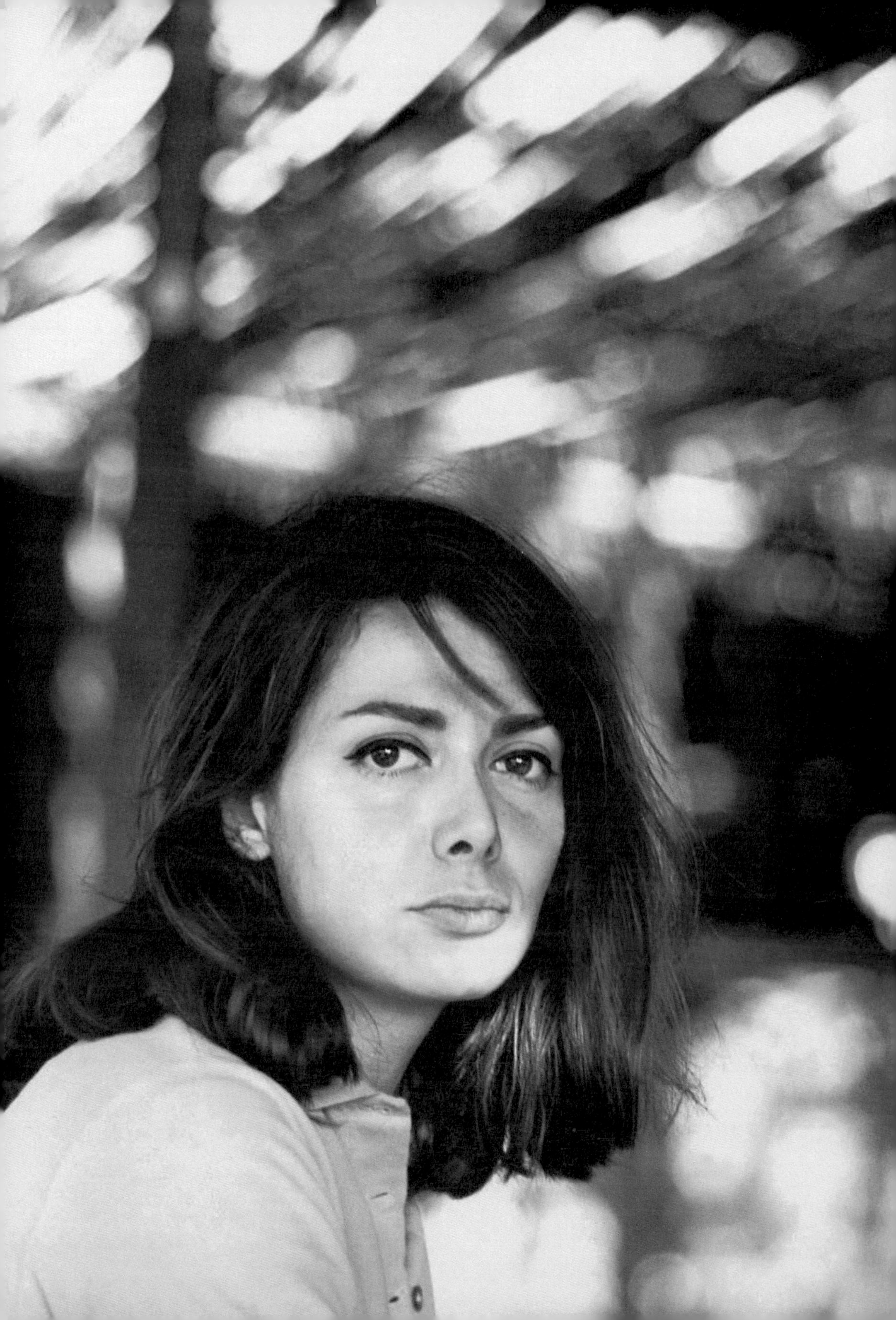

SOLO EXHIBITIONS

1964
- Galleria Il Segno, Rome
- Errepi, Bologna

1965
- Galleria dell'Ariete, Milan

1968
- Galerie E. M. Thelen, Essen

1969
- *Un' Area di Nebbia*, Marlborough Gallery, Rome

1970
- *Luce + Calore = Tempo di Fusione*, Galleria del Naviglio, Milan
- Galerie E. M. Thelen, Essen

1973
- *Pebbles*, Leo Castelli Gallery, New York

1975
- *Stripes*, Leo Castelli Gallery, New York
- *Stripes*, Castelli Graphics, New York
- Saman Gallery, Genoa

1976
- Galerie Françoise Lambert, Milan
- *Hypothesis about Time*, Leo Castelli Gallery, New York
- Van Abbemuseum, Eindhoven

1977
- Galleria Marilena Bonomo, Bari

1978
- Saman Gallery, Genoa
- Galerie Konrad Fischer, Düsseldorf
- Leo Castelli Gallery, New York

1979
- Galleria Ugo Ferranti, Rome

1980
- Galerie Françoise Lambert, Milan

1981
- Leo Castelli Gallery, New York
- Galleria Ugo Ferranti, Rome

1986
- Leo Castelli Greene Street Gallery, New York

1992
- *Laura Grisi. The Mirrored Series*, Leo Castelli Gallery, New York
- *Laura Grisi. From the 70s to the 90s*, Nohra Haime Gallery, New York

1994
- Galerie Konrad Fischer, Düsseldorf

1995
- Galleria Ugo Ferranti, Rome

2018
- *Laura Grisi. Le opere filmiche, 1968–1972*, cur. Elena Volpato, Galleria Civica d'Arte Moderna e Contemporanea, Turin
- *Hypothesis on Infinity*, P420, Bologna

2021
- *The Measuring of Time*, cur. Marco Scotini, Muzeum Susch, Susch

2022
- MAMCO, Geneva

GROUP EXHIBITIONS

1965
- IX Quadriennale nazionale d'arte, Rome*

1966
- 33th Venice Biennale, Venice*
- *Italy: New Tendencies*, Galleria Bonino, New York*
- *Rassegna arti figurative,* Amalfi*

1967
- *Mostra Nazionale di Pittura–Premio Provincia di Trento,* Trento*
- Museo sperimentale d'Arte contemporanea, Galleria Civica d'Arte Moderna, Turin*

1968
- *Young Italians*, cur. Alan Solomon, Institute of Contemporary Art, Boston; Jewish Museum, New York*
- *Teatro delle mostre,* Galleria La Tartaruga, Rome
- Galerie E. M. Thelen, Essen
- *Prospect 68,* Kunsthalle, Düsseldorf*

1969
- *I Materiali*, Qui Arte Contemporanea, Rome
- *Nuovi Materiali, Nuove Tecniche*, Caorle*
- *Plane und Projecte als Kunst (Plans and Projects as Art),* Kunsthalle, Bern; Actionsraum 1, Munich
- Galleria Diagramma, Milan

1970
- *5a Rassegna d'arte del Mezzogiorno–Grafica italiana*, Palazzo Reale, Naples*
- *Kunst nach Planen*, Kunsthaus, Hamburg
- *Arte e Critica 70*, cur. Nello Ponente, Modena*

1971
- *Earth Air Fire Water: Elements of Art*, Museum of Fine Arts, Boston*

1972
- *Mappa 72*, Incontri internazionali d'arte, Rome*
- *Pollution. Per una nuova estetica dell'inquinamento*, cur. Daniela Palazzoli, Piazza Santo Stefano,
- Bologna*

1973
- X Quadriennale nazionale d'arte, Rome*
- *Italy Two: Art Around 70*, Philadelphia Civic Center, Philadelphia*
- *Contemporanea*, Villa Borghese, Rome*

1974
- *De Matematica*, cur. Filiberto Menna and Bruno d'Amore, Galleria L'Obelisco, Rome*
- *Grafica Internazionale,* Museo d'Arte Moderna, Turin

1977
- *Time,* Philadelphia College of Art, Philadelphia

1978
- *Le figure del tempo*, Galleria de' Foscherari, Bologna*
- *Numerals 1924–1977*, Leo Castelli Gallery, New York; touring in 1978–1979 to Yale University Art Gallery, New Haven (CT); Dartmouth College Museum and Galleries, Hopkins Center, Hanover (NH); University Art Gallery, University of North Dakota, Grand Forks (ND); Minneapolis College of Art and Design, Minneapolis (MN);

Fine Arts Gallery, University of California, Irvine (CA); Art Museum of South Texas, Corpus Christi (TX); Center for the Visual Art Gallery, Illinois State University, Normal (IL); Center for the Arts, Muhlenberg College, Allentown (PA); New Gallery of Contemporary Art, Cleveland (OH)*

1979
- *Intricate Structure/Repeated Image, Part I*, Tyler School of Art, Temple University, Philadelphia*

1980
- *Intricate Structure/Repeated Image, Part II*, Tyler School of Art, Temple University, Philadelphia*
- *Cronografie: Il tempo e la memoria,* special project during the 39th Venice Biennale, Venice*

1981
- *Linea della ricerca artistica in Italia 1960–1980*, Palazzo delle Esposizioni, Rome*
- *Erweiterte Fotografie,* 5. Internationale Biennale, Secession, Vienna*

1982
- Saman Gallery, Genoa
- *Castelli and His Artists–Twenty-Five Years*, Aspen Center for the Visual Arts, Aspen (CL); touring to La Jolla Museum of Contemporary Art, La Jolla (CA); Leo Castelli Gallery, New York; Portland Center for the Visual Arts, Portland (OR); Laguna Gloria Art Museum, Austin (TX)*

1983
- *Drawing–Photographs,* Leo Castelli Gallery, New York

1985
- *Il Museo sperimentale di Torino: arte italiana negli anni sessanta nelle collezioni della Galleria Civica d'Arte Moderna,* Castello di Rivoli, Rivoli*

1986
- XI Quadriennale nazionale d'arte, Rome*
- 42nd Venice Biennale, Venice*
- *Surrealismo,* Barbara Braathen Gallery, New York

1987
- *Thirtieth Anniversary Show, The First Fifteen Years: Part 2,* Leo Castelli Greene Street Gallery, New York
- *Leo Castelli y sus artistas,* Centro cultural Arte contemporaneo, Mexico City*
- *Leo Castelli: A Tribute Exhibition*, Butler Institute of American Art, Youngstown (OH)
- *Three Decades of Exploration: Homage to Leo Castelli,* Fort Lauderdale Museum, Fort Lauderdale (FL)*

1988
- *In Memory of Toini Castelli,* The Mayor Gallery, London*

1990
- *The Artists of Leo Castelli,* Nichido Gallery, Tokyo*
- *Artificial Nature*, Deste Foundation for Contemporary Art, Athens

1991
- *The Conceptual Eye: Becher, Charlesworth, Grisi, Luyten, Starn Twins*, Barbara Mathes Gallery, New York

1996
- *Omaggio a Leo Castelli. Da Rauschenberg a Warhol, da Flavin a Judd, 20 artisti a New York negli anni sessanta,* Padiglione d'arte contemporanea–PAC, Milan*

1998
- *Fortieth Anniversary Show*, Leo Castelli Gallery, New York*

2010
- *Quadro scultura–scultura quadro*, Galleria nazionale d'Arte Moderna, Rome

2013
- *Anni '70 Arte a Roma*, Palazzo delle Esposizioni, Rome*

2014
- Graham Foundation, Chicago

2015
- *Brera Anni Sessanta-Settanta*, Accademia di Brera, Milan

2017
- *Vero Amore, Pop Art italiana dalle Collezioni della GAM*, cur. Riccardo Passoni, Galleria Civica d'Arte Moderna e Contemporanea, Turin

2018
- *100% Italia, Cent'anni di capolavori*, Museo Ettore Fico, Turin
- *Matriz do tempo real*, cur. Jacopo Crivelli Visconti, MAC USP, São Paulo*

2019
- *After Leaving, Before Arriving*, 12th Kaunas Biennial, Kaunas*
- *A Woman Looking at Men Looking at Women*, cur. Kasia Redzisz, Muzeum Susch, Susch
- *She Devil XI, We Will Survive*, Studio Stefania Miscetti, Rome

2020
- *Earthkeeping/Earthshaking–Art, Feminisms, and Ecology*, cur. Giulia Lamoni and Vanessa Badagliacca, Galerias Municipais, Lisbon*
- *Flower Blast*, cur. Annette Lagler and Myriam Kroll, Ludwig Forum, Aachen
- *I sei anni di Marcello Rumma 1965–1970*, MADRE–Museo d'Arte Contemporanea Donnaregina, Naples

2021
- *Io dico io*, Galleria nazionale d'Arte Moderna e Contemporanea, Rome*
- *Multiples, Inc.*, cur. Dieter Schwarz, Marian Goodman Gallery, New York*

2022
- 59th Venice Biennale, cur. Cecilia Alemani, Venice*
- *Vita Nuova. New Stakes in Italian Art, 1960–1975,* cur. Valérie Da Costa, MAMAC, Nice*

PUBLIC COLLECTIONS

- Brooklyn Museum, New York
- Galleria Civica d'Arte Moderna e Contemporanea, Turin
- Galleria d'Arte Moderna, Rome
- Ludwig Forum for International Art, Aachen
- Museum of Modern Art, New York
- Van Abbemuseum, Eindhoven
- Frederick R. Weisman Art Foundation, Los Angeles

ARTIST'S BOOKS & MONOGRAPH

- *Pasos por Buenos Aires*, Capricornio, Buenos Aires 1959
- *I Denti del Tigre*, Lerici Editore, Milan 1964
- "L'aria è la certezza visiva di uno spazio," in *Qui-Arte Contemporanea*, no. 6, Rome, September 1969
- *Distillations: 3 Months of Looking*, Artestudio, Macerata 1970; limited edition of 300 signed copies
- *Distillations: Choice and Choosing 16 from 5000*, Artestudio, Macerata 1970; limited edition of 300 signed copies
- *Endless Dialogue*, Saman Edizione e Vanni Scheiwiller, Milan 1978
- Germano Celant, *Laura Grisi. A Selection of Works with Notes by the Artist*, trans. Marguerite Shore, Rizzoli, New York 1990

EXHIBITION CATALOGUES

- Nello Ponente, *Laura Grisi*, Galleria Il Segno, Rome 1964
- Renato Barilli, *Laura Grisi*, Galleria dell'Ariete, Milan 1965
- Udo Kultermann, *Laura Grisi*, Galerie E. M. Thelen, Essen 1968
- Maurizio Calvesi, *Teatro delle mostre*, Lerici Editore, Rome 1969 (group exhibition)
- *Laura Grisi*, Galleria del Naviglio, Milan 1970
- Giulio Carlo Argan, *Laura Grisi*, Galerie E. M. Thelen, Essen 1970
- *Laura Grisi*, Van Abbemuseum, Eindhoven 1976
- Calvin Tomkins and Piero Dorazio, *Omaggio a Leo Castelli. Da Rauschenberg a Warhol, da Flavin a Judd, 20 artisti a New York negli anni sessanta*, Padiglione d'arte contemporanea–PAC, Skira, Milan 1996 (group exhibition)

BOOKS

- Alberto Boatto, *Poetiche europee dell'oggettività, L'Arte moderna, Vol. XIII*, Fabbri Editore, Milan 1969
- Udo Kultermann, *Nuove forme della pittura*, Feltrinelli, Milan 1969, published in German by Ernst Wasmuth Verlag, Tübingen
- José Pierre, *Le Pop Art*, Fernand Hazan Éditeur, Paris 1975
- Germano Celant, *Precronistoria 1966-69*, Centro Di, Florence 1976
- *Soho: Downtown Manhattan*, Akademie der Kunst, Berliner Festwochen, Berlin 1976
- *Art Actuel*, Editions Skira, Geneva 1977
- Germano Celant, *Off Media, Nuova tecniche artistiche: video, disco, libro*, Edizioni Dedalo, Bari 1977
- Achille Bonito Oliva, *Autocritico Automobile: attraverso le avanguardie*, Il Formichiere, Milan 1977
- Germano Celant, *Identité italienne. L'Art en Italie depuis 1959*, Musée national d'art moderne, Centre Pompidou, Paris 1981
- Arturo Schwarz et al., *Arte e alchimia*, La Biennale, Venice/Electa, Milan 1986
- Raffaele Perna, *In forma di fotografia. Ricerche artistiche in Italia da 1960 al 1970*, Derive Approdi, Rome 2009
- Lara Conte and Francesca Gallo, *Artiste italiane e immagini in movimento. Identità, sguardi, sperimentazioni*, Mimesis Edizioni, Aurora, Milan 2021

NEWSPAPERS & MAGAZINES

- In the 1960s–1970s, Laura Grisi's work and exhibitions were often analyzed and reviewed in art magazines such as *Art International*, *Art Press*, *Artforum*, *Arts*, *Avanti*, *Das Kunstwerk*, *Domus*, *Flash Art*, *L'Œil*, *Marcatré*, *Qui–Arte Contemporanea*, and *Studio International*. Among the art critics and authors who have written about Laura Grisi in the 1960s and 1970s are Achille Bonito Oliva, Germano Celant, Gillo Dorfles, Maurizio Fagiolo dell'Arco, Alain Jouffroy, Henry Martin, Nello Ponente, Pierre Restany, and Tommaso Trini.

* indicates when a publication accompanies the exhibition.

Invitation cards to solo exhibitions, 1969–1995; cover of *I Denti del Tigre* published in 1964

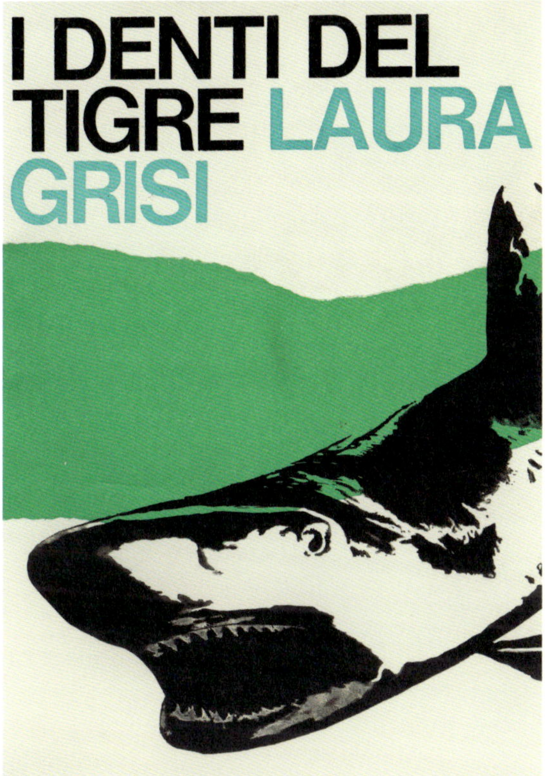

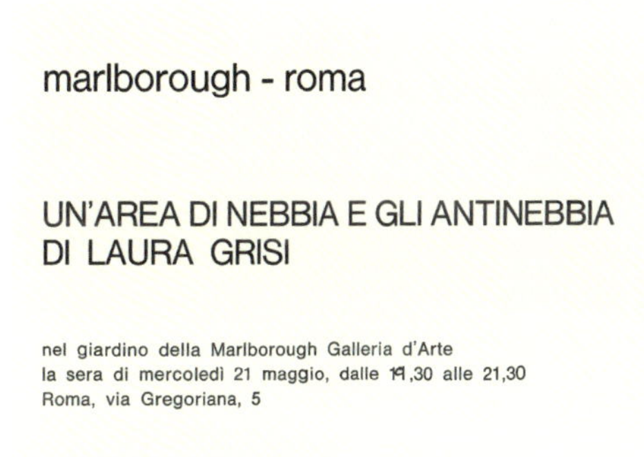

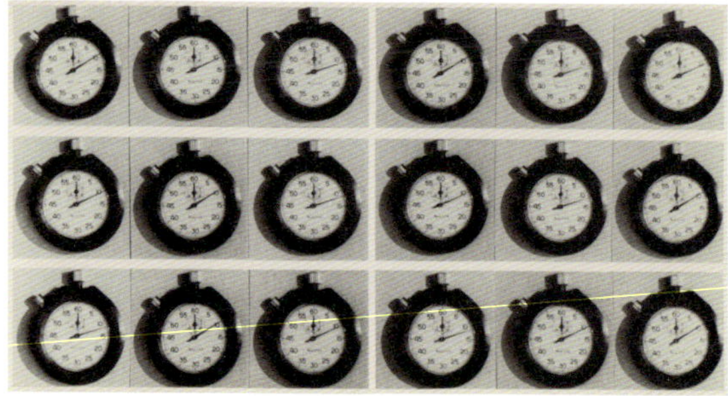

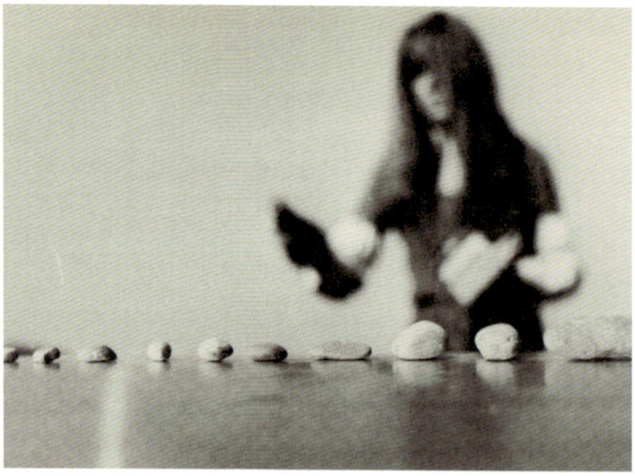

LAURA GRISI
"HYPOTHESIS ABOUT TIME"
24 APRIL-15 MAY, 1976

LEO CASTELLI
420 WEST BROADWAY
NEW YORK 10012

Van Abbemuseum
Bilderdijklaan 10
Eindhoven / Nederland

LAURA GRISI

U bent van harte welkom
op de opening vrijdag
10 september, 20.30 uur

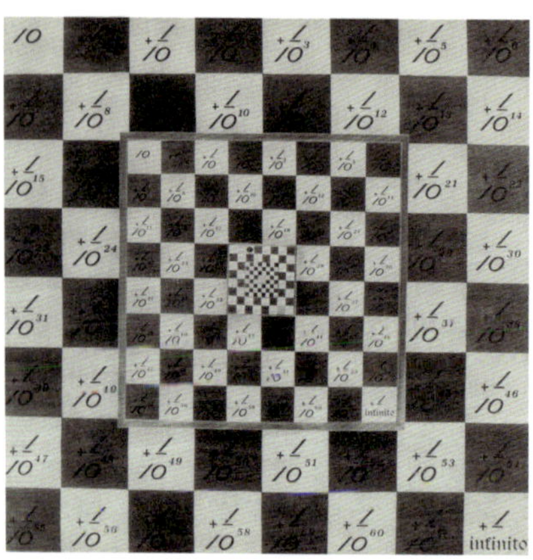

LAURA GRISI

BEI KONRAD FISCHER
PLATANENSTR. 7
4000 DÜSSELDORF
TEL. 68 59 08

SAMSTAG, 16. SEPTEMBER
BIS 10. OKTOBER 1978

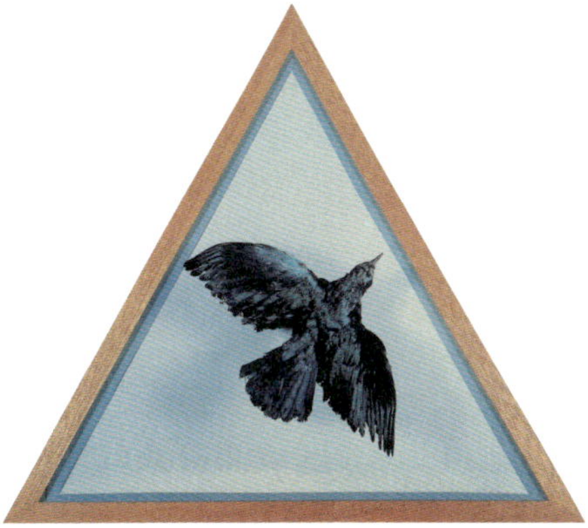

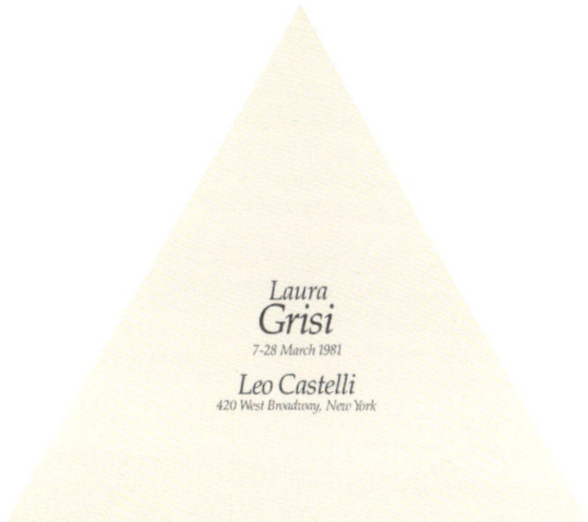
Laura
Grisi
7-28 March 1981
Leo Castelli
420 West Broadway, New York

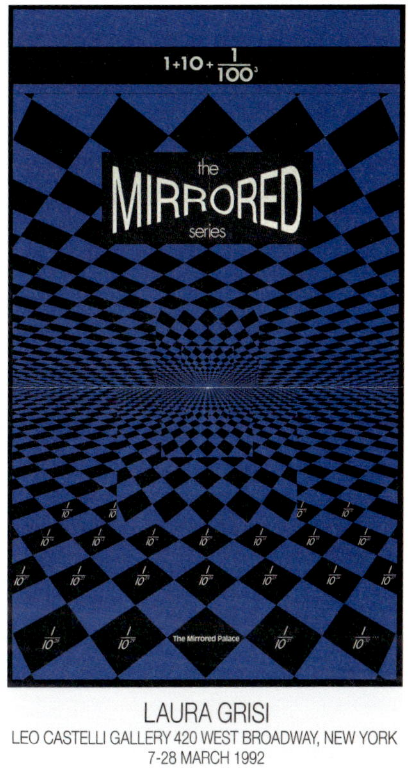
the
MIRRORED
series
The Mirrored Palace
LAURA GRISI
LEO CASTELLI GALLERY 420 WEST BROADWAY, NEW YORK
7-28 MARCH 1992

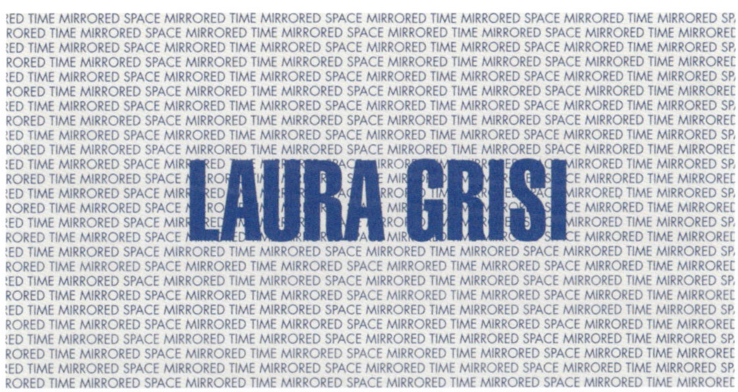
LAURA GRISI
MIRRORED TIME MIRRORED SPACE

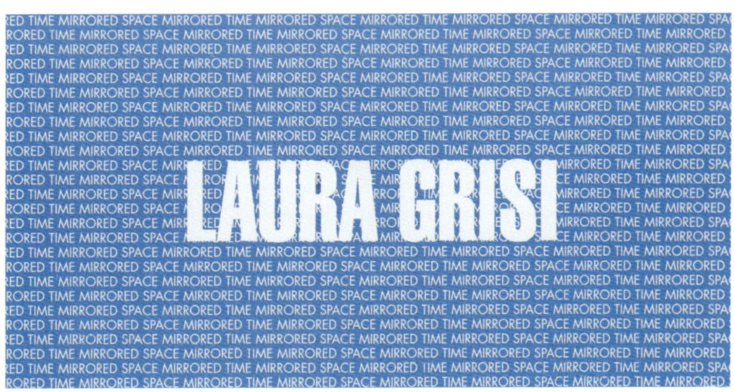
LAURA GRISI
MIRRORED TIME MIRRORED SPACE

List of Works

These pages only list the artworks created by Laura Grisi between 1964 and 1999; all archival images and documentation reproduced are fully captioned on the relevant pages.

The works whose titles are preceded by an asterisk were shown in the exhibition *Laura Grisi. The Measuring of Time* held at Muzeum Susch, which also included photographs from the 1950s–1960s and printed matter (artist's books, archive material).

Laura Grisi is represented by P420, Bologna.

1
Volume of Air, 1968
Fluorescent white-painted wood walls, white ceiling, white floor, white neon tubes
450 × 450 × 450 cm

54–55
**Grande Reflex*, 1964
Acrylic and felt pen on canvas
165 × 130.5 cm

56–57
**Untitled*, (1964–1965)
Mixed media on card
70.5 × 100.5 cm

58
Untitled, 1966
Acrylic and mixed media on card
100 × 70 cm

59
Untitled, (1966)
Acrylic and mixed media on card
100 × 70 cm

60
Untitled, (1966)
Acrylic, graphite, and felt tip pen on card
92 × 62 cm

61
Untitled, 1966
Acrylic and mixed media on card
100 × 70.5 cm

62
**Untitled*, (1965–1966)
Acrylic and mixed media on card
70 × 100 cm

Untitled, (1965–1966)
Mixed media on card
70.5 × 100.5 cm

63
Untitled, (1965–1966)
Acrylic and mixed media on card
62 × 52.5 cm

65
**Untitled*, 1964
Mixed media on card
70.5 × 100.5 cm

**Untitled*, (1964–1965)
Mixed media on card
70.5 × 100.5 cm

66–67
**Grass Field*, 1966
Acrylic on canvas, Plexiglas, sliding panels
98 × 62 × 12 cm
Grażyna Kulczyk Collection

68–69
Untitled, (1965–1966)
Acrylic and mixed media on card
Diptych
38.5 × 100 cm each part

70
Transparent Door, 1965
Acrylic on canvas, Plexiglas, sliding panel
165 × 394 × 10 cm

71
**Landscape Omaggio a Gainsborough*, 1966
Acrylic on canvas, Plexiglas, sliding panels
200 × 190 × 9 cm
Museo Sperimentale, Galleria Civica d'Arte Moderna e Contemporanea, Turin

72–73
Untitled, 1966
Acrylic on canvas, Plexiglas, sliding panels
44 × 31 × 7 cm

74
Untitled, (1965–1966)
Acrylic and mixed media on card
70 × 100 cm

**Untitled*, (1965–1966)
Acrylic and mixed media on card
70.5 × 100.5 cm

75
Untitled, 1966
Acrylic and mixed media on card
100 × 70.5 cm

76–77
**Seascape*, 1966
Acrylic on canvas, Plexiglas, sliding panels
100 × 122 × 12 cm

80–81
**Geometric Landscape*, 1966
Acrylic on canvas, Plexiglas, collage, sliding panels
205 × 305 × 10 cm

82–83
**Seascape Omaggio a Constable*, 1966
Acrylic on canvas, Plexiglas, collage, sliding panels
220 × 330 cm

84
**Untitled*, 1965–1966
Acrylic and felt pen on canvas
130 × 80 cm

85
**Sphere with Grass Field*, 1966
Acrylic on canvas and mixed media on card
92 × 61 × 3 cm
Sphere in Plexiglas
ø 43 cm

87
**Glosty (East Village Series)*, 1966
Neon, acrylic on card, canvas, ondulux, wood, revolving Plexiglas
163 × 131 × 15.5 cm
Grażyna Kulczyk Collection

88
**Subway*, 1967
Neon, Plexiglas, aluminum, sliding panel
163 × 103 × 22 cm
Grażyna Kulczyk Collection

89
**East Village*, 1967
Acrylic on canvas, neon, Plexiglas, aluminum
163 × 167 × 22 cm

92
St. Marks Place (East Village Series), 1967
Neon, Plexiglas, aluminum, sliding panels
175 × 185.5 × 21 cm
The Emami Group Collection

93
No. 470, Angolare, 1967
Neon, Plexiglas, aluminum
106 × 174 × 25 cm

Antinebbia, 1967
Plexiglas, neon, steel
200 × 30 × 30 cm

94
***Model Car Racing*, 1967**
Plexiglas, neon, aluminum box
80 × 170 × 13 cm

***Blue*, 1967**
Plexiglas, neon, aluminum
17 × 66 × 47 cm

95
***Model Car Racing*, 1967**
Plexiglas, neon, aluminum box
49 × 73 × 13 cm

***Model Car Racing*, 1967**
Plexiglas, neon, aluminum box
73 × 40 × 15 cm

96
***Model Car Racing*, 1967**
Plexiglas, neon, aluminum box
80 × 170 × 13 cm

97
***Top Floor*, 1967**
Neon, Plexiglas, aluminum
173 × 140 × 22 cm
Ludwig Forum for International Art, loan from the Peter and Irene Ludwig Foundation, Aachen

100–101
******Un' Area di Nebbia (A Space of Fog)*, 1968**
Artificial fog, spiral neon tubing, Plexiglas, steel
Dimensions variable
Private Collection, Rome

102
***Spiral Light*, 1968**
Neon, Plexiglas, steel
232 × 30 × 30 cm

103
******Sunset Light*, 1967**
Neon, Plexiglas, steel
219 × 30 × 30 cm

104–105
******Rainbow*, 1968**
Prisms, light projector (15 × 17 × 34 cm)
Dimensions variable

106
***Sunset Light*, 1967**
Neon, Plexiglas, steel
219 × 30 × 30 cm

107
***Sunset Light*, 1967**
Neon, Plexiglas, steel
52 × 16 × 16 cm

***Sunset Light*, 1967**
Neon, Plexiglas, steel
52 × 16 × 16 cm

108
***Light Melting Time*, 1968**
Lead sheet (300 × 250 cm), 64 Osram lamps
Dimensions variable

116–119
******Refraction*, 1968**
Four water-filled containers in Plexiglas (28 × 95 cm each), enamel-painted iron and steel, free-floating aluminum tubes (53 × 1.3 cm each), painted iron base (33 × 168 × 170 cm)
Black-and-white print on cardboard panel (101.5 × 192 cm)

121
******Drops of Water*, 1968**
Drip system and painted metal vessel
ø 200 cm

122–124
******The Measuring of Time*, 1969**
16mm film, black and white
5'45"

125
******Whirlpool*, 1969**
16mm film screened on floor, color, 3'
Dimensions variable

126
******Wind Speed 40 Knots*, 1968**
16mm film, black and white
4'45"

127
******Wind Speed 40 Knots*, 1968**
Environment of black painted wood and wind machines
Dimensions variable

152
******Sounds (Ten Stones Ten Materials)*, 1971**
Pencil and felt pen on paper
22 × 28 cm

******Sounds (Ten Stones Ten Materials)*, 1971**
Pencil and felt pen on paper
28 × 22 cm

******Sounds (Ten Stones Ten Materials)*, 1971**
Pencil and felt pen on paper
28 × 22 cm

154
******Sounds*, 1971**
Magnetic recording on two cassettes, 4 tracks
15' each track

155
******Sounds (Ten Stones)*, 1971**
Color photograph mounted on board
24 × 30.5 cm

******Sounds (Tree)*, 1971**
Color photograph mounted on board
24 × 30.5 cm

159
******Pebbles*, 1973 (detail)**
150 color photographs
25 frames, 8 × 13 cm each
120 × 490 cm overall

160
******From One to Four Pebbles*, 1972**
16mm film, color
4'30'

161–163
******Drawing for Pebbles*, 1973**
Ink on paper and photo collage
24 parts, 31 × 23 cm each
Dimensions variable

164–166
******Hypothesis about Time (Ipotesi sul tempo)*, 1975**
360 photographs mounted on board
20 parts, 28 × 120 cm each

168–169
******Tempo reale*, 1975**
Photo collage
173 × 23.5 cm

170–171
******Stripes*, 1974**
Ink on canvas
13 parts, 302 × 34 each
Dimensions variable

173
Top: *Hypothesis about Space*, 1975
266 color photographs mounted on board, 12 × 12.5 cm each
Dimensions variable

174–175
**Drawing for Time*, 1975 (details)
Ink and photo collage on paper
20 parts, 31 × 23 cm each

176–178
Le dimensioni immaginarie–Rotazione all'infinito/Ipotesi Spazio-Tempo, 1977
Ink and photo collage on paper
7 parts, 70 × 50 cm each

180–181
**Chessboard*, 1977 (details)
Photo collage
16 parts, 40 × 40 cm each

182–183
Endless Dialogue–Index I, 1977
Ink on paper
9 parts, 45 × 45 cm each
135 × 135 cm overall

184
Reflectivity, 1977 (detail)
7 color photographs and 8 ink on paper drawings mounted on canvas
15 parts, 71 × 51 cm each

185
Riflessività, 1978
Photo collage and mixed media on paper
22.5 × 22 cm

186–187
The Minimum Discernible (Double Horizon), 1977
12 photographs and 4 ink drawings
25 × 20 cm each
The Place Collection

226–227
Blue Triangles, 1981
Color photographs, ink on card
28 parts, 23 × 26 cm each
46 × 214 cm overall

228
Untitled, 1980
Mixed media and collage on paper
27 × 27 cm

229
Triangle with Two Birds, 1980
119 drawings in ink on paper, 2 color photographs, wood
121 parts, 23 × 16 cm each
254 × 294 cm overall

Blue Triangle, 1980
Ink on cardboard, color photographs, wood
121 parts, 23 × 26 cm each
254 × 294 cm overall

231
Borromini's Violin, 1985
Wood, canvas, wax, bronze, marble
218 × 153 × 14.5 cm

232
Classical Simmetry, 1985
Wood, wax, bronze, granite, plaster
218 × 147 × 22 cm
Private Collection, Turin

233
Apollinaire's Secret, 1985
Wood, wax, aluminum, bronze, brass, marble, granite, plaster
218 × 153 × 17 cm

234
Time Geometry, 1985
Wood, brass, marble
42 × 36 × 11 cm

Moondial, 1985
Wood, granite, marble
36.5 × 33 × 16.5 cm

Urbino, 1985
Wood, brass, Plexiglas
33 × 26 × 22 cm

237
Scheherazade Part 1, 1982
Color photographs, wood, and collage
37 parts, 21 × 24.5 each
150 × 136 cm overall

239
Regatta, 1999
Silkscreen on anodized aluminum and Forex
173 × 178 cm

240
One Minute, 1975–1994
Silkscreen on anodized aluminum
225 × 25 cm

241
One Minute, 1975–1994
Silkscreen on anodized aluminum
225 × 25 cm

One Minute, 1975–1994
Silkscreen on anodized aluminum
225 × 25 cm

242
Time4Time, 1994
Silkscreen on anodized aluminum, 3 parts, 225 × 63 cm each
225 × 189 cm overall

243
Time4Time, 1994
Silkscreen on anodized aluminum, 3 parts, 225 × 63 cm each
225 × 189 cm overall

244–245
Mirrored Time, 1994
Silkscreen on anodized aluminum, 5 parts, 175 × 62 cm each
175 × 310 cm overall

This book is published on
the occasion of the exhibition
Laura Grisi:
The Measuring of Time
Muzeum Susch
June 5–December 5, 2021

Curated by Marco Scotini

An exhibition of works by
Laura Grisi is organized in
Fall 2022 at MAMCO, Geneva.

MUZEUM SUSCH /
ART STATIONS FOUNDATION CH

Founder and Chairwoman
of the Foundation Board
Grażyna Kulczyk

Director Instituto Susch
and Curator at Large
Anke Kempkes

Curator of Acziun Susch
Joanna Leśnierowska

Associate Curator Instituto Susch
and Temporars Susch
Pierre-Henri Foulon

Curator of Publicaziuns Susch
Ph.D. Agnieszka Sosnowska

Advisor
Maciek Chorążak

Producer
Aleksandra Wojtaszek

Administration Manager
Marzena Mikosz

Display of the exhibition
Laura Grisi:
The Measuring of Time
Vincenzo Treccosti

Public Relations
Lara Facco, Milan
Scott & Co., London

Muzeum Susch
Surpunt 78
CH-7542 Susch
www.muzeumsusch.ch

MUZEUM
SUSCH

Kulturförderung Graubünden.
Amt für Kultur
Promoziun da la cultura dal
Grischun. Uffizi da cultura
Promozione della cultura dei
Grigioni. Ufficio della cultura

SWISSLOS

MAMCO GENEVA

Director, Lionel Bovier

Museum Management
and Development
– Administrator, Valérie Mallet
– Development Manager,
  Nicole Boissonnas
– Development Assistant,
  Damien Grimm
– Library, Archives, and Museum
  Resources, Chloë Gouëdard
– Digital Communication,
  Julien Gremaud
– Press and Communication,
  Viviane Reybier

Exhibitions and Collection
– Chief Curator, Julien Fronsacq
– Honorary Curator,
  Françoise Ninghetto
– Collection Curator, Sophie Costes
– Curator, Paul Bernard
– Chief Exhibition Productions,
  Cyrille Maillot
– Exhibition Productions
  and Collection Registrar,
  Filipe Dos Santos
– Transport Registrar,
  Benoît Charron

Public and Education Services
– Public Services Manager,
  Yann Abrecht
– Public Services Coordinators,
  Mathilde Acevedo, Daniel Maury
– Education Services Manager,
  Charlotte Morel
– Education Services Coordinator,
  Julie Cudet
– Curator in Charge of
  Publications, Thierry Davila

Facility Management and
Surveillance
– Chief of Facility Management,
  Antonio Magalhes
– Facility Management, Maria de
  Fatima Braganca, Joana Gomes
  Da Silva
– Surveillance, Carlos Martins
  Fonseca, Luc Schuwey

MAMCO is overseen by FONDAMCO,
chaired by Philippe Bertherat and
made up of FONDATION MAMCO,
the Canton, and the City of Geneva.

MAMCO Geneva
10, rue des Vieux-Grenadiers
CH–1205 Geneva
www.mamco.ch

MAMCO
GENEVE

PUBLICATION

Editors
Marco Scotini, with Clément Dirié

Editorial Coordination
Clément Dirié

Editing and Proofreading
Clare Manchester

Translation from the Italian
Nicola Rudge Iannelli
(Marco Scotini)

Translation from the French
Susan Pickford (Valérie Da Costa)

Design
Gavillet&Cie/Devaud

Assistance
Morgane Cachin

Typeface
Metodo (www.optimo.ch)

Color Separation & Print
Musumeci S.p.A, Quart (Aosta)

Cover
The Measuring of Time, 1969
Seascape, 1966

Photo Credits
Archives Van Abbemuseum, Eindhoven/Hans Biezen: p. 172–173; Archivio L'Attico/Fabio Sargentini, Rome: p. 46t; Carl Brunn: p. 97; Mimmo Capone: p. 179b; Bevan Davies: p. 228t; Carlo Favero: p. 24–29, 32–34, 54–55, 56–57, 58, 59, 60, 61, 62, 63, 65, 66–67, 68–69, 72–73, 74, 75, 76–77, 80–81, 82–83, 84, 85, 87, 88l, 89, 92, 95, 96, 102, 103, 106, 107, 118–119, 148–149, 150–151, 152, 159, 161, 164–165, 166, 168–169, 170–171, 174–175, 176–178, 180–181, 182–183, 185, 226–227, 228b; Julien Gremaud / JRP|Editions: p. 35, 42–43, 78–79, 90–91, 98–99, 100–101, 104–105, 116–117, 121, 122–123, 156–157, 162–163; George Hirose: p. 236b; Sebastiano Luciano: p. 237, 240–241, 242–243, 244–245; Eric Pollitzer: p. 158; Paolo Robino: p. 71

Courtesy
Laura Grisi Estate, Rome: p. 1, 23, 24–29, 31, 32–34, 36–41, 46b, 47, 53, 64, 70, 88r, 93, 94, 108–109, 110–111, 112–113, 114–115, 120, 147, 148–149, 150–151, 153, 167, 179t, 184, 225, 229, 230, 231, 232, 233, 234t, 235, 236t, 238, 239, 259, 263–265, 272; Laura Grisi Estate, Rome, and P420, Bologna: p. 54–55, 56–57, 58, 59, 60, 61, 62, 63, 65, 68–69, 72–73, 74, 75, 76–77, 80–81, 82–83, 84, 85, 89, 95, 96, 102, 103, 104–105, 106, 107, 116–119, 121, 122–123, 124, 125, 126, 127, 152, 154, 155, 159, 160, 161–163, 164–166, 168–169, 170–171, 174–175, 176–178, 180–181, 182–183, 185, 226–227, 228b, 234b, 237, 239, 240, 241, 242, 243, 244–245; Galleria Civica d'Arte Moderna e Contemporanea, Museo Sperimentale: p. 71; Private Collection, Turin: p. 232; The Emami Group Collection: p. 92; Grażyna Kulczyk Collection: p. 66–67, 87, 88l; Ludwig Forum for International Art, loan from the Peter and Irene Ludwig Foundation, Aachen: p. 97; The Place Collection: p. 186–187; Private Collection, Rome: p. 100–101

ACKNOWLEDGMENTS

Muzeum Susch would like to thank the following individuals without whom the exhibition and accompanying projects would have not been possible: Fausto Grisi, Clément Dirié, Ursula Esposito, Fabrizio Padovani, Alessandro Pasotti, Sefora Tarì, Chiara Tiberio, and Brando Quilici.

Printed in Europe.

Published by
JRP|Editions
Rue des Bains 39
CH-1205 Geneva
info@jrp-editions.com
www.jrp-editions.com

ISBN 978-3-03764-566-6

JRP|Editions books are available internationally at selected bookstores and from the following distribution partners:

Switzerland
AVA Verlagsauslieferung AG
avainfo@ava.ch
www.ava.ch

Germany and Austria
Vice Versa Distribution GmbH
info@viceversaartbooks.com
www.viceversaartbooks.com

France
Les presses du réel
info@lespressesdureel.com
www.lespressesdureel.com

UK, other European countries
Cornerhouse Publications, HOME
publications@cornerhouse.org
www.cornerhousepublications.org

USA, Canada, Asia and Australia
ARTBOOK|D.A.P.
orders@dapinc.com
www.artbook.com

Laura Grisi in her installation *Rainbow*, 1968 →

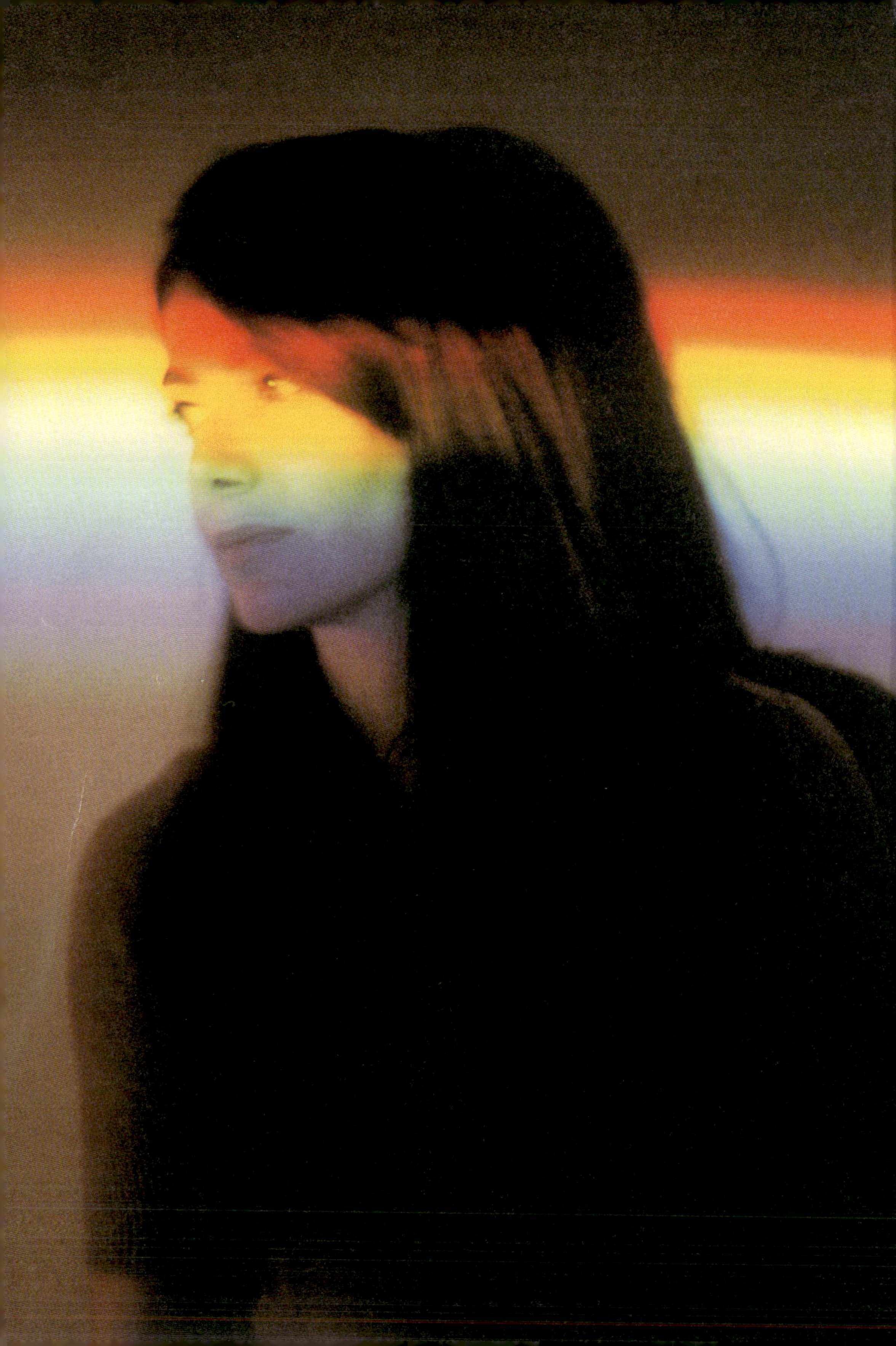